THE PSYCHOANALYTIC
STUDY OF SOCIETY

Volume I

THE PSYCHOANALYTIC STUDY OF SOCIETY

VOLUME I

Founded as

PSYCHOANALYSIS AND THE SOCIAL SCIENCES

(Volumes I-V)

by Géza Róheim

Edited by

Warner Muensterberger, Ph.D. and Sidney Axelrad, D.S.Sc.

INTERNATIONAL UNIVERSITIES PRESS, INC.
New York   New York

EDITORS' NOTE

The title of the series, *Psychoanalysis and the Social Sciences,* has been changed to *The Psychoanalytic Study of Society.*

The causes for this change are more than stylistic. In the years since the late Géza Róheim founded *Psychoanalysis and the Social Sciences,* psychoanalytic thought and theory have broadened in a direction which makes psychoanalysis not just one of the ancillary means of studying and enriching the social sciences, but which makes it possible to study the institutions of any social structure and of any culture. We refer chiefly to the development of ego psychology, and the awakening interests of psychoanalysts in problems of defense mechanisms and adaptation. They have given new dimensions to psychoanalytic observation and research.

There has been an increasing absorption of psychoanalytic concepts within the social sciences, particularly within sociology, anthropology, and social psychology, and a number of cross-cultural studies have been undertaken which test and illuminate psychoanalytic hypotheses.

In former years, it was the psychoanalyst who, using the data and hypotheses derived from his clinical observation, would deal with problems and issues which were within the provinces of the humanities and the social sciences. Today, there is an increasing trend among social scientists to examine problems and aspects of social structure, of culture and of institutions, making use of the concepts and propositions of psychoanalysis. It is this shift which has necessitated the change in title.

This series plans to remain within the body of hypotheses and the type of data derived from the insight and technique of classical psychoanalysis. It is the aim of the editors that this publication provide the meeting ground for the work of the social scientist and the psychoanalyst, and that the range of subjcet matter be somewhat wider than that found in the first five volumes of our series.

Warner Muensterberger
Sidney Axelrad

CONTENTS

SOCIAL ADAPTATION

CHARACTERISTICS OF TOTALITARIANISM

ROBERT WAELDER, Ph.D.

In a previous paper (1951) I have tried to describe the characteristics of totalitarianism, the conditions for its emergence and its impact upon men, both those reared under a different system and "re-educated" under totalitarianism, and those who had grown up under a totalitarian system and had accepted its doctrines as their natural spiritual and philosophical habitat. The basic propositions were not new; they had been clearly seen by nineteenth-century authors whom later writers on the subject had often overlooked. I tried to carry their analysis one step further, from the level of political analysis to that of an analysis of the psychological processes which underlie the political attitudes.

The Nature of Totalitarianism

The first subject was the distinction between authoritarianism and totalitarianism; the term, authoritarianism, should refer to a system exemplified, among others, by the Poland of Pilsudski and Rydz-Smigly, the Hungary of Horthy, the Austria of Dollfuss and Schuschnigg, the Spain of Franco, the Portugal of Salazar. Totalitarianism, on the other hand, was meant to refer to Soviet Russia and Communist China, to Nazi Germany, and, in weaker examples, to Fascist Italy or, more recently, nationalist Egypt. The difference between the two types is not measured in the number or the severity of restrictions imposed upon the people nor in the extent of the private sphere allowed to them. As a rule, the private sphere is wider in the authoritarian than in the totalitarian system, but this is not necessarily so, because genuine totalitarianism may at times choose to leave relatively wide areas free from interference (as was, e.g., the case in Fascist Italy, at least until the last years when Italy became a German satellite); it may do so because of personal allegiances of the rulers or for reasons of expediency or out of sheer weakness. It is not the extent of the unregulated sector that makes the difference.

The difference is more fundamental than this; it consists of the different impact of the system upon its victims, i.e., upon those who are opposed to its policies or, at least, not convinced of their value. One can say that authoritarianism is oppressive for its victims, sometimes very oppressive, but not degrading or demoralizing, while totalitarianism is just that.

This difference was brought out, implicitly, by Benjamin de Constant-Rebècque in a treatise published in 1814: the two systems which he compared are the old-fashioned despotism of the *ancien régime* and the "usurption" of the Bonapartist Empire. The latter, said Constant, had deprived the people even of the "right of silence."

In an authoritarian system the subjects are compelled to obey the orders of the authorities: to pay their taxes, confiscatory though they may be (without representation); to surrender their property when so required; to render military service at whatever terms are imposed; and, in general, to carry out loyally what they are asked to do; and they have to abstain from revolutionary activities and sometimes also from criticism of the government. But they are *not* required to say that they love the hand that beats them; *they may be whipped, but they do not have to kiss the rod.* This latter requirement, however, is added under totalitarianism.

Totalitarianism denies to its subjects this last refuge of human dignity; the whole coercive power of the rulers is used, mercilessly, not only to ensure obedience to orders as in authoritarianism but also, in addition to it, to extract continuous expressions of enthusiastic approval from them. The public spectacle of persons accused of treason or sabotage in the purge trials in Soviet Russia in the 1930's, or of exploitation and similar sins committed in the past, in the numerable orchestrated lynchings of landlords and other persons in Communist China, with the humble confessions of the accused and their supplication for a lenient punishment are cases in point. They are only the extreme manifestations of pressures that in a less ferocious degree permeate daily life; the people must not merely passively obey but actively approve. A Communist paper in Poland was recently reported as having referred to nonconformist writers who had taken more advantage of the liberalization in cultural matters—the "thaw"—than the Polish Communist Party thought either permissible from their own point of view or wise in view of Russian supervision: we will judge them not only by what they say but also *by what they do not say.*

Shakespeare's Henry V, visiting the camp on the eve of the battle of Agincourt, says to a group of soldiers: Every subject's duty is his king's; every subject's soul is his own. Authoritarianism is the system that is adamant in demanding *every subject's duty* but is willing to let the subject's soul be his own; totalitarianism, on the other hand, insists on every subject's *duty and soul.*

The Essence of "Brain Washing"

The request for the soul, i.e., the attempt to change the allegiance of a person whose allegiances have already been formed, has recently been called brain washing and there has been much speculation how it is brought about. Everybody is, of course, familiar with techniques of propaganda and advertising, but despite the alarms recently sounded by some authors about the power of unrecognized propaganda (the "hidden persuaders"), it is doubtful whether the ordinary means of persuasion, without a monopoly of propaganda and without the power of physical coercion—both enjoyed by totalitarian governments but quite out of the reach of manufacturers trying to promote a product, or of political parties in pluralist democracies—can ever gain any great and lasting power over men's minds. The limits of skullduggery in a competitive market of ideas, without the help of the executioner, have probably been properly defined in the famous saying of Lincoln. Even the influence of the hypnotist over his object—considerably greater than that of any ad-man over the public—has not been considered to be great enough to force a person to a behavior inconsistent with his previous character; in the long discussion, about half a century ago, of the question whether a hypnotist could make a criminal out of an average law-abiding person, students of hypnotism seemed to discount this possibility.

The question remains how one can influence the thinking of adults radically and lastingly. Sheer physical force can, of course, induce most people to behave in the desired way; many, though not all, people have under torture confessed to crimes they had not committed, and have denounced their kith and kin as supposedly guilty of the same crimes. But what force had produced in these cases was behavior—speech or signature—not belief; the person who made such confessions and denunciations did not, as far as we know, actually believe that, e.g., she was a witch and her husband a sorcerer. How can thinking be changed against the evidence of the senses and how can the most basic allegiances be changed?

The answer to this question is latent in the quoted lines of Benjamin Constant. It is true that one cannot really force another person's thought but merely his hand or his tongue; and that he may submit to coercion and yet think his own thoughts. But one can force him to repeat required statements over and over again, and while this does not alter the *theoretical* freedom of his thought, it does create a situation which is *psychologically* very difficult for most people to bear because it involves constant tensions; one must all the time be careful lest one may give oneself away to the watchful eyes of the inquisitor—through a slip of the tongue, a lack of enthusiasm in one's facial expression, or the forgetting of a required formula or ritual. Professional revolutionaries are used to the perpetual need for high-tension self-control, and they may even enjoy it, and diplomats are expected to practice it; but both are specially selected and highly trained individuals, and both can relax from time to time in the contact with their own. Not much opportunity for relaxation is available to the average person in a totalitarian state where neighbors cannot be trusted, children may have taken to the idea of watching over their parents' loyalty, and where even confidences between husband and wife may become a source of disaster if the relationship should ever deteriorate.

The average person finds this constant tension hardly bearable and will eagerly seize the way out that is offered to him, viz., to embrace the ruling philosophy and to learn to believe in it. There are many rationalizations to make the step more palatable and to disguise before oneself and one's *amour-propre* the true nature of the surrender; after all, friends have embraced the new philosophy and prominent people in the land have aligned themselves behind it; why should one be different from all the others? Is it not just being stubborn and uncooperative to say "no" when everybody else says "yes"? What right does one have to think differently where all the others seem to agree?

Once one has accepted the ruling creed, one can perform the required rituals with full conviction. There is no more danger of giving oneself away; life is easy once again. One will all the more easily take this way out the less firm one's previous convictions have been. The skeptic, the opportunist, the relativist, the liberal are therefore an easier prey to totalitarian "brain washing" than the devout religious believer, the totalitarian of another persuasion or, for that matter, the psychotic.

Thus, brain washing, in the main, consists simply in forcing people to perpetual professions of belief in certain doctrines. Force is usually sufficient to have them go through these motions, and what people are forced to say over and over again they will very often end up believing.

One is reminded of the James-Lange theory of affects according to which expression *causes* the sentiment: we do not laugh because we are amused, but we are amused because we are laughing. One is also reminded of Alfred North Whitehead's four stages of religious development: ritual, stories, belief, and systematization. In general, the observance of certain rituals—e.g., the folding of the hands in prayer—is often the first step in the religious instruction of a child; belief comes later and is often the more firmly entrenched the more there was of an early conditioning in ritual.

The available data seem to support our conclusion that brain washing operates through enforced professions of belief.

In a recent presentation of the results of an Army study on the defection of American prisoners in the hand of the Chinese Communists during the Korean war, Eugene Kinkead (1959) describes the political instruction of prisoners; they were taught Marxism: "Repetition was used both in classes and in individual instruction. Prisoners were required to memorize certain material, such as the contents of a pamphlet on Communist ideology, and they were examined on this material day in and day out, week in and week out. While they are being crammed with this literature and questioned on it over and again, the prisoners were . . . allowed to read nothing else" (p. 106).

Kinkead reports the following incident: the Communist instructor had told the class how the "South Koreans had treacherously attacked the peaceful North Koreans" as a consequence of the plan of "Wall Street" capitalists to start a war in order to raise stock market prices. A prisoner raised the question how it happened, if South Korea was the aggressor, that the North Koreans had penetrated forty miles deep into South Korean territory at the end of the first day of fighting. The instructor ordered him to recant, and as the soldier refused, the instructor had the whole group stand until this man would give in. After a few hours, with pressure from his comrades mounting, the soldier yielded and recanted. He had then, for several days, to write every day a long piece of self-criticism and to apologize for his conduct (p. 108).

Kinkead's report illustrates also another aspect of the process of brain washing, which distinguishes it from propaganda in nontotalitarian countries; i.e., in brain washing, the object is treated *like a child* who, in traditionalist education, has to accept explanations and to abide by rules without questioning. This kind of treatment is, of course, profoundly humiliating for those being submitted to it. In any kind of propaganda other than brain washing, on the other hand, the approach is essentially on an adult level, appealing to existing allegiances and moral principles, and to reason, spurious though the appeal may be.

The Conditions of Totalitarianism

The conditions for the adoption of totalitarianist attitudes follow from their nature. Totalitarianism appears whenever there is a "monism of value," i.e., a concentration of human will upon the achievement of *one* goal. Whenever there is a "pluralism of value," i.e., whenever people are given to many, often conflicting, pursuits, the resulting political system cannot be totalitarian. Lord Acton had expressed this principle in 1862: "Whenever a single definite object is made the supreme end of the State, be it the advantage of a class, the safety or the power of the country, the greatest happiness of the greatest number or the support of a speculative idea, the State becomes for the time inevitably absolute" (p. 184).

There is no reason why, if complete power is in our hands, we should refrain from using it for the achievement of our purposes unless we feel some doubt about the worthiness of our purposes—in which case we are not fully committed to them—or feel allegiance not only to these goals but also to some other principles or ideas, e.g., to the idea that violence should not be used because it is felt to be morally condemnable and a source of evil even if used for right ends, or self-defeating in the long run; or if we believe that respect for human dignity is as important as the goal that we might pursue at its expense. In these latter instances we are not pursuing one goal *exclusively* but are trying to steer our way in the midst of different, partially conflicting, values. Even the difference between authoritarianism and totalitarianism must be seen in this light. True monism of values, *undivided allegiance* to one goal only, will always find its expression in totalitarianism.[1]

Authoritarianism indicates a condition short of complete monism; for a political system to stop at the authoritarian level without going all the way toward totalitarianism there must be, in addition to dedication to the goals of the State, some respect of individual human dignity, or some feeling that there should be a private sphere which the State should not enter; in short, some reason why those who wield full coercive power should be content with their subjects' duty and not demand their subjects' soul, too.[2]

[1] A readiness to "liberalize" controls under the Soviet system, e.g., by permitting free, or relatively free, discussion in so-called cultural matters—literature, painting, music—if advocated not merely as an expedient of smoother political control must therefore appear from a Bolshevist viewpoint as the introduction of an extraneous value, hence as treason.

[2] Sometimes, of course, the comparative restraint of authoritarian rulers may merely be a consequence of their limited strength; they do not dare to go any further. But there are cases of self-restraint, too.

Totalitarianism is probably older than pluralist systems and perhaps also older than authoritarianism, which has a slight touch of pluralism, as it were. One wonders to what degree the idea of liberty in Western civilization may be an end product of the separation of secular and spiritual authority that was inaugurated by the word of Jesus: Render therefore unto Caesar the things that are Caesar's; and unto God the things that are God's. This separation has permeated the life of Europe under the Latin Church and has permitted a degree of liberty to develop in the shadow of the long struggle between Crown and Papacy; and with the decline of the influence of the churches, the spiritual authority which they had wielded became a stray good, for everybody to pick up and keep it if he could.

In the Eastern Church, on the other hand, spiritual and secular authority have remained in one hand, according to the famous word of a Byzantine emperor: *imperator sum et sacerdos*.[3] We still see today in the greater part of what was the domain of Eastern Christendom that unlimited physical coercive power and the authority to define proper beliefs rest in the same hands, viz., the ruling men of the Communist party.

The dedication to one, and only one, goal, to the exclusion of all other considerations, can be brought about in two ways: one is, of course, the conviction of men that only one thing matters, at least for the time being, and that everything else must be postponed or subordinated to it; in our age, the idea of socialism and the idea of nationalism have played this role, and totalitarianism has been practiced in the name of one or the other. We may call this the *ideological* case of totalitarianism. It is well enough known today, through the experience of the last four decades. But there seems to be less awareness of another case of totalitarianism, or potential totalitarianism. Domination of the mind by one goal can come about not only as a consequence of an ideology but also through extreme circumstances which tend to reduce the leeway of human actions so that it may all come down to concern for one thing without which nothing else is possible, i.e., to the question of coping with extreme danger, the issue of survival. If ship-wrecks are stranded on a deserted island, if a mountain-climbing party is faced with an avalanche, or a nation sees destruction or slavery stare in its face, many issues of property, income, status, convenience, or individual rights may be brushed aside if they stand in the way, or seem to stand in

---

[3] I am aware of the fact that the statement is apocryphal and that Byzantine scholars would question whether this state really fully applied except perhaps under the iconoclast emperors, and again, toward the end of Byzantine history, under the Palaeologi. But if not exactly true, the formula is a good enough approximation to the truth.

the way, of survival. Extreme dangers have always called forth the temporary suspension of individual rights. Roman constitutional practice had it regularized; the Senate voted emergency powers to the consuls with the standing formula: *Caveant consules ne quid detrimenti capiat res publica.* Beyond that Rome had the institution of temporary dictatorship.

Resort to Potentially Totalitarian Measures in the Struggle against Totalitarianism

This may throw some light upon a discussion that has been going on in the United States for some years. In a fight against totalitarianism, we are told, we must beware lest we become totalitarian in the process of fighting it: "The defeat of totalitarianism . . . must come about by due process of law and not by destroying freedom and the ways of freedom through adopting the methods of totalitarianism" (Kallen, 1954). This is an appeal that is certain to win the favor of an audience, like proclamations in favor of peace, democracy, or economy in government, because like those it implies that what one desires can be had without a price; one can oppose such declarations only at the penalty of unpopularity. Every reduction of freedom, in the face of enemy threat, every measure of political control, however mild in itself, is immediately denounced from many quarters as a step toward totalitarianism and *therefore* automatically disqualified in a fight against totalitarianism; in fact, it is denounced as indication that we are losing the fight in the very act of waging it.

The policies so denounced may, or may not, be effective remedies which fight off the disease without causing evils greater than those they cure. That depends on the respective policy and on the situation in which it is applied. But the *general* assumption, implicit in the criticism, that we *must* be able to counter the threat without ourselves curtailing any liberties, and that any curtailment of liberties necessarily means defeat in the ultimate sense because we would already have succumbed to totalitarianism of the domestic variety, and that delivery from the external threat of totalitarianism, if so purchased, would therefore be necessarily worthless—this assumption shows a fundamental misunderstanding of the nature of emergencies and the prerequisites of coping with them. One cannot take it for granted that it will *always* be possible to defend oneself successfully against a totalitarian threat without concentrating command and imposing discipline. Whenever possible, it is certainly desirable, for the kind of people that we are, to defend ourselves while maintaining the whole fabric of individual liberties. It was possible in the last war because the United States was then not immediately threatened, i.e., because the emergency was not critical enough. But even then the guarantees of liberties and due process broke down in cases in which an immediate and serious threat was felt; the deportation of the West Coast Japanese is the most significant example.[4]

The insistence that in the defense against totalitarianism we must never make any step, however small, toward totalitarian organization ourselves, by exercising pressures on individuals, is obviously based on one of two assumptions; either it is taken for granted that we do not face, and never will face, an emergency serious enough to require enforced discipline to deal with it; or that there is nothing to choose between the permanent loss of all our rights to our enemies and the temporary curtailment of some of our liberties at the hand of our fellow citizens, and that we may therefore just as well risk the former if we can avoid it only at the price of the latter. In short, the critics either do not believe in any great danger or they hate or fear other Americans at least as much as they fear the enemy. Better the crescent of the Turk than the tiara of the Pope, the Eastern Christians used to say in the last days of the Byzantine Empire; their descendents who lived under Turkish rule would probably have taken a different view of the matter if they had still any decisions to make.

TOTALITARIANISM AND PARANOIA

We have distinguished between totalitarianism as product of an ideology and totalitarianism as the result of extreme danger. Psychologically, the two types are essentially one because in the mind of the ideologist the condition against which he fights or which might recur if he relaxed in his vigilance —e.g., so-called capitalism for the Communists—is so profoundly evil that its prevalence would mean moral or spiritual death for him. The monistic ideologist therefore feels himself always in an emergency; but as different from the threat that is felt by the shipwrecks, the stranded mountain climbers, or the nation under actual threat of subjugation or extinction—say, the Romans at the time of Cincinnatus—the emergency of the ideologist exists only in his interpretation and in most instances does not appear as emergency to outsiders. Perhaps the best *objective* criterion for this difference is the fact that these other emergencies are all temporary and once they have passed, the people will again pursue variegated goals, while the *emergency of the ideologist never ends.*

[4] That such situations are used, or abused, by private interests, prejudices and hatreds or by sheer hysteria, and that such factors may extend the action, in scope, severity or time, beyond the limits of self-preservative necessity is of course also true, but it does not alter the fact that there is a core due to self-preservation.

But the permanent concentration on one goal with the elimination or subordination of all others is the sign of a *distortion of the human form;* popular speech indicates this impression by attributing to such people a "one-track mind." The corresponding scientific expression would be "overvalued idea"; i.e., we have to do with *paranoid* types.[5]

I do not mean to suggest that the individuals in question are paranoid schizophrenics or that they suffer from Kraepelinian paranoia in the sense of delusions of grandeur, or delusions of persecution or delusional jealousy. But they may be called paranoid for the following reasons:

They make one ideal or aspiration absolute, to the neglect of all others, like the paranoid querulist who sacrifices his position and his career, the future of his family and the lives of innocent people to his fight for his right and for the redress of grievances which in themselves may well be real. In such cases, a man fights for a goal which we may consider worthy in itself, but he lacks a *sense of proportion.*[6] The old saying, *fiat justicia, pereat mundus,* is a questionable principle at best and must in any case not be applied to minor issues. Justice is a noble value, but so are respect for life, peace, humility, the protection of the innocent or the preservation of the legal order. Only in extreme circumstances will we feel that everything else can and must be disregarded for the sake of the one: e.g., if the injustice was monstrous, or if peace is not obtainable anyway, and in similar contingencies. But short of extreme conditions it is in some kind of *balance* that a sane mind seeks the solution of a conflict; he will not pursue any goal beyond any limit because he is aware of the fact that there are many mutually contradictory values in the world, that the realization of one goes at the expense of another one, and that there is a point where the price paid for the realization of one value is too great; e.g., where justice could be bought only at too high a price in human suffering, etc.

[5] The paranoid element in millenarian movements throughout history has recently been pointed out by Norman Cohn (1957), who considers the following characteristics as pathognomic: "The megalomanic view of oneself as the Elect, wholly good, abominably persecuted yet assured of ultimate triumph; the attribution of gigantic and demonic powers to the adversary; the refusal to accept the ineluctable limitations and imperfections of human existence, such as transience, dissension, conflict, fallibility, whether intellectual or moral; the obsession with inerrable prophesies . . ." (p. 309).

[6] Cp. to this the following words by Edward Shils (1958): "It has not been the substantive values sought by ideological politics which have done such damage. Rather it has been the rigidity, the exclusiveness, and the extremity with which particular values have been sought. There is nothing evil about loyalty to one's community, national or ethnic or cultural, nor is there anything wicked in the appreciation of equality or the devotion to any particular ideal. What is so malign is the elevation of one value, such as equality or national or ethnic solidarity, to supremacy over all others, and the insistence on its exclusive dominion in every sphere of life."

The lack of proportion, in the monistic ideologist, goes hand in hand with an unawareness of complexity; it is justified by beliefs which are not accessible to correction by experience. When such people are confronted with facts at variance with their theories, they do not change their theories but find ways to explain away the facts;[7] their attitude runs the gamut from strong bias due to chance experience, indoctrination, and emotional preference to complete inaccessibility to influence by reason (Waelder, 1949). More transient advocates of the doctrine may be found at the former, but the enduring protagonists are likely to be found at the latter, end of the spectrum. With them, the basic tenets of the ideology are *a priori* true and no event that would contradict any part of them is even theoretically thinkable.

Thus, when an American group headed by Herbert Hoover distributed food in Russia during the famine of 1921, with the U. S. government contributing to the expense of the operation, the Communists did not conclude that humanitarian sentiment existed in the United States and influenced the actions of private groups and of the government; this was theoretically impossible because government actions are determined by class interest and a humanitarian act from a "capitalist" state to a "workers' state" is a double impossibility. Hence, the food distribution must have been caused by other motives, presumably by a desire to plant spies in the Soviet Union and by the need of the capitalists to get rid of surplus goods.

Or, when it became difficult to deny that the living standards of American workers had risen substantially over the subsistence level, this was not taken to indicate that a market economy can provide for the economic betterment of the masses. Marx had proved that all value comes from labor and equals the amount of labor expended; hence, the value of a man's labor is equal to the cost of keeping him alive and in working condition. Wages,

---

[7] The way the mind of the believer operates can easily be observed in analysis. During the Second World War, e.g., a large company decided, apparently under political pressure, to open to Negroes some job categories that had heretofore been reserved to whites; thereupon the white union went on strike. These developments were deeply disturbing to a convinced Marxist who was then in analysis with me. Racial tensions, according to his convictions, were a product of capitalism; the natural condition of men was brotherhood. Racial tensions between workers were an artifact, manufactured, or, at the very least, worked up out of proportion by the capitalists who acted according to the principle: divide and conquer. How could it be that a capitalist company was ready to give job equality to Negroes and that workers opposed it?

For days he walked around in a state of bewilderment. He then strolled around near the factories in the evenings and started conversations with striking workers. In this way, he learned about a few trivial incidents which he interpreted as indicating sympathy with the strike on the part of the company. From this he inferred that the strike had actually been engineered, behind the scenes, by the company, and with this idea which immediately hardened into conviction his mind came to rest.

under capitalism, must therefore remain on the level of the costs of subsistence (the iron wage law) and the visible rise of living conditions among
American workers must be due to the operation of extrasystemic factors—
presumably, enormous war profits made by the capitalists during the two
World Wars which enabled them to let the workers share in some of their
loot.

Or, finally, if businessmen do not behave the way they should according
to the theory of class warfare but devote themselves, not to building a
united front against the "proletariat" and against the "workers' state,"
the Soviet Union, but to their own competitive enterprises, it does not indicate that the Marxist theory of classes is wrong, at least as far as the businessmen are concerned, but merely that the capitalist class is so decadent a class
that it no longer shows the characteristics of a real class. It is all like in an
old Jewish story: two men from different Jewish communities in old Russia
competed with each other in praising the merits of their respective rabbis;
sometimes one, sometimes the other, had the better of the argument. Finally,
one man has an unbeatable trump card: his rabbi is a man of such high
virtue that God Himself had talked to him. Nothing is left to the other man
than to question the accuracy of the story; perhaps it is not true? "The rabbi
told it to me himself," says the first man. "Perhaps he did not tell the truth,"
counters the other. "You are a fool," says the first man contemptuously,
"do you think God would talk to a liar?"

A believer in Communism might be asked whether he can conceive,
theoretically, of any event that would invalidate Marxist-Leninist theory.
Convinced Communists do not understand the question; Marxist "teachings"
are "scientific" Truth, so how could they ever be invalidated?[8]

It is for these reasons that the protagonists of ideological monism, as a
rule, impress us as being of paranoid type; those ideologists who are not of
this bent of mind shrink back, sooner or later, from the costs of realizing
their ideas—the sacrifices, the injustices, the distortions of truth.

The rank and file of the followers, on the other hand, are average people,

---

[8] The Communist's attitude to his doctrine cannot be compared to the attitude
of others, who have not accepted a monistic ideology, to their respective political or
economic ideas, nor, in general, to the attitude of average people to their views
in any empirical matter. It is only comparable to the attitude we all have to
mathematical theorems. Here we behave in the same way. We think that two and
two make four, and if we should ever make the experience that after having put two
objects and again two objects in a place, we find afterwards five of them there,
we would think that the fifth was put there by another person or by ourselves in
inadvertence, or has somehow been produced from other matter, or, if need be,
may even have been dropped from outer space, but we will not consider the
possibility that the arithmetic is wrong. The Communist feels this way about
Marxist-Leninist doctrine.

of many kinds of psychological make-up, who have felt the appeal of the ideal, who are pleased to hear that their aspirations can be fully fulfilled, without cost or without serious cost, who are impressed by the determination and self-confidence of the leader and have subordinated themselves to him, putting him in place of their consciences, as was described by Freud (1921).

Totalitarianism may thus be said to be *either the consequence of the imperatives of survival or the outgrowth of a paranoid system.*

Paranoid thinking is a source both of strength and of weakness. It gives strength through the polarization of all tendencies in one direction and the complete intellectual conviction which eliminates doubts and ambiguities; here, clearly, the native hue of resolution is not sicklied over with the pale cast of thought. But it is a source of weakness, too, because of the failure properly to appraise those aspects of reality that run counter to basic theoretical tenets.

In the real paranoiacs and the paranoid schizophrenics, seen in our psychiatric hospitals, there is no doubt that the liabilities far outweigh the assets. But it is often different with the paranoid personalities under discussion; with them, paranoid thought may be limited to one, or a few, propositions, and some such persons combine paranoid thought in a few fundamental tenets on matters outside the experience of average people with an ice-cold realism in other matters, particularly in matters of power and strategy; Lenin is a perfect example of this combination.[9] In such instances, the simple paranoid ideology gives to its devotees the unfaltering conviction of the eternal righteousness of their cause, and thereby a ruthlessness undisturbed by pangs of conscience, a determination to stop short of nothing in the pursuit of their goals. The very impossibility to reach the totalitarian by any kind of argument is a further source of strength because it drives those in his power into despair and, finally, except in the case of those who are morally supported by firm beliefs of their own, to inner capitulation.

"Strong ideas" that carry everything before them and become a tornado of history are often paranoid ideas. Once the paranoia has gone out of them and the idea is merely based on ordinary considerations of expediency and reasoning, strength has left them, too, and the end of the power of the idea over the minds of men is in sight. The last decades of the Tsarist autocracy provide an example of the latter condition. The system was no longer able to prevent opposition from forming itself and growing rapidly until it finally

---

[9] Cohn (1957, p. 309f.) comments: "National-Socialist and Communist leaders, despite the hard-headed realism which has characterized their tactics, have also exhibited and imparted to their followers a truly psychotic irrationality wherever the eschatological phantasy itself has been involved."

encompassed practically the entire educated middle class. The Tsarist government wavered between relative tolerance of and retreat from the popular demands and sudden outbursts of oppression. But either the determination or the power to annihilate the opposition was lacking. Power, presumably, was lacking because determination was lacking or, rather, was held only by very few. With very few exceptions, the supporters of the autocracy no longer believed in the divine ordination of kings which had been its ideological basis and justification; they stood for the Tsar not for transcendent but for purely practical reasons, above all because they feared the consequences of revolution or reform. The lack of faith in the ultimate right of the system encouraged opposition and weakened the hand of its defenders.

But there was a time when the divine right of kings was an immensely strong idea against which nobody dared to take a stand. In the peasant revolt in England in 1381, under the reign of Richard II, the peasants forced their prisoners to swear an oath of allegiance to the king and to the common people of England. We can hardly judge whether they actually believed, or merely pretended to believe, that the Crown was on their side; but in any case, revolution against the royal principle or against the person of the monarch was apparently out of the question. At most there could be revolution against the lords in the name of the king. Today, the idea of socialism seems to hold a similar power over the minds of men in a large part of the earth. Opposition against the leadership in the Soviet world appears therefore to be possible, at the present time, only in the name of socialism, not as opposition against socialism.

It is difficult to believe that men who are fully convinced that the basic propositions of Marxism-Leninism are absolute truth should ever voluntarily grant a substantial degree of freedom of expression to those who hold views fundamentally different from their own, because such freedom must mean, from their point of view, that dangerous errors have a chance to work mischief. The enormous tolerance of our society in political, religious, philosophical and social matters is partly due to doubt[10]—to the very wise distrust

[10] Cp. the words written by Freud in 1921 about religious intolerance (p. 98f.): "However difficult we may find it personally, we ought not to reproach believers too severely on this account; people who are unbelieving or indifferent are much better off psychologically in this matter. If to-day that intolerance no longer shows itself so violent and cruel as in former centuries, we can scarcely conclude that there has been a softening in human manners. The cause is rather to be found in the undeniable weakening of religious feelings and the libidinal ties which depend upon them. If another group tie takes the place of the religious one—and the socialistic tie seems to be succeeding in doing so—then there will be the same intolerance towards outsiders as in the age of the Wars of Religion; and if differences between scientific opinions could ever attain a similar significance for groups, the same result would again be repeated with this new motivation."

in our own judgment and to the suspicion that our convictions, no matter how well founded they may seem to us, may yet be mistaken and are indeed likely to appear as at least partly mistaken to a later age—and partly to the multiplicity of our values,[11] which lets us cherish not only different and partly contradictory substantive goals but also the very freedom of choice itself. These two characteristics—doubt and pluralism of values—seem to be interconnected, as the cognitive and the emotive aspect of our approach to the world, just as the opposites, intellectual dogmatism and devotion to one aspiration to the exclusion of all others, appear in their more extreme manifestations as the interconnected characteristics of the paranoid attitude.

BIBLIOGRAPHY

Acton, John E., E. Dahlberg Acton, 1st Baron (1862), Nationality. *Essays on Freedom and Power*. Glencoe, Ill.: Free Press, 1949.

Cohn, N. (1957), *The Pursuit of the Millennium*. London: Secker & Warburg.

Constant-Rebècque, B. de (1814), *De l'esprit de conquête et de l'usurpation dans leur rapport avec la civilisation Européenne*. Paris: Nicolle et Le Normant; fourth ed.

Freud, S. (1921), Group Psychology and the Analysis of the Ego. *Standard Edition, 18*:67-143. London: Hogarth Press, 1955.

Kallen, H. M. (1954), In: Considerations Regarding the Loyalty Oath as a Manifestation of Current Social Tensions and Anxiety. *Group for the Advancement of Psychiatry, Symposium No. 1*.

Kinkead, E. (1959), *In All Wars But One*. New York: W. W. Norton.

Shils, E. (1958), Ideology and Civility: On the Politics of the Intellectual. *Sewanee Rev., 66*.

Waelder, R. (1949), Notes on Prejudice. *Vassar Alumnae Magazine, 34*:2-5, 23-24.

—— (1951), Authoritarianism and Totalitarianism. In: *Psychoanalysis and Culture*, ed. G. B. Wilbur & W. Muensterberger. New York: International Universities Press.

[11] The Communist conviction that "capitalism" is "decadent" contains a nucleus of truth. If we take capitalism to mean a pluralist society, and decadence to mean the existence of intrinsic weaknesses, the statement comes down to this: pluralist societies have intrinsic weaknesses, and this is correct. Totalitarian societies, of course, are not free from weaknesses of their own which are best visible in the very long run.

TOTALITARIAN IDEOLOGY AS A DEFENSE TECHNIQUE

NORBERT BROMBERG, M.D.

Ideologies of all kinds are usually propounded with such an air of certainty and finality that the impression is often conveyed that they are the products of pure reason, the inescapable conclusions derived from the logical marshalling of scientifically derived data. Actually, nothing could be farther from the truth. The term "ideology" was first used as a designation for the analysis of ideas, or for the doctrine that ideas are exclusively derived through sensation. Like many others, this term has since undergone an evolution which has altered its meaning to some extent. However, it still does not imply any of the irrefutable certainty with which it is endowed by many. Representative dictionaries define ideology as visionary or idle theorizing or a speculative or impractical theory or system of theories. A political ideology would, therefore, be no more than a system of political, economic and social theories and values from which are derived objectives that form the nucleus of a political program.

Of course, social values and political and economic ideologies are arrived at no differently than are any others, be they about beauty, or sex, or money, or strength, etc. Schilder (1936) states,

> Psycho-analysis has shown the way in which ideologies are built up. They arise from the libidinous situation in early childhood and are therefore in close relation to the emotional attitude of the child towards his parents and the other persons around him. A part of these ideologies are built up by identification and others by imitation. They are very often reactions of the parental ideologies when there is an open conflict between parents and child. Very often they have the complicated genesis of a neurotic symptom, and represent in a symbolic way the libidinous forces as well as the repressing ones.

Based on a paper read at the Fall Meeting of the American Psychoanalytic Association, December 5, 1958.

From the Department of Psychiatry, Albert Einstein College of Medicine, and the Psychiatric Service of the Bronx Municipal Hospital Center.

[At another point he says,] Ideologies are not only a theoretical belief but they have a profound influence upon our actions and are very often the deciding factor in the organization of our lives. . . .

The truth of this statement can readily be seen if one considers the current international political scene. Not only have millions of lives already been sacrificed in recent years for one or another totalitarian political ideology, but many more millions may momentarily be sacrificed in the name of one of these.

When a totalitarian ideology dominates the immediate or general environment of an individual, he may adopt it by identification, or as a practical expedient for survival, or by conviction resulting from the unavailability of accurate data with which to correct information distorted by propaganda. When, on the other hand, a person espouses a totalitarian ideology in the face of available data patently contradictory to the tenets of this ideology, we are obviously dealing with distortions of reality that probably meet some of his particular psychic needs. Thus, when an intelligent and educated man accepts a dictum of a would-be artist that (a) there is a master race, and (b) that it is threatened by a conspiracy initiated by a group called the Elders of Zion, there must be some psychological reason for the fact that these ideas are acceptable to him in the face of expert evidence and testimony to the contrary. Again, when an intelligent and well-informed American maintains that the electoral system of the U.S.S.R. is a more democratic one than that of his own country, we must assume that he does this violence to the political realities because of some special psychological factors.

This assumption is supported by what Adorno et al. (1950) consider the most crucial result of their study concerning "the potentially fascistic individual." That result is

    . . . the demonstration of close correspondence in the type of approach and outlook a subject is likely to have in a great variety of areas, ranging from the most intimate features of family and sex adjustment through relationships to other people in general, to religion and to social and political philosophy. Thus, a basically hierarchical, authoritarian, exploitive parent-child relationship is apt to carry over into a power-oriented, exploitively dependent attitude toward one's sex partner and one's God and may well culminate in a political philosophy and social outlook which has no room for anything but a desperate clinging to what appears to be strong and a disdainful rejection of whatever is relegated to the bottom.

It may be noted, parenthetically, that the reason the fascistic type of totalitarianism was selected for this study is at least partly related to the fact that it was sponsored by the American Jewish Committee which is interested in the cause and "cure" of anti-Semitism. Up to the time of that study, this form of prejudice had revealed itself most brutally in the Nazi type of totalitarianism. More recent events have revealed that, even in this respect, the Communist form of totalitarianism does not differ psychologically from other forms. Their conclusions, therefore, regarding the potentially fascistic individual really relate with equal validity to any potentially totalitarian one.

While the conclusions quoted are far from surprising to the psychoanalyst, it is interesting to have them statistically validated in a careful nonpsychoanalytic study. What that kind of study, of course, cannot do, is to elucidate the detailed genetic, topographic, and dynamic factors which underlie these findings. Efforts in this direction have, however, been made by some analysts.

Waelder (1951), for instance, clearly demonstrates the important role that the superego plays in the acceptance of totalitarian ideology. He points out that psychologically, the distinguishing feature between authoritarianism and totalitarianism is that the latter is "a system in which power is not subject to any of the limitations or restrictions which are characteristic for Western civilization, and in which temporal and spiritual authority are united in one hand." In psychoanalytic terms, this means that the individual's superego is required to defer to the moral authority of the dictator. If the dictator imposes restrictions which serve an ideal or purpose which is not part of a person's superego, he feels their pressure as external and therefore oppressive or even tyrannical. But if the ideal is internalized and part of the superego, the restrictions which serve it do not interfere with a sense of freedom.

Waelder further points out a feature of totalitarian ideals which is unacceptable to anti-totalitarians both per se and because it contains the seeds of the tyranny and the ruthlessness of the methods used to achieve those ideals. He calls this ethical monism. It is manifested in Communist ideology in that the latter recognizes no other values outside its socioeconomic goals; just as the greatness of the German nation, as the Nazis saw it, was the only ideal that their ideology accepted. On the other hand, Waelder points out, that

> . . . Western man is a pluralist who believes in a polyphonic system of values, both moral and hedonistic, which often are in conflict with each other . . .
> . . . but Western man is not embarrassed by these contradictions. He feels that the world of human aspirations is highly complex, no less so than the visible world of things, and that nothing can be gained but much can be lost by trying to simplify it.

Since the successful introduction of any other values into a monistic ethic would undo it, any disagreement is perceived by the ethical monist as a vital threat. Hence, as Waelder observes, monism always tends toward concentrated power, ruthlessness in its use, and totalitarianism.

Talmon (1952) cites the ethical monism of totalitarian ideology as the source of what he calls the paradox of freedom. He formulates this by posing the question whether human freedom is actually compatible with an exclusive pattern of social existence, even if this pattern aims at the progress to man's perfection and complete social harmony professed by the "totalitarianism of the Left." Moreover, Talmon points out that this aim or ideal is an entirely unrealistic one. History has already demonstrated the unrealistic nature of the Nazi ideal of a millenium of the Third Reich.

This leads us to two general questions: (1) What moves the totalitarian to adopt his narrow, rigid, perfectionistic and unrealistic ideal? (2) What motivates his cruel ways of trying to achieve it? The answers to both of these questions are, of course, quite complex.

In a study of the Russian trials confessions, Bonnard (1954) interprets the doomed defendants' clinging to the Soviet ideal as "an example of the defence mechanism of 'identification with the (idealized) aggressor.'" As will be shown later, there is reason to believe that this mechanism plays a part, in some instances, in the adoption of the totalitarian ideal in the first place.

Bychowski, who has written extensively on dictatorship and dictators (1948, 1955), makes a further contribution to the answers to these questions in his emphasis on the paranoid features in the totalitarian. Using historical illustrative material, he points out that Robespierre, for instance, like most dictators, felt rejected, despised, and humiliated since his childhood. Aggressive impulses derived from this as well as from latent homosexual strivings were given superego acceptance in the following way. The then-prevalent ideal of the basic goodness of man, as most eminently enunciated by Rousseau, was adopted by the dictator. This he elaborated to mean that everything that the people wish is good and that all who disagree are evil and must be destroyed. The dictator became the sole authority as to what the people need and wish by virtue of his complete identification with them. His grievances became their grievances, and vice versa. The same became true, in his mind, of his aggressive impulses and wishes. These were further intensified as well as justified by his projection of them onto all opponents who thereby appeared to him dangerous and completely evil. Consciously, of course, the restrictions on their freedom, freedom to live even, were justified on the grounds of the ideal that the good of the people is the only good and paramount to everything.

It is the thesis of this study that the espousal of totalitarian ideologies, with their unrealistically idealistic and perfectionistic theoretical goals on the one hand, and their cruelly tyrannical practices on the other, provides for some individuals a defensive device against anxiety that would otherwise eventuate from the expression of libidinal and aggressive drives on their part in relation to their parents or parental surrogates.

Certain essential features are common to all these people. In the first place, we always find that, in their upbringing, they have been severely deprived and frustrated from their earliest days on. In large part, this is due not only to a rejection of the child, but also to a particular kind of inconsistent handling. The latter is largely the result of a specific inconsistency that one or both parents manifest: an incongruence between professed principles of conduct and actual behavior. Thus, a parent may advocate honesty but actually behave dishonestly in many respects; preach altruism, but behave selfishly; admonished self-denial but be self-indulgent and greedy; profess devotion to the child's welfare but dominate and control him by instilling feelings of inadequacy, indebtedness, and guilt in him. Another contributing factor that is invariably present is the long-standing history of open conflict between the parents. This schism between them is frequently aggravated by sharp differences in their characters—a circumstance which again makes it difficult for the child to find reconciliation. Finally, the element of object loss often obtains due to the death or the physical or emotional separation of at least one of the parents from the child. All of this obviously calls for a series of choices on the part of the child throughout his development. What is most significant about these choices is that they begin to be foisted on him prematurely. That is, the infant is forced to cope with a variety of severe and frequent frustrations before he is equipped to do so in a way that would not set up undesirable patterns of behavior.

To understand the evolution of the chain of defenses culminating in those under special consideration here, we have to start practically from the beginning of the individual's life. It must be remembered that the marital strife, the differences in the characters of the parents, and the frequently found tendency of at least one of them to be alternately seductive and suppressive usually antedate the birth of the child. These influences, therefore, begin to bear on him from the earliest moments on (Spitz, 1957). The consequences of this, I have discussed, in part, in another connection (Bromberg, 1959). To summarize them, we must first recall Freud's (1923) statement that the earliest form of object cathexis is hardly distinguishable from identification. What he apparently means by this relates to the observation that the child's earliest form of relating to an object is based on oral incorporation. The most primitive form of perception, furthermore, is modeled on oral incorporation, the psychic counterpart of which is introjection. In the maturer individual, perception by introjection can be achieved without further change in the perceiver. In the primitive organism, however, perception simultaneously involves a change in the organism, at least to some extent, in imitation of the characteristics of the object. Such a change is, of course, the essence of identification. Hence, the indistinguishability between the earliest form of object relatedness and identification.

Theoretically, if every wish of the infant were immediately gratified, he could continue his fantasies of omnipotence without becoming aware of the existence of any other objects. It is deprivation and the consequent frustration that force upon him recognition of the fact that objects exist outside himself. Since the kind of patient under discussion is subjected to very early, repeated, and sometimes severe frustration, the earliest and most primitive form of relating to an object, introjection, becomes fixated and a model for later object relations. In addition to their effect on object representation, frequent early experiences of deprivation and frustration have certain consequences for the process of self-representation. Since primitive perception is indistinguishable from identification, object and self tend to be indistinguishable. When the infant introjects a frustrating "bad" object, therefore, he also fantasies himself as "bad." Moreover, if we bear in mind that early introjections are characterized by powerful oral-sadistic strivings which dominate this stage of development, it becomes apparent how the idea of being devoured, closely linked to the wish to devour, would stir up great anxiety. These factors, by the way, doubtless provide the roots of the marked orality invariably encountered later on in these individuals.

Even the infant is believed to make efforts to defend himself against various forms of pain by such precursors of denial as negative hallucinations and magical thinking (Kestenberg, 1953). The older child goes on to denial by fantasy, a combination of the denial of some disagreeable reality and an imagined reversal of the unwelcome facts. Eventually he achieves denial by word and act. But these forms are normal stages in the development of the ego. Hence, the last of these is discharged when "the organization of the mature ego becomes unified through synthesis. . . . and is resumed only if the relation to reality has been gravely disturbed and the function of reality-testing suspended," according to Anna Freud (1936). However, it is well known that the mechanism of denial may be resorted to in conditions in which reality testing is not completely suspended. This is made possible, it seems to me, when it is bolstered by other defenses. In the type of character structures under consideration here, these are notably, identification with the aggressor (Anna Freud, 1936), or with the frustrator (Spitz, 1957), or with the idealized aggressor (Bonnard, 1954), idealization, projection, and displacement.

One of the earliest of these is identification with the aggressor, the groundwork for which is laid in primary identification, and in early gesture identification, at age nine to twelve months, when the child also acquires the first understanding of commands and prohibitions. Finally, as an adaptive device to these and to most situations requiring mastery or defense, there appears the mechanism of identification with the aggressor at the end of the first year of life (Spitz, 1957). An important aspect of this process is that conflict between external object and ego is internalized, thereby contributing to the development of the superego, at least to its preliminary phase.

As in the case of the mechanism of denial, this identificatory process is a normal, indeed, indispensable one for the psychic development of the child. However, when the forces promoting it are excessive, it tends to persist beyond the period of its usual usefulness. Thus, after reality testing becomes established, it would seem that the denial of objectionable features in a libidinal object can be maintained only under the pressure of the need to identify with it. Indeed, the interdependence of the two defenses is so great that it is almost equally true to say that the identification with the frustrator is not possible without the denial of his objectionable traits.

In some instances, however, it seems that even denial is not enough to support the identification and, what may be considered as another defense mechanism, idealization, is brought into play. Pubertal idealization, whether traceable through aim inhibition back to the repression of infantile sensual components (Freud, 1921), or to a primitive form of idealization consisting of a tender attitude to part objects (Glover, 1928), is well known. This is generally considered a form of sublimation, but can also appear as a defense. Greenson (1954) cites a pathological form of this process in adults who, "predisposed . . . by the history of excessive deprivation, frustration and satisfaction in early childhood, and the violent parental discord," tend to idealize the parent of the opposite sex, while they actively hate the parent of the same sex. They are impelled in these directions by a poorly resolved positive oedipus complex on the one hand, and by a need to repress strong homosexual and aggressive impulses toward the parent of the same sex, on the other hand.

But among the group of patients on which this communication is based, some hated the parent of the opposite sex and idealized the other parent, during their childhood, even though very much the same forces were operative in them as in Greenson's cases. The one important element common to the histories of all of these children is that the parent of the opposite sex had actually or virtually deserted them as a result of a divorce or the absence of any effective interest in them. This strongly suggests that these children had to turn to the one remaining parent, no matter how frustrating, out of the reality fear of complete abandonment. In order to surmount the powerful forces mentioned above, which tend to counteract such an attachment, an even greater force had to be brought to bear. This is the defense mechanism of idealization of the less frustrating libidinal object. Further evidence of the validity of this concept is provided by the following. In every one of these cases, the idealization ceased and the parent was perceived more realistically when the patient became more independent of that love object either financially or emotionally, or both. Thus, it is reasonable to suspect that, even when the attachment is to the parent of the opposite sex, the defense mechanism of idealization to avoid objective danger is also operative if the parent of the same sex is seen as the more depriving and frustrating one. By "also operative" is meant, of course, that it obtains in addition to the forces already outlined as determining the course of the attitudes toward the parent in these cases.

With the help of all the defenses mentioned the child and later the adult may manage to maintain a precarious balance of instinctual forces. As though in reaction to the inconsistencies in and between the parents, the patient's attitudes toward them become fixed, rigid, and oversimplified. The "good" parent is idealized and seen as devoid of any negative traits, and the "bad" one is seen as totally evil and without any redeeming features. In addition to the defense mechanisms already briefly discussed, this split is facilitated by the displacement onto the accepted parent of all the desirable traits of the hated one. At the same time, all the objectionable traits of the "bad" parent are projected onto the "good" one, with whom the patient identifies. This further justifies the hatred for the "bad" parent as well as the tendency to evade him rather than deal with him as an object in reality.

One special form that this evasion may take, in certain instances, is the displacement of the whole interpersonal conflict on the more impersonal arena of conflict of political ideologies. The espousal of a totalitarian ideology is particularly apt for this purpose because it recognizes only the totally good versus the totally bad and gives sanction and encouragement to hatred and cruelty toward that which is regarded as bad. By identifying the hated parent with the opposing order and one of its leaders, while he identifies himself and the idealized parent with the totalitarian movement and leadership, such a person gains, moreover, a considerable degree of superegolike sanction for his aggressive impulses as well as for his passive, homosexual strivings. That recourse to the involvement of political ideology is not always necessary, is illustrated by a case that cannot be discussed in detail. Suffice it to say that in that instance, adherence to a totalitarian ideology was obviated by the patient's propensity for finding adequate expression of her conflictful identifications in her stormy relations with various love objects. In the case to be described, which for reasons of discretion will be briefer than I would prefer, the involvement of a totalitarian ideology was helpful to the patient in coping with anxieties resulting from his conflictful identifications.

II

This twenty-five-year-old man was born to parents between whom there was much disharmony. The mother was a dull, bovine woman, with marked intellectual and emotional limitations. She professed love and interest in her only son, but very early relinquished almost total responsibility for his care to one of her daughters. During the boy's childhood and early adolescence she was alternately seductive and rejecting of him. She liked to think of herself as a devoted mother, but had little interest in his thoughts or activities. She constantly complained to him about his father. Her most frequent grievances were that her husband neglected her and was not generous in providing material assistance to her relatives. In general, she was an unhappy, complaining woman, with few intellectual and emotional resources.

The patient's father was a so-called "self-made" man who had built up a large and prosperous business. His success was to a large extent due to his deserved reputation for honesty and fairness. Though a capitalist and entrepreneur, he considered himself a social democrat, opposed to the exploitation of labor. At home he was the undisputed head of the family. While he professed great interest and solicitude for them, he used his preoccupation with business affairs as an excuse for spending very little time with his wife and children.

The patient's birth was greeted with much joy, especially by the father and the children who were all girls in their late teens and older. He soon became the pet of his sisters, one of whom practically took over the role of mother. The way in which the mother handled the boy as well as the ubiquitous propinquity of females in the home was erotically stimulating to him, so that eventually he began to spend much of his time peeping through keyholes to spy on them while they undressed. The positive aspect of his relationship with his father, on the other hand, while real, was somewhat curtailed by the father's deep involvement in his business affairs, and by his relatively advanced age. Both of these factors limited the amount and the degree of involvement that the father was able to achieve in the interests and activities of a little boy.

Against this background, the boy's misinterpretation of his father's attitude toward two physical disabilities which the patient had, created in him a markedly negative attitude toward his father. The disabilities involved a deformity of a limb and a maldevelopment of the genital apparatus. Both of these were regarded with a secretive attitude which gave the child the impression that they were a great disgrace. Moreover, he misinterpreted his father's frequent expressions of concern over the genital maldevelopment as a castration threat. Thus, in spite of all his genuine interest, tolerance for the patient's foibles, and his financial generosity, the father was the object of increasing hatred by his son. He thought of his father as a cruelly ruthless, avaricious, and hypocritical tyrant, without love for his fellow men, including his own family. The father's undeniable kindness to the patient was waved aside as merely his wish to have an heir to whom the business might be passed on, as though that were a completely selfish and reprehensible desire. More specifically, the gifts of money to him were derided as evidence of hypocritical unfairness to his sisters, though there was every indication that they were treated with equal generosity.

Indeed, he considered his sisters, his mother, and (partly because he identified with them) himself grossly mistreated by his father. He saw his mother as a faultless victim of his father's cruelty, and in his early adolescence he often expressed the desire to rescue her from it. During that period of his life he felt particularly lonesome since his sisters had married and left the home and his father continued to spend very little time in it. He had no friends so that he found himself forced to lean heavily on his mother for companionship. While this was a far from satisfactory situation, it was given support by his fervent idealization of her.

In his late adolescence, the patient witnessed a spirited discussion between his father and a young man who was extolling the virtues of Communism. He was profoundly impressed by what struck him as the vigor, courage, and success with which the younger man stood up to the older. From that time on, the patient became increasingly interested in Communism. After several years this interest waned and eventually ended as he achieved a more realistic understanding of his parents, his siblings, and himself. He gave up his violent hatred of his father and the idealized image of his mother as well as his unconscious rivalry with his sisters. Along with these, also, went his guilt over his wealth. He established some deeper relations with members of his family and others. Finally, he recognized the unrealistic and contradictory nature of many aspects of Communist theory and practice which he had denied heretofore and saw how he had employed them in his efforts to cope with his personal and interpersonal emotional conflicts.

III

A review of this history reveals that its unfolding hinges on the use of certain defenses, notably denial, identification, and projection in a repeated pattern.

In the first place, it is apparent that, in addition to whatever constitutional predisposition there may have been operative in this direction, certain genetic factors conspired to incline the patient to a marked feminine identification. These factors include the seductiveness of the sisters and also of the mother, who used to complain to him of her husband's alleged ill treatment of her. This was followed by their virtual rejection of him because the mother remained with her husband and the sisters left him to take other men for their husbands. To these motives for his feminine leanings was added a form of identification and projection resembling that designated by Edward Bibring[1] as "altruistic surrender," as a means of dealing with his envy and rivalry with his sisters for his father's love. It was doubtless helpful, also, in dealing with his guilt in accepting considerable sums of money from his father while deeply hating him. I speak of his complaints that his father did not give his sisters a fair share of the profits of the business as only resembling "altruistic surrender" because it did not really please him when his sisters achieved any financial gain, either from the father or from any other source.

Still another way of dealing with his guilt feelings, if one may call them that, was by means of identification with the aggressor, supplemented by the projection of guilt. This was manifested most graphically on a number of occasions when he inveighed against his father with particular violence, charging him with being an unfair, selfish, greedy, and hypocritically rapacious man who robbed his employees of their just due. Each instance of this type of flare-up coincided with a period during which a desire to steal some money from his father was gradually increasing in intensity and usually culminated in an actual theft. Anna Freud (1936) cites examples of this kind of behavior and indicates that it is a manifestation of an intermediate stage in the development of the superego. The maturer superego, under such circumstances, turns its severity inward instead of outward and becomes less

---

[1] Quoted by Anna Freud (1936).

intolerant of other people. Such an eventuality, of course, must coincide with the evolution of an ego able to endure the psychic pain resulting from self-criticism.

To help him ward off the guilty anxieties which the father's real love and kindness tended to increase, the patient probably chose to see him as an essentially evil and therefore repelling figure. This was achieved by a denial of the father's good traits and a projection onto him of the patient's own greed, envy, ambition, and hostility. Denial was also involved and supplemented by projection in the idealization of the mother in so far as that process is "merely his substitute for the lost narcissism of his childhood—the time when he was his own ideal" (Freud, 1914). The idealization, of course, helped him cope with his oedipal strivings (Freud, 1921). But it doubtless was also the product of the fear of isolation and abandonment which threatened him at the same time.

If one takes an over-all view of developments up to this point, one cannot help but recognize that, aside from the patient's identifications and projections in relation to each of his parents, he achieved a kind of partial cross-identification of them. In other words, he seemed to have displaced all the objectionable traits of the mother to the father, and all the admirable traits of the father to the mother. Thus, his love objects were either black or white, either totally good or totally bad. Admittedly, this is a very neat arrangement for those who find the anxiety evoked by ambivalence intolerable, and for whom the mechanisms for evading it come readily to hand. But even this helpful arrangement has its disadvantages. It is not easy to maintain.

This was certainly true in the case of this patient. The force of reality was too insistent. Though, in his fantasy, he endowed his mother with all the virtues he wished she had, the fact was that she was preoccupied with her own needs and desires, that she had little interest in his problems and affairs, and that she warded off his attempts to get close to her. On the other hand, his father was generous, accepting, and eager to be helpful to him. Moreover, the patient was not willing to put in jeopardy the advantages that his father supplied. Thus, he did not allow himself to give any outward expression of his hostility to him.

The political arena, therefore, provided an almost tailor-made medium for the exercise of his feelings. He identified himself and the women in his family with the proletariat, in this country, according to his lights, a weak and inferior, but noble class in conflict with the powerful, tyrannical, capitalistic class, personified more immediately by his father and more eminently by the President of the United States. In this struggle he saw the workers and himself aided by the Communist movement and by Stalin as its leader. The individuals personifying the conflicting ideologies were too far removed from him to compel or enable reality testing. In the human environment that he sought out, this was discouraged, as were, moreover, any deep meaningful social relationships. It did encourage the idealization of an impersonal political movement which could be courted, and abjectly served as a devoted swain might a fair maid. It is true that a cause can be a very "jealous mistress," but the demands it makes are of a different order than those made by a "flesh and blood" love and superficially suit much better the needs of some people with the character structure described.

BIBLIOGRAPHY

Adorno, T. W., Frenkel-Brunswik, E., Levinson, D. J., & Sanford, R. N. (1950), *The Authoritarian Personality*. New York: Harper.

Bonnard, A. (1954), The Metapsychology of the Russian Trials Confessions. *Int. J. Psychoanal.*, *35*:208.

Bromberg, N. (1959), Stimulus-Response Cycles and Ego Development; with Special Reference to the Masochistic Ego. *J. Amer. Psychoanal. Assn.*, 7:227.

Bychowski, G. (1948), *Dictators and Disciples*. New York: International Universities Press.

—— (1955), Dictatorship and Paranoia. *Psychoanalysis and the Social Sciences*, *4*:127. New York: International Universities Press.

Freud, A. (1936), *The Ego and the Mechanisms of Defense*. New York: International Universities Press, 1946.

Freud, S. (1914), On Narcissism: An Introduction. *Collected Papers, 4*. London: Hogarth Press, 1950.

—— (1921), *Group Psychology and the Analysis of the Ego*. London: Hogarth Press, 1948.

—— (1923), *The Ego and the Id*. London: Hogarth Press, 1940.

Glover, E. (1928), A Note on Idealization. In: *On the Early Development of the Mind*. New York: International Universities Press, 1956.

Greenson, R. (1954), The Struggle Against Identification. *J. Amer. Psychoanal. Assn.*, *2*:200.

Kestenberg, J. S. (1953), Notes on Ego Development. *Int. J. Psychoanal.*, *34*:1.

Schilder, P. (1936), The Analysis of Ideologies as a Psychotherapeutic Method, Especially in Group Treatment. *Amer. J. Psychiat.*, *93*:601.

Spitz, R. A. (1957), *No and Yes*. New York: International Universities Press.

Talmon, J. L. (1952), *The Rise of Totalitarian Democracy*. Boston: Beacon Press.

Waelder, R. (1951), Authoritarianism and Totalitarianism. In: *Psychoanalysis and Culture*, ed. G. B. Wilbur & W. Muensterberger. New York: International Universities Press.

THE EFFICIENT SOLDIER

K. R. EISSLER, M.D.

After having listened for weeks and months to the unending complaints of soldiers and observed their incapacity to withstand the hardship and strain of training, I thought it opportune to find out what may render a soldier efficient. I was able to list many reasons which I thought responsible for soldiers' breaking down in the course of training, reasons pertaining to the time preceding their induction as well as to that of their training. But I could not have adduced one single reason for what made a "good" soldier—one who did not develop neurotic symptoms, who was ready to undergo the terrific strain of training, and who not only did not resent but was even perhaps eager to make a sacrifice for the good of his country which needed his service most urgently—the soldier who was called by his army environment "normal."[1] While there was no difficulty in the neuropsychiatrist's becoming familiar with the failing soldier, it was questionable how to proceed in order to find out who was a good soldier.

Author's Note.—The following paper is a chapter of an unpublished book I wrote twelve years ago. In perusing this part of the manuscript for the first time since it was written, I experienced feelings stranger than those the reader may have. Our interests have changed, though—regrettably—interest in military matters has been reawakened. But clinical experience and theoretical progress have thrown new light on the controversial problem I take up in this paper. I doubt I would have written it today in this form, and I was surprised by the "radicalism" (which I have tried to soften at places) of my former presentation.

Though the paper would have aroused greater interest if it had been published at the time it was written than it will today, its theme is not without bearing on present-day problems. It also might have had a greater chance of approval when the experiences of wartime were more alive in psychiatrists than they are today, when repressive forces have pushed them to the background and most people live as if the great war was an atypical intermezzo. Anyone who has served in the ground forces will not blame me for the poverty of the psychiatric interviews I set forth, but will understand the mere trickle of material I was able to get out of eight efficient soldiers.

[1] For literature on successful or "normal" soldiers see: Billings et al. (1943), Needles (1945a), McNeel and Dancey (1945), Sheps (1944), Steinberg and Wittman (1943), Schwab et al. (1944). Special attention must be called to the excellent paper by Janis (1945), who discusses some of the then current defense mechanisms by which apparently a large number of soldiers succeeded in maintaining their equilibrium. Since this article was written two important texts that contain the essence of the psychoanalytic view on adjustment and adaptation have been published in English. See Nunberg (1932) and Hartmann (1939b).

39

It turned out that there was a fairly reliable method for determining who were the best trainees. One had only to select the best of those trainees who were accepted for officer candidate school. This group, which was in the upper bracket of the ratings, must have been superior in terms of military achievement and adaptability. These soldiers had been examined by special boards, and their ratings were computed on the basis of manifold factors, such as efficiency during previous service, personal impression, intelligence, and other factors. The rating the candidates received was usually not based on a scientific study of their personality—they had not been examined by a psychiatrist or psychologist—although intelligence tests had been used in selecting them. The final score was based rather on a collection of behavioristic data than on a scientifically guided examination of the personality type. This made the psychiatric examination of the subjects even more promising.

It could be assumed that these candidates had impressed their examiners, who were laymen, as particularly able and efficient. It is further concluded that since their civilian record had also been considered they had given the same impression in their civilian environment. Although efficiency and psychological normality do not coincide, they are closely allied, unless what is involved is an unusually high degree of efficiency or efficiency in an unusual area: efficient rope dancing will under no circumstances be considered normal. But these subjects had been efficient in pursuits in which the average male citizen within certain age limits was expected to be efficient. Therefore it may be permissible to discuss normality and efficiency concomitantly in this context.

Efficiency is a behavioristic index. It is applicable to machines. It derives its significance primarily from the content of goals. It is meaningful exclusively in the context of purposes to achieve certain goals. Further, it pertains primarily to actions and is without connection with motivations. Efficiency when applied to human psychology is one of the few categories which readily submit to quantitative measurement. The situation becomes more complicated, however, when the efficiency of a soldier is scrutinized. In order to be an efficient soldier a man must serve simultaneously many purposes. A soldier may be efficient in long marches, but inefficient in the handling of rifles; he may be efficient as a private, but fail as a noncommissioned officer. Under what conditions, then, should we call a soldier efficient? The ideal would be achieved if a soldier were equally capable of being subordinate or superior, if he could function equally efficiently in both roles, and even be ready to switch from one role to the other as conditions required. The candidates for officer training schools had proved their efficiency in their roles as subordinates, and according to military selection they were the best prospects of becoming good leaders. Hence, they came close to the ideal, of military efficiency, although their value as leaders or superiors had not yet been proved *de facto*.[2]

The subjective image of efficiency certainly does not coincide with the psychological reality. Efficiency, in ordinary thinking, connotes rationality, health, reason or adjustment. Efficiency is considered an asset, a virtue, an enviable good. However, there are people whose efficiency may annoy us. These are the ones who cover up their emotions and their whole personality setup behind a persistent patterning of their behavior in accordance with the exigencies of reality demands.

Furthermore, the way in which a person's behavior falls short of ideal efficiency is one of his most individual features. We can often learn more about a person's personality from his failures than from his successes. Since efficiency is defined exclusively in terms of goals, efficiency with respect to one goal may by its very operation promote inefficiency by entailing neglect of other and perhaps equally important goals. This outcome was frequently encountered in the military context. Efficiency in the teaching of military skills was often observed in instructors who failed gravely to maintain good morale.

The military situation presents particularly serious pitfalls. Some of Germany's military leaders who undoubtedly were highly efficient within a narrow military frame of reference were declared by high tribunals to have been inefficient in the preservation of human rights, which was no less their duty. In everyday language, however, efficiency pertains rather to the achievement of mostly physical or measurable goals, and the realm of moral, ethical, spiritual, or artistic values is exempt from the application of that concept.[3]

Efficiency as measured in attainment of external goals frequently exists in circumstances detrimental to internal freedom or the adequate evolvement of emotional life. Popular thinking does not embrace the idea of a very efficient person's possibly being very sick. Nevertheless, the analysis of patients reveals that just their greatest achievements—in terms of performance accepted by the community as efficient—sometimes are the direct outgrowth

---

[2] But cf. Boring (1945): "The old military maxim that every soldier should be trained to do everything so well that he can replace any comrade or superior who becomes a casualty simply does not work. It is an ideal goal." (p. 170).

[3] For suggestions regarding the organization of society in such a way as to make performances serving these values coincide with efficiency, see Charles Horton Cooley (1918).

or derivative of their central psychopathology.[4] Yet efficiency is one of the qualities expected in the "normal" person. "Normality," however, is the most elusive concept of psychiatry.[5]

It would be of interest to know since when occidental society has had at its disposition a word to signify normal behavior. Words denoting deviant behavior certainly were among the vocabulary of antiquity. But I surmise that in earlier phases of occidental history, man was considered a far too individual configuration ever to be expected to follow consistently a predetermined set of rules of conduct. In most participants of present-day civilization, however, the concept of normal behavior will be encountered as a permanent fixture of their conceptual inventory. The concept is used quite freely and without much deliberation. It can be seen that in people's practical thinking normal behavior will frequently coincide with what they would like people to do or what they have been accustomed to consider as the only possible reasonable reaction to certain stimuli. Rarely does anyone who uses the term in everyday language become aware of the subjective arbitrariness of the way he applies the concept.

I only once have had the opportunity to conduct (part of) an analysis of a man who considered himself essentially "normal." In the first interview he gave the impression of a person not laboring under any undue psychopathology. His request to undergo psychoanalysis seemed justified by the necessity of his knowing about mental science for professional reasons. His general history seemed to confirm the impression. Yet in the course of his treatment, it became evident that he was suffering from a very severe disorder which made him less accessible to therapy than those who started out their treatment with the knowledge that they were sick.[6]

It was my clinical experience with this patient which made me decide not to attempt again the analysis of a socialized normal person. Therefore I

---

[4] This study of efficiency will consider exclusively the personality aspect. There is an entirely different approach possible, namely, the study of external conditions which will favor efficiency in the soldier. For literature and an excellent presentation of all problems involved, consult Boring (1945). Furthermore, the problem of the connection between outstanding qualities and efficiency in the army will not be discussed. For the contribution of the "gifted" to the army, see Terman and Oden (1947). For military careers of normal university students see the forthcoming monograph by John P. Monks. For the extent to which efficiency in specialists can be improved by proper selection and training, see Bray (1948).

[5] See Hacker (1945), Thibaut (1943), Ryle (1947), Reider (1950).

[6] Cf. Glover (1932): "Normality may be a form of madness which goes unrecognized because it happens to be a good adaptation to reality" (p. 248). See also Jones (1931): ". . . one is often astonished to observe how a comparatively good functioning of the personality can exist with an extensive neurosis, or even psychosis, that is not manifest" (p. 3).

welcomed the possibility of delving into the problem of normal behavior when I obtained permission to interview the trainees with the highest score among the candidates for officers training. I assumed that if the term "normal" had any rational applicability at all, it might be applied to this group of trainees, who had shown an amazing degree of flexibility and capacity to adjust behavior to the exigencies of unusual and highly varied situations.[7] This particular quality which is called adjustment or mental health may serve as an index of normality of behavior. Those who use terms adjustment, mental health, normal behavior, as final categories of human behavior all too frequently forget to investigate the motives which lead to that adaptation of an action to the requirements of a situation.[8]

Indeed, quite opposite impulses may lead to actions which appear outwardly to be well adjusted. Such actions may be caused by interest in the situation or fear of humiliation or a compulsion to do what one is told to do. Certainly from the psychiatric point of view actions per se can only be registered; their interpretation depends on motivation. Only rarely is the action such that it may be considered that only one series of motivations could have led to it. This, however, applies only to actions of significant pathology, in which it is assumed that the motivations underlying the actions must be of similar pathology. The closer, however, the action pattern falls into what is acceptable or even commendable from society's viewpoint, the less can safely be said about the probability that a certain motivation led to that pattern.[9]

Eight subjects were interviewed. All of them held top ranks in the rating

[7] Hacker (1945) pointed out the two meanings normality alternately takes: the statistical average or the ideal. The way I have used the term in the above statement would fall into the latter meaning. For a discussion of the variety of meanings of the term in biology, see Ivy (1944). Ivy differentiates: the normative and the clinical or pathological view; the arbitrary and the nonarbitrary statistical view. This could *mutatis mutandis* be applied to psychology. Ivy's differentiation of the statistically usual condition and the statistically usual response to a stimulus or insult impressed me as particularly valuable for clinical psychopathology.

[8] See Cantor (1941). Quite generally it must be stated that there seem to be two broad kinds of approach toward the problem of normality: one looks at normality as something absolute, the other as something relative. For an example of the former, see Maeder (1941); of the latter, Hartmann (1939a).

[9] Cf. Wegrocki (1939): "The delusions of the psychotic and the delusions of the Northwest Coast Indian cannot by any means be equated. Mechanisms like the conviction of grandeur are abnormal not by virtue of unique, abnormal qualia but by virtue of their *function in the total economy of the personality.*" However, from the viewpoint of psychoanalysis the following statement must be rejected. "The true paranoiac reaction represents a *choice of the abnormal;* the reaction of the Haida chief represents no such choice—there is but one path for him to follow" (*author's italics*).

for candidates for officer training. The goal of the interview was frankly told to the eight subjects. Discretion was assured. In most instances I did not even know the name of the soldier, and this was told to him so that he might have the greatest possible assurance that there was no trick involved to check on the advisability of sending him to Officers' Training School. In addition, the subjects were assured that they might refuse to answer any or all questions and that if they desired, they might come for a second interview—which did not happen in a single instance.

Most of the subjects evidently had trouble in relaxing during the interview. Almost all of them perspired during most of the period; some were shaky. In general the interviews proceeded slowly, against a tacit but heavy resistance. Rarely did the conversation reach the point of a free and easy flow, although all subjects assured the interviewer that they were most eager to cooperate.

Perhaps it was the subjects' distrust of the situation and their simultaneous desire to please the interviewer by trying to appear or to be frank and honest which not only made the interviews poor in scientific results but also created a scarcely describable unpleasant atmosphere. The impression was received that the subjects did not consciously object to communication with the interviewer but that they were genuinely lacking in the capacity for self-expression.[10]

It was interesting to note the reaction of most of the subjects when they were told that they should start to talk about themselves with whatever they would like to say. The usual response was the bare naming of their family status and the date of induction, or similar data. These were, they insisted, the only things they thought worth saying about themselves. It was plain that they were greatly hampered in verbalizing interior processes, as if their power of description had been completely absorbed by external data.[11] Only the insertion of questions kept the interview going, and no appeal to express the sequence of thoughts as they came and went was of any avail. In the following I wish to present briefly some case histories of this series. (The sequence in which the cases were interviewed was: 2, 8, 3, 7, 4, 6, 5, 1.)

[10] I first thought that the difficulty I encountered in interviewing these eight subjects might have been caused by a wrong technique of interviewing on my part. But Hooton (1945), in his report on the findings in normal college students selected for the "Grant" study, describes difficulties which the psychiatrists encountered in interviewing normal subjects. These difficulties, although by no means identical with mine, may nevertheless have been similar.

[11] This finding may possibly constitute a serious argument against Roger's non-directive therapy (1942).

Case No. 1

Soldier, twenty-nine years old, married for six years, has a daughter three years old; one nineteen-year-old brother was rejected for military service because of a heart murmur since the age of seven. Father was fifty-three years old, mother one year younger. Both parents were in fairly good health and were born in this country. The family was of Swiss, English, and German descent. His father ran a large farm and was in comfortable circumstances. Soldier graduated from high school at the age of fifteen or sixteen. Since he was allergic to hay and repeatedly suffered from hay fever, he made his professional plans dependent on leaving the farm. He became a teacher and obtained a certificate prior to having reached the legally prescribed age. He was later appointed principal of a school. Apparently he had been more than averagely successful in his profession. He had devoted much time to various sports activities. He was a coach on several teams. Because of these sports activities he neglected his social life and visited with his friends only once a week. He would have enjoyed having more opportunity to mix with his friends. He had met his wife when he attended college. His child was not a planned baby, but he showed no untoward reaction in the course of his wife's pregnancy. He regularly practiced coitus interruptus. There were some sexual difficulties at the beginning of his married life, since both he and his wife were inexperienced in sexual matters. The soldier had had no pre- or extramarital intercourse. He had expected to be inducted one year prior to his actual induction. When he was called in, however, it took him by surprise. He was in the process of taking his master's degree, which would have put him into a financially more favorable position, and he was promised deferment. His superintendent tried to get a deferment for him, but the necessary steps were undertaken too late. He quickly became accustomed to army life. He spontaneously mentioned two points of criticism: first that the army did not grant the soldier any possibility of taking the initiative; and, secondly, that the trainees did not get enough sleep. The latter wore him down. He believed he had been in better physical condition before his training started than at the end of it. While on bivouac he fell sick with an upper respiratory infection and was hospitalized. On return to duty, he was assigned to a new organization and had difficulty forming adequate contacts because firm groups had already been established. The excessive cursing and swearing in his military environment was painful to him and he tried to swear as little as possible, but could not completely keep away from it. There were two instances of disciplinary difficulties, once when his shoes were dusty and the other time when his rifle was not properly cleaned. Both instances occurred at an inspection and he was punished for one and ordered to do some extra duty. There was no reaction of resentment. Carrying the heavy pack caused him pain when he had to do it for the first time. He suffered from blisters on his feet caused by marching. This did not interfere with his progress in training.

The soldier had a history of pneumonia at the ages of one, two, and ten, and of occasional upper respiratory infections. He claimed that family life at home was very peaceful. There were no disagreements or arguments between his parents. His mother seems to have been the more active parent in the home. He attended a Protestant church but had no strict church affiliation. He received physical punishment from his mother up to the age of twelve and later from his father. He often had the feeling that the punishment was not warranted but he believed at the time of the interview that his parents were justified in the way they had treated him. When he was asked how he had felt as a child when suffering corporal punishment, he started to cough and tears came to his eyes, which he claimed was caused by hay fever from which he had suffered for the last two days.

The soldier had been a Republican. He resented Roosevelt's accumulation of power by the "packing" of the Supreme Court. But after the President's death he changed his mind and thought that he had been a farsighted statesman. The soldier had recently developed away from isolationism.

Comment: Notwithstanding the many details further exploration of this soldier's history might have revealed, two areas of manifest psychopathology were brought forth in that interview: hay fever and coitus interruptus. There was a predilection of the respiratory system in the history of physical disorders. The coitus interruptus is susceptible, among others, of the interpretation of a defense against the experience of a strong orgastic sensation. The informant doubted that he ever felt in his penis during ejaculation a sensation more pleasurable than that in any other part of his body. Hay fever apparently made it possible for him to leave the parental home, which in turn led him to start a career in which he claimed to have attained achievements above average. A poorly repressed reaction against parental punishment was obvious. The soldier had the appearance of a stable personality, but the two main symptoms he mentioned suggested that his success was based on compensatory mechanisms. One cannot tell what his reaction might have been if he had reached a higher level of physical gratification during intercourse or if the hay fever defense mechanism had been blocked. I would surmise that his effort to overcome the unpleasantness he encountered in training was a camouflaged competitive struggle with his father.

It is remarkable that this soldier could remember but one incident of defeat in his life—in a tennis tournament. He claimed that the outcome of the tournament was not particularly important to him.

Case No. 2

This soldier was twenty-five years old, the second oldest of seven children. One brother was three years older and one two years younger; his oldest sister was five years younger than he. His father had died five months before the soldier's induction, from carcinoma of the pancreas. Although his father's death had not been sudden, the soldier was still depressed. He had not cried at his father's death, and evidently was still engaged in a delayed mourning reaction at the time of the interview. He was aware that he had not yet overcome his father's death. His father, a Methodist, ran a small country store in the Middle West. He was strict with the children, but to a lesser extent than his mother. The soldier was punished physically by his father every three to four months, mainly for fights with his younger brother. He felt angry whenever he was licked by his father and twice he seriously thought of running away from home, but never did. It never entered his mind to go A.W.O.L. from the Army. His mother, however, was the real disciplinarian. She was a thin, small woman who always threatened she would denounce him to his father for minor misdemeanors, but usually did not follow up her threats. She was far less liberal than his father and did not permit the children to smoke or to play on Sundays. She developed arthritis when he was nine years old, and her fingers became stiff. Recently she had difficulty in walking. She was taken care of by two younger sisters of the soldier.

The soldier graduated from high school. In his last year of school, he was a bellboy at a hotel. After graduation he worked full time in the hotel and became assistant manager within two years. Then he entered an airplane factory, first as a timekeeper and then as a foreman. He was proud of having worked for an aircraft factory which had the highest rating of all. He had to supervise twenty-five girl workers. He claimed the reason that he was not deferred was that he had not yet reached the age of twenty-six, and although he knew that there were quite a few who dodged the draft, he did not feel angry about his induction. Yet he wished that some of the draft dodgers had been with him in training.

His older brother developed in a way which was quite different from his. The brother was a social climber. He was a good talker and got access to the wealthy crowd. By some ingenious scheme he made good money. He went into the Navy and was commissioned. The soldier too would have preferred naval service. He was originally selected for it, but when he came to the induction center he was told that the quota had been changed. He thought it was a tough break to be assigned to the infantry. In the Navy one gets at least one hot meal a day and there are no foxholes and C-rations.

The soldier's main interests were devoted to his family. He had been married for five years and had a boy of three. He never had extramarital intercourse. There was a history of premarital intercourse with his wife, two months prior to marriage. He was quite dependent on his wife. When she left to stay with her mother in her second month of pregnancy, which she took badly, and did not return after two months as planned because she felt too sick to travel, he cried for twenty minutes. She followed him to camp but left the baby, against his desires, with its grandmother. She had gone home five weeks prior to the interview. He felt at a loss after her departure, but gradually he became accustomed to her absence. They were in daily correspondence. There was a history of masturbation about which he felt very bad and humiliated. The last time he had masturbated was shortly before his engagement. The feelings of guilt about masturbation were evidently still alive in him.

His oldest sister was married to an unreliable man who fought with his wife and in-laws and had to change jobs incessantly because of his argumentative disposition. The sister next to the oldest was happily married to a soldier.

The informant could not remember ever having been sick. He was in excellent physical shape when he entered the Army. He went hunting in fall, and was accustomed to taking long hikes. He was a passionate tennis player. During training he had difficulty in bearing up under the heat since he was accustomed to working in an air-conditioned office. He reacted with nausea to salt tablets, but felt better when he replaced them by generously salting his food. His mouth became dry and full of sand on hikes. He knew about that particular difficulty beforehand from a man who worked at his plant and who had been discharged from the Army because of age.

During the first hour of the hand grenade course, the soldier whose turn at practice was before his was injured because a grenade fell short. Being the first to throw after this accident, he was afraid, but after one throw his fear vanished.

His platoon was very proud that no soldier in it was excused from any training activity and that no one ever fell out on hikes. Hence "it was impossible for me to fall out," he said. After three weeks of training, he was on guard duty at night and had scarcely slept at all. The next day he frequently dozed off and felt exhausted but recovered toward evening. That day, however, was so trying for him that it brought him close to giving up. He did not oppose military discipline. He did not feel irritated by the orders of the officers and cadremen, but the anger of other soldiers and their incessant complaints got on his nerves. He knew perfectly well that officers and cadremen only did what they were told to do. He knew this from his own experience as foreman at the factory plant. The foreman had an iron system and they had to keep strict discipline. Most foremen were hated by their men. He always tried to avoid this and was as liberal as possible to others. When a workman accomplished in fifty minutes what others did in sixty, he gave the man a ten-minute break. He could not stand the idea that anyone might be angry at him and he went out of his way to make everyone like him. He had no friends but one. After his marriage he gradually drifted away from this pal. He also became less closely attached to his mother than before. He visited her twice a week. He became able to do things she considered a great sin, such as taking five or six drinks in a night club. But he did not know what he ought to consider a sin. There was a history of compulsive traits, such as taking care to step (or not to step) on cracks in the pavement when he was on a newspaper route. But later he stopped paying attention to this because he had to think about so many things. Since he had all his life stayed away from men who drank and caroused with women, he had trouble getting accustomed to army life and particularly to foul language. He had to participate in swearing. "In the Army," he said, "you have to swear because you would not know what to say if you didn't do it." Yet he made it a point that he never used a word worse than "hell." He was not afraid of combat service. He had learned that only one out of ten sees combat overseas and he thought that he might be one of the nine. He had found out that training was not so hard as it was always being made out to be by others. When he was told that something particularly difficult was on the training schedule the next day, he found that it turned out not to be so hard. He thought that since so many had gone through it, he too would be able to accomplish it.

Comment: In this instance, again, it became evident that there was some problem that had its center in his father that provided the general background of the soldier's conflicts. Anger was not conspicuous in him since the shadow of his father's death was still on his mind. Furthermore, his mother's compulsive strictness seems to have drawn most of the soldier's anger toward her, and the conflict concerning the father was partly relieved by competition with an older brother. Be this as it may, the soldier had developed an attitude of outward dependence on his wife. It did not become clear what enabled him to bear up under the anguish which was caused by his separation from her. His situation became eased by a partial identification with military authority on the grounds of his previous civilian occupation as a foreman. Evidently he possessed an appropriate defense mechanism against growing anger by saying to himself: "They cannot help it and just do what they are told to do." The recollection of the man who was discharged because of age and who had complained about the hardship of hikes stimulated his competitive spirit, which was further buttressed by the excellent group morale. It is interesting to note that the idea of hostile feelings against him in others was intolerable, which in turn drove him toward an effort to fulfill his duties. His dependence on and passivity toward his wife apparently helped him in keeping himself free of feelings of guilt about some of the unavoidable transgressions of the strict code of conduct which was implanted in him by his father's teachings. It is possible that his mild depression about his father's recent death protected him against aggressive feelings which otherwise might have been precipitated by the strictness of army discipline. It is regrettable that the intricate working of this soldier's defenses could not be studied. Evidently he was wrestling with two problems: the aftereffects of his father's death and the necessity of having to live away from his wife. Since the hardship of military life may have mitigated feelings of guilt there is the interesting possibility that a recent traumatic event and the presence of a neurotic conflict may rather have facilitated the soldier's behaving in conformity with military expectations than militated against it.

Case No. 3

This soldier, a Southerner, was eighteen years old and single. He was a short, puny fellow with red cheeks and nose. Just looking at him one got the impression that here was a neurotic young man whom one would expect to have considerable difficulty in the Army. His father was forty years old, an engineer, and had always been interested in the Army. He had participated in the First World War for three months as an enlisted man and had been an officer prior to Pearl Harbor. He had been overseas. He was the absolute ideal of the soldier. The soldier had a brother four years younger. Two of his paternal uncles were only a few years older than he.

The soldier claimed that he liked the Army. He had seen a lot of military life as the family joined the father at the various camps where he was stationed before going overseas. The father had not been in combat and was in this country at the time of the interview. In spite of the soldier's liking the Army there was one incident when he felt bad—the evening of Christmas Day he felt homesick. But another soldier turned the light on and gave him some religious pamphlets to read. Then he felt better and was able to go to sleep easily. He thought he might have been down in the dumps prior to Christmas Day, but he could not remember it. He had been a churchgoer before his induction. He was certain that going to church had a good influence on him. "It is the least," he said, "a man can do for himself."

The Army had always been his ideal. As a child he preferred playing soldier to all other games. He was proud of having his father in uniform and he wanted to make the Army his career. He feared lest he be too short in stature to be acceptable as an officer. He would be greatly disappointed if he did not obtain a commission. Even if his failure were the result of all applicants' being rejected because there was temporarily no need for officers, it would be a tremendous blow to him. He really liked training, except for "chickenshit." After their return from a long hike, all of them were called into the company street because one man was called to a detail. The same thing was repeated shortly thereafter. "But that," he said, "is because they want to teach you discipline." Yet he felt angry about a recent order to fix bayonets and carry the rifle on the shoulder as on parade. "Now that we have been here for three months, they teach us drill. But my friends could pour out more about that. I like the Army. I always wanted to come in," was his comment. He claimed he would not mind going overseas. There was a history of a few mild superstitions he had learned from his mother, such as not to open an umbrella in the house or walking beneath a ladder. In earlier years he wore a rabbit's foot and was in the habit of stepping on cracks in the pavement.

At the age of twelve he was seduced by an older girl. He remembered the event only vaguely. Apparently there was an unsuccessful attempt at intercourse. He had masturbated rarely and only out of curiosity. He had never been in love. When other trainees talked about their experiences with girls, he became curious and wanted to know how it was, but had no difficulty in mastering his desires. He was interested in sports, but not in dancing. He had wet dreams once a month. He dreamed frequently about muddy waters and snakes lying on the ground. He and his uncle went out frequently to kill snakes when he was ten years old. Once his uncle was bitten by a snake. The uncle killed snakes by throwing stones at them or he took one in his hands and threw it against a tree.

The soldier had had the usual childhood diseases. Occasionally he had a headache lasting not longer than a half an hour. Sometimes he was constipated. His mother believed in doctoring and dispensed laxatives freely. She supervised his personal hygiene up to the age of twelve and entered the bathroom when he was present. He went to college for eighteen months. He was just an average student. He was called "Stinky" and "Shorty" but did not mind it. Only when he played ball did he regret not being taller, because he was certain he would have been able to play better. "It is something I can't do anything about," he said.

He admired his mother for her many abilities such as in planning meals and entertaining guests. He thought he would never be able to function in these respects as well as his mother did; moreover, he did not want to. He wanted to marry and have a family. His wife would know how to run the house.

Although he thought his father was perfect, he believed he would be just as good as he when he reached his father's age. He knew of only one fault in his father, namely, that he was stubborn, but he thought that he himself was stubborn too. His younger brother was his closest companion before he went to college. They shared the same room and slept in a double bed.

Comment: This type of soldier was rarely met in this country. His immaturity was very plain, but nevertheless he became an efficient soldier because of a strong identification with his father, who was an officer. Under the direct or indirect influence of his father, a military career became his professional ideal, which was so firmly embedded that it carried him through all the strain of training. Without that ideal he probably would have failed fairly quickly. But it was of interest to observe how a strong ideal could make him independent of all the bywork of immaturity and neurotic symptomatology. Yet it was quite possible that troubles were in store for him and that after he obtained a commission underlying conflicts would manifest themselves. The feebleness of military traditions in the United States may account for a possibly larger number of soldiers incapacitated by neuropsychiatric disorders in this country than in others. This soldier certainly showed that an integrated tradition may prevent manifestation of psychopathology.

This soldier's biographical outline may be valuable, from yet another viewpoint. Wright (1942) discusses some theories regarding the periodicity of wars. Discussing Spengler he writes: "The warrior does not wish to fight again himself and prejudices his son against war, but the grandsons are taught to think of war as romantic" (p. 230). Whether this notion is at all correct or not, it suggests a further proposition. In modern history a great deal seems to depend on whether the father's absence from home because of warfare occurs before his children are born or after. If a child has witnessed his mother's abandonment by his father who had to leave for the army, then the likelihood that the grownup will develop antiwar attitudes is great. But the likelihood is so great as to amount almost to certainty that father's leaving, and particularly his return, will have had in most instances a traumatic effect on the child. If the father's military service occurs before he has any children, and particularly if it occurs before he is married, the child in all probability will hear only an idealized report of his father's experiences (Gregory, 1944). The chances of a positive attitude toward war will then be quite great. This may be at the bottom of the theory that grandchildren of a soldier generation are taught to think of war as romantic. In the instance under discussion, the soldier was not traumatized by his father's military service in the First World War since he was born in 1926. When his father left home prior to World War II, the boy had reached a developmental phase when positive identification with his father certainly was the adequate response, particularly in view of the glorification of military values which he had witnessed in his childhood without suffering a trauma.

However, in order to gauge the future it must be kept in mind that an indefinite number of American children had a rather confusing experience at the end of World War II. Those fathers who were not sent overseas but were joined by their families in the zone of the interior spent more time with their children and came closer to them than they would have in civilian life. For many of these children the end of the war coincided with the abrupt discontinuance of a very gratifying relationship with their fathers. Therefore, for this indefinite number, there is the bizarre situation that war is associated with a particularly cordial and gratifying relationship to their father.

Case No. 4

This soldier was a quiet-spoken man who occasionally showed a smile of embarrassment during the interview. He started to pick up things from the desk where he was seated and dropped them again, or bent a pipe cleaner, when he felt embarrassed by a question. These little mannerisms were rather inconspicuous and did not attract much attention.

He had entered the Army thirteen months prior to the interview. He was selected as a cadreman at the end of the training cycle and since then had been promoted to sergeant. Recently he had been told that he had been made available for overseas service and therefore he was advised to apply for the officers' candidate school.

His parents were born in the northern part of the Middle West, and he had spent most of his life in one of the larger cities of that section. He was of American-English-German descent. He was above average in his scholastic achievements. He never was interested in factory employment, but went to work in a bank in his home town. Later he followed friends to the west coast where he continued his occupation. Starting out as a page boy, he quickly advanced to junior teller. Later he entered an aircraft plant, for which he worked for several years as a buyer traveling from one city to another. He was successful, but admitted that he occasionally made mistakes for which he received "quite a lashing."

His father was very reticent and never showed any emotion. The soldier thought that his father could have been more successful in business if he had been more outspoken. He was successful in business but lost part of his property in the 1929 crash. He then became an inspector for a larger concern and lived in a financially secure situation, owning some real estate.

The soldier's mother was a domineering type to whose authority the family always had submitted. He was never spanked by his father and the severest punishment he received from him was to be deprived of little things he liked. His mother punished him occasionally in a mild way. His two sisters, respectively eleven and nine years his junior, were both married and both of them had children. The soldier had been married for seven years and he had two boys, five and two years old; he was in the habit of spanking his older boy, whom he described as being mischievous and careless when crossing the street. His wife joined him at camp during the holidays. He did not want her to stay with him because of the expense and unfavorable housing conditions. He also feared some detrimental influence on his children. His hobbies were photography and attending baseball games. He himself liked to play football and hockey. There was no history of family quarrels or disagreements. Only after he had reached the age of seventeen did he get closer to his sisters.

During the training he felt physically exhausted because he was not prepared for the strain involved. He claimed that his training cycle was used for frequent experiments in night problems. This, he thought, was an additional severe burden. He had no difficulty with officers and cadremen. When other soldiers complained about the strict discipline or the reprimands they received, he regularly found out that they were not accustomed to working in the business world. He thought that officers should be far stricter than they actually were, and he favored a firmer discipline than was customary. He claimed that the "lashings" he received at his civilian job were far worse than those ever meted out in the Army. For instance, shortly before his induction, he had ordered some items without authority to do so. He got a "terrific beating" for it. In his criticism of the Army he was vague. He disliked the repetitiveness but could recall distinctly only one incident worthy of criticism, when fifteen soldiers were ordered to do the same job over and over again because of disagreement among superior officers about certain details.

He was on sick call only once, for a sprained ankle. He was satisfied with the medical treatment he received. He had never been sick before induction except for two or three infectious diseases during childhood. Yet he frequently caught colds since his induction. He had no pain in back or feet during his training.

He was a devout Catholic, went to confession four times a year, and never missed Sunday Mass. He denied having engaged in masturbation or pre- or extramarital affairs.

It took a great deal of encouragement to get him to speak about an incident in which he was suspected of draft evasion because he had lost his registration card without requesting a duplicate. He feared lest this neglect might have gone on his Army record and have a bearing on his prospect as a candidate for officers' school. He admitted that his wife thought him completely unemotional, but he thought that her reproach was due to her Mediterranean descent. Her family was excessively emotional and therefore she misjudged his own emotional level. The soldier made a strong point that he was "completely normal." At the end of the interview he reported having suffered from short-lasting depressions when things did not work out on his job the way he expected. During such times he lost sleep and ate less than usual. But he snapped out of the depression as soon as something enjoyable happened. He got angry at times, but never expressed it. He just felt it and then the anger disappeared quickly. As to his sexual experience, he claimed that he had a pleasant feeling in the lower part of the stomach and in the groin as well as in the upper part of his legs during ejaculation, but he was certain that he had no sensations in the genital.

Comment: This soldier was remarkable because he represented, in appearance, conduct, and the major parts of his history, what may be called the "ideal clean American boy." He fulfilled all his duties punctually; he was devout in his religion; he lived up to the official sexual standards. Even when he participated occasionally in a party and got mildly drunk, he acted in a socially acceptable way and did not abandon his role of being a smoothly fitting cog in the social machinery. Except for a slight indication that his perfect "social adjustment" was possibly colored by some masochistic propensities, which showed up in his elaborations on and glorification of the "lashings and beatings" he had received in his civilian job, there was nothing that would have stood in the way of calling him a model boy. The price he had to pay for that adjustment was quite large. He had surrendered to society at the expense of his emotional life. I would surmise that his wife was right that he was "completely unemotional." His physical experience during intercourse may serve as proof of the marked deformation his personality had suffered in the process of adjustment.

Only little could be learned from his history as to the dynamic background on which such a personality type develops. There was the father, who had apparently developed a similar state of unemotionality. There was the domineering mother, who, without resort to punishment, prevented his deviating from the ideal and took proper care of his growing into the socially patterned mold. The compulsiveness of his personality was obvious from the impression he made during the interview. He denied compulsive symptoms. It was my impression that he was the type of "normal" person who, in analysis, once the superficial defenses are overcome, shows indications of psychopathology which makes a speedy conclusion of analysis advisable. He was the ideal soldier, but I doubt that this country would have won the war had all members of the armed forces been as he was.

Case No. 5

This twenty-nine-year-old soldier was superficially reminiscent of the last described. The clinical impression he made was more favorable and he appeared to have integrated some behavior patterns conducive to adjustment. He had married nine years ago after a courtship of eighteen months. His wife was the first girl with whom he went steadily. After an acquaintance of half a year he discovered that he was in love with her. He had two girls, aged six and two respectively.

His father had died after an appendectomy at the age of forty-nine, seven months before the soldier got married. His siblings seemed to have developed adequately. His oldest brothers were twins, aged thirty-four. Three brothers were serving in the Army. None of them seemed to have met difficulties. One of the twin brothers was not eligible for service because of stomach ulcers. One sister, aged thirty-two, worked successfully in an office. One brother, aged twenty-four, was a prisoner of war. One nineteen-year-old brother was a trainee in the Air Corps.

The soldier grew up in the Middle West. He had no difficulties at school and worked his way through two years of college with the help of a loan he received from his sister, to whom he felt the closest of his siblings. He did not want to be helped by his father and made a point that he had repaid the loan to his sister although she considered it a gift. Because of the depression, he did not see much prospect in any job and therefore he chose to train for the same sort of work his sister did, since she never was unemployed during the depression. After holding two other jobs for a short while, he became purchasing agent for a large company and was successful above average. He described his life at home as peaceful and congenial. There was some friendly kidding of his mother by his father because they belonged to different political parties, his mother feeling more strongly about politics than his father. His mother was a Republican, mainly under the influence of her German-born father. The soldier followed his father in political opinions but felt equally close to both parents.

He was a devout Catholic, attended Mass every Sunday, and went to confession regularly. The worst sins he believed he had ever committed were a few instances of masturbation between the age of seventeen and his engagement and the occasional use of birth control. He tried to avoid pregnancies by following the biological rhythm, but since his wife's cycle was not regular he felt insecure. Both of his children were planned, and he would have liked to have four or five children. Intercourse occurred once a week. He considered himself more passionate than his wife, although he thought he was rather cold in his sexual feelings. There was no history of pre- or extramarital intercourse. He never had difficulties in intercourse. As a result of an accident in early puberty, his wife's hymen was torn. He was informed about it only after marriage. He and his wife were perfectly attuned. Arguments never occurred. His wife joined him at camp in his fifth week of training, without the children. She stayed for a short while. Several times he had pangs of homesickness, but did not show undue reactions to the separation from his wife.

He occasionally had inconsequential headaches. One or two years before induction he had an appendectomy. Simultaneously warts were removed from his rectum. The latter operation had to be repeated a few months later. He had had mild abdominal distress for two years prior to the appendectomy, but had no difficulty after the operation. This surgery occurred a few months after his second oldest brother was circumcised. The soldier did not know whether he had been circumcised or not. From what he had noticed, he thought that other soldiers had larger foreskins than he. At Christmas in 1943 his wife asked him to build some toy as a present for one of his daughters.

He worked on it at the factory and got a finger into a machine. He suffered no pain, but noticed the bleeding. He was told that part of the finger had to be removed. He did not experience any untoward effect from the amputation.

He did not change jobs in order to avoid induction. When told that he would be inducted, he was determined to go through training successfully. He accepted it as part of his responsibility. The first few weeks he felt uneasy about his new environment. He suffered moderate muscle pains and occasional pain in his ankles. But neither physical nor mental pain was considered by him as undue hardship. He described the training he received as excellent and was quite impressed by its thoroughness. He had no criticism to offer nor any suggestions as to possible improvements of military life. He was reprimanded only once, for dropping a stack of rifles, and was punished with some extra detail, but did not resent this disciplinary measure. He never dropped out on hikes, although he was short-winded and was bothered by pounding of the heart.

During his school years he played baseball. Later he played golf twice a week and worked around his yard. He helped neighbors in keeping up their gardens. His life in general was sedentary. His hobby was public speaking, and he paid special attention to the enlargement of his vocabulary. At school he took leading roles in stage performances and thought that public speaking would help him in later life. He suffered mildly from stage fright and tried hard to overcome his nervousness. He thought that the worst thing that had happened to him was his father's death. He cried at the funeral and wept frequently during the following weeks. He was deeply attached to his father, although he was something of a disciplinarian. He was a good provider and was an integral part of the family. When the soldier began to date with girls, his father permitted him to go out twice a week only. The soldier did not rebel, but was satisfied in knowing how often he could go out without having to ask for permission. He had admired his father, who had worked his way up from small circumstances as a farmer. The father moved to town and left some wealth to the soldier's mother. His mother ran a small store for many years.

At the beginning of the interview, when told to say whatever he wanted about himself, he gave his occupation and then said a few words about his marriage. Then he paused and remarked that this was all he thought necessary to say. Prompted to give further information, he spoke about the high position he held in a fraternity. He perspired profusely during the interview, but claimed he felt perfectly at ease. He thought that his perspiring was due to his being accustomed to living in a higher altitude than that of the camp.

To make the parallel points with the previous subject perfect, he reported that during ejaculation he had a pleasant sensation all over, with no point of his body yielding any special sensation of physical lust.

Comment: It might be worth while to speculate on what made this soldier appear more human than the previous one. There were more indications in his comportment of at least some expressions of emotions, even if distorted, such as excessive perspiration. Likewise, his history suggested some individual deviation from an expected model pattern, such as the stage fright and his ensuing attempts at conquering it. Even his accident while working on a gift for a child strikes a human note. Although he surrendered to military authority and found that everything was perfect in the army, at least his body rebelled against some of the imposition, and he felt pain and a pounding of his heart. The little disagreements between his parents about politics and his father's giving him a reliable, though strict, frame of reference, as shown in the limitation of dating to twice a week, seemed to have been favorable factors in the psychological background. His open manifestation of grief after his father's death should be mentioned here too. His contact with the interviewer was more intense than that of the former subject and he showed an alert interest and was frank and direct in his answers. Nevertheless, the seed of psychopathology was noticeable. His ignorance of whether he had been circumcised or not, the indication of mild psychosomatic symptoms, a possible accident proneness, the deformation of the sexual experience, a successfully combated phobia reaction, may show that there was a possibly strong latent neuroticism present. But in general it seemed that this soldier had attained a higher integrative level than the previous subject. In a tentative comparison of the backgrounds of the two the following factors should be mentioned: the former subject was the oldest in his family, followed by two sisters, whereas the latter had older brothers and one younger brother. The latter was offered better opportunities of masculine identifications particularly in view of an adequate father who was not overshadowed by a domineering mother as was the case with the former. There seemed to have been at least a modicum of sexual liberty, as he had dared to masturbate a few times, whereas the former at least claimed never to have indulged in masturbation. In my experience, proved absence of masturbation in the male is a pathognomonic sign.

Case No. 6

This soldier presented a picture markedly different from the preceding. He was eighteen years old, rather short, husky, round-headed, with dark eyes and vivacious gestures. He often smiled in an open and appealing manner, was cooperative and ready to give information to the best of his ability. His parents were fifty years old; both were born in the Balkans. His father, who spoke with a slight accent, came to this country at the age of nineteen, and his mother, who spoke

English fluently, at the age of ten. The father was an inspector for the railroad. The soldier had two unmarried sisters, aged twenty-five and twenty-one. His father had not been a soldier in the First World War because he was engaged in essential civilian work. At the age of twelve the boy developed the idea that it would be nice to be a soldier. He thought that the idea had originally been a fancy, as other children want to become engineers or streetcar conductors, but after reading about the Army, he became serious in his plans and at the age of fifteen he decided to make the Army his career. He surmised that stories about his grandfather and uncles having been soldiers in the old country might have had an influence on his decision. His father opposed the idea because a soldier was not looked up to by other people, and would have preferred his son's becoming a lawyer. His mother did not take any stand in the matter and encouraged him to make up his own mind, since "he knows more about the world than she," his education being superior to hers. Yet both parents were certain that he would be disappointed in army life and they spoke about the army as if it were a matter of parades, wearing uniforms, and mock heroism.

The soldier, however, never thought about the army in such terms. He enlisted immediately upon graduation from high school, but was told he would be called after his eighteenth birthday. His training period was uneventful. He had some pain in his foot during the tenth week of training, when he suffered from blisters; he counteracted this by holding the foot in a different position and thus it did not interfere with his marching. For a short while he felt discomfort because he was allergic to pollen.[12] When he was scheduled for X-rays, the discomfort had ceased and he did not keep his appointment. He felt frightened by the recoil of the M-1 rifle, but he figured that the rifle was just an instrument of wood and steel and, therefore, could be mastered by the human mind.

He expressed some criticism of the Army. He was certain he had observed some instances of abuse of trainees by noncommissioned officers who were bucking for promotion. He objected to soldiers' being subjected to personal ambitions of officers. He further thought that the training in firing of the rifle was not sufficient, and he was desirous of obtaining more of it. Previous training in R.O.T.C. made it easy for him to adjust to army discipline. His absorbing interest in R.O.T.C. prevented him from earning better than average grades in other work. His great interest in R.O.T.C. can be seen from the only dream he can remember, one which he dreamed when he was receiving R.O.T.C. training. Then he dreamed that he was promoted to a lieutenant colonel. The dream pictured the celebration which customarily takes place on such occasions.

His sexual history was uneventful. Shortly after he began to masturbate, during his second year of high school, a friend took him out

[12] Cf. Hooton (1945, p. 22); 22.2 per cent of the subjects of the Grant study suffered from asthma or hay fever.

and provided him with a girl, with whom he had intercourse. Religious scruples prevented him from repeating the experience and caused him to stop masturbating. He claimed he had not been particularly interested in girls since he was preoccupied by his work in R.O.T.C. and he had been warned by his parents. He did not smoke because he grudged the expense. He went to church regularly. Life at home was congenial. Years ago his father occasionally became drunk, but his mother condoned it; he was not abusive during these episodes but was in high spirits and sang. Occasionally his father criticized his two older sisters for using make-up. His sisters were good-looking, went out with men who worked in the same office, but only rarely, and were not attached to any particular man.

At the age of seven the soldier went in quick succession through pneumonia, measles, and a tonsillectomy. There was a period of amnesia during the time he spent at the hospital because of pneumonia. There was a history of frequent bronchitis and sporadic hay fever. He remembered having lived a short time with his grandparents at the age of five, when his mother was suffering from pleurisy and was hospitalized. At first he suffered from being separated from his mother but became quickly accustomed to the new environment. His hobbies were the construction of airplanes and the writing of movie scripts.

Comment: This soldier evidently was greatly helped in his army service by an old fantasy he had developed years ago. Service in the army gratified this fantasy. The hint he dropped by mentioning that he had heard about his grandfather's and uncles' army service may be suggestive of idealization of a grandparent in disfavor of the father. His father's foreign accent, his occasional drunkenness, his mother's condoning attitude as if her husband were a little child, may have aroused in the soldier the desire for a strong and virile father image. By entering a career which coincided with that of an idealized grandfather, he may have temporarily solved the problem. His criticism of the noncommissioned officers may have pointed in the same direction. Yet in his instance we see that the army situation fitted into the soldier's unconscious requirements. The army offered him the opportunity to act out an unconscious fantasy, which, from the army's viewpoint, led to constructive behavior. Since recognition by the army was an aim that made an unconscious fantasy concrete, he was driven to be successful, and even his allergy was not permitted to stand between him and success. Certainly army life was enjoyable to him, because every day brought him closer to the fulfillment of an old wish, namely, to show that he was as good as his grandfather, which meant to be better than his father. Yet in his instance there was no indication of a surrender to reality; it was rather a symbiotic coincidence of individual and army pathology. Hence, there was far more of activity in his dealings with the army than in the two previous reports.

In the last three instances differences in the relationship to their fathers may account for differences in the relations to the army. The father of this soldier behaved in a way which demanded open criticism. This circumstance may have helped the soldier in finding his own personal ideal divorced from the paternal pattern, which might have endowed him with a greater degree of independence and forestalled the surrender which was characteristic of the two other instances. In them the fathers did not offer much of masculine behavior favorable to the development of a virile ideal in the child. However, the behavior of the fathers did not challenge open criticism, but stayed within the boundaries of the socially permissible. This may have favored or necessitated the identification with a rather feeble father image and militated against the search for a more satisfactory ideal.

Apologies are in order for drawing such far-reaching conclusions from superficial clinical evidence. Furthermore, attention should be paid to the fact that it probably was not a mere coincidence that this soldier came from a middle-class family which had not yet been Americanized. The upbringing of his sisters showed the strong influence of European traditions, which in turn may be closely related to his evolving a military ideal. The soldier spoke fluently the language of his parents' native country.

Case No. 7

This soldier's history will be briefly presented in order to show that even serious psychopathology did not make a successful training record impossible. In this instance the psychiatric situation was so complicated that even a tentative guess becomes hazardous.

The soldier, twenty-five years old, was the only boy in the family. There were two older and three younger sisters. Two baby brothers died in infancy. The death of the first one was not remembered by him, but the second was. It occurred when he was in the fifth grade. He remembered having seen the baby before and after its death. He disclaimed any particular or strong emotional reaction to the event. He did not feel close to any of his sisters except the second oldest, one and a half years his senior. He was told by others that he was his parents' favored child, but his parents denied this and he himself never thought so.

After graduation from high school he wanted to study medicine but did not possess the necessary means. He held a variety of jobs and became a tool and die maker. There was a history of frequent employment changes. Before his induction into the army he took a correspondence course seeking to become a mechanical engineer.

He claimed that he only rarely lost his temper, but frequently felt angry without showing it openly. He was often subject to moody spells that lasted three to four days. These usually occurred in connection with some mishap on the job, such as the inadequate turning out of a tool at which he had worked for three or four weeks. When he got into an argument with fellow workers and felt an angry spell coming on, he would leave work, go home, tell his wife what was the matter, and return to work the next day. He had his last blue spell when his wife convinced him that she knew people who were accepted as officer candidates in spite of their suffering from chronic sinus trouble, but he was told that this would make him ineligible. He got into arguments with fellow trainees but avoided fights in order not to endanger his application for officer training. Once he was threatened by a corporal with court-martial. He had started to yell at the corporal for removing a cleaning rod which he needed to clean a rifle.

At the age of twenty, three months after surgery for an inguinal hernia, he became married. His wife was two years older than he. They had a three-and-a-half-year-old girl. The soldier had had premarital intercourse a few times. Yet he did not fall in love prior to meeting his wife. Out of respect for her, he abstained from premarital intercourse with her. He claimed that his marital relationship was good. But it turned out that his wife resented his moody spells and that he occasionally got angry at her because she did not take proper care of herself and did not obey her doctor's orders when she was ill. There was a history of two instances of sexual unfaithfulness, once before he joined the Army, when his wife was visiting her parents, and once in the fourth week of training. Both instances occurred in conjunction with drinking. He started to masturbate at the age of thirteen after he heard some boys talking about the subject. He felt ashamed and thought it was childish "because one doesn't get any satisfaction in that way." He admitted that in masturbation he obtained a pleasurable sensation in his genital, which he described as tingling. Yet during intercourse he had no particular sensation in his penis but felt a soothing, pleasurable sensation all over his body. His wife knew about his second escapade. He had to tell her since he had a growth on his penis one month later. In the dispensary he was told that he might have contracted lues, but one week later he was informed a blood test proved negative. His wife was shocked that he might have contracted a venereal disease, but no consequences as to their relationship developed.

He was critical of the training he had received. He should have had more opportunity for firing the rifle; his squad leader was not interested in instruction, etc. He had pain in his feet, his shoes were too large. Once he was called a goldbrick in a dispensary. He claimed there were many goldbricks in the army but he was not. He was quite afraid of being called a goldbrick and did not dare fall out on marches. Pride prevented him from doing so. At the beginning of his training he tried to avoid passing an officer because he felt awkward about saluting. He had the feeling that his hand got way out when he saluted as if it were a Hitler salute. After a few trials he got accustomed to it. When saluting he had the feeling of saluting the uniform and not the man. It was as in his boy scout days, when the flag was saluted and not a superior.

One week before his wife joined him at camp, he had a trivial accident. He tripped over a barbed wire and bruised himself with his bayonet. Three days after the sexual adventure he had his latest attack of splitting headache, from which he suffered two to three times annually. Recently he started to suffer from colds and the flu.

His father was a hard-working man with little education. He had learned to read and to write by himself. He was a railroad engineer. The soldier admired him for his technical knowledge and abilities, although his spelling was poor. The father had little time to spend on him. There were occasional arguments between the parents about politics. His father dismissed his opinions as boyish. He engaged his mother's help in obtaining permission from his father to do things which the father opposed. His father slapped him on two occasions, once when he was impudent to his mother and once when he slid down a road against his father's prohibition. He had a good understanding with his mother, although she sometimes meted out physical punishment. His mother suffered from high blood pressure, which resulted in headaches and weakness whenever she became excited even about trivialities.

In earlier years he believed in the Bible and took it literally. Later he accepted evolution and combined Bible and science. "For God one day is a million years." He could swear that there was a God because he had been saved twice. Four years earlier he went on a skiing party. He fell into a snowdrift. He felt chilled and went back to the car. From then on he had no memory until twelve hours later when he woke up. He had been taken to a physician without a pulse or heartbeat but was apparently miraculously saved. He claimed that eleven vertebrae had been dislocated. He was under a chiropractor's treatment for three years. The other instance of his being saved occurred when his truck skidded on an icy road. Everything was smashed but he got away with only slight bruises.

During training he had an extensive *déjà vu* experience. When he was in the course of rapid firing, he always knew what the next step would be. First he knew he would achieve the maximum possible in the test. When he achieved this, he knew a lieutenant would come up to him. When this happened he knew that the officer would commend him. A while later he knew he had dreamed the entire scene before he had come into the army. In the dream, it was a lieutenant of his size looking like him. Such things had happened two or three times before, at work, and he had concluded that he must have earlier dreamed the events which he could accurately predict. When asked how he thought a dream could depict the future, he replied that this was exactly what he could not explain and therefore he tried to forget such episodes.

In this context it is noteworthy that he had regularly gotten into arguments in a specific sort of situation. Whenever someone claimed that a certain thing could not be done, he felt compelled to argue and to try to prove that it could. This happened particularly in discussions on sports activities.

Comment: In a superficial psychiatric investigation of this soldier, psychopathology was discovered which must be called serious in spite of the good training record. Apparently his psychopathology did not interfere with his bearing up under the specific stress to which he was exposed. His main clinical symptoms were: psychosomatic disturbances, accident proneness, *déjà vu* experiences, and mood swings. The deformity of sexual experiences would probably not be considered a severe clinical symptom according to prevailing standards. The *déjà vu* experience must be evaluated as serious in this instance. It occurred in a person who was deeply involved in a magical-superstitious system having the center in two instances of miraculous saving. It must be assumed that further probing into the background of the *déjà vu* experiences and his theory of having dreamed the events in question—the dream was not a memory, but a conclusion on his part— would have uncovered a series of paranoid ideas.

As far as can be concluded from this superficial inventory, one must assume that the central traumatic events of the past were the early deaths of two younger brothers. The soldier was preoccupied with the problem of achieving the impossible, which was a frequent cause of argument with his friends and which, after all, was the initial step in his last *déjà vu* experience. But the impossible had become the possible in reality when two male competitors died shortly after their arrival and the only surviving subsequent competitors were girls. This would understandably result in the feeling of being chosen and elected for miraculous survival even if the truck in which one is riding is smashed to bits. His own accident proneness may be interpreted as a testing of omnipotence as well as a gratification of guilt feelings. What kept this soldier going was apparently an optimism, based on magical convictions but guilt-laden, a crude product of a primitive destructive impulse. The short-lasting depressions were precipitated by a threat to the magical optimism or magical feeling of omnipotence.

The conflict surrounding his parental relationship could be but dimly perceived. His engaging of his mother in counteracting paternal opposition, his rage about paternal punishment, his dependence on mother and wife, his sporadic rebellion against his wife and his using her as a means to restore his optimism—all of these must have been important factors in the background of his psychopathology, but simultaneously useful means in maintaining a satisfactory achievement level in terms of external behavior. Since, apparently, his frame of reference was almost exclusively that of competitive values, the level of integration must have been low in spite of commendable conduct.

Case No. 8

The last case of this series will not be reported. It would not have introduced any new aspect. There was a rather restless family background with frequent arguments between the parents regarding disagreements on religion; arguments between the soldier and his wife; a history of past phobias, continuing until adolescence; an active role on the part of the subject in attempting to straighten out parental arguments; mild disciplinary difficulties during his training period; and a very good occupational record.

It may be worth while to present general albeit superficial impressions which were gained from this series. These impressions certainly are not meant as definite rules of selection or prognosis of military fitness, but reflect certain general features which seemed to prevail among the majority of those who were interviewed.[13] The family background was characterized by stability in many instances. There were no striking, open disagreements between the parents. At least, the child obtained the impression that the relationship between his parents was harmonious. Whatever tension may have been present did not interfere with the open, official family equilibrium. At the same time, however, there was not always complete agreement between the parents. The differences between them manifested themselves as divergences of political or religious beliefs, sometimes showing up as mere distinctions of outlook on life in general. These differences appeared to be of importance in so far as they gave the child the opportunity of learning to discriminate between father and mother and to develop well-separated representations of them. From clinical experience it is known that the archaic configuration which encompasses both parents and makes one picture of them conduces to fixation to infantile levels and militates against a mature orientation in the grownup. If the conflict between the parents is so intense as to make it impossible for the child to perceive any common features in them, this in turn will result in irreconcilable identifications in the child and will necessarily lead to a permanent conflict of severe degree. The optimum for the child will lie between these two extremes; a harmonious relationship between parents and the presence of sufficiently distinctive features to prevent the child from taking his parents together as an unstructured unit.

August Aichhorn held the view in one of his seminars that a certain degree

---

[13] The general clinical impressions received from this series seem not to contradict those which McNeel and Dancey (1945) reported on front-line soldiers.

of ambivalence on the part of a child toward his parents is a prerequisite of a healthy development. Ambivalence is usually regarded as the great obstacle to harmonious relationship to the world; indeed, a marked ambivalence in the neurotic and the delinquent persistently interferes with wholesome attachments to objects. But reviewing my series of subjects I was reminded of Aichhorn's views and felt that their correctness had been confirmed. Most of the subjects were prevented from establishing an open and severe fixation to one of the parents rather than the other. An auspicious unlikeness of the parents kept them in a state of moderate tension which was psychologically beneficial. Thus, being prevented from too great a reliance on one of the parents and kept in continuous mild ambivalence toward both of them, the children were forced to acquire a favorable degree of independence. This showed up in their early and quick attainment of financial independence from their parents. Economically the family background was characterized by middle-class status, which saved the child from material want without permitting his being spoiled by unlimited gratifications of demands for purchasable goods.

Another area in which there was significant similarity among the subjects was their sexual activities. There was a short period of masturbation, and sexual gratification was derived exclusively from the spouse. In view of the widespread promiscuity in present American society, this feature was most remarkable. It may be objected that this impression was created by the subject's unwillingness to report the truth, and that a longer-lasting and more thoroughgoing exploration would have revealed the usual history of prolonged premarital experimentation and occasional unfaithfulness.[14] This may be correct and cannot be directly disproved, but if reliance can be put on the feeling an interviewer has as to the sincerity of an interviewed subject, I should be inclined to believe that the outline of their sexual history was roughly correct as it was presented. I surmise that further examination would have shown a manifoldness of activities the sexual character of which did not dawn on the subject. I can imagine that voyeuristic or exhibitionistic or other pregenital behavior did occur. This would not disprove the impression that as far as genital activities were concerned, the subjects had followed officially promulgated standards more closely than the majority of the population can be assumed to. The clinical dwarfing of genital activities was not accompanied with conspicuous neurotic symptoms, as in the case of hysteria. Nor did the subjects report extensive conflicts between cravings and

[14] For the variety of types of sexual behavior correlated to class membership, education, church membership, etc., within the American community, see Kinsey et al. (1948).

prohibitions. In most instances they related not having been especially pre-occupied with their sexual desires. They appeared to be inhibited in that respect. They were somehow reminiscent of a certain type of woman that is particularly endowed with tolerating frigidity without compensatory neurotic symptomatology or character defect. There was no indication that the subjects really had learned to master genital aspirations. According to their account, they just did not feel very strongly drawn toward genital activities. The dislocation of the orgastic genital sensations to other parts of the body proved that their seeming adjustment was based on inhibition and not on mastery.

If their histories are compared with those of the average neurotic, it is evident in what respects the latter is at a disadvantage. The young man of our time who suffers from conspicuous neurotic symptoms usually goes through spells of increased sexual tension, is exposed to manifold tempta-tions, fights against his cravings, and is finally victimized by an inadequate, unsatisfactory discharge which grants him but a short respite before being followed by a level of tension if anything higher than that when the vicious circle started. This is a permanent drain on the energy available for realistic pursuits.[15] The type that prevailed in this series had a far greater amount of energy invested in external reality. Whether this was a true sublimation or not could not be decided from the clinical material at hand. It would rather appear to be a reaction formation patterned according to compulsive mechanisms, but fitted into realistic exigencies.

I believe that this type is on the wane in this country. They represent the remnants of former puritanism, which in the last century and a half has suffered such a crushing defeat and has not been replaced by a new frame of moral reference endowed with binding power upon the majority of the American community. True, some patients, suffering from severe neurotic symptoms come from exactly this group. However, if my clinical judgment does not lead me astray, my observation leads me to believe that the key to whether in our time an upbringing in a puritanic environment will lead to conspicuous psychopathology lies in whether the child is kept in social isolation, that is to say, in whether or not the child becomes aware during its early development that the parental standards are not coincidental with those of the environment in general. If there has been such isolation, untoward reactions will set in immediately once the child is compelled to function in that larger environment. In addition, it seems that those puritanic parents who keep their children in isolation are those in whom the puritanic

[15] See Jeanne Lampl-de Groot (1936) for the optimal relations between instinctual intensity, discharge, and efficiency.

principle has suffered some weakening. Doubting the potency of their own philosophy, they must alert their children to all kinds of imagined dangers. It is the combination of the child's exposure to identification with a parent in whom an extreme moral demand had not been well integrated, but overcompensated, with the factual narrowness of the experiential field which sows the seed of later extreme symptoms. In the puritanic type which will later be successful in terms of external behavior, the child has early opportunity to find out that the parental standards have only narrowly circumscribed validity. The child may even derive some pride in discovering these distinctive features in his own parental environment, whereas the other type dragged along the parental morality as a loathsome burden from the very beginning.

In the case of our subjects, their fathers did not seem overly concerned about their children's moral development in spite of the strictness they exerted. It was further significant that almost all of the subjects had succeeded in competing successfully with their fathers. Many of them had established themselves in situations socially and financially superior to those of their progenitors. In some cases, the father or mother had become dependent on them for support, which made them feel proud and enforced their feelings of superiority.

Church affiliation and the importance of religious training were conspicuous. While this feature should not be overrated—it was found as conspicuously in those who failed utterly in adapting themselves to the new environment—it is probably not irrelevant, since it seems likely that a person brought up puritanically who nevertheless rebelled against church membership would hardly be disposed to ready conformity with rigid army rules.

The result of my inquiry into the psychology of soldiers who kept their bearing under trying conditions and constituted a distinctive group with regard to their performance and their contributions to the national emergency does not indicate an essential qualitative difference between the neurotic and what is called, from society's viewpoint, normal. To be sure, the quantitative difference in the energies invested in various patterns of mechanisms may have been great. But by and large it could be said that what is called in present society "normal behavior" is a specific disorder which fits into particular social configurations and which involves a neglect and dwarfing of the internal microcosm in favor of submission to the external macrocosm.

It can be proved that the subjects of this study were specimens of a particular psychopathology. Before doing so, I wish to cite an opinion which is frequently encountered. Hooton (1945), in commenting upon the difference in number between those "normal" subjects who were desirous of discussing their problems with a psychiatrist and those who had never sought such discussions but were thought by the psychiatrist to be in need of them, wrote: ". . . the present reporter is certainly no psychologist, far less a psychiatrist; he therefore offers timorously the trivial suggestion that the experts in these fields may sometimes discern personality difficulties that are not really there, but are rather the projections of similar difficulties that said psychiatrists themselves experience" (pp. 73-74). This suggestion may indeed be trivial, but it is frequently heard and socially portentous. It is one of the greatest obstacles to the social integration of modern psychiatry. In the present instance, a group of soldiers successful far above the average has been presented. In spite of a general consensus by the whole community that they are to be regarded as prototypes of normality, the psychiatrist finds himself professionally obliged to view these very men as specimens of significant psychopathology. Hooton's argument can be easily refuted in this instance. The psychiatrist's conclusion was based on the subjects' statements. It is not a matter of interpretations or an esoteric method of diagnosis. Furthermore, the subjects' statements were in answer to definite and clear-cut questions and there was no reason to doubt the correctness of these answers since, if anything, the social situation required denial of symptoms. All the subjects described an experience of orgasm which was objectively inadequate. Without going into the difficult problem of the relationship between biology and psychology, this much can be safely stated: namely, that there are certain biologically prescribed experiences, the adequacy or inadequacy of which can be directly gauged. One of these experiences is the genital orgasm. To be sure whether a subject has genital experiences or not may depend on the culture in which he lives, on his philosophy, his ethical principles, and many other factors, and therefore the fact of abstinence per se cannot be used as a measure of mental health. But if a subject has a genital experience leading to an ejaculation, this biological occurrence must result in a well-definable subjective state unless the subject is to be classified as suffering from psychopathology.[16] The adequate subjective state must fulfill two conditions, at least. It must lead to a certain form of pleasure, and the lustful pleasure must take place at a certain anatomical area which is physiologically endowed with the evolvement of the pleasurable sensation. There may be uncertainty about many details concerning the adequate experience of orgasm, but these two factors are an unquestioned minimum and biologically determined. Now, it is remarkable that not one of the subjects described his orgasmic experience as having taken place at the

[16] Cf. Agoston (1946), Keiser (1947), and Bose (1937).

biologically proper place. From the subject's point of view this displacement
served an appropriate function: it preserved him from anxiety, fright, and
trauma. But the fact that the orgasmic experience had to be deformed is a
clinical proof that the ego had been injured in one of its most important
functions.

Here is a point where the authority of the biologist may be called in.
King (1945), when discussing the meaning of normal writes: "The normal
. . . is . . . to be defined as that which functions in accordance with its
inherent design." [17] It is difficult to find many "inherent designs" in the
psychic apparatus's functioning. One is the gaining of pleasure during the
activation of certain functions. Within the framework of biology, sexual
occurrences may be meaningful only inasmuch as they serve purposes of
propagation. Hence, in the eyes of the biologist all the subjects of this series
may have been normal. None of them complained about or reported any
physical deficiency regarding the propagative performance: their erectile
and ejaculatory potency was uninjured as far as could be determined. Yet
it would be a grave mistake if the evaluation of sexual behavior were limited
to the biological aspect and "normal" sexual behavior were defined exclusively in terms of sequences of physiological and cellular changes.[18]
Furthermore, the sexual life of these soldiers may be considered normal from
the viewpoint of the sociologist. It leads to propagation, it sufficed the
purpose of maintaining the family group, it did not lead to dissension or
isolation of the subgroup from the supraordinated group. And nevertheless
the psychiatrist must insist that in these subjects sexual experiences did not
occur in accordance with their "inherent design," notwithstanding the
absence of any subjective complaints and although a psychologically "normal" experience might have led to conflict in the subject as well as in his

[17] I do not agree with King's definition. Its applicability to psychology is limited,
the experience of orgasm being one of the few instances where it may serve a fruitful
purpose. The participants in the Grant study at Harvard for the research project of
normal college students, though agreeing with King, reached the following conclusion: "The 'normal' individual . . . is regarded as the balanced person whose combination of traits of all sorts allows him to function effectively in a variety of ways"
(Heath, 1945). It would be difficult to prove that effective functioning on the community level ever occurs in accordance with any inherent design.

[18] Kinsey et al. (1948) come close to such a viewpoint. The authors write: ". . . all
cases of ejaculation have been taken as evidence of orgasm, without regard to the
different levels at which the orgasms have occurred" (pp. 159-160). Kinsey's conceptual approach serves the purpose of his study, if I am not mistaken. Inclusion of a
psychological viewpoint would have made his research impossible as well as confused
the data he wanted to obtain. If I regard Kinsey's definition as inadequate for the
purpose of evaluating the sex life of the subjects of this series, this does not imply a
criticism of Kinsey's investigation, which aimed at a problem different from the one
under investigation here.

partner. If a man is not taken as a machinelike composite designed to serve a variety of external purposes, such as he must as a law-abiding citizen, a husband, a father, or a soldier, then the orgasmic experience becomes an event of supreme significance. It will then be considered the resultant of the sum total of all adaptive mechanisms correlated to the internal microcosm in which man lives. These subjects could never be called normal except in disregard of how they were living within themselves. Viewed in terms of the totality of human existence these men would never have been warrantable as prototypes of normality. From the viewpoint of the internal microcosm the orgasmic experience becomes the final step in the consummation of the "you" relationship, when biologically and psychologically all borders which usually separate human beings evanesce and two become one. Any deviation within the subjective experience coincides with a fundamental deviation in the relationship to the "you," and therefore it is imperative to consider the eight subjects as representatives of serious psychopathology.[19]

So far our attempts at finding out something about the psychology of the efficient soldier have not carried us far. The general result pointed to a negative rather than a positive statement, namely, the fact that efficiency is possible in spite of psychopathology and that quite possibly even that which is arbitrarily called normality is a special instance of psychopathology. If so, what the specific nature of that psychopathology is has escaped our knowledge.

Following the psychoanalytic principle of investigating the pathological in order to get knowledge of the normal,[20] we may find the three following case histories useful. They deal with patients who required extensive psycho-

[19] Without wishing to discuss here Reich's theories regarding orgasm and the conclusions he drew therefrom regarding psychotherapeutic techniques, I wish to refer to his great contribution in demonstrating that the biological sequences of sexual events per se are not decisive unless imbedded in certain psychological experiences (Reich, 1927, p. 206; 1933).

[20] Cf. Freud (1932): ". . . we are familiar with the view that pathology, with its magnification and exaggeration, can make us aware of normal phenomena which we should otherwise have missed. Where pathology displays a breach or a cleft, under normal conditions there may well be a link" (p. 84). I am uncertain whether the translation of the terms *Bruch, Riss* and *Gliederung* which Freud uses as *breach, cleft* and *link* convey the full meaning of what Freud had in mind. The terms *rupture, tear* and *articulation* impress me as better suited since they convey the idea of different *states* of the same substance rather than opposites, the articulated, organized, structured, state rather than the disrupted state. Because structure is the mode of organization of a whole organism, it may escape our attention. Its distortion in psychopathology renders its observation possible. This becomes clear in Freud's reference to psychotics as "fissured and splintered structures" who "know more of internal psychic reality [than we] and can tell us much that would otherwise be inaccessible to us" (p. 85).

therapy, but whose military performance was far above average and in outstanding disproportion to their psychopathology.[21]

The first patient is encountered not on the American scene but on the European; nevertheless the underlying mechanism of his remarkable resistance to a particularly harrowing military experience deserves attention because of its general significance and the possibility of its occurrence in any section of occidental culture.

The subject was driven to seek psychiatric treatment at the late age of sixty when he had fallen into a severe depression which threatened to incapacitate him in his profession and at times brought him to the verge of suicide. His condition was worse in the morning and subsided somewhat toward the late afternoon. His appetite was poor. His sleep did not yield rest and was lacking in any refreshing effect. There were the usual unpleasant and annoying feelings of physical discomfort, the conviction that there was no hope, and dread of the future. This depression had put a halt to a brilliant career. During the premorbid phase, the subject had achieved nearly everything he had desired to obtain from life. He was happily married with a congenial woman, socially and intellectually his equal. He had children. His professional achievements were far above average. He had encompassed a broad sector of human life. He was well versed in many artistic fields. He was effective as a collector of art. He had been successful with women and had enjoyed many affairs. He was not lacking in friends devoted to him and had maintained sincere relationships with them. Up to the beginning of his depression even a keen observer would not have discovered any blemish in his life. He was an only child, and enjoyed the advantages and suffered the disadvantages of such status. He had received a large share of maternal affection and his father gave him all possible encouragement in cultural pursuits. After graduation from school he volunteered for the Army. He felt that his concentration on mental work had entailed some neglect of *savoir-vivre*. By serving in the army he intended to acquire self-reliance and confidence which would enable him to overcome some timidity and clumsiness in social contacts. He expected from army discipline the acquisition of graceful, social manners. In accordance with his intentions, he selected a regiment which was famous for its exclusiveness and for having aristocrats in its ranks. Since he was a Jew and rather short and of not appealing physical appearance, he aroused open hostility as soon as he joined his outfit. The regimental commander took his presence as an affront, humiliated him publicly, tried to involve him in some subordination, and exposed him to particular stresses in order to enforce his removal or compel him to resign. Yet nothing could pre-

[21] The three subjects seemed to be beyond the scope of what Farrell and Appel (1944) had in mind when they wrote: ". . . among all troops on duty in continental United States, a significant percentage admitted current nailbiting; say they are troubled by sick headaches; have been bothered by nightmares; by 'upset stomachs'; by nervousness; by frequent insomnia. . . ."

vail on him to discontinue the plan he had set in his mind and he bore up unflinchingly despite his exposure to what amounted to torture. This was all the more remarkable since there was no external necessity for his staying in that regiment, neither in terms of prestige, being a member of the middle class, nor of future career, having never intended to make the Army his profession. Yet he continued to endure his sufferings, and his efforts were rewarded by his passing the graduation examinations and obtaining the commission for which he had had to undergo so much of humiliation and pain. It is because of this harrowing episode of military service that this patient's history becomes important in this context.

During his treatment the question of course was raised of what had enabled him to endure all the hardship involved in his military service. The answer was found when the precipitating factor of his depression had been determined. About half a year before the onset of his depression he had suffered the first serious defeat of his lifetime. Whereas prior to that time as far as he could remember he had been victorious in all matters of import to him, it had then happened that he was unable to achieve a cherished goal in his relationship to a woman to whom he had become strongly attached. After a brief but happy and mutually gratifying love relationship, his mistress decided to get married. The patient, for obvious reasons, did not wish to interpose any obstacle to her plan, but nourished the secret hope that she would one day return to him. It was not so much a matter of his love continuing to be directed toward her, but of a severe injury to his pride and sense of importance to a person whom he had loved and by whom he had been loved. For about half a year he was able to sustain the hope that perhaps what had first appeared to be defeat might end in victory, but gradually it became impossible for him to maintain that illusion and to deceive himself. The woman had definitely broken away, and there was no indication that she felt any sort of attachment to him.

The consequences of being confronted with defeat were disastrous. He was completely unprepared to adjust to it. It turned out that his philosophy was based on the assumption that any problem or difficulty in life could be solved by effort. The fact that complications of reality might be beyond solution by personal ingenuity, endeavors, and effort had not found any place in his outlook on life. The recognition of a limitation to his power threatened to destroy the basis of his very existence. It further turned out that all his past successes had served the purpose of confirming his basic, operational assumption, which he had developed under the auspices of a stern, authoritative father who had intimated in his preachings the close association between fulfillment of duty, investment of energy, and success. Actually he had learned by experience that he could defeat his early enemy, his father, by making a supreme effort to comply with the various paternal demands to the minutest detail. Thus he stripped his father of the power of reprimanding him, which meant to him, the power of attacking him and, hence, victory. His father, however, did not forbear to predict that his son would end in a catastrophe whenever he was guilty of the slightest deviation from his father's expectations. That imaginary but predicted catastrophe was what the patient felt was approaching when it had become a certainty that, in spite of all his wishing, planning and scheming, he was not going to be rewarded by real events' falling into line with his anticipations. The patient became aware that the same reaction would have set in forty years earlier if he had not succeeded in obtaining the commission for which he was striving. Only because of the very serious psychopathology underlying all his efforts to conquer reality was he able to withstand the extreme strain put on him during his military service. Without the need for confirmation of his magic theories he certainly would have lost patience with the foolish pettiness of a biased and prejudiced group to which he did not feel the slightest personal attachment or loyalty. Yet all his subsequent successes—and they were considerable—followed the identical pattern.

It must be said that an early failure of his philosophy, let us say on the occasion of his military endeavors, would have been of advantage to this subject. It would have forced him to face an issue which inevitably would come up one day. No other case, I believe, could demonstrate so impressively the utter fallacy of Alexander's and French's (1946) application of the adage "Nothing succeeds like success" to psychotherapy or psychoanalysis. Each success brought this patient closer to doom, and the first step of wholesome reorientation would have been for him to permit himself to suffer defeat.

On the other hand, his career illustrates impressively how psychopathology may lead to the attainment of socially constructive and desirable goals, even over long periods of time. No sincere and faithful service to an ideal, no wholesome integration of reality, could have led a man to greater effort than this patient invested in all his dealings with reality. The magic mechanisms constituted a firm tie to anything of import in his personal, volitional field. No wonder that under such circumstances he was often capable of bending reality to conform with his goals. It must be concluded from the patient's episode of depression that success on the level of social reality must be divorced from any conceptual relationship to mental health, a statement which certainly cannot be reversed. Hence, the fact that a soldier or officer was successful in the army was not per se an index of his status in terms of mental health. Likewise, failure for neuropsychiatric reasons in connection with military service should not necessarily have been correlated with psychopathology,[22] but may in individual instances have indicated an improve-

[22] N. Lionel Blitzsten emphasized in his seminars the necessity of a program of indoctrination to bring to public attention that the mere fact of a soldier's having been returned home because of a neuropsychiatric diagnosis did not permit any conclusions regarding the severity of the disorder from which he may have been suffering.

ment or the initiation of a constructive step forward. Therefore I believe that broad conclusions as to the national mental health, which were drawn from the N-P rate of soldiers, were premature and should have awaited thoroughgoing preparatory investigations. In this context it may be mentioned that according to a statistical examination a significant proportion of soldiers who had been discharged from the Army for N-P reasons, went to work after their discharge although they had not been employed prior to their induction (Brill, Tate, and Menninger, 1945).

The second patient in this group deserves attention from various viewpoints. He was twenty-seven years old when he sought continuation of his psychoanalysis, which had been started in a sanitarium. About half a year previously, he had shown marked, generalized anxiety without definite content. He had threatened suicide, but did not show any serious intention of carrying it out. He was wrongly diagnosed as suffering from schizophrenia, and sixteen metrazol shock treatments were instituted. His symptoms did not subside, and he was then treated in a sanitarium by psychoanalysis. He became quite enthusiastic about that treatment and recovered at least to such an extent that continuation of treatment outside of the hospital could be recommended.

His history revealed that he had suffered from a severe emotional disorder for many years. He had been unable to accept authority from his childhood on. He had had the greatest difficulty at school; he had failed in mathematics and had not been able to graduate from high school. He had stolen and associated with a "bad" crowd. Later he drank and gambled and lacked the ability to concentrate on work. He was overwhelmed by sporadic attacks of anxiety and feelings of severe discomfiture. He had no confidence in himself. He attached himself to those he considered stronger than himself, oscillating between the stronger in virtue and the stronger in vice.

He was the middle of three brothers. The older and the younger were successful at school and in their occupations. The older brother served as a substitute for a father ideal. There was marked unlikeness between the parents. The mother was a sophisticated, refined, ambitious, and compulsive person, of Anglo-Saxon extraction; the father was a negligent, happy-go-lucky, and unsophisticated Irishman who was a chronic alcoholic of moderate degree. The older brother was idealized by the patient and became his mainstay in threatening reality situations. The family was economically close to the upper border of the middle class, the father earning a steady income as a salesman.

The dynamic background of the patient's disorder never became clear, although he was quite eager to conform to the requirements of psychoanalytic therapy. He never missed an appointment and was ready to report his trains of thought. Yet he was repetitive in his ideation, blunt and obtuse in his emotional responses. In view of the large

proportion of delinquent symptomatology in his history an attempt
was made to break through what appeared to be a defense armor of
character symptoms, yet the emotional obtuseness did not give way. It
became evident to me that he had no chance of recovery by psychoanalysis. I surmised that the impediment met in his psychotherapy
was a personality change due to repeated shock treatments. Since the
patient repeatedly stated that his "psychoanalytic" treatment was the
only hope which kept him going, the treatment was continued in spite
of the slim chance of its ever resulting in a clinical success. Only two
active therapeutic steps besides reassurance and superficial appeasement of anxiety occurred during the course of his treatment, which
lasted about half a year. The one concerned his insight that he was
not a manifest homosexual, which he violently feared to be, and the
second referred to conclusive evidence that he went into a panic
whenever reality took a turn which brought him close to the realization of any of his daydreams. His favored daydream over many years
had been to be a famous pilot, and to bask in public attention and
fame. One day the patient declared without specific provocation that
he would volunteer for the Air Force. No objection to that plan was
raised by the therapist, although he was convinced that in view of the
patient's past history and his repeated flunking in mathematics he was
bound to fail in the course of his training, if, indeed, he was ever accepted at all by the Air Force as a candidate. Subsequent events, however, blatantly disproved that conviction.

It may be of general interest to record that already during the
premilitary period this patient showed all but one of the nine signs
which Billings et al. (1943) thought pathognomonic and differentiating the probable misfit from his counterpart. These are, according to
Billings's statistics: (1) hypochondriasis; (2) excessive general sweating; (3) irregular work record; (4) underactivity; (5) disturbed
sexual development; (6) difficulty in making friends; (7) two or
more morbid fears; (8) lack of definite ambition; (9) voluntary en-
listment. This patient likewise would have ranked at the low end of
Whitehorn's personality scale (1946). Whitehorn suggested not to
forget in the evaluation of soldiers that neurotic symptoms may be
counterbalanced by assets. Therefore the soldier's personality must be
gauged as to (1) tolerance or capacity for enduring frustration, tension, or anxiety; (2) neurotic and immature attitudes; (3) enthusiasms, loyalties, group identifications, and morale vs. resentments and
aversions; (4) mental capacity, intelligence, special knowledge and
skills. Although this patient was low in the assets enumerated by
Whitehorn but high in the negative factors, he went through training
without failing one single examination. He earned his wings. He func-
tioned excellently throughout the war except for a short-lasting episode of imbalance of the eye muscles which kept him from flying for a
few weeks (cf. Harrington, 1947). His assignments were by no means
easy, although he was never engaged in combat. He lived under un-

favorable conditions at isolated places and had to bear the full impact of material and psychological hazards to which pilots were exposed. As time went on, personnel dropped out to his right and left because they could not withstand the terrific strain, but he went on outwardly unperturbed and to the satisfaction of his superiors, except for the one aforementioned episode.

The letters he sent home and what he reported later were in marked contradiction to the stolidness of his outward demeanor. Behind the mask of composure and devotion to duty, he fell from one depression into another; one crisis followed the other. Oddly enough, he had not even grasped the mathematics he was taught in the training school. He claimed in his letters that he learned it by rote and applied it mechanically in test examinations. He informed me that he felt terrified during flights because he labored under the compulsion to do the very opposite of what he should do in view of what the instruments on the panel board indicated. Such obsessions gripped him when he cruised alone through the vastness of space. Yet it turned out that he did not feel alone in such circumstances. He felt in contact with me. It was unclear whether this feeling amounted to a delusion that I extended protective power over him. On the other hand, he was preoccupied during flight in a competitive struggle with God. Flying became a kind of gamble of whether he could be stronger than God, or a sort of test whether God would help him.

In spite of the great success he had achieved during his service, his behavior and complaints after his return to civilian life proved that no change for the better had taken place with respect to his personality structure, if such proof were necessary in view of what he had reported during the years he spent with the Air Force.

As far as I can see there were two factors responsible for the astounding performance he was capable of. One, I believe, must be credited to the shock treatment he had received. I feel certain that that treatment had facilitated his functioning as an automaton. I doubt very much that he would have been able to learn extensive and complicated mathematical operations by rote and to apply them mechanically, had not that individual factor of rebellion and demand to understand what one is doing been burned out by the shock treatment. If a person refuses to act on a mechanical level and therefore fails, it is not necessarily the index of a deficit. On the other hand, if a person submits to the necessity of so acting and therefore succeeds, it is not necessarily an index of an asset. It might be our "sanity," our good sense, our feeling of status as human beings, which would prevent the vast majority of us from matching this patient's military accomplishments.

The other factor which perhaps underlay his military success may have been a contribution of the psychoanalytic treatment, namely, a willingness to experience the realization of a cherished daydream. Being a pilot was an old fantasy he had nurtured and advanced over many years. I was ignorant of the meaning of that fantasy and its unconscious root. There is no doubt that the great emotional meaning and the imagery surrounding a pilot was intimately connected with his survival as a member of the Air Force.[23] I am certain that this patient would have failed in any other branch of the armed services. He would never have been able to go through infantry training successfully.[24] It was probably the coincidence of fantasy and reality, the ultimate enjoyment and usufruct of a hidden and continuously flowing source of energy, which attached him for the first time in his life to something he was doing in reality and which made him stubbornly cling to it despite the displeasure and anguish it created.

I may however, be overrating the effect of my repeated demonstration to him that panic was aroused in him by the imminent realization of daydreams. It is probable, as mentioned before, that in the course of shock treatment his ego lost some of its capacity to evolve a feeling of guilt when enjoying the gratification of an unconscious and forbidden desire. He probably served his unconscious in automatonlike fashion as he was wont to do in his contact with demands put on him by external reality. The seemingly strong emotional reactions he reported home in his letters and the delusionlike fantasies he produced regarding me do not necessarily contradict such a view. His complaints at least were monotonous repetitions of what, over many years, he had claimed his emotional crises to be, but the undoubtedly new element was that he did not follow up the crises by corresponding actions and therefore acted in accordance with the requirements of reality.

Summarizing, it may be said that this patient was able to carry out a difficult and responsible assignment over many years (except for a short

[23] Similar observations were made by others. Anderson (1947) studied the particular combination of psychopathology and successful flying. He writes: "The war produced many competent flyers who actively disliked flying almost from their first experience but were deterred from renouncing it. . . . In many the pseudo-love of flying was born of an inability to obtain officer's training elsewhere." Flying served as a compensation for inadequacies and as an outlet for aggression. ". . . many individuals correctly classified as psychopathic personalities have made creditable records in combat aviation." He further found that flying had a special fascination for persons with schizoid make-up in connection with their desire to detach themselves. Anderson also reports that premilitary instability and psychiatric disorder per se did not militate against even great success in combat flying.

[24] Cf. Murray (1944). For some beginning of a comparative psychiatry of the various military branches, see Console (1946). A comparative psychiatry of the armed forces would have been a great contribution to the solution of many military problems. As far as can be seen from the little done in that field there seems to have been a tendency among psychiatrists to consider the hardships of their own patients greater than that of soldiers serving in other branches of the Army.

period of what probably was a neurotic ocular dysfunction), although or because his level of performance was lowered and reduced to a mechanical and automatonlike one. In addition, the particular duties to which he had been assigned coincided with a fantasy he had nourished over many years. Whereas the first patient of this series achieved his success by an overflow of magic interest and impulses with which he met his military duties, this patient became capable of functioning to the satisfaction of military standards because a personality change induced by shock treatment lowered the interest he took in the world at large so that it became less meaningful to him and therefore aroused less rebellion and contrariness.

The situation encountered in this case, although it seemingly involves a purely medical question, really touches on one of the central problems of our time.

Here a medical procedure (shock treatment) endows a patient with the capacity to perform on a level far above average, at the price of losing the individual facets of his personality. Sullivan (1940), in writing about the modern surgical and shock treatments, stated: "These sundry procedures, to my way of thinking, produce 'beneficial' results by reducing the patient's capacity for being human. The philosophy is something to the effect that it is better to be a contented imbecile than a schizophrenic" (p. 73, n. 51). The problem could not be stated more aptly or succinctly. Only an indiscriminate urge to eradicate schizophrenic symptoms (not unlike the orthodox raging against heresies) and an arbitrary glorification of utilitarian values regardless of their meanings to the subject who is supposed to pursue them can lead one to justify a medical treatment which is devoid of any feeling for the dignity of man. Without shock treatment this subject probably would not have been able to function, as he did, as a valuable pilot over the course of years; yet under the impact of shock treatment, although not yet deprived of the capacity to evolve a delusion or produce anxiety, he lost the capacity to react to his individual, internal, microcosm and thus came closer to what quite possibly may become the ideal of modern man, namely, a machinelike structure dependable in the management of certain sectors of reality. There is the question whether this reduction of the human personality is desirable, permissible, or socially useful, even if it results in the patient's performance of socially highly esteemed pursuits. The ethical question which underlies this problem will be further discussed in a later context, but here it may be remarked only that one way of becoming efficient in present society is to blot out individuality, to scar organic reactability, to surrender to expedience, and to act in accordance with a social pattern in disregard of the constellation within the internal microcosm.

The third and last patient certainly was the most interesting. Unfortunately, reasons of discretion prevent me from submitting his history in as detailed form as it deserves.

This subject, who never was treated by me but with whom I was well acquainted, started out in life in a way which permitted the worst prognosis. He lived on an extremely low performance level up to preadolescence. He did not wash himself, did not comply with minimal demands of the parental home, did not want to eat, was unable to go to school, had innumerable compulsions and transitory paranoid ideas, suffered from facial tics, and had some moderately severe speech impediments. Needless to say, the entire clinical picture was filled out with intense anxiety. He was barely accessible to any educatory influence and his way of growing up was reminiscent of that of a little animal. Fortunately for him, his parents' wealth permitted the application of the arsenal of modern psychiatry—which at that time, again fortunately, had not yet been enriched by lobotomy and the various techniques of shock treatment—including intensive psychoanalysis over many years, special teachers, expert supervision during his free time, and compliance with any advice the treating physician might give, in so far as it involved things materially acquirable.

The patient's condition improved after three to four years of treatment to such an extent that he could be sent to a private school, which he attended with moderate success. His social relationships improved markedly. He established friendships, kept himself presentable, developed a variety of mental interests, and took in general a vastly friendlier and more constructive attitude toward his environment. His fears became allayed so much that he could eat hearty meals and he gained considerable weight.

Yet, in spite of this marked clinical success, the factor of artificiality could not be overlooked. He was not really independent, and there was no indication that anything was growing in him which ultimately might result in self-reliance and self-assertiveness. What was really happening was that he incessantly took from his parents, although he used it in a more constructive way than before. Whereas everything that had been invested in him before his clinical recovery had started was spoiled, destroyed, or sullied, he now continued to let things flow through his confines, but returned them in a more presentable way. However, there was no indication of any point of crystallization around which attitudes might develop that would enable him to exist without that continuous flow of things. He had developed, so to speak, from an ugly parasite into one that was more aesthetically pleasing and no longer repulsive, but his existence continued to be essentially parasitic.

The rise to power of Hitler forced the patient to reorganize his existence. He had to leave his native country and establish an existence abroad without any parental help. He went through the tribulations of that adjustment period with what must be called heroism. He worked under the most unfavorable conditions, doing heavy labor.

and supported himself. With the outbreak of war he immediately made an effort to be inducted, and succeeded after several attempts. He was assigned to the infantry and went through basic training without apparent difficulty. Then he was shifted through the entire zone of interior from one organization to another. Even this did not spoil his good humor. Finally he was ordered overseas and joined an infantry organization in combat. Fate did not spare him opportunities to prove his mettle. He went through harrowing experiences, such as hour-long exposure to heavy artillery fire, encirclement by the enemy, and several close brushes with death. Yet, neither physical exhaustion nor the constant threat of capture and death wore him down, and he went through weeks of acute peril, when his outfit was close to disorganization and panic and he got but little encouragement from others, without apparent production of symptoms.

He had got married before going overseas. After his separation from the Army he learned an occupation and continued to behave in a well-adjusted way. In social contact with him there were no direct visible signs of any outstanding disorder, except for sporadic tics and an occasional speech impediment. It is scarcely possible to grasp by empathy that his early condition of complete asociality and animallike behavior, destructiveness and extreme psychopathology, and his endurance of and resistance to extreme danger and physical want and exhaustion barely twenty years later were states pertaining to the same individual. The development of this patient is a real challenge to a clinical psychiatrist.

There was evidence that his improvement was not equivalent to a true recovery. The persistence of tics and the speech impediment warned against any such assumption. Tics are excellent forms of neurotic discharge; they serve as vents of energy which is superfluous or cannot be integrated. Their great value consists in most instances in their being a means of keeping the psychic apparatus free of surplus energy without actual detriment to intended performances. They may cause social disgrace or evoke ridicule, but those who suffer from them are, in a surprisingly large number of instances, not called upon to pay the high price of displeasure and deficient performance which most neurotics must suffer. Hence, the patient's adequate performances must not be overrated in view of the existing tics, although significance of the symptom in terms of its social impact was minimal. The tic might even have gone unnoticed by the untrained. But since it is known that the dynamic value of tics in terms of psychopathology is always very high, it makes the riddle of this patient's clinical problem even greater. As far as I can evaluate his situation the following elements of his history must be considered.

The patient had the fantasy, in previous years at a time when there was no indication of his coming to this country, that he would one day in the future become the president of the United States, and thus acquire such power as to create a worldwide association of nations which would eradicate the world's evil under his leadership. This fantasy appeared frequently in his conversation and was precipitated by acquaintance with the life of Abraham Lincoln. He was incapable of grasping the irrationality of that fantasy, which evidently was a sequence to the flow of paranoid imagery that possessed him in early years. Hence, quite possibly the catastrophe which befell him and his family in their native country may have had a gratifying effect, since it brought him suddenly into that country from which he expected salvation.

In addition, his fear and hatred of the Nazis must be considered. The Nazis, representing to those whom they persecuted the archaic resurgence of the deepest childhood fears and the revivification of the most accursed nightmares of earliest years, actually gave to many of their victims an opportunity to invest their paranoid trends. The opportunity is tempting to delve into a comparison of the type in which the Nazis precipitated clinically manifest paranoid ideas with the type in which they helped to get rid of such ideas by offering a realistic configuration to which the previously imaginary productions could be displaced.

As a hypochondriac may feel relieved upon eventually obtaining a physical diagnosis, so a strongly paranoid person may feel greatly alleviated if at last he meets in actual form and realistic shape the ogre of his infancy which had surrounded him everywhere and always elusively up to the time a real persecutor made his appearance.[25] Furthermore, the fear of the real persecutor is shared by others, and the paranoid, who had had to bear his fears in isolation without a companion, suddenly finds himself in good company. What was ill-defined and unlimited becomes a configuration which can be dealt with by means effective in reality, such as flight. I should surmise that it resulted in a feeling of triumph for the patient when he escaped from Hitler and reached this country. To be sure, he had applied a variety of defense mechanisms before in order to escape his fears. But this time when he escaped he really left his persecutor behind; he knew where the enemy was and could turn his hatred against a real object. Hence, his "extratherapeutic" recovery probably set in during that first episode when he defeated his enemy by successful flight.

[25] For the problem of the spontaneous disappearance of delusions, see Robbins (1937). In a comprehensive context Hartmann (1939b) has discussed the theoretical aspect of regressive phenomena which occur in the service of adaptation to reality. "The turning toward reality can also mean protection from fantastic fears; it can serve the purpose of overcoming anxiety" (p. 42; my own translation). Kris (1941) stated: "Real danger is, on the average, faced better than vague apprehension; the fantastic or imaginary elements of anxiety are deflated by the impact of the concrete situation."

It is quite possible that fear of reality never can reach that degree of utter pain and distress which is attained by neurotic and psychotic fears. Hence, in certain circumstances even a very neurotic individual may be better endowed to cope with anxiety aroused by external dangers than the fairly unneurotic. The neurotic knows all too well what anxiety is, and, indeed, he has spent plenty of time and effort in abating anxiety; furthermore, this new anxiety of real danger does not reach the excruciating peak of the neurotic anxiety over imaginary dangers. The comparatively healthy person is rather handicapped if compared with the neurotic in this respect. The sudden upsurge of great quantities of anxiety is new to him and finds him unprepared to deal with it. This is not the case with the neurotic, whose reality anxiety taps the sources of neurotic anxiety. The neurotic, of course, labors under severe handicaps. But I can very well imagine that this man was in a favorable position in fighting against the Nazis. He faced in combat a realistic enemy toward whom he felt a tremendous hatred. At the same time he was a member of a powerful organization which undertook reality steps to exterminate the reality enemy-ogre. He had fooled the hideous enemy once before and escaped. This time it was he who returned and not the enemy; it was he who would take terrible vengeance and kill utterly whatever had stood in his way and caused distress.

The patient rendered valuable service to his outfit. Yet there occurred outbreaks of severe aggression beyond military necessity. Reality permitted him to act out marked destructiveness without the necessity of suffering feelings of guilt. Combat, and probably the totality of army service, was one great process of catharsis to him. As a punctured empyema spurts out the whole pus, so did he spurt out fear, destruction, and hatred.

It was extremely interesting to watch this man, after his return to civilian life, develop against the communists attitudes similar to those he had held against the Nazis. It seemed that he had learned to select reality enemies in accordance with current ideologies. In his phillipics he applied the current arguments and did not show any significant deviation from average standards besides some exaggerations and compulsive reiterations. There was for a short while the danger that he would develop a parasitic attitude toward the Veterans Administration, but the effort to establish himself in a self-supporting position was strong enough to counteract such a tendency. It seemed that the war experience had relieved him of considerable anxiety on the basis: "If I was able to get through all that without harm, then nothing can happen to me." The ordeal had restored a feeling of omnipotence which must have been present in an early phase of existence.

It seemed that the real experience of omnipotence had a more salutary effect on him, at least temporarily, than the imaginary. Does this not confirm Alexander's motto: "Nothing succeeds like success"? It does to a certain extent, if magic solutions can be accepted as valid. No doubt, there are very many patients who can keep their even severe psychopathology in abeyance if their egos are engrossed by extensive narcissistic gratifications. This patient had an opportunity to experience gratifications which man in general is rarely privileged to enjoy. The combination of historical and personal factors led him to witness the destruction of an extremely hated enemy which had become the representative of archaic and despicable images. Generally, that conflict must be brought to naught by internal changes; in his instance, he was permitted to bring the conflict temporarily to an end by experiences in reality. How long that solution brought about by a massive projection would last cannot be said. It certainly was not a solution on the level of a healthy ego change, but a grandiose wish fulfillment which granted temporary peace. Again, it was by a historical coincidence that the wish fulfillment could be accepted without the feelings of guilt which regularly set in when wish fulfillments are attempted on a fantasy basis. Reality provided him with an enemy whose evilness was greater than his own unconscious destructiveness; for this reason a *carte blanche* was granted him by his own superego. The historical coincidence provided him with a situation in which a feeling of guilt would have been aroused rather by his not killing than by killing.

This comment should not be taken as depreciating the great contribution of the preceding psychoanalytic treatment. Initially the patient was in a condition in which no external event could have precipitated any kind of adjustment. Psychoanalysis substituted reactability for rigid fixity. But the great question in every psychotherapy is whether the final solution will be on a reality level or will take place on a fantastic-imaginary level. The end product may in both instances be very similar, or even the same in terms of appearance—the surface a patient will show to the community or even to his closest companions. Nevertheless, from the viewpoint of a true psychology the two solutions are as different as day and night. No doubt, the patient's ego was stronger than ever after he had gone through army service and combat. But I am inclined to agree with Waelder (1934) that this kind of ego strength is a pseudo strength. Perhaps there are patients for whom the only solution is to be found in the development of that pseudo strength.

Another indication of his change in attitude toward reality may be seen in his temporary pursuit of writing short stories. The plots of these stories were good, that is to say, they followed a course of action which was accessible to empathy by others and lacked the bizarreness which was so typical of the earlier productions of his imagination. But the plots showed a direct and crude transposition of his personal problems into a literary form. Whereas his earlier imaginary productions were crude elaborations of his unconscious, the new ones contained more secondary elaborations, but still his short stories did not undergo that removal from the unconscious systems which is necessary for artistic production. They still lingered on the "dream" or "symptom" level.

It was noteworthy that his marriage proceeded satisfactorily as long as he had cause for a reality feeling of guilt toward his spouse because of unemployment. As soon as he became the supporter, the first signs of conflict manifested themselves.

This third patient demonstrated that there is, so to speak, no limit to the psychopathology that can be fitted into army service and even into prolonged combat activity, under certain conditions. It depended in this instance on the coincidence of reality and unconscious factors, on intense hatred and destructiveness which could not only be accepted without feeling of guilt, but also yielded gratification of superego demands. The army situation and combat became the stage for a series of cathartic processes which endowed the ego with a rich fund of pseudo strength.

In this context it may be of interest to report a reaction observed in neuropsychiatric battle casualties (See Henderson and Moore, 1944). When they were asked how soon they would be well enough to return to the islands for combat, 72 per cent answered that they would never be able to return. They were suffering, according to the authors, mainly from anxiety states. Twenty per cent answered, "Yes, but . . ." or "Yes, if . . . my [sc. symptom] didn't bother me too much." (These were patients suffering from hysteria.) Eight per cent, however, said they were ready to return: ". . . almost all were or had been psychotic."

These three patients, then, are instances of how extraordinarily far human beings can go in dealing with certain limited and particular reality problems even when they seem most exaggeratedly unfitted because of psychopathology for coping with the problems that everyone confronts. From their cases, perhaps, something can be learned about what it may be possible to do in an emergency, in rendering resistant to the disorganizing impact of prolonged combat experience soldiers who cannot, because of shortness of time, be prepared for warfare by effecting adequate structural personality changes. It would, it seems, be a matter of properly directed magic, a technique which can be learned only from the sick who has seemingly recovered by the upsurge of pseudo ego strength. The subject seems important enough to elaborate further on its theoretical aspect.

Needles (1945a), who at the outset thought he had found a significant difference between military neuropsychiatric casualties and untainted control cases, later revised his opinion and wrote: "There is no essential difference between the early breakdowns and the soldier with a relatively long survival period." This was his conclusion after examining neurotic soldiers whose time of combat equaled or exceeded that of the so-called healthy soldiers. Seven case histories were briefly outlined by him. As far as can be seen there was a great variety of clinical pictures among his subjects. Some of them may be roughly characterized by the following catchwords: the soldier who simulated health; the soldier who would have accepted death as a redemption from his neurotic suffering; the soldier who found fulfillment in obedience; the soldier who was driven by the desire of revenge for his brother's death; the soldier who was kept going by alcohol.

Some of the syndromes described by Needles can be found among the last three cases I have presented, but his material was richer and more apt to permit general conclusions than mine. Nevertheless, I would raise doubts regarding his thesis of the absence of essential differences between the, so to speak, unsuccessful neurotic and successful neurotic soldier. While it is correct to stress those psychological factors which are common to even highly different behavior patterns, at the same time the differences must also be ascertained, if psychological research is not to come to a standstill. To be sure, the great merit of Needles's paper in demonstrating the stupendous neuroses existing in successful combat soldiers must not be belittled. Still, even in the light of his findings, which were particularly surprising and scarcely anticipated by anyone, I must admit that my last two cases strike me as extremely amazing. Their psychopathology has been only most cursorily presented and therefore the reader may not share this impression. Yet it must be repeated that the war performance of both soldiers was unexpected in the extreme, and if anyone had dared to predict it, he would have met no acceptance in any quarter. This paradox—of unusually severe psychopathology ensuing in stamina seemingly greater than in many of those who unquestionably were healthier—may become even more puzzling if it is suggested that Needles's and Whitehorn's conclusions which seem to be in agreement are highly questionable. Both of them have the idea of neurotic symptoms being counterbalanced by assets. This idea probably is patterned after some biological findings. It is a matter of actual observation that an organism may compensate for a deficiency in one structure by the hypertrophy of another. The final result may then be a function identical with that of an uninjured organism, or, under favorable conditions, the compensatory mechanism may outbalance the deficit and even lead to greater achievements than the organism would have been capable without the previous deficit. Acquired immunity is an example which may fall into this category. If this analogy were really applicable to the psychological situation here encountered, the efficiency in spite of psychopathology would lose its surprising quality. But in reality the situation was quite different. It was the psychopathology per se that made it possible for these soldiers to bear up under the reality stress.

This can be seen in Needles's Case No. 2, who felt so miserable and tortured by obsessional thinking that he became suicidal and was unaware of fear during combat. It would be wrong to say that it was *in spite* of his psychopathology that he was able to go through combat. It is far more correct to say that it was *because* of his obsessional thinking that he remained free of fear. To be sure, it would be wrong to conclude that obsessional thinking predisposes toward fearlessness in combat, but in these selected interviews it seems so. Certainly in my reported series of three sick soldiers there must have been unusual combinations of psychopathological features which led to success. But the unusual combination lay not outside of their psychopathology, but in it.

In the first case the necessity of proving omnipotence by effort was simultaneously one of the most important symptoms *and* the tool with which he mastered reality; in the second, the automatonlike surrender to one sector of reality and the loss or individual reactability were the crux of his psychopathology *and* the prerequisite of efficient action; in the third, the displacement of paranoid symptoms onto the Nazis was the end result of a paranoid disorder *and* the driving force of relentless striving toward the destruction of the enemy.

The stringent conclusion from this state of affairs is that psychopathology and efficiency, disorder and achievement, do not exclude each other. In terms of emotional, biased thinking, psychopathology is bad and efficiency is normal and good, and therefore we are constrained to assume that they exclude each other. If we see a very sick person engaged in a brilliant performance, we are impelled to assume counterpoises, compensations, and what not, because the idea that something that makes us feel bad could produce something that makes us feel good is contradictory to our magical thinking. But this way of thinking led to attributing therapeutic value to modern shock therapy. The patient worked again after the assault on his central nervous system, whether by knife, drug, or electricity, and therefore the therapy must have been good. Yet this way of thinking does not strike me as more correct than the conviction that the burning of heretics is good because it increases the percentage of true believers.

In summary, I wish to state that psychopathology may lead to performance constructive in terms of society's needs. Psychopathology, however, is always essentially detrimental in terms of the internal microcosm. Efficiency is a category which is meaningful predominantly in terms of the individual's relationship to his external world. In view of Freud's (1932) statement of "the underlying identity, subsisting between pathological and so-called normal processes" (p. 198),[26] I tentatively conclude from the cases of the three soldiers who were eminent in their military performance that efficiency, mastery of reality, in short what present society calls normality, is a balanced mixture of the following three factors: the urge to prove one's omnipotence at all costs; the surrender with or without inner struggle to the exigencies of the moment or the future, enforced by the blotting out of individuality; and the projection of a fear into a sector of reality which becomes the goal of an aggressive impulse without the superego's raising a feeling of guilt.[27] These seem to be the three features of psychopathology which are engaged in the personality's successful dealing with reality. The feeling of omnipotence, in this instance, is based on a superficial and temporary fusion of the three systems (Angel, 1934). The ego gratifies the id by offering itself as the exclusively lovable object. The superego in its persistent endeavor to enforce its rule dogmatically, that is to say, its demand to be uncompromisingly omnipotent is drained toward external reality. By surrendering to reality the ego enjoys masochistic pleasure and the superego is pacified by submitting to the displeasure of reality. By attaching a paranoid projection to a sector of reality the id is drained of aggression and the superego is placated by rationalization.

Thus it can be seen that each of the three sets of adaptive mechanisms is supported to a certain extent by each province of the personality. The three sets, however, seem to be mutually exclusive: the ego feels omnipotent, surrenders to reality, and transforms reality according to the id's wishes. However, the ego, where it is unconscious, permits itself to be as contradictory as the id is commonly observed to be. The rational part that complies with logic and bows to consistency is actually very small. That area is surrounded by primitive and archaic adaptations. They may easily be thrown out of balance. If any one of them arouses feelings of guilt or anxiety, then successful bearing on reality becomes disturbed. Yet the feeling of omnipo-

---

[26] In German the passage reads as follows: ". . . die innere Identität zwischen den pathologischen und den sogenannten normalen Vorgängen", meaning "the intrinsic identity of pathological and so-called normal processes."

[27] Cf. Nunberg (1937): "The impulsion of the super-ego for dominating the ego, its need for power, is displaced onto the ego, which now becomes capable of making a better adjustment to the instinctual world as well as to the external world." In the Symposium (1937) many references will be found to the effect of therapy on the personality, and hence only indirectly to the psychological condition under which a person functions adequately.

tence is prone to pacify anxiety, the paranoid projection to drain aggression, and the surrender to reality to eliminate feelings of guilt.[28] The cooperation of these three psychopathological adaptive structures can be impressively observed in a person who masters reality by the integration of a religion, particularly if it is based on revelation. He surrenders to the dogma without objection. He obtains a feeling of omnipotence by his direct communication with God, and he displaces a paranoid delusion onto a socially accepted and, under favorable conditions, socially constructive system of ideas. It can likewise be observed in the religious person to what extreme forms of psychopathology it may lead when one of the factors enumerated does not continue to serve the inherent function. Yet as long as their balanced working together continues, the person will obtain an unmatched tool particularly adapted for the mastery of reality.

I believe the following quotation from such an authority as William James will be of interest in this context. He writes about "the Christian *par excellence,* the mystic and ascetic saint."

> There is a state of mind, known to religious men, but to no others, in which the will to assert ourselves and hold our own has been displaced by a willingness to close our mouths and be as nothing in the floods and waterspouts of God. In this state of mind, what we most dreaded has become the habitation of our safety, and the hour of our moral death has turned into our spiritual birthday. The time for tension in our soul is over, and that of happy relaxation, of calm, deep breathing, of an external present, with no discordant future to be anxious about has arrived. Fear is not held in abeyance as it is by mere morality, it is positively expunged and washed away. . . . Now in those states of mind which fall short of religion, the surrender is submitted to as an imposition of necessity, and the sacrifice is undergone at the very best without complaint. In the religious life, on the contrary, surrender and sacrifice are positively espoused, even unnecessary givings-up are added in order that the happiness may increase. *Religion thus makes easy and felicitous what in any case is necessary* [James, 1902, pp. 47 n., 51; italics by James].

James, indeed seems to illustrate the three psychopathological adaptations when he describes the practical difficulties of all religious phenomena. They are: "1. to 'realize the reality' of one's higher part; 2. to identify one's self with it exclusively; and 3. to identify it with all the rest of ideal being"

---

[28] I do not see any great advantage to our knowledge and understanding if the difference between the successful and the unsuccessful soldier is called character. See Michaels: (1946): "It may well be the law of self-preservation that compels the soldier to push on, but it is character that enables him to carry on despite most adversities."

(p. 509, n. 1). The realization of the reality of the higher part corresponds to the condition of the feeling of omnipotence; the process of identification with it corresponds to the surrender; and, further, the inclusion of the rest of ideal being corresponds to the paranoid delusion.

This coincidence—of three pathological mechanisms in three patients who were enabled by their psychopathology to conquer a particular onerous reality situation, with three basic psychological tasks which religious man must according to James fulfill in order to extend it to its greatest operational efficiency—may increase the credibility of my thesis.

In the last three subjects of my series the mechanisms or sets of mechanisms were observed in isolated working.[29] In this lay their weakness. The first patient was lacking in the ability of surrendering to reality. Therefore, he could not accept a frustration. The second patient was lacking in the aspiration toward fulfilled omnipotence. He could function only if reality pressed itself on him and forced him into certain activities. This made him dependent on the accidental combinations of reality. Moreover, his ability to surrender was limited to a few situations which corresponded to daydreams. Outside of that comparatively narrow sector his capacity for surrender was blocked and he had to resort to flight or other mechanisms of escape.

In the third instance adequate functioning was limited to a sector in which an aggressive paranoid idea could be invested. As in the second case, the patient was dependent on particular combinations of reality factors. Furthermore, the weakest spot in his adaptive setup lay in his necessity of draining direct aggression into that sector of reality which he engulfed in his paranoidlike way, in order to maintain a constructive contact at all. If reality had taken a turn in which the paranoid drain had become blocked, for example, a permanent defeat in battle, a manifest psychosis or at least a manifest regression to his former level would have necessarily ensued. A surrender to reality or a feeling of omnipotence aroused by effort was not available to him.

A general weakness to be observed in all three patients was the low degree of internalization of the adaptive mechanisms.[30] The first patient would have been more secure if the feeling of omnipotence had not depended on a reality success but on the realization of an internal value; the second patient needed a specific sector of external reality or an external force to which to surrender, but the surrender to an inner frame of reference would have

[29] That is to say, their adaptation depended mainly on a single mechanism. Notwithstanding the preponderance of single mechanisms, in each of them, traces of the other mechanism were also observable.

[30] For the great importance of internalization to adjustment, see Hartmann (1939b), particularly pp. 57-59).

broadened the operational basis of the mechanism; in the third instance there was no sufficient internalization of aggression, and adaptation was dependent on the exigencies of reality that might or might not provide appropriate channels of discharge.

In the religious person as outlined by James the three sets of adaptive mechanisms reach perfection. They protect the ego against all dangers. There is no surprise, no frustration, possible. The self is constantly triumphant. Facing death, the martyr does not envisage annihilation, but perfection. This becomes possible when the feeling of omnipotence is caused by the superego's victory over the ego, as happens when the surrender of the ego leads to submission to the superego and when the delusional projection of value systems engulfs the whole of reality.[31] The balanced cooperation of all three adaptations will rarely be encountered in clinical reality. It must be assumed that the majority of people will maintain their constructive contact with reality by reliance on one or two of them. Furthermore, the adaptation will not be as extreme, exclusive, and rigid—that is to say, pathological—as in the clinical material presented here. In the series of eight "normal" soldiers initially discussed, the same kind of psychopathology could be dimly observed. However, the value of these case histories is greatly reduced by their particular incompleteness—even the best psychiatric interview is to be considered incomplete in a discussion that pertains to the unconscious part of the ego—and the least that can be said is that the material obtained in the interviews does not disprove my thesis.

It is worth while to review briefly the place which the term "normality" takes in Freud's work. The two different contexts in which the concept is used may be roughly distinguished as first, methodological, and, second, clinical. Freud (1917) speaks of *normal* prototypes, such as the dream vs. narcissistic mental disorders, or grief vs. melancholia. The concept of normality, here, serves as an operational tool to investigate by its contrast certain psychopathological phenomena, but not as a yardstick or measure of clinical evaluation.[32] This was unmistakably expressed when Freud (1917) wrote: "We are able to learn in various ways how advantageous it is for our researches to institute comparisons with certain states and phenomena which may be conceived of as *normal prototypes* of morbid affections" (p. 137, italics by Freud). The concept of normal for the purpose of gaining insight

---

[31] This one-sided description must, of course, be complemented by the dynamics of the id in all three adaptations.

[32] The dream remained for Freud psychopathology. "A dream . . . is a psychosis, with all the absurdities, delusions and illusions of a psychosis. No doubt it is a psychosis which has only a short duration, etc.," (1938, p. 61).

into contrasting structures does not throw any light on the subject matter of this study.

The clinical application of the concept occurs rather rarely in Freud's writings except in his comprehensive paper on the efficacy and limitations of psychoanalytic therapy (Freud, 1937). The term is used in a variety of meanings which may be briefly outlined:

1. *Descriptive meaning* (normality as a subjective feeling) in order to characterize a patient's feelings after the termination of his analysis; Freud writes that the patient "felt normal" (1937, p. 318). Here the term is used descriptively for a subjective state among other data such as behavior, in order to evaluate the effect of treatment.

2. *Structural meaning* (absolute psychic normality). Freud raised the question whether an analysis could ever result in a condition in which all the patient's repressions had been lifted and every memory gap filled. In such circumstances further therapy would not bring forth any changes. The patient would have reached a level of absolute psychic normality (1937, p. 320).

3. *Economic meaning* (fictitious normality ego[33]). Freud in evaluating the difficulties encountered in the process of analysis established a scale one end of which was marked by the ego of the psychotic. His ego structure has undergone extensive and intensive modification of such degree as to make a psychoanalytic treatment impossible. On the other end of the scale there would be a fictitious normality ego which follows *all* the necessities of treatment, that is to say, is inexhaustible in its loyalty to the analytic process and therefore is unlimitedly willing to bear displeasure for the sake of its recovery and thus would be apt to execute uncompromisingly the requirements of the psychoanalytic procedure. In psychoanalytic practice, egos approaching to a varying degree the psychotic are encountered.

4. *Dynamic meaning* (harmony of the ego). It is not the goal of a psychoanalytic treatment to enforce the disappearance of a drive the warding off of which had resulted in the patient's neurotic symptomatology. The drive should be brought into the harmony of the ego, that is to say, should be mastered and tamed. However, if the ego is weakened the drive may seek substitute gratification by means of *abnormal* ways (Freud, 1937, p. 327). Hence, this aspect would result in normality pertaining to temporary states of balance between ego and id, states which can be attained by the ego only under particular conditions, since sleep (a "normal" occurrence) would already upset this kind of equilibrium.

[33] See Freud (1937, pp. 337 and 342), where his term *fiktives Normal-Ich* (*Ges. W.*, XVI, p. 185) is translated as "imaginary normal ego."

5. *Functional meaning* (degrees of normality). The patient's recovery may be obstructed by the analyst's own deficiencies. The analyst should have a high measure of psychic normality. It can be measured by his ability in "discerning his patient's situation correctly and reacting to it in a manner conducive to cure" (Freud, 1937, p. 351).

6. *Social meaning* (schematic normality) (Freud, 1937, p. 354). Depending on society and particular goals, certain concepts of normality may be conceived, such as absence of conflicts or passions in a person. Such definitions certainly have no clinical validity and appear arbitrary from the scientific viewpoint, although the one who conceives of them may try to base them on objective data.

It is impressive to notice how precisely Freud indicated in which sense he wished the term to be understood whenever he spoke of normality. Further, he points out each time where the data may be obtained which will indicate the distance from or closeness to a normal condition, that is to say, he gives the frame of reference to which the respective meaning of the term belongs whenever the term has a nondescriptive meaning. Further, there seems to be no indication that he thought the *clinical* reality of "normal" to be essentially divorced from the interplay of those forces which are so well observed in the neurotic and the psychotic.

With regard to the question of conflict and adjustment I wish to refer to an allied topic. In reading biographies of indubitably creative masters and in paying special attention to situations in which patients present particular skills in constructive achievements one gains the inescapable impression that these pursuits—which must be considered accomplishments or achievements (*Leistungen*) in contrast to symptoms—are the final outcome of particularly intense conflicts. The psychological circumstances in which the conflict (and its solution) exhausts itself completely in the formation of an autoplastic change such as a symptom are quite different from those in which it leads to the realization of an artistic value in which others can participate. But the two outcomes seem to have in common that they grow out of conflicts. The discovery of what the difference is that leads in the one case to a useless and painful symptom and in another to a highly appreciated structure would be of great value.

Health is a fictitious concept in the psychic stratum; perhaps it has a proper place in the biological. There are defenses which cause displeasure or pleasure and there are defenses which favor the survival of the individual or of the species or lead to the individual's destruction. We need the concept of health for practical purposes and the concept requires redefinition probably with each important historical change and probably with

each new developmental phase of the individual. I do not see how the
concept can theoretically be defined in a meaningful way and still stay
in accordance with the principles of scientific psychology. This, however,
does not negate the need—nor, perhaps, the possibility—of outlining the
conditions under which man has the greatest chance to continue functioning
even when exposed to the weight of trying excessive stimulation coming
from either external or internal sources. While the ability so to function
may be made the cornerstone of the concept of health, I wished to
demonstrate that such functioning can, and, as I surmise, even must, be
bought at the price of unquestionably severe psychopathology. Thus this
paper may be taken as an attempt at trying out the operational value of the
concept of the psychopathology of normality.

* * *

As I reread this manuscript I asked myself whether I still adhere
to the views set forth here. In the analyst's daily work, of course, one
concentrates on the problem of uncovering, and removing, the causes
of the disturbance of the adjustive processes. Accordingly, I have no
doubt paid less attention to the problem the paper deals with since
the end of the war. At a time when a large number of people had to
face unusual demands of adjustment—and actually met them in one
way or another—attention was necessarily drawn to the problem by
the acuteness of the reality situation.

The psychopathology I observed in inquiring into this problem
might have been caused indirectly by the unusualness of the adjustive
demand, and the field of inquiry may therefore not have been as
suitable for evolving a theory of adjustment as I thought at that time.
The pathology of the external situation, so to speak, may have required in turn the activation of psychopathology in the individual.

Further, it may be objected that I have based my main inferences
upon the otherwise very fruitful principles of deriving insight into
the normal from the study of the pathological and it may be suggested
that this principle is to be complemented in the instance of the
particular psychological inquiry under discussion. The development
of ego psychology may have changed the general perspective. To cite
an example: when Freud wrote his Leonardo study in 1910, he was
mainly interested in that part of the genius "which he shared with
all men" (Freud, 1925, p. 119), whereas in his last historical work he
raised the question of what it is that makes a man great (Freud, 1937-
1939, pp. 169-176). He did not have in mind the factor of endowment in the form of skills and talents, but precisely the problem of
what makes the personality of a genius different from the average.
Likewise it may be asked what the differences are between the adjustive processes that are observable within certain syndromes and
those that occur under internal conditions that are not pathological.

In other words the issue to be decided would be whether or not the observations I made during the interviews with the eight selected soldiers are indicative of processes that, though reduced or abridged when compared with gross instances of psychopathology, are still equivalents of what is found clinically in such instances. This question I should not venture to decide at present, though I retain the impression that it will one day be answered in the affirmative.

However, I feel less certain that the clinical material regarding these eight soldiers is really convincing. But even if further research should confirm my hunch, I am certain that the mechanisms I have set forth are not sufficient to cover the area I have assigned to them. Many more mechanisms and factors will be found within psychopathology that in minutiae make their contribution to mental adjustment in the normal. The limitation in my presentation to just three mechanisms may have been the result of the extremely specific character of the situations to which the individuals had to adjust.

BIBLIOGRAPHY

Agoston, T. (1946), The Fear of Post-orgastic Emptiness. *Psychoanal. Rev.,* 33:197-214.

Alexander, F. & French, T. M. (1946), *Psychoanalytic Therapy.* New York: Ronald Press.

Anderson, R. C. (1947), The Motivations of the Flyer and His Reaction to the Stresses of Flight. *J. Aviation Med., 18:18-30.*

Angel, A. (1934), Einige Bemerkungen über den Optimismus. *Int. Z. Psychoanal., 20:191-199.*

Billings, E. G.; Ebaugh, F. G.; Morgan, D. W.; O'Kelly, L. I.; Short, G. B.; & Golding, F. C. (1943), Comparison of One Hundred Psychiatric Patients and One Hundred Enlisted Men. *War Med., 4:283-298.*

Boring, E. G. (ed.) (1945), *Psychology for the Armed Services.* Washington: The Infantry Journal.

Bose, G. (1937), The Duration of Coitus. *Int. J. Psychoanal., 18:235-255.*

Bray, C. W. (1948), *Psychology and Military Proficiency.* Princeton, N.J.: Princeton University Press.

Brill, N. Q.; Tate, M. C.; & Menninger, W. C. (1945), Enlisted Men Discharged from the Army Because of Psychoneuroses. *J. Amer. Med. Assn., 128:633-637.*

Cantor, N. (1941), What Is a Normal Mind? *Amer. J. Orthopsychiat., 11:676-683.*

Console, W. A. (1946), Psychiatric Reactions to Aerial Combat and Their Sequelae. *Conn. Med. J., 10:900-902.*

Cooley, C. H. (1918), *Social Process.* New York: Scribner.

Farrell, M. J. & Appel, J. W. (1944), Current Trends in Military Neuropsychiatry. *Amer. J. Psychiat., 101:12-19.*

Freud, S. (1910), Leonardo da Vinci and a Memory of His Childhood. *Standard Edition, 11:59-137.* London: Hogarth Press, 1957.

—— (1916), Metapsychological Supplement to the Theory of Dreams. *Collected Papers, 4:137-151.* London: Hogarth Press, 1948.

—— (1917), Mourning and Melancholia. *Collected Papers, 4*:152-170. London: Hogarth Press, 1948.

—— (1925), *An Autobiographical Study*. London: Hogarth Press, 1950.

—— (1932), *New Introductory Lectures on Psychoanalysis*. New York: W. W. Norton, 1933.

—— (1937), Analysis Terminable and Interminable. *Collected Papers, 5*:316-357. London: Hogarth Press, 1950.

—— (1938), *An Outline of Psychoanalysis*. New York: W. W. Norton, 1949.

—— (1937-1939), *Moses and Monotheism*. New York: Knopf, 1939.

Glover, E. (1932), Medico-Psychological Aspects of Normality. *On the Early Development of Mind*. New York: International Universities Press, 1956.

Gregory, E. (1944), The Idealization of the Absent. *Amer. J. Sociol., 50*:53-54.

Hacker, F. J. (1945), The Concept of Normality and Its Practical Significance. *Amer. J. Orthopsychiat., 15*:47-64.

Harrington, D. O. (1947), Ocular Manifestations of Psychosomatic Disorders. *J. Amer. Med. Assn., 133*:669-675.

Hartmann, H. (1939a), Psycho-Analysis and the Concept of Health. *Int. J. Psychoanal., 20*:308-321.

—— (1939b), *Ego Psychology and the Problem of Adaptation*. New York: International Universities Press, 1958.

Heath, C. W. (1945), *What People Are: A Study of Normal Young Men*. Cambridge: Harvard University Press.

Henderson, J. L. & Moore, M. (1944), The Psycho-neuroses of War. *Mil. Surgeon, 95*:349-356.

Hooton, E. (1945), *Young Man, You Are Normal*. New York: Putnam.

Ivy, A. C. (1944), What Is Normal or Normality? *Quart. Bull. Northw. Univ. Med. School, 18*:22-32.

James, W. (1902), *The Varieties of Religious Experience*. New York: Longmans Green, 1935.

Janis, I. L. (1945), Psychodynamic Aspects of Adjustment to Army Life. *Psychiatry, 8*:159-176.

Jones, E. (1931), The Concept of a Normal Mind. *Int. J. Psychoanal., 23*:1-8, 1942.

Keiser, S. (1947), On the Psychopathology of Orgasm. *Psychoanal. Quart., 16*:378-390.

King, C. D. (1945), The Meaning of Normal. *Yale J. Biol. Med., 17*:493-501.

Kinsey, A. C.; Pomeroy, W. B.; & Martin, C. W. (1948), *Sexual Behavior in the Human Male*. Philadelphia: Saunders.

Kris, E. (1941), Morale in Germany. *Amer. J. Sociol., 47*:452-461.

Lampl-de Groot, J. (1936), Hemmung und Narzissmus. *Int. Z. Psychoanal., 22*:198-222.

Maeder, L. (1941), Diagnostic Criteria—The Concept of Normal and Abnormal. *Family, 22*:171-179.

McNeel, B. H. & Dancey, T. E. (1945), The Personality of the Successful Soldier. *Amer. J. Psychiat., 102*:337-342.

Michaels, J. (1946), Strength Through Character. *Amer. J. Orthopsychiat., 16*:350-355.

Murray, J. M. (1944), Psychiatric Aspects of Aviation Medicine. *Psychiatry, 7*:1-7.

Needles, W. (1945a), The Successful Neurotic Soldier. *Bull. U.S. Army Med. Dept.*, 4:673-682.

—— (1945b), A Statistical Study of One Hundred Neuropsychiatric Casualties from the Normandy Campaign. *Amer. J. Psychiat.*, 102:214-221.

Nunberg, H. (1932), *Principles of Psychoanalysis*. New York: International Universities Press, 1955.

—— (1937), The Theory of the Therapeutic Results of Psycho-Analysis. *Int. J. Psychoanal.*, 18: 161-169.

Reich, W. (1927), *Die Funktion des Orgasmus*. Vienna: Internationaler Psychoanalytischer Verlag.

—— (1933), *Character Analysis*. New York: Orgone Institute, 2nd ed., 1945.

Reider, N. (1950), The Concept of Normality. *Psychoanal. Quart.*, 19:43-51.

Robbins, B. S. (1937), Escape into Reality: A Clinical Note on Spontaneous Social Recovery. *Psychoanal. Quart.*, 6:353-364.

Rogers, C. R. (1942), *Counseling and Psychotherapy; Newer Concepts in Practice*. Boston: Houghton Mifflin.

Ryle, J. A. (1947), The Meaning of Normal. *Lancet, 1*:1-5.

Schwab, R. S.; Finesinger, J. E.; & Brazier, M. (1944), Psychoneuroses Precipitated by Combat. *U.S. Naval Med. Bull.*, 42:535-544.

Sheps, J. G. (1944), A Psychiatric Study of Successful Soldiers. *J. Amer. Med. Assn.*, 126:271-273.

Steinberg, D. L. & Wittman, M. P. (1943), Etiologic Factors in the Adjustment of Men in the Armed Forces. *War Med.*, 4:129-139.

Sullivan, H. S. (1940), Conceptions of Modern Psychiatry. *Psychiatry, 3*:1-117.

Symposium (1937), The Theory of Therapeutic Results of Psycho-Analysis. *Int. J. Psychoanal.*, 18:125-189.

Terman, L. M. & Oden, M. H. (1947), *The Gifted Child Grows Up*. Stanford University Press.

Thibaut, J. W. (1943), The Concept of Normality in Clinical Psychology. *Psychol. Rev.*, 50:338-344.

Waelder, R. (1934), The Problem of Freedom in Psycho-Analysis and the Problem of Reality-Testing. *Int. J. Psychoanal.*, 17:89-108.

Wegrocki, H. J. (1939), A Critique of Cultural and Statistical Concepts of Abnormality. *J. Abn. Soc. Psychol.*, 34:166-178.

Whitehorn, J. C. (1946), Changing Concepts of Psychoneurosis in Relation to Military Psychiatry. In: *Neuropsychiatry* (Res. Publ. Assn. Nerv. Ment. Dis., 25:1-10). Baltimore: William & Wilkins.

Wright, Q. (1942), *A Study of War*. Chicago: University of Chicago Press.

A CROSS-CULTURAL STUDY OF THE RELATIONSHIP BETWEEN VALUES AND MODAL CONSCIENCE

MONICA BYCHOWSKI HOLMES

I

THE CONCEPTUAL AND THEORETICAL FRAMEWORK

Our major theoretical framework for this study will be F. Kluckhohn's (1950) value-orientation scheme and McCord's formulations on conscience structure.[1] Since in this study we will be investigating the relationship between values and modal conscience, it is necessary to understand exactly how we mean to use these concepts and the nature of their relationship to national character. Some students of national character have delineated the values or the major institutions and have then equated this configuration of cultural patterns with character; some have deduced national character from the study of a single technique in the socialization process; and some have written as though they expect absolute uniformity among all the people of a given nation. In an attempt to avoid these errors we must define as explicitly as possible what we mean by national character and how we expect to derive it.

In order for people to be able to communicate with each other they need not only a common language, but also a set of implicit and explicit ideas and expectations with regard to each other, which they share in common. As Bateson (1948) puts it: ". . . some degree of uniformity of character structure occurs among the individuals who participate in any given set of cultural behaviors . . ." (p. 131). We assume, then, that if ego and alter are to coexist, there must be some degree of consistency in their expectations and actions toward one another. The random characteristics of individuals

---

This manuscript was first presented in 1958 as an honors thesis in the Department of Social Relations at Harvard University. Grateful acknowledgment is due to Dr. D. McClelland for his direction of this paper, to Drs. F. Kluckhohn and C. Kluckhohn, and to Dr. W. McCord, without whose seminars and lectures this work would not have been possible.

[1] Unpublished material presented in a seminar at Harvard University in 1957-58.

98

must give way to certain patterned regularities of behavior if the individuals of a given group are to function positively in relation to one another. We can assume, then, that there are certain shared elements of personality among the people of a given culture, because, for survival, they must have certain expectations toward one another. But as Gorer (1953) has pointed out: "A normative statement does not imply universality, is not meant to be applicable to every member of the society being investigated; it does imply that members of a given society at a given place and at a given time act *consistently* in relation to certain norms or ideals of behavior . . ." (p. 59). Implicit in this statement of Gorer's is the view that in dealing with national character, we are dealing somehow with the problem of frequency. Because this problem of frequency must be taken into account and because there has been so much popular misconception about national character, we propose instead to deal with the more specific concept of modal personality.

The concept of modal personality is a construct; it does not conform to any one concrete person, but is rather a descriptive statement about a number of people and an attempt to extract these few features of personality which are common to most of them. We can then agree with Inkeles and Levinson (1954) in their essential definition of national character. It "refers to relatively enduring personality characteristics and patterns that are modal among the adult members of the society" (p. 983). Furthermore, as Inkeles and Levinson point out, it is quite possible that there can be a plurality of modes within the society. Consequently, it seems vital to make explicit which class we are speaking about when we describe a modal pattern for a nation, and it is further necessary to point out that the dominant class in terms of influence might not always be the dominant one numerically. Thus, when we discuss certain American personality features, we shall be speaking of the middle class, which happens to be dominant in both number and influence. On the other hand, in France, for example, we shall be dealing with the values of the upper-class aristocracy, who are certainly not dominant numerically, but who, we feel, have had the greatest influence in that the rest of the population admires and tries to emulate their patterns.

Briefly now we must turn to the further consideration of how we expect to study modal personality and how it can best be inferred. The study of national character has been defined by Mead (1953) as "the attempt to delineate the regularities in character among the members of a national group attributable to the factors of shared nationality and accompanying institutional correlates" (p. 646), and that seems to have led to a serious confusion as to what exactly is being studied. There has been in the past a tendency to confuse the fact that we attempt a construction of national character because of the underlying assumption that there is some measure of uniformity due to "like factors of shared nationality and accompanying institutional correlates," and the fact that the study of the institutions gives us perhaps national culture but not national character. As Inkeles and Levinson (1954) have pointed out, there has in general been "failure to view modal personality as analytically distinct from other aspects of psychosocial analysis. Ordinarily, a society is described and analyzed chiefly in socio-cultural terms, that is, in terms of the normative patterning of beliefs, values, institutional practices" (p. 988). Furthermore, little attention has been given to the personality structure of the adults of the society; rather, attention has been given to child-training techniques. While we believe that there is an intimate connection between national culture on the one hand and national character on the other, that each influences and shapes the other, it seems necessary to keep them at least analytically distinct.

We expect to study national culture by the investigation of the dominant value profile of each group. We have then predicted certain meaningful relationships between the value profile of a culture and personality; in fact, we will be dealing with only one aspect of personality: conscience. A little further on we shall describe how we conceptualize modal conscience; the point to make clear here is that we have used this psychological variable because we do not think that the study of values tells us about personality structure. While we believe that the values of a people influence deeply their life view, their child-training patterns, and personality patterns, they are not, however, personality itself. If we say that an individual is "doing-oriented," this does not tell us much about his ego or superego structure. Perhaps it is possible to infer his personality structure from his value profile— and indeed we shall try to show that this can be done—but at the present time there is no systematic formulation for making these inferences.

Before describing our conceptualization of modal conscience, we must first present a justification for the use of the value scheme and at least some brief description of F. Kluckhohn's value-orientation scheme, which is to be one of our major conceptual and analytical tools. As Vogt (1955) has pointed out, value orientations serve as selectors, regulators, and discriminators of goals. Hence the adults of any one generation have certain conscious and unconscious goals as to what and how they wish the next generation to learn. Out of all the great potentiality for variability in human behavior, the values of a culture tend to present some patterns of behavior in a more favorable light. We agree with Vogt (1955) who points out that values act "as regulators in the system by continually defining and redefining the limits of permissible behavior. In this function they provide the fundamental basis for a set of moral norms" (p. 5). Although we shall be concerned mainly with the structure of conscience, rather than with its content, or "moral norms," clearly this regulative function of values makes them a useful tool in the study of conscience. The values that an individual or a social group hold afford the group a common ethos by dictating the culturally prescribed ways of feeling, thinking, and acting. As C. Kluckhohn (1951) has said: "There is a philosophy behind the way of life of each individual and every relatively homogeneous group at any given point in their history. This gives, with varying degrees of explicitness or implicitness, some sense of coherence or unity both in cognitive and affective dimensions" (pp. 409-410).

The underlying assumption of almost all work in the national character field has been that the early years are vital in the formation of the child, that the mechanics of child training tend to be similar in a single society or in a specific subgroup of the society (such as the American middle class), and that therefore we can speak of some uniformity of personality. However, it seems a serious mistake to arrive at modal personality on the basis of the mechanics of child training. It is the values which work on the mechanics: whether a culture in general has a long nursing period or not is a reflection of the basic values of the culture; we can expect, for instance, that a culture such as our own which has a strong Future orientation will want each generation to reach maturity quickly and will therefore thrust it into the future as soon as possible by having a relatively short nursing period. Thus, it seems to us that if we are to get at modal conscience, it is more valid to proceed from the values of a culture to conscience, rather than from mechanics of child training to conscience.

F. Kluckhohn has postulated that there are at least five basic problems which all human societies must solve: (1) the relation to time; (2) the relation of man to man; (3) the valued form of activity; (4) the position about human nature; and (5) the relation to nature. Each of these problems has three possible solutions, and to a certain degree each solution exists in each culture, but it makes a vital difference which of the solutions is the first-order orientation, how large a gap there is between the first- and second-order orientation, or whether the two are equal in emphasis. The possible solutions to each of the five problems are as follows. (1) *The relation to time:* Past, Present, Future; (2) *The relation of man to man:* Individualistic, Collateral, Lineal; (3) *The valued form of activity:* Being, Being-in-Becoming, and Doing; (4) *Belief about basic human nature:* man is seen as Evil, Mixed, Good, and along with each of these there is a choice as to whether man's nature is mutable or immutable; and finally (5) *The relation of man to nature:* man is Subjugated to Nature, in Harmony with Nature, or has Mastery over Nature. Having presented the value-orientation scheme, we shall devote some attention to our other system of conceptualization—the conscience-orientation scheme. We shall now turn to a consideration of Freud's superego theory and our modification of it for use in cross-cultural study.

Just as conscience is a vital part of the personality of the single individual, so it is our contention that it is a vital part of the character structure of the group of individuals who make up society. We must first turn our attention to the formation of the superego in the individual, since society is made up after all of a group of individuals who, due to the fact that they have been molded by similar institutions, share the same values and character structure. The study of the individual has shown that there can be great differences in both the content and structure of the superego. In order to account for these differences we must diverge somewhat from Freud's original formulations on the nature of the superego. It is our contention that his formulation of the origins of the superego is not universal. While we owe it to Freud's genius that the content, the functions of the superego in the total personality, the processes of introjection and identification, and the aggression of the superego have been set before us and made clear; his discussion of structure and formation seems limited. We intend to make an attempt at augmenting Freud's superego theory; in so doing we shall be following McCord's recent formulations.

McCord designed a moral decisions test which he administered to a group of air force men in the summer of 1957. The test consisted of about thirty stories, each of which presented some type of moral problem; the respondent was asked to say what he would do in each case and to describe the grounds on which he made his choice. After correlating the data McCord found that there were four distinct types of responses: hedonistic, authoritarian, other-directed, and integral. Our present task is to define these four conscience types, and to attempt a reconstruction of how a specific conscience style becomes part of the personality of a given individual. In other words, individuals differ in the grounds on which they make a moral choice, and we must assume that somehow these differences are attributable to differences in the socialization process and to basic differences in superego structure.

The hedonist bases his moral decisions on an evaluation of the relative amount of pain and pleasure which he can expect from following a certain course of action. A moral choice is considered to be good if it brings pleasure, and if one is not made to suffer for this pleasure content at a later date. We can readily see that this attitude is much akin to the attitude of the infant. The more he can "get," the more highly he is indulged, the more inherently satisfied he is with his life position and with his environment. We would expect the hedonist to come from a family where he is highly indulged, where the pleasure principle is so long fostered that later it becomes the prime consideration in the evaluation of a situation. As we shall attempt to show later, there is a strong relationship between the values of a culture and the modal conscience of its people. Thus, the hedonist will most often appear in a culture where much emphasis is placed on the pleasure principle, on self-enjoyment, on immediate gratification. Such a culture is one where the first-order Time and Activity Orientations would be Present and Being. When these values predominate we could expect a long nursing period, much gratification of childhood needs, and a lack of rigid discipline in any of the socialization spheres. We would expect that the attitude toward human nature will be that it is mixed and mutable, that sexual training will not be repressive because the values of the people do not suggest man's inherent sinfulness.

We must realize, however, that no culture could perpetuate itself if its members had a hedonistic conscience, unless there was some sort of very specific social control. We would like to suggest that this control is external, felt to be ego-alien, and is primarily control by the family. Since in this kind of Being-Present-oriented culture the family is highly gratifying to the individual, there is no feared loss of love and a minimal intensification of the oedipal problem; rather the family has control over the individual because it is the prime source of his satisfaction and he continues to be dependent on it for his need gratification. Thus, if he is not caught at an act, the family exercises no control over him; he does not feel the guilt that is felt by the individual who has internalized parental principles.[2] We would therefore expect that a hedonistic modal conscience can be extant, without bringing about social disruption, only in those cultures where the adults are ever present, where people live in small groups in which all individuals are economically and socially interdependent. On the other hand, one could expect a socially disorganized area in those cultures or subgroups in which there is a hedonistic modal conscience and no lineality or collaterality as a form of social control. We would like to suggest that in the American urban lower class where there is a Present-Being first-order orientation, and yet very little lineal control, this combination of values is a contributing factor to the increasing amount of delinquency.

Our prediction is, then, that the hedonistic modal conscience occurs in

[2] Note the similarity between our distinction here and Bettelheim's (1955) discussion of superego development in the behavior disorders.

those societies in which the individual is highly gratified in his early years, so that the pleasure principle is given much strength and free rein. Furthermore, since there is an emphasis on impulse release and gratification, punishment tends to be highly sporadic and inconsistent, and parental demands are low. There is high impulse release of all kinds by the parents, so that we can expect this impulsiveness to lead to alternation between parental warmth and aggressiveness. Hence, frustration tolerance is not very great, and the dominant mode of social control is the actual presence of the lineal or extended family group. There is no emphasis on the postponement of gratification for some later goal; and since the baby is given the feeling that the adults exist for his own pleasure, there is little need to internalize their standards. Love-oriented techniques of discipline are not employed; rather direct punishment and withholding of awards are the recognized means of making a child conform to recognized social standards. If he is not caught in his transgression, there can be no punishment; and since the child has not internalized these injunctions, there is no guilt. His act goes unpunished and since he has derived pleasure from it, the activity is reinforced. Consequently, it is only morally wrong to him if he has been apprehended and punished. In a society where individuals work closely together, and where the children spend most of their time in the presence of adults, such an act, one can expect, will soon be noticed and punished. The child is so highly gratified by these same adults, he soon learns that the act is not worth the punishment and it is possible to find a substitute activity. In this way the hedonistic conscience is developed in the child, so that when he comes to make a moral decision the act is evaluated only in terms of pain and pleasure, pain being, of course, connected with apprehension.

In turning now to the authoritarian conscience type, we are essentially dealing with the type that Freud thought to be universal. The parents here are not so highly gratifying as they were in the case of the hedonist; rather they are high in their demands and withdraw love when these are not met, so that the child fears the loss of their love and in order to retain it he internalizes their values and injunctions. Even when the parents are not actually present, the internalized superego does not permit the transgression of its injunctions without severe punishment through guilt. It is among this type that we can expect to find an explicit and fairly rigid moral code; this internalization of the code comes directly from the internalization of parental standards, and a transgression from the code implies the dreaded loss of love and retaliation by the father. The superego is, however, more tyrannical even than the parental injunctions, because it is difficult for the child to appraise exactly what is wrong when the parents get angry. The parents are angry at one specific act and the child generalizes this anger to everything else which occurred at the same time. Thus, the parent may request that the child leave the ash tray alone and this may be interpreted by the child to mean that he should leave off all exploratory behavior. Then too, parental inhibitions occur before the child's intellectual capacities have developed to the point where he can understand the reasons for the prohibitions. Thus, he cannot appraise the reality of the taboos before they are introjected.

If the dominant form of control in the hedonistic society is that of the family, then the dominant form of control in the authoritarian society is this internalized moral code, and a feeling of obligation to others. This moral code has an element of compulsion to it; the authoritarian modal conscience is essentially what Piaget (1932) has described as moral realism. At this stage of moral realism a rule is seen to be absolute, there are no extenuating circumstances, and it has the authority of a categorical imperative. It is perhaps significant to note that in their recent study, Levin, Sears and Maccoby (1957) found that oldest and only children had the most strongly developed consciences, but they had also had more physical punishment and deprivation of privileges. Thus, there seems to be some correlation between parental sternness and strength of conscience, when signs of conscience are measured in terms of the child's resisting temptation when he is alone, teaching the moral code to other children, and feelings of guilt. It must be kept in mind, however, that this parental sternness is effective in bringing about the internalization of demands only if it is fused with love so that the child experiences this sternness as a withdrawal of love. In subsequent sections we shall see that the three cultures which we have found to have an authoritarian modal conscience—pre-Civil War America, Germany, and Ireland—all have this highly explicit moral code which has an element of compulsion to it, and all have this parental sternness and emphasis on obedience which is fused with love and the use of love-oriented techniques of punishment.

We use the highly charged word "authoritarian" here because it is the only one which fully denotes the authority that the moral code has in the personality structure of the individual, and because at any time the moral code may be represented by a single individual who becomes the national hero and who is the repersonification of the father. Consequently, by authoritarian we mean that fear of the loss of parental love and retaliation for the child's own aggressive impulses leads to the internalization of a strict moral code; under special circumstances this code can be embodied in a single individual. The authoritarian, then, must follow the dominant code or personality of his time. This code can embody the dictates of religion, politics.

or parental injunctions; the important point is that they must be in line with the dominant authority. Unfortunately, it is beyond the scope of this study, but it might be fruitful to investigate what happens to the authoritarian individual who is socialized by his parents under one specific moral code, when in the course of his lifetime this code is radically changed, as had occurred in modern Russia. We would predict that for the authoritarian the content of the code does not matter, as long as he remains in line with whoever is in power.

In comparing the hedonistic and authoritarian conscience types it is important to note that the anxiety of the hedonist has to do with reality: he fears some form of external punishment or deprivation which may really be forthcoming; the anxiety of the authoritarian is moral anxiety: he fears his own superego and the violation of the moral code of this internal gyroscope. Whereas the hedonistic parent makes low demands on the child, the authoritarian is consistent and high in his demands. The hedonist lives, as much as society will allow, by the pleasure principle; the authoritarian represses and relegates to the unconscious his pleasure. Thus, the hedonist with his Present-Being orientation accepts life as it is; the authoritarian must put the stamp of order on his world. As the study by Adorno et al. (1950) has shown, the authoritarian has a desire for consistency, he cannot tolerate ambiguity, his moral code is based on well-ordered imperatives. It is the authoritarian who needs order, who has a moral code which is so well defined that consequently he has few moral conflicts and does not have to exercise freedom in deciding what is the best course of action. The authoritarian does not make moral decisions on the basis of his own autonomous choice; rather, he is compelled to them by the rigid code which is inherent in his personality structure. He must obey the imperatives of those in authority, because his superego tolerates no other solution.

While the hedonist bases his moral choice on the relative amount of pain and pleasure which will result from a proposed plan of action, and the authoritarian bases his choice on its agreement with his highly internalized imperative moral code, the other-directed individual bases his choice on its agreement with the values of his peers and contemporaries. The other-directed child is made to feel that the good life consists of being loved by others; social aloneness and ostracism induce intolerable anxiety. His self-concept is weak; he conceives of and values the self in terms of the love that this self receives from others. As Riesman (1955) has said: "This mode of keeping in touch with others permits a close behavioral conformity, not through drill in behavior, . . . but rather through an exceptional sensitivity to the actions and wishes of others. Of course it matters very much who these 'others' are: . . . His need is for approval and direction from others—and contemporary others rather than ancestors" (p. 38).

In contrast to the authoritarian, the other-directed individual is not compelled to observe the dictates of a well-internalized moral code; the parents of the other-directed child "make him feel guilty not so much about violation of inner standards as about failure to be popular or otherwise to manage his relations with these other children" (Riesman, 1955, p. 37). What the authoritarian and other-directed have in common is that both are dependent upon direction from others; however, the authoritarian internalizes this direction in the form of the moral code, whereas the other-directed does not have this internal gyroscope. Among the authoritarians the superego, having replaced the parents, will not tolerate digression from its stern commands; among the other-directed the parents replace themselves, implicitly telling the child that his first duty is to be attuned to others. In both cases the primary and original goal is to maintain parental love. For the authoritarian this goal is never altered except of course in so far as the superego stands in lieu of parental approval and authority; for the other-directed, however, the approval of the peer group is originally a means to parental love; ultimately it becomes an end in itself.

A comparison between the other-directed and the hedonistic modal consciences will serve further to illuminate each of these orientations. In both the moral code is not internalized; control is of an external nature. Both conscience orientations can be conceived more readily in terms of shame than of guilt. The hedonist refrains from an act and judges it to be wrong only if he knows he will be caught; the other-directed judges an act to be wrong only if he knows it will bring about the disapproval of his peers. In the other-directed culture if the neighbors do not know what the person has done and if he has no cause to fear that they will find out, there is no anxiety. However, he often distorts reality and is plagued by the fear that they will discover what he has done. Thus, while the anxiety of the hedonist is based on reality, the anxiety of the other-directed we might term social anxiety. The hedonist is secure in the love of his lineal or extended family, and gives up his pleasure only when direct punishment is forthcoming; the other-directed individual is insecure in his love relations and so it is the fear of group disapproval and the need for its approval which motivate his actions.

Our concept of the integral conscience type is quite similar to Riesman's (1955) concept of autonomy. However, Riesman presents his concept as a utopian ideal and he neglects to mention that in a culture where all are free to choose their own goals, these goals might be highly advantageous for the individual and dangerous to the society as a whole. In other words, Riesman's concept of autonomy has behind it the tradition of Greek philosophy: the belief that it is part of man's nature to live in society; that the good society is one in which all members harmoniously realize their nature; and if they do so, there can be no conflict of interests. Our own conception of the integral conscience type is much more in the tradition of Locke and his conception of a social contract: what may be best for each individual, will not necessarily be best for the whole society. Consequently, whereas Riesman's conception of autonomy is an ideal, our own conceptualization of integrity involves the dual problem of the individual fulfilling himself, yet refraining from doing so in a manner injurious to the other members of society.

The integral individual, then, is one who acts not by measuring relative pain and pleasure, not out of acquiescence to the demands of an authoritarian superego, not out of a need for compliance with and the approval of his peers, but rather because he needs to act in accordance with his own self-image. He is concerned with what *he* thinks about an action, not with what anyone else may think. His socialization is slow so that he does not swallow whole, as it were, the injunctions of the parents. In fact, we could say that his morality, instead of stemming from the demands of the superego, stems from the rational cognitive functions of the ego. The injunctions of the parents are carefully thought over and reformulated for individual use; the acceptance of social and political authority is also conditional. Thus, the internalized, well-defined moral principles of the integral individual may at the behavioral level cause him to deviate from authority, from the approval of others, and from his own evaluation of pleasure and pain.

Both the integral and the authoritarian conscience are structured on well-internalized principles, but the differences between them are great. The authoritarian lives by the well-structured moral code of his society; the integral has each time to decide anew through the process of evaluation which course of action he must take. The difference can be seen in terms of Piaget's (1932) conceptualization of moral realism and moral relativism. In the stage of moral realism, for the person with an authoritarian conscience, a rule has absolute status, is unquestionable and unchangeable, and wrongness is positively correlated with the amount of damage done. In the stage of moral relativism, obedience to rules is seen as a matter of individual concern, and the intention behind the offense must be considered. For the authoritarian, a rule holds a certain magic and seems to have something intrinsic in it, a power which demands obedience; for the integral, a rule is seen as something which is made by men out of the necessity created by social living, and such a rule has no virtue in itself.

This difference between the authoritarian and integral conscience orientations can be further understood if we contrast the Hebraic and the Aristotelian conceptions of God. In the Hebraic tradition God is first and foremost a giver of the Law, an ultimate moral authority. He is a God who intervenes in the course of history, so that the element of power and of the supernatural is very strong here; his intervention is not intelligible to human reason. The fundamental good is not happiness, but rather it is the conformity to God's will. The emphasis in the Hebraic tradition is on *duty* and obedience; Job's great error is to demand justification of God's action. Revelation is the best form of knowledge; it is not possible or necessary to understand everything through reason. The Judaic ethic of morality involves, then, an element of command and authority which is not entirely clear to man's reason. This is like the authoritarian child whose duty it is to obey parental injunctions which are not intelligible to him, and little effort is made by the parents to explain the *why* of an order. For such a child, the Law is the ultimate moral authority and its power over him is the power that he both fears and craves when he identifies with this law and internalizes it.

In the Greek ethic, there is no concept of duty; man's goal is to fulfill himself, to realize his nature and potential. And, since reason is the essence of man's nature, his goal is to cultivate this reason. Thus, to the Greek cult of reason, the notion of revelation as a form of knowledge is totally foreign. Nothing is to be absorbed by man which is not intelligible to his reason; in the same way the integral absorbs no principle until it has been cognitively understood. Aristotle's God is a prime mover; he is not a providential God, but rather a philosophical creation. There is in this conceptualization of God no Divine intervention, no miracles; rather, it is a universe of reason. In the Greek tradition, moral ethics can be upheld only by reason and there is no one universal natural law; whereas in the Hebraic tradition there is a universal moral code which man accepts on faith and which it is his duty to obey.

Freudian superego theory has been criticized since, aside from its monolithic universality and lack of concern with structural differention, there is little or no conception of development. We are not prepared to say, without clinical observation, whether the theory of conscience which has here been put forth involves evolution or not. It is possible to conceive of hedonism as a first stage in conscience development, in which the small child is primarily concerned with its own pleasure and is detained from action only by direct adult presence. In the evolutionary scheme authoritarianism would be the second stage, at which the child fears the loss of parental love and fears the retaliation of the parent of the same sex due to the oedipal strivings toward the parent of the opposite sex and therefore identifies with the parent of the same sex. The third stage would be that of other-direction, in which the parents are no longer so important and in which the collateral peer group becomes dominant in guiding thought and action. The final stage would be the integral, in which after the individual's cognitive capacities have been fully developed he begins to act on the basis of his conception of his own self-image. Except for the first stage of hedonism, the other three are roughly parallel to Piaget's (1932) evolutionary stages: expiatory, equalitarian, and the final stage of equity. We do not believe that this evolution of conscience is mandatory, however, and as we shall see later it seems to us that the values of a culture determine in large part the modal conscience. Thus, in a Present-Being-oriented culture, we would expect a hedonistic modal conscience with no impetus toward evolution to another stage. We are also not prepared to assert that an individual with an integral conscience has passed through the other three conscience orientations, although this seems quite possible. The concept of evolution implies also that each successive stage is somehow better than the last; we definitely wish to avoid such value judgment. Each conscience style has its own way of bringing about the control of the individual, and each has its own disadvantages both for the individual and for society. We see no reason to assert, for instance, that the other-directed modal conscience is any better than the hedonistic modal conscience, when the latter is predominant in a small tightly knit community. Hence, until further clinical evidence can be gathered, we will not deal further with this concept of conscience stage and of evolution.

Before we turn to the problem of the relations between values and modal conscience, we must devote some attention to a problem which has only recently been found in the literature: the problem of the relation of aggression to morality. It has been observed by various writers ever since Freud formulated his conception of the superego that there is a large component of aggression in it. Some studies, e.g., that by Adorno et al. (1950), have shown that the most aggressive individuals are often the most moralistic (see especially Chapter 21). Then too, when society demands justice and the death of the criminal, there is an element of aggression in this which cannot simply be explained by saying that society is moral and wishes to see justice done. Some writers, e.g., Reiwald (1950), believe that all of criminal law is based on man's aggression, and that the law is just an institutionalized means for the release of this aggression (see also Flugel, 1945). Reiwald conceives of criminal punishment as a festival: a prescribed excess which permits a breach of the prohibition against aggression. In psychoanalytic theory, society is aggressive toward the criminal because he acts out certain tendencies which are latent in all men; to let his actions go unpunished is to give sanction to these "dangerous" sexual and aggressive tendencies. We are certainly in no position to offer a clear-cut theory of the relations between morality and aggression, but we must try to conceptualize the relation between aggression and each of our four conscience types. It is our basic thesis that man's innate aggression has a very different fate under each of these four conscience orientations.

In the culture where the modal conscience is hedonistic we have suggested that the child is highly gratified by the parents; since there is little frustration, we would expect that aggression against the parents does not become great. Where aggression appears, it is probably suppressed by the group. We have already suggested that a culture with a hedonistic modal conscience can function successfully only if there is strong family interdependence and control; hence we would expect that aggression in the ingroup would simply not be tolerated. Aggression when it became manifest in the child would be firmly disapproved of, and so the hedonistic child whose desire it is to avoid punishment would refrain from aggression against any member of the ingroup. We would expect that aggression in such a culture would be displaced onto certain selected members of the society, such as witches, or onto an outgroup. In the case of the culture with a hedonistic modal conscience in which there is little family control, we can expect that due to their low frustration tolerance, individuals will act aggressively whenever this seems to be the easiest means of attaining the desired end. Again, this could at least in part explain the reason for the increasingly aggressive and sadistic nature of crimes perpetrated by lower-class American delinquents.

In the culture with the authoritarian modal conscience we would expect a larger component of aggression in morality. As Levin, Sears, and Maccoby (1957, Ch. 7) have pointed out, when the parent is stern and aggressive toward the child, he provides an aggressive role-model for the child. Thus, in the authoritarian culture where rules are arbitrarily imposed on the child, he internalizes the aggression of the parent along with the rule so that the two get fused. The child in order to avoid the retaliation of the parent of the same sex identifies with this same parent. He fears the aggression of the parent towards him and when he internalizes the injunctions of the parent he also internalizes this aggression. At the same time, his own aggression against the parent has been aroused since this parent has frustrated his desires toward the parent of the opposite sex. Consequently, when he internalizes parental demands he is internalizing a high content of his own and the parent's aggression. Then too, we have postulated that the individual with an authoritarian conscience is made to feel a sense of obligation to others, a strong sense of duty. When in the authoritarian the feeling of obligation towards others is weakened we might expect a stronger component and release of aggression.

It has long been recognized also that there is a certain component of aggression or sadism in the authority figure; thus we could expect that the aggression of the authority could be introjected along with its moral imperatives. And we can expect that when the child identifies with and introjects an authoritarian figure, he then desires to be this way himself; that is, he wishes to dominate as he in his turn has been dominated. As Flugel (1945) has said, "punishment is (or at least professes to be) itself a moral institution; and it is exercised by just such impressive authoritarian figures . . . as those whose precepts and attitudes we introjected to form our superego" (p. 38). We can see, then, that aggression becomes fused with morality in the authoritarian because in introjecting the moral code of the parent the child is also introjecting the image of the aggressive-authoritarian parent. Morality for the authoritarian *is* aggressive; it is an imposition made by the parent upon the child. Since the authoritarian has been forced to identify with a power figure due to his own weakness, he has a contempt for those weaker than he. And toward those weaker ones he expresses his aggression, just as the parent expressed his moral aggression toward the child when the latter was weak. We see, then, how through the identification with a power figure aggression is fused with morality in the authoritarian; how this aggression is expressed in moral indignation toward the weaker members of society; and how the imperative, pertaining to duty toward others, might lead to hostility against these same others. Moreover, the libidinal strivings of the authoritarian are repressed and not allowed into play by the rigid superego, so that a vigilant watch must be kept over anyone who might transgress the moral code and thus threaten the superego with loss of control.

In contrast to the authoritarian who externalizes his aggressive tendencies and fuses them with morality, we would not expect this of the other-directed. The other-directed person cannot afford to antagonize anyone. His ethic is one of humility and compliancy. In effect, he is a humanitarian; aggression is a threat to the other-directed individual, since an aggressive act might cause him to lose someone's love and esteem. Consequently, he is ready to give in, to blame himself; in politics he is the type of person who wants all the inside news but won't commit himself to any stand because he fears it might not be that of the majority. Thus, while the aggression of the authoritarian is displaced onto the weaker members of society, the other-directed turns it against the self. In the authoritarian culture aggression is controlled by the feeling of obligation toward others, the problem being that this obligation fosters a store of hostility; in the other-directed culture aggression is controlled by the need for love and approval from others, and is turned against the self.

In the integral, aggression is most often well controlled, since his ego has taken over in large part the functions of the superego. This emphasis on rational mastery would discourage aggression and tend to keep it under careful control. It is possible, however, that such individuals would not hesitate to use aggression if this were the only way to do justice to their own self-image. In general, however, we would expect that in the culture with an integral modal conscience aggression would be absolutely discouraged in the training of children, and that children would be taught to get what they need by rational mastery. It is also quite possible that due to the emphasis on rationality and the ego functions, verbal aggression would be encouraged and rewarded, so that this could be the predominant form of draining off individual aggression.

In Section III we shall attempt to relate this discussion of conscience types to our previous discussion of values. The hypotheses about the relationship between values and modal conscience have grown directly out of the preliminary investigation on America and France which is to be presented in that section. We must first turn our attention to the methodology of this study: how the value profiles were derived, and how we expect to test the validity of our hypotheses.

II

COMMENTS ON METHODOLOGY

In order to discern the value profile of each individual culture we have coded stories from children's school readers. If a society is to persist through time it must inculcate each new generation with the values held by the older generation. One of the basic ways in which this occurs is through the school. It has long been recognized, for instance, that the school in American culture has been the chief mode of stamping some sort of homogeneity on the various ingredients which have gone into the "melting pot." Yet strangely enough, little attention has been paid to how it is that the school aids in the value-forming and molding process, particularly to that which is implicit in what these children learn.[3] It is our conviction that the values which a society holds will be found in these readers; some of this occurs on a highly conscious level, some on an unconscious level.

Essentially, this approach is the same as studying folk tales and myths of a "primitive" culture; but in modern states we feel it is more valid to study the readers than to contrast the fairy tales of the cultures. All children have to go to school, but the reading of Grimm's fairy tales, for instance, may be a regional or class phenomenon. Although we have said that we will in each culture be primarily concerned with a specific class, these readers often have a culture-wide appeal. In France, for instance, the educational system is such that all children learn out of the same readers. What goes into the readers is determined by upper-class officials, but all French children are exposed to them. Hence, children's readers are one possible way of studying national culture; certainly this is not the only way. National culture has been studied through the means of novels, movies, newspapers, plays; but the readers are the only one of these media which affect the entire population including the very young children. Since both values and conscience are formed very early in life, it seems highly important to study just what values are presented to the children through these readers.

The stories used in this work come from two different samples. In Section III, where we are concerned with the formulation of hypotheses, we have scored twenty-five stories which were not selected at random, and the cultural identity of each story was known at the time of coding. Furthermore, under influence of the McGuffey readers where the distinction between "good" and "bad" characters is so striking, we decided to score all major characters separately on their value orientations. In Section IV, where we are concerned with the testing of hypotheses, we have scored twenty-one stories for each of the cultures. The stories were selected at random by McClelland and were all translated into English with a disguise of all names and places so that there would be no bias incurred through previous knowledge of the cultural affinity of the stories. Hence all these stories were coded at once; and then, since each story had a code number, we were able to sort the stories into their cultural groups. We found also that it was unnecessary to score each major character separately since it was possible to score each story as a whole.

To test the significance of our findings a special variation of the chi-square formula has been used which is applicable only in those cases where

[3] Notable exceptions are McClelland's (unpublished) research and Child, Potter, and Levine (1954).

it is expected that there will be a 1:1 ratio between the two variables. Our hypotheses deal only with the first- and second-order values in a given orientation; hence in each orientation we are only interested in testing whether or not there is a significant difference between the first and second rank-order values. For example, if we were considering a culture whose values in the Time Orientation were Past > Present > Future we would ask whether given the possibility of either Past or Present only, leaving the Future orientation out of consideration, the number of Past responses was significantly greater (than could reasonably be ascribed to chance) than the number of Present responses. Where the difference is not statistically significant we say that any such difference *might* well be due to chance, but we reserve judgment on the matter.

The basic method of the study is to determine the dominant value profile of each culture by the coding of children's third-grade readers. Then we have formulated certain hypotheses as to the relationship between values and modal conscience; Section IV represents an attempt to test the hypotheses on the authoritarian modal conscience, and finally there is a discussion of the relations between the predictions and our findings. Instead of testing the actual population to see whether it is authoritarian we have assumed on the basis of the literature and our definition of the authoritarian modal conscience that the Irish and the Germans have such a modal conscience. Then we have ascertained their respective value profiles from the readers, in order to see whether or not we would find those values which we predicted would be crucial in fostering authoritarianism to be dominant.

Hence, we must ask two questions about the results on each culture. We want to know first of all whether the values which were predicted to be crucial in determining a certain conscience structure are significantly higher than any other values in that culture. And second, if they are, we can only say that this culture fits our conceptualization of a particular conscience structure, as we have hypothesized it. Except in the authoritarian case we cannot say, however, whether those values are indeed the ones which foster a particular modal conscience and we must withhold judgment as to the validity of our predictions. On the other hand, if the predicted values of a particular culture are not significantly greater than its other values, we can only say this particular culture does not meet our criterion for a certain conscience type; but we are in no position to reject our hypotheses as to the values which foster that conscience.

In the present work we have confined ourselves to a study of each conscience type and the development of a possible method of ascertaining modal conscience. Our main concern has been with demonstrating the way in which we conceptualize modal conscience within a cultural context. In formulating our hypotheses it seemed best to study the relationship between values and conscience on a longitudinal as well as a cross-cultural scale, since we wanted to know whether a change in modal conscience had been accompanied by a shift in the value profile. We chose America inasmuch as this was the only country for which we had readers dating from over 100 years ago; and since there has been much discussion in the literature about the change in the American modal conscience over this time span, we wanted to know whether there had also been a shift in the value profile. If indeed the type of modal conscience is, at least in part, determined by the values of a culture, then we would expect that a change in conscience would have to be attendant upon a shift in the value profile.

In all cases third-grade readers were used, except in so far as there were not enough stories in the third-grade reader, and then fourth-grade stories were used. There is a certain problem in using the readers as a measure of values since in France and Ireland the choice of readers to be used in each grade is centrally determined; on a specific day all children of a specific grade will be reading material out of the same book. In Germany education and the choice of books is centrally determined in each separate state; therefore our particular West German stories may be less influential on German children as a whole than any French story would be on all French children. In America the choice of readers is left to the individual school and teacher. Hence, we are dealing with three levels of reader use, ranging from central to local choice. We view these stories as a projective system in so far as the writers project their own values into the stories. This circumstance presents further problems because, as we have already mentioned, a culture can be multi-modal in its value profile; hence we will be dealing with the values of a specific class in each case. In those cultures where the readers are written and published by members of the same social class as we are concerned with in our discussion, there is no problem. However, where the readers are written by the members of a class other than the one under scrutiny, there is always the question of whether the readers reflect the values of the class in which we are interested, or whether they reflect the different class values of the writers and educators who compile them. In the cases of both America and Germany, we are interested in the dominant middle-class values, and most probably the readers are written by middle-class people. Similarly in France, where education is primarily the concern of the elite, the content of the readers is probably determined by people who either belong to the upper class themselves or else are highly influenced by aristocratic values, so that this is in accord with our intention to study upper-class values in France. In Ireland, however, we are faced with a problem: we shall be dealing with the small farmers of the Irish Free State. No information is available on who makes up these readers, but we seriously doubt that it is the peasants. There is some consolation in the expectation that Ireland is probably much more uni-modal in its value profile than America, France, or Germany, but at the present time we have no way of validating this, except that in the Irish case Catholicism is both salient and universal and hence a great factor in homogeneity.

Two further points should be noted. One may question the validity of a cross-cultural study in which there is no equation of social classes. In each case the class chosen for study is dominant in some way, and the one on which there is the most available information. Hence, in America and Germany the middle class is dominant numerically and in sphere of influence; in France the upper class is dominant in its influence and in the ideals it generates; in Ireland the small farmers and peasants are dominant numerically. Since we are not interested in a comparison of these cultures as such, but rather in the relationships between values and modal conscience, it makes no difference that we are not in each case speaking of the same social class. In other words, if we are concerned in one culture with the values of a particular class and their relation to hedonism, it should make no theoretical difference that in another culture where we wish to delineate other-directedness we are dealing with a different social class. A lower-class value profile of one culture may be the same as the middle-class value profile of another; in that case we would expect the modal conscience in both groups to be the same. Hence, it is not the social class which matters, but rather the value profile and its relationship to the modal conscience.

Finally, we wish to make explicit that we are not concerned with a full description and study of each culture; we are under no illusion that any culture is herein adequately studied or described in all its full complexity. Our problem is a highly specific one and we have for the most part paid attention only to those factors which we felt to be either directly or indirectly influential in the formation and development of conscience. While we feel that insight into the modal conscience of a culture is invaluable for a better understanding of that culture, we are only very indirectly concerned with such understanding of specific cultures. If we were to study the effects of coercive bowel training on a group of individual children, such a study would undoubtedly lead to greater insight into the problems of each individual child; but that would not be the main objective of such a study. Similarly, new insight into a culture might be a by-product of this study, but this is not the primary goal; rather the intention is to study the possibility that there exist meaningful relationships between values and modal conscience. The cultures herein are our means of study and not our ultimate end.

Furthermore, we wish to point out that for the sake of brevity we will refer, e.g., to "American culture" rather than the "American middle-class," though in the case of each "culture" we are referring to a specific class. An investigation of a whole culture would have to deal with all classes, their variant value profiles, the consequently variant conscience structures, and the effects of each class on the others. Since we are dealing with only one class in each case, the problem of variant values and conscience type is not discussed.

III

PRELIMINARY INVESTIGATION: AMERICA AND FRANCE

Contemporary writers such as Riesman (1955) and Whyte (1956) are highly concerned with the changes in American character; whether the change is described in terms of a move from inner-direction to other-direction, or a move from the Protestant ethic to the social ethic, there is much talk about change in modal personality on the American scene. It is one of the aims of this chapter to see how American values are changing and to see how these changes affect the modal conscience. In terms of values, we would predict that American values in the pre-Civil War period were: a strong first-order Future with a large gap between that Future and the second-order Present, which is greater than the third-order Past. In the Relational Orientation we would expect a strong first-order Individualism, which is greater than the second-order Lineality, and which is greater than the third-order Collaterality. In the Activity orientation we would expect a strong first-order Doing, which is far greater than the second-order Being, and the third-order Being-in-Becoming. In the Human Nature Orientation we would predict that the view is that man is evil but perfectible, the basic Protestant ethic; and finally, in the Nature Orientation we would expect that Mastery over Nature is greater than Subjugation, which is greater than Harmony with Nature.

It is our contention that in present-day America, although the Future is still most emphasized, the second-order Present orientation has come much more into focus. There is less future optimism, and more of a feeling that the future holds the unknown and perhaps even the unpleasant. The frontier and the constant opportunity to push forward "bred the temper of the pioneers; the temper of the discounter of the future, who was to some extent bound to be a disparager of the past . . . movement became a virtue, stability a rather contemptible attitude of mind" (Brogan, 1944, p. 5). We think that the depression brought about the suspicion that perhaps the future will not be golden, that things are not getting better; and the pioneer spirit is giving way to a concern with the present. People are not willing to make long-term investments; there is a far greater emphasis on present-day security than on future possibility.

For our study of conscience this American emphasis on the future and repudiation of the past is highly important, because it means that the child-rearing techniques and practices of the older generation are already invalid. Americans have a terror of being called old-fashioned, and so since the young mother cannot ask her own mother what to do she must ask her own contemporaries. Americans have a fear that they will not hit the standard; they conform compulsively because there are no broad standards for all to accept. It is this in part which has created the other-directed American modal conscience, the inability to take the experience of the past as a guide, and the consequent need to look to the peer group. As Maurois (1936) has said about America: "It has been said that the American people adopt a scientific idea as they adopt a type of shoes . . . Freudianism, behaviorism, the humanism of Babbitt, the relativism of Einstein . . ." (p. 111).[4] Thus, we see that American emphasis on the future and repudiation of the past are at least in part responsible for the other-directed conscience and for the compulsive conformity. However, this does not explain why the Americans were once inner-directed and then shifted to other-direction. By looking at the relation of man to man we may gain some insight into this problem.

It is our hypothesis that although Americans have always been Individualistic, the second-order orientation used to be Lineal, whereas now it is Collateral. In Riesman's (1955) terms, the inner-directed—which is like our authoritarian—conscience is developed when the child is socialized by the parents. He identifies, usually, with the parent of the same sex and introjects his principles and values. Since these values are internalized, the person has a standard for action which is very much his own; and so he is not obsessively concerned with obtaining from his contemporaries a constant flow of guidance and approval (p. 57ff.). As the Lineal orientation in America has become a remote third-order value, so the direction from the peer group has grown steadily.

[4] Translated from the French by the author, this holds true of all quotes from Maurois and from the French readers.

It is our contention that we will find much more parent-child interaction in the McGuffey readers, and more peer group interaction in the modern ones. This shift from Lineality to Collaterality, from discipline by the parents to discipline by the peer group, has brought many important changes. For the inner-directed child, self-discipline and accomplishment were stressed. He lived in relative isolation from his peers even though he went to school with them; playmates were most often siblings; children were usually with their parents. The model child was polite, studied hard, and was clean. Study was so important that children who played much were criticized: fun was definitely not the goal of life. Essentially, we would like to suggest that this is the type of child that we will find in the McGuffey readers; and the contrast with the present-day other-directed type will be sharp.

The other-directed child is encouraged to be self-expressive, to play, and to "have fun." His accomplishments are relatively unimportant, whereas morals and relations to the group are stressed. The inner-directed Lineally-oriented child was most often with his parents or with one other child. The other-directed Collateral child is most often found in a group; he is almost never alone; conformity is rewarded rather than ambition and individual hard work. This new concern with the child "having fun" is reflected in another change of value orientation: the valued form of activity.

We would like to suggest that in present-day America the gap has become smaller between the first-order Doing orientation and the second-order Being orientation. Riesman (1955) has said that the meaning of work has changed: the inner-directed person thought in terms of objects, the other-directed thinks in terms of people (p. 151ff.). With this shift in emphasis to work with people came the American idea of "having fun." The right to play and to have a good time is a right which has been inalienably granted to American children. As we shall see at the end of this section, we predict that a culture with a strong Being orientation will tend to foster a hedonistic conscience. In America, the importance of the peer group seems to counteract the tendency toward a modal conscience, which might otherwise be hedonistic. The American other-directed child is inhibited to the extent that he fears the disapproval of the group; but the stronger the Being orientation becomes, the stronger will be the tendency to inhibition due to fear of the possible pain to be encountered. Perhaps the reason, at least in part, for the great increase in juvenile delinquency in this country lies in the increasing importance of the Being orientation. In most cultures in which there is a strong first-order Being orientation, e.g., in the Italian and Mexican, there are strong family ties to counteract this in terms of conscience. The family acts as the chief censor; people live in the same location for years, so that everyone knows them well and disapproves when they break a sanction; there is not the anomie of the large American city. But in America the social influence of the family is not strong enough to counteract the dangers of a Being-oriented hedonistic society. The new emphasis on fun and the rising influence of the Being orientation have received much encouragement from a change in another set of value orientations: the attitude toward human nature.

In pre-Civil War America human nature was believed to be evil. Parents exercised constant control and discipline lest the child regress to his former evil state. The goal of life was to work hard, and men were supposed to work because idleness and sloth might lead them to further sin and corruption. For the authoritarian inner-directed man, God was the supreme master; and it was part of American Individualism that each one was responsible for himself, for his own success or failure, and in order to succeed he needed only to curb his evil impulses and answer directly to God. There has been a radical change in this value orientation; the belief now is that human nature is mixed: neither wholly good nor wholly bad. This is highly important for our study of conscience because it means that the American no longer feels that he has to hold himself in such tight control. A slip can be understood and even forgiven. Indeed, Margaret Mead (1942) has suggested that we are moving fast from being a guilt culture to a shame culture. This is actually in accord with everything we have said so far: the authoritarian child of the past who derived his conscience from parental demands and inhibitions had a strongly internalized conscience which caused him to feel guilt whenever he transgressed its demands; the other-directed child, who is no longer made to feel his own sinfulness and who is punished primarily by the disapproval of his peers, is made to feel shame. Only if his peers catch him at what is disapproved, does the child worry about what he has done. Thus, the shift toward the belief that human nature is mixed has given impetus to the other-directed modal conscience, because it afforded the opportunity to relax standards, to emphasize "fun," and the belief that children are best off when they are in a group of their peers.

It is only in the sphere of the attitude toward nature that we do not see any major shift in emphasis. Americans have always valued Mastery over Nature: they build bridges to span water, make roads to span distance, and have a generally confident attitude toward life. The American is taught that it is his duty to overcome obstacles, and, as Florence Kluckhohn (1950) has pointed out, Americans exploit and improve on their environment. They are not really innovators. The Americans are great believers in man's ability to overcome illness and disease, and this is reflected in their attitude toward their children. Americans will do anything for their children: if teeth are bad, then they are given braces; if noses are too big, plastic surgery is done; and above all, there is the belief that the child must surpass his father in stature and achievement. As Gorer (1948) has pointed out, the American home is really child-centered: nothing and no one is to interfere with the "fun" of the American child (p. 70ff.). Of course, this attitude toward children stems from several other values too: the emphasis on the Future, for, after all, children are the future; the emphasis on Doing, early independence, and the grooming of children for achievement. But this child-centeredness of the American home stems, at least in part, from the value attached to Mastery over Nature and the belief that both external nature and human nature are to be manipulated to the best possible advantage of society.

In this section, we have attempted a first set of hypotheses concerning the relationship between values and modal conscience; we have tried to show how a shift in values on the American scene has brought about a shift from the pre-Civil War inner-directed authoritarian conscience to the present-day other-directed conscience. We shall now examine the actual data to determine whether they bear out these relationships between values and conscience, and the predicted shift in the American modal conscience.

Looking first at the McGuffey readers we see that in every value orientation the results are in the predicted direction. As was expected, the data show a strong break between the Future and Present orientation. All twenty-seven social characters have a Future orientation: they are either planning for the future or they are able to postpone immediate gratification for later, deeper pleasure or for the sake of self-control. The parents are very much concerned with the children's future; strong value is placed on education as a means of achieving future success. In two consecutive stories about two schoolmates the "good" boy thinks of his education and his future, whereas the "bad" boy loafs, does not think about his future, and ends up as "a poor wanderer without money and without friends." The moral of this story is that even the very young must plan for their futures: "Many young persons seem to think it of not much consequence if they do not improve their time well in youth, mainly expecting that they can make it up by diligence when they are older." In another story two brothers are contrasted: one lives for his present pleasure; the other is aware of the future and so when their father presents each of them with a tree to take care of, the "bad" Present-oriented boy lets his die; the other Future-oriented son takes care of his tree for years, until finally it bears wonderful fruit.

All fifteen "bad" children are Present-oriented. They are either unconcerned with the future, or they are unable to postpone immediate gratification. Of the twenty-five stories, five are concerned primarily with just this postponement, so that the child does something for someone else and in this way is given a deeper satisfaction. One boy finds some strawberries in the woods

TABLE 1

Pre-Civil War United States
Results of the Scoring of Twenty-Five Stories

	Stories	"Good" Characters	"Bad" Characters	Total
Time Orientation				
Future		27	0	27
Present		0	15	15
Past		0	0	0
Total				42
Relational Orientation				
Individualism		19	10	29
Lineality		8	0	8
Collaterality		0	5	5
Total				42
Activity Orientation				
Doing		23	1	24
Being		1	14	15
Being-in-Becoming		1	0	1
Total				40
*Human Nature Orientation				
Evil	22			22
Mixed	0			2
Good	2			2
Total				24
Nature Orientation				
Mastery		10	0	10
Subjugation		1	7	8
Harmony		0	0	0
Total				18

*Scored by story rather than by character.

and is sorely tempted to eat them instantly, but instead he gives them to his sick mother. Such stories emphasize the Lineal filial relationship, but also the necessity of being able to account for one's actions to one's own conscience at some future date. In three other stories a little girl gives her last apple to her siblings, another gives her pet dove to a little sick girl, and a boy gives away his beloved rabbit. In every case there is the temptation to give in to present selfish desire; but in the "good" child the thought of future consequences is what guides his action.

The ethics in these stories are absolute: there are parents who always embody the good, and children who are supposed to be models; and then there are those children who are absolutely "bad." It is highly significant that in seventeen of the twenty-five stories coded, parents are given the role of socializers and teachers, and interaction takes place solely or primarily with them. In fourteen of the stories a child is seen in interaction with another child; of these, six of the stories deal with interaction among siblings, who are always loving to each other or else learn a lesson from the example of one of the others. In only eight of the stories do we see unrelated children with each other; of these, three of the stories deal with the bad effects of the peer group: ". . . instead of going to school, he was in the habit of playing truant . . . He would . . . spend his time with idle boys . . . He was led by them to hire a boat . . ."; one of the stories is concerned with an older child helping a younger with his schoolwork; three are concerned with a "good" child who is criticizing and trying to influence a "bad" child to love school or to be honest; and in only one story do we find children playing together constructively. Although individual action is prized above all by both good and bad characters, there is in the good characters a strong Lineal orientation and emphasis on obeying parents, while it is only bad characters who tend toward the Collateral or peer-group orientation. The story of Frank exemplifies this high value placed on the Lineal orientation and on obeying parents: ". . . and then all the hot water would have run out . . . , and might have scalded me. I am very glad, mother, that I did as you bid me." These results tend to show that, as was predicted, pre-Civil War American children were socialized primarily by their parents, and peer-group interaction was slight and often discouraged. In fact, strong value is placed on the child acting on his inner principles, rather than upon pressure from the group. As one story, where the "bad" boy is trying to get the "good" one into a fight, demonstrates: "Robert had told all the boys that Henry was a coward, and they laughed at him a great deal. Henry had learned, however, that true courage was shown most in bearing reproach, when not deserved, and that he ought to be afraid of nothing but doing wrong."

The data on the valued form of activity demonstrate that out of the forty characters coded on this orientation all but two of the twenty-five good characters are Doing-oriented. Parents value children who work, study hard, achieve their goals, and make themselves useful. "Good" children are those who fulfill these expectations; "bad" children are those who do not. The cardinal sin is idleness. In the following conversation between Mary and Jane it is not difficult to see which child is "good":

Jane: I can never leave my play, to waste time over a dull lesson . . . *Mary:* Why, Jane, how can you speak so? Which do you consider most important your lessons, or your play? *Jane:* I like to play best. *Mary:* But you will not be able to play always. And what will you do then? *Jane:* When it comes to that, I will study or work. *Mary:* But you will not know how. [And Mary goes on to tell Jane the following story:] Ants work hard in summer to lay up their winter stores. But grasshoppers do not work in summer, and they die when winter comes. A grasshopper once asked an ant to give him some food to keep him from starving. "What did you do all summer," said the ant? "I sang," said the grasshopper. "Well, now you may dance," said the ant.

The value on Future planning, on Individualistic self-sufficiency, and on purposeful Doing can easily be seen. In another story a little girl loses her father's love because she is so lazy and only wants to play; it is the boy who actively takes care of his tree that reaps its fruit; and the "idle are poor and miserable," whereas the "industrious are happy and prosperous." ". . . if you are not diligent it is one of the surest evidences that your heart is not right with God. You are placed in this world to improve your time. In Youth, you must be preparing for *future usefulness.* And if you do not improve the advantages you enjoy, you sin against your Maker." Indeed, we even have a story whose title and moral is that "Industry [is] a Treasure."

It is easy to see that this value attached to Doing, to individual work, and to achievement embodies the Protestant ethic. Competition among children is valued: in one story the mother gets her daughter to learn to write, only because the child is aware of the fact that her cousin already knows how. And she is told that it will depend entirely on herself how quickly she can learn. Only the individual himself is responsible for his own success or failure, in a world where success is passionately worshiped. If he does not succeed, it is his own fault and he feels guilty. And the surest means to success is hard work and diligence with respect to school. In one story the parents were "greatly troubled, lest their only son would never learn to read and to write. They could not teach him themselves, and they were too poor to send him to school." When the rich boy comes and offers to teach him: "Joe and his mother were ready to fall on their knees to thank Charles." In another story a boy who is too poor to buy a school book is "very much troubled," but then he goes out to shovel snow, earns money, buys the book, and "from that time, Henry was always the first in all his classes, he knew no such word as fail, but always succeeded in all he attempted." On the other hand, we see that of the fifteen "bad" children all but one had a Being orientation. Children who gratify their immediate desires, who spend much time playing, who are not useful and ambitious are regarded as "bad."

As has been previously mentioned, each story was coded only once for the Human Nature orientation. It is highly significant that of the twenty-four stories coded, twenty-two are based on the idea that human nature is evil: either the child does something which is disapproved of, or it is feared that he will do evil. There is little trust in his natural goodness; children must be taught and guided continuously if they are to grow up as social beings. The child is seen as a selfish asocial being, and it is the duty of the parents to instill a conscience in him. In one story, an analogy is made between an alarm clock and conscience: "Just so it is with conscience. If we obey its voice, even in the most trifling things, we always hear it, clear and strong. But if we allow ourselves to do what we have some fears may not be quite right, we shall grow more and more sleepy, until the voice of conscience has no longer power to wake us." Thus, since human nature is seen as basically evil, there is always the danger of regression to the asocial state and so only by constant work and vigilance can a child stay out of trouble. The ultimate goal is to give the child a conscience which is as authoritarian and militant against sin as the parents were. We have further broken down the stories to determine what it is that is most frequently approved and disapproved of, and then what the typical means of punishment are.

In eleven of the twenty-four stories coded for this orientation the problem lies in the child's indolence, and lack of initiative and drive in doing something. The goal is to install an inner conscience which nags every time the child loafs or demonstrates his childish Being-Present orientation. In one story the father gives each of his sons a peach and then asks what they did with them; we see here the difference between the well-socialized oldest child and the still "primitive" youngest child:

> *Oldest,* "I have taken good care to keep the stone, and I intend to raise a tree of my own." [The value on Doing, on Future planning, and Individualistic activity is here unmistakable.] "Well done," replied the father. "Provide for the future by taking care of the present." "I ate mine," said the youngest, "and threw away the stone, and then mother gave me half of hers." "Indeed, my boy," observed the father, I cannot say much for your prudence, but you acted in a natural and childlike manner, as might have been expected."

We see here that the young child is seen as evil and primitive and that much work must be done before he can be made to arrive at the "good" adult level. Human nature may be evil, but it is also seen as mutable; it is because of this that so much emphasis is placed on training the child.

Of the remaining thirteen stories, four deal with the importance of obeying the parents. Only by obeying what the wiser and older parent says can the child internalize the proper values and principles. He is not supposed to argue, cajole, or plead; he is expected to acquiesce graciously to parental demands and inhibitions. In one story a child who disobeyed his parents is almost drowned; finally: "He became regular at school, learned to attend to his books, and, above all, to obey his parents." Children who disobey get into trouble and meet the severe rebukes with which the indolent are met. Of the remaining nine stories, three deal with the importance of honesty and unselfishness. Children are tempted to keep and hold on to what belongs to them and what does not, and much emphasis is placed on the fact that "the eye of God is always upon us"; conscience must be vigilant and always appeased. The only successful way to do this is to give up beloved possessions for the sake of others, and never to take someone else's property. Private property is seen as a sacred thing; each child always has his own individual toy, peach, or pet, so that individualism is given further impetus here. The remaining two stories deal with the importance of being guided by inner principle. First, the child must obey his parents; if he does this, he will internalize their values and injunctions; after this he is expected to be guided only by his own internal gyroscope. This attitude is exemplified in a story where the father is criticizing his daughter for making a birthday present for her cousin: ". . . to make a present . . . because everybody gives her something; because she expects something; and because your grandmother says she likes to see people generous, seems to me . . . to be rather foolish." In the last analysis, the internal gyroscope is supposed to guide one and not the expectations and desires of others.

Of the eighteen stories which could be coded for type of punishment and reward, nine show a combination of love and material reward. If the child is "good," he gains approval and some type of material reward; if he is "bad," both of these are withdrawn. It is of interest to note that Gorer (1948) has intuitively arrived at the same conclusions (p. 106ff.). He says that Americans feel a need to be worthy of love, that love is conditional upon success, that there is a deep confusion between the two. In each of these nine stories the "good" child is rewarded by this combination of approval from his elders, and gains in material wealth. The boy who cultivates his tree gains the greater love of his father, and the fruit of the tree; the boy who remains honest gains approval of his elders and is given some oranges; the boy who tried to steal the oranges is rebuked and gets nothing. In five more of the eighteen stories, love alone is given or withheld. One father who is angry with his daughter for her indolence withdraws his love in the following manner: ". . . instead of smiling at her, he turned away his head with a frown, and put her hand out of his . . ." In reaction the little girl "hung down her head and wept very bitterly. She did not dare to look at her father, all that evening, and she did not cease crying, till she fell asleep." She then becomes industrious and after three days feels worthy of his love again: "Gently touching him she let him know that she was waiting to be again received as his favorite girl." This use of love-oriented techniques of discipline would again tend to reinforce our basic hypothesis that pre-Civil War Americans had an authoritarian conscience, since we know that love-oriented techniques have been shown to be most effective in inculcating guilt and the compulsion to act from parental principles. It is further important to note that in only one of the stories is there a use of comparison with the achievement of another peer, which is the type of discipline we would expect to find most often in an other-directed group.

In turning now to the other three stories where the child is punished by natural forces as a consequence of his own misdeeds, we must also look at the results of the relation to nature orientation. Of the eighteen characters which could be scored on this orientation, eleven were "good" and seven were "bad." Of the eleven "good" characters ten gained a mastery over nature, and the eleventh was threatened with harm by nature only if he did not obey his parents. The "good" child is successful, and part of this success is to master the land. Industrious people are those who have a good harvest, whose trees bear fruit, who find strawberries in obscure parts of the woods; and who in general "get from" rather than fear Nature. In sharp contrast to this, we see that all of the seven "bad" characters are either punished by natural forces or else Nature wins over them. The boy who disobeys his parents is nearly drowned, another one nearly has a table fall on him, and a third is nearly kicked by a horse. Moreover, the indolent are subjugated to Nature: their trees wither and die, the land will not yield for them. Perhaps the best example is one story where the "coward" is just about to drown (he is subjugated to the waters), when the courageous boy saves him (he is master over the waters). Thus, we see that mastery over Nature is the valued orientation, and is given to those who are "good." The fact that several children are punished through Nature by their own deeds also serves to place the burden of control on the individual: they act and then they must pay for the consequences of this act. It is as though Nature were being personified as the punishing conscience, for really in these stories it is only the child who is punishing himself. Thus, as was postulated in the beginning of this study, mastery over Nature equals mastery over self.

We have seen that every value orientation turned out in the predicted direction, and that these values combine in a very particular way to form the authoritarian American modal conscience. Our next task is to take the longitudinal

TABLE 2

Present-Day America
Results of the Scoring of Twenty-Five Stories

	Stories	Adults	Children	Total
Time Orientation				
Future		5	22	27
Present		3	16	19
Past		0	0	0
Total				46
Relational Orientation				
Individualism		8	31	39
Lineality		0	0	0
Collaterality		0	7	7
Total				46
Activity Orientation				
Doing		6	20	26
Being		2	18	20
Being-in-Becoming		0	0	0
Total				46
*Human Nature Orientation				
Evil	0			0
Mixed	6			6
Good	19			19
Total				25
Nature Orientation				
Mastery		0	15	15
Subjugation		1	0	1
Harmony		0	1	1
Total				17

*Scored by story rather than by character.

approach and to see if American values have shifted in the predicted direction, and if so, how these new emphases combine to form the other-directed modal conscience which has been postulated for the present-day American.

If we turn to the data on the Time Orientation, we see that indeed as predicted the Future orientation is still dominant, but the Present-time orientation has become very important. We think that the country as a whole is becoming more concerned with the immediate present, less sure that the future will be indubitably glorious. Certainly, children appear to be more concerned with the present than they were 100 years ago. Third-grade children of today seem to be encouraged to live for the moment; of all the children in these stories only four think of the future in terms of several years from the present. It is interesting to note that all four of these children are the "littlest" ones in the story, and there is something they cannot do. Thus, they look eagerly to the time when they can "do things" too. In a culture where early independence is highly valued, so that the child gains competence early, the youngest child who is perhaps kept as a baby the longest seems to resent this. But not even all parents are Future-oriented; of the eight stories for which parents were coded because they had a central part, five are Future-oriented, and three are Present-oriented. One can only speculate as to the significance of this shift, in the direction of present time, for the development of conscience. For the authoritarian child of 100 years ago, who was from a very early age made aware of the importance of what he would become both externally and internally, conscience development must have been quite different from that of the modern child who is allowed to live from day to day. The only possible development for the latter group lies in the direction of hedonism or other-direction. The child who lives from day to day must be ready to shift his standards whenever the climate of opinion or of opportunity shifts; the authoritarian child has internal principles which were inculcated by parents who wished these principles to serve the child long after the parents had ceased to be physically present. Thus, we would predict that the more the Present time orientation is valued in America, the less possible it will be to have the authoritarian conscience.

In sharp contrast to the McGuffey readers where the parents played a vital role in seventeen of the twenty-five stories, only eight of the present-day American stories concern parents at all. This difference becomes even stronger when we make the further distinction that in not one of the modern readers do we find a child alone with his parent(s), whereas in eight of the McGuffey stories we find a child solely in interaction with his parent(s). In the McGuffey readers we had only one story in which children played together constructively; here we have eight stories which are mainly concerned with the necessity and value of friends. In one of these stories the girl has to plan a complicated series of actions in order to get a friend, because she is sure that no one wants to be her friend: ". . . there were girls she would like to have for friends. But all those girls had been friends for years and years. Judy was not sure they wanted a new friend." Both Judy's mother and brother worry about her lack of friends and question her about it several times; finally she devises a plan to attract a friend by the use of her pet ducks: "Well, my little ducks! I hope you didn't mind taking a walk. It was the only way I knew to make a friend." In another story two little girls are ready to cry because they venture in on the wrong party and everyone is a "stranger." In another of these eight stories a little boy is first laughed at when he exhibits his trick pig and then applauded. When he is laughed at the writer says: "Poor Jim! A hundred people laughing at him!" When he wins the prize the comment is: "Happy Jim! A hundred people clapping for him!" But whether Jim is laughed at or applauded, the important thing to note is that he is in the public eye, and the approval or disapproval of his peers determines his affective state. In two more stories the child is sort of on the periphery of the group; he strives to become popular and when he does, it is the happiest, most important moment for him: "When David went home from school that day, he didn't feel new and strange any longer. He knew he liked this school." No one was concerned with whether or not the children in the McGuffey reader had friends or felt strange; whereas here this is one of the prime emphases.

Children appear with other children in twenty-two of the stories; of these, six stories are concerned with the relations of siblings to each other. In the other sixteen stories children play with a combination of their own siblings and peers who are outside of the family unit. Whereas in the McGuffey readers play with peers not belonging to the family unit was interpreted as "idleness," here it is much encouraged. Parents arrange parties, take their children's friends out with them, children sleep over at each others' houses, and peer-group activity is highly valued. Only the child who is outside the group is unfortunate, and then his goal is to gain the group's approval. Indeed, the importance of the Collateral peer-group relationship over the Lineal one is felt by one little girl who has just spent the night with her friend: "She thought . . . she would walk right by as if she didn't know the folks in that house [her own home] at all."

It is due to this rising importance of the peer group that Riesman has suggested the existence of the other-directed child. We see here that the peer group and making friends is now highly valued, whereas 100 years ago it was supposed to get the child in trouble because of the fear of "bad" influence. When parents raise their children to believe that friends and peer-group approval are vital, it is obvious that the child will do anything to keep this approval. Thus, it is no longer the parents' principles which are important, only the group's. We then get the situation where a parent's demands are meaningless, because the child has only to say: "But Johnny does it," and after all, the parent has already taught his child that what Johnny does, and Johnny's approval, is the most important thing of all. As Gorer (1948) has pointed out: "the fiats and prohibitions of the greater number of American parents are constantly being overruled by an appeal to the authority and example of the neighbors. In this way each generation of Americans acquires in early childhood attitudes which will subsequently reinforce the belief in divided authority, . . . and the supreme importance of the neighbors as guides and exemplars" (p. 87).

In the Activity orientation we again see a sharp contrast between the McGuffey readers and the modern ones. Whereas in the former only "bad" characters were Being-oriented, in the latter group twenty of the forty-six characters are Being-oriented, and we must remember that there is no distinction between good and bad characters in the modern readers. The Being-orientation is a strong one and it is not disapproved of. We shall leave the discussion of the first-order Doing orientation until after we have studied the French, since it is on the basis of these first-order orientations that we plan to compare the two cultures. At the present time we are concerned primarily with the shift in American values, and as the shift has occurred primarily in the rising importance of the second-order orientations (Collateral, Present time, Being, Mixed Human Nature), we must concern ourselves for the moment mainly with these.

Whether on the basis of the coded data, or on an impressionistic level from merely reading these stories, one is left with the unmistakable impression that children must play and "have fun." It seems to us that the American conception of the child has changed radically in the last 100 years. Whereas in the McGuffey readers the child was seen as a little adult who must as soon as possible assume adult status and responsibilities, now the child is expected to be just that. Of course, this shift in attitude supports our hypothesis that the Present orientation has become stronger in recent years. The more Future-oriented a culture is, the more quickly it must attempt to push its children toward maturity. In nine of the modern stories, the parent or the children themselves have planned a party, a picnic, or some sort of amusement. This is, of course, closely connected with the fact that high value is placed on the child being in a group; and it is significant to note that never can a child "have fun" alone; the presence of the peer group is indispensable to a good time. In one story two children are ill and unable to attend the class Christmas party; Christmas is almost ruined for them until someone suggests that the party be taken to them. When this occurs everyone is happy —the parents because their children are so well liked, the two children because they can be in the middle of the "fun," and the group because it has become whole again. In another story a brother and sister are supposed to baby-sit with their little brother. They spend the afternoon "trying to think of something to make Tommy happy," and finally they are rewarded when Tommy says: "I've been having fun." Perhaps the best example of this rising concern with "fun" is a story where one boy is asked to stay home with his sister; he mentions to his mother that he was planning to go fishing. Apparently his individual rights and his "good time" are so important that it never occurs to the mother to tell him to stay home anyway. This high value on the Being orientation, the way it is structured, tends to support the other-directed conscience: to have a "good time" is vital, but one can only have a "good time" when the peer group is present; to be isolated from the group, morally or physically, is the worst possible form of punishment.

Turning now to the Human Nature orientation, our original prediction that children who play are not considered evil is once again supported. It is interesting to note that Mead's and Wolfenstein's (1955) study of American child-rearing literature has led them to the same conclusions. In pre-Civil War America there was a belief in infant depravity and the need to break the child's will through obedience training; fun was suspect and taboo. At the present time, however, this "goodness morality" has been replaced by the almost equally compulsive "fun morality" (Part III, Chs. 9, 10). In fact, there is no preoccupation with sin in our stories at all. We see also that in six of the twenty-five stories human nature is seen as mixed, and in nineteen it is seen as good. It will be remembered that our original hypothesis was that human nature would be seen primarily as a mixture of good and evil. Perhaps it is because these stories do not deal with any children who do wrong or must be reprimanded, or perhaps it is because the value on human nature as a mixture of good and evil is so difficult to code, that this result does not come out in the expected direction. We do not think that Americans really regard human nature as completely good; but even bearing this difficulty in mind, it is highly significant to note that whereas fifteen out of the forty-two characters in the McGuffey readers were definitely presented as "bad," not one character in forty-six in the modern readers is seen as "bad." One could argue that this is because modern educators wish to reinforce values only by positive example; but still this does not satisfactorily explain the preoccupation with sin 100 years ago, and the absence of such preoccupation today. Unmistakably, the shift lies in the predicted direction: that of a greater tolerance for and acceptance of human nature. It is possible that Americans regard their children as being essentially good, with potential for evil which may be brought out by bad environmental conditions. This would explain, at least in part, the reason for

America's ready acceptance of all theories which attribute the neuroses, schizophrenia, and all other maladjustments to the faults of the parents. In this case, the child would really be seen as a good being, who is corrupted by adult influences. In any case, we can say from the results that the American view of human nature has become more lenient, more permissive. As we have mentioned before, with this change alone one would expect the disappearance of the authoritarian inner-directed modal conscience because it is only when human nature is regarded as essentially evil that parents are high in their demands and maintain the vigilant watch which is later to be transmitted to the child's own conscience.

It was possible to score only seventeen of the forty-six characters for the relation to Nature orientation; of these seventeen we see that fifteen are able to master Nature. This is actually connected with the strong Doing orientation in American culture: American children are most often seen as trying to achieve or accomplish something. Of these, ten characters are concerned with the training and mastery of animals. The new preoccupation with pets tends to support our prediction about the shift toward a Being orientation; children are supposed to "have fun" and part of this "fun" is a pet. Unfortunately, our judgment about the relation of this orientation to conscience style must remain suspended. Since these readers do not deal with stories of "bad" children, there is no mention of type of punishment and reward. Therefore, we cannot see whether love-oriented techniques or material reward or punishment by Nature is employed. Since we found that these children interact more frequently with their peers than with their parents, our original hypothesis that punishment lies in the withdrawal of and rejection by the group still stands. However, it is not verifiable from the data.

Having completed our longitudinal study of the change in emphases in American values, we must now take the comparative approach between two cultures. As has been previously mentioned, in discussing America, we have often left out the discussion of the first-order orientation because we were primarily concerned with the rising strength of, or shift in, the second-order orientation. We must never forget, however, that America is still primarily Future, Individualistically, and Doing oriented. Thus, in order to understand more fully the conscience change in our own culture we must now turn to the study of French culture, which is radically different in its first-order value orientations.

In the realm of the Time orientation it is our hypothesis that the French have a first-order Past, second-order Future, and third-order Present Time orientation. The French value tradition: both that of French "civilization" as a whole, and that of the individual family. As Mead and Métraux (1954) have pointed out, the French have a "conception of stability in which the past is continually incorporated into the present and provides models for the future" (p. 53). Thus, it is on the basis of tradition and the past that the Frenchman orients his life. If one speaks to a Frenchman about the present economic crisis in France, his invariable response is to skirt the subject and instead to begin a discussion on the French Revolution and past glory. French education emphasizes the importance of being well acquainted with the old masters; and as Mead (1942) has pointed out, whereas in America the teacher is representative of the future, in France she is custodian of tradition and of the past. Furthermore, French child rearing stresses the belief that what happens in an individual's past vitally shapes his future. A person who is inadequate or foolish is said to be a person who has had a difficult childhood, or who did not belong to the *foyer*. There is "the belief that only those born and reared in a French foyer in France can be completely French and can fully understand and be understood by other Frenchmen. . . . The Frenchman going abroad may acquire a new citizenship without—in French eyes—ceasing to be French, and the stranger in France, no matter how well he has learned all that can be explicitly taught, remains 'a little different from the others' " (Mead and Métraux, 1954, p. 53). The individual's past is so important that it can never be absolved in the present. The French have a keen sense of belonging to an ancient civilization and of the importance of their collective past. Curtius (1932) has observed that "The cult of the dead is a striking feature in the character of France . . . among the most impressive sights of Paris are the graveyards: Montparnasse, Montmartre, and above all Père-Lachaise. . . . The French reverence for the past is not a romanticism which simply gazes back at the past, it is an instinct which is close to reality, and shapes both the present and the future" (pp. 229-230). We have only to think of the Panthéon, Les Invalides, and the Arc de Triomphe and we are made further aware of this cult of the dead and of the past. The funeral is called *pompe funèbre*.

If the importance of the past is irrevocable, the child's education should be very carefully planned with his future well in mind. The French protect and guide their children much longer than Americans do. They do not value early independence for children, but they are deeply concerned with the child's ultimate future. Americans wish to hurry time, to thrust themselves into the future; the French identify with their past, but are aware of the necessity of future planning. It is highly important that we make a distinction here between authoritarian and integral conscience types in relation to the Time orientation. In a Future-oriented society where the children are given much independence, there is the unconscious fear that they will slip away

before the parent has completed his job of socialization. Thus, rules and regulations must be internalized quickly, often before the child is cognitively
mature enough to reappraise the parental standards. On the other hand, in
a society where past time is most highly valued, the children are not pushed
into quick internalization of values, the parents know they have a long period
of time in which to socialize the child, and so values are sorted out, reap-
praised, and slowly internalized. Of the two conscience styles presently under
consideration the authoritarian is more likely to be developed in a Future-
oriented society, whereas the integral is most likely to be developed in a
Past-oriented society. For the French, the goal of education is to give the
child "the ability to make *selective* use of the traditional in a personal way;
or, alternatively—to become an innovator through the use of models other
than the traditional ones" (Mead and Métraux, 1954, p. 36). The authoritarian child is never given a chance to find out what he thinks, his security
lies in knowing what the authorities think; the integral child is given time
slowly to develop his own system of values, so that his security lies in acting
in accordance with his own self-image.

We should like to suggest, then, that the integral conscience can be derived only in a Past-oriented society, whereas a Future-oriented society seems
most likely to produce an authoritarian or other-directed conscience. Which
of these two will evolve depends on the valued Relational orientation. If it
is Lineal and the parents are the prime punishers and rewarders, then the
development is most likely to be authoritarian; if it is Collateral and the
peers are the prime socializers, then the development is most likely to be
other-directed. Turning now to the French Relational orientation we would
predict that it is first-order Lineal, second-order Individualistic, and third-
order Collateral. The French child's early years are spent primarily in the
confines of the *foyer;* the parents have, and are acutely aware of, their responsibility in socializing the child. As Mead and Métraux (1954) have
pointed out, the French attitude toward adoption is one of suspicion; only
the child brought up from birth in a *foyer* by its natural parents has a real
chance for *bonheur.* The world outside the *foyer* is seen as dangerous, a place
where the child can be easily hurt. It is the duty of the parents to prepare the
child to live effectively in this outside world.

As has been mentioned before, in a Lineal society where certain broad
standards are accepted and understood, there is much more opportunity for
individuality than in the individualistic society where so much is left up to
the individual that he has no foundation and so must continually look to
others for guidance and comparison. Those who have deplored American
conformity have long looked to France as the country of individuality. This

individuality is clearly reflected in their government and their inability to unite behind a single political party. Frenchmen look at Americans with contempt and cite *Babbitt* because to them conformity is a horror. Maurois (1936, p. 18) has pointed out that Americans have a high respect for law, whereas the French rebel against all laws, each Frenchman being indeed a law unto himself.

In France then, because of this Lineal orientation, there is much better identification between father and son. The French father is home for a two-hour luncheon every day, guides his son, and often the son goes into the father's profession. In America, where everyone is expected to "get ahead," the son is supposed to surpass the father. Maurois (1936) in comparing the French and Americans has expressed this difference between American first-order Individualism and French Lineality: "Here one scarcely finds, as in France, the old family business, transmitted from father to son for several generations" (p. 23). We saw that in America 100 years ago the Lineal orientation was strong, but due to the necessity of moving on, of climbing up, of rebelling against the past, of surpassing the parents, this orientation was never a first-order one. The Americans, because they value individualism, have always had to conform to a standard, whether authoritarian in the past, or other-directed in present-day America. The French, however, with their Lineal and Past Time orientation, are given a firm foundation and then develop individuality. Hence we postulate that in a society where Individualism is the first-order orientation and Lineality the second, there is great probability of an authoritarian conscience; whereas in a society where Lineality is the first-order orientation and Individualism second, there is much greater chance for the integral conscience.

The French integral conscience is further fostered by their very strong first-order Being-in-Becoming value. For the Frenchman the fulfillment and development of his own potential and capabilities are the most important part of life. As Mead and Métraux (1954) have observed: "A common image of parent and child in their educational relationship is that of gardener and plant which he is cultivating" (p. 30). The French value intellectual awareness, the *sens critique*, the development of aesthetic tastes and interests. "For the French, development is a lifelong process, the individual can continue to evolve indefinitely" (p. 27); the French are concerned with what a person is internally rather than with what he has accomplished. The goal of the French parent is not to make the child obey, but to make the child willing to learn from and be guided by the parents' greater experience. The child is never asked to swallow whole beliefs which are passed down as absolutes; rather it is expected that his standards will be continuously modified and thought over as he matures. Whereas American parents 100 years ago forced obedience and were concerned with morality, French parents are more interested in intellectual and aesthetic development, and it is from this very interest in aesthetic and intellectual development that Frenchmen derive their love of *civilisation* and general excellence. As Curtius (1932) has pointed out: "The values of French literature do not lie in the absolute greatness of individual personalities, but in the elevation of the collective level, and in the inward continuity of the intellectual tradition. It is characteristic that to the question: 'who was the greatest Frenchman?' no one can find an answer. France has produced no Dante, no Shakespeare, no Cervantes, no Goethe. Instead of this, however, she possesses a literature which forms an unbroken and vital unity" (p. 119).

Whether we take the Americans of 100 years ago or today's Americans, it is perhaps this difference in the Activity orientation which alienates them most from the French. It is to be remembered that the French Being-in-Becoming first-order value is the American third. When Americans had a fairly strong Lineal orientation, parents demanded strict obedience because they wanted the child to be a "success." Idleness was a sin, industry a virtue, because the one led to failure, the other to success. The French are not so much concerned with obedience because they do not have to push all their children into one narrow channel or pattern. Whereas the prime aim of American parents is to raise a social and financial success, "the primary aim of French education is to develop *l'indépendence et l'esprit critique* (Mead and Métraux, 1954, p. 33). Whereas in America it is the cowboy and entrepreneur who is the ideal, in France it is the mature intellectual. Americans turn to the expert for guidance and attend lectures on "culture," the French value solitude and their own company and opinion; Americans engage in "recreation," Frenchmen speak of leisure. As Maurois (1936) has pointed out, the American when he is in trouble must act, the Frenchman must think things out: "the American is obliged to kill time, to forget his troubles by doing a number of things" (p. 56). "That which they [Americans] lack, is a long heritage of culture and of leisure which would give them a surer instinct of values" (p. 58). It is in part because the American values achievement and success so intensely that Fromm (1947) has evolved his concept of the "market personality" and Riesman that of the other-directed. In order to be a success one must be ready to change one's standards continuously: alter's expectation, if alter is the boss, is that ego will agree with him. The Frenchman who values nothing more highly than his own opinions, whose aim in life is to fulfill himself, can afford an integral conscience; the American cannot.

Turning now to the attitude toward human nature, we have predicted that the French believe human nature to be a mixture of good and evil, just as present-day Americans do. They regret but are highly tolerant of human frailty, they understand crimes of passion, and other excesses of emotion. The French value the Golden Mean and are equally opposed to the puritanical denial of early Americans and the present American's indulgence of children. Human beings are seen to have the potentiality for good as well as for evil, the potentiality for *bonheur* and *malheur*, and it is only through careful training and education that *bonheur* will prevail. The goal is to build a rational self-image, to control one's own self: in effect, the development of the integral conscience is in every way encouraged. All of the things which humanity enjoys—sex, food, drink—are seen as valuable and good, as long as none is practiced in excess. A mature sexual relationship between a man and woman, where each partner is gratified, is highly valued. At least in part because of their emphasis on the Past and the Being-in-Becoming value, the French ideal of womanhood is the mature woman who is warm, receptive, and a real sensual and intellectual partner. The *sagesse française* about which the Frenchman talks has to do with a certain wisdom of life and maturity which is gained through experience and knowledge of the world. The Americans, on the other hand, value the young glamor girl, in part because of their Future orientation and consequent adoration of youth, but also, it seems to us, because the young girl is still asexual, or rather her sexuality is pregenital.

We have postulated that the French view themselves most often as being part of Nature. They seem to view Nature neither as something to be mastered, nor as something to which man is subjugated. They derive an aesthetic pleasure from Nature, and the Frenchman has no fears that if he mentions liking flowers, someone will think him a homosexual. Perhaps it is no accident that the first artists who really concerned themselves with the exploration into the sensuality of Nature were the French impressionists. The American mastery over Nature can readily be seen to be closely connected with the value placed on "doing"; the French feeling of unity with Nature stems directly from the value attached to aesthetic and intellectual contemplation.

We must turn our attention now to an analysis of the French data, and see if the results bear out the above hypotheses. We see from Table 3 that the hypothesis about a Past Time orientation is not borne out. We must of course bear in mind that in children's stories it might be difficult to present a Past Time orientation and since all stories which deal with past ages or history were left out, this might have biased the data. Nevertheless, we must, until further study can be done, withhold judgment. It is significant to note, however, that whereas no character was Past-oriented in either of the Ameri-

TABLE 3

Present-Day France
Results of the Scoring of Twenty-Five Stories

	Stories	Characters
Time Orientation		
Future		17
Present		12
Past		16
Total		45
Relational Orientation		
Individualism		18
Lineality		27
Collaterality		0
Total		45
Activity Orientation		
Doing		10
Being		11
Being-in-Becoming		24
Total		45
*Human Nature Orientation		
Evil	0	
Mixed	19	
Good	1	
Total	20	
Nature Orientation		
Mastery		2
Subjugation		1
Harmony		6
Total		9

*Scored by story rather than by character.

can groups, in the French we do have sixteen out of forty-five who are Past-oriented. Of the twenty-five stories, five are told by adult men who are reminiscing with a certain nostalgia about their childhood. Of the seventeen characters with a Future orientation, sixteen are adults who are placed in the Future category because they evince some concern with the child's personal qualities and thus an implicit concern with his future. This may not, however, be a real Future orientation. We can conclude only that the hypothesis is not borne out by the data, although it is true that in the French there is concern with the past, while there is none in our two American groups. One further thing should be noted. As Erikson (1950, Ch. VIII) has pointed out, Americans are always on the move; they change homes and travel frequently. In seven of the present-day American stories there was some mention of travel, going on a car trip, or changing homes. On the other hand, in the French stories there is very little movement, a desire for stability. It seems to us that this difference can, at least in part, be attributed to the difference between a fast-moving Future-oriented society and a Past-oriented one which therefore values tradition and stability. Certainly, the response of this child, in one of the French stories, to a car trip is very much unlike the American children who always greet the prospect with enthusiasm: "the car stopped at many places . . . its habitual state was one of immobility. I did not complain; when it moved, I did not feel at ease—my taste for stability makes me prefer that which lasts and is still."

Our data on the Relational orientation show that twenty-seven of the forty-five characters have a Lineal orientation. Ten of the twenty-five stories are primarily concerned with the *foyer* or family unit, and unlike in the American stories much tender emotion is expressed. In three of these stories we have the separate role of the mother and father clearly defined: the father is the initiator of action, he is seen as succoring and responsible for the family welfare and yet as a certain mysterious being with emotions not often revealed to his family; the mother is seen as the person who preserves the image of the good father in front of the children, who is gentle, and most immediately concerned with the child's needs. One of these stories depicts father and mother in very much the same roles as Gorer (in Mead and Métraux, 1953) has described them. The father is upholding justice, in view of the injustice done to his friends by the landlord; the child's reaction is significant: "I must say that at that moment he seemed very beautiful to me, very proud—we were all in back of him, fascinated, marveling—Papa began to smile, his calm became frightening, we all understood that he was in a towering rage, such a beautiful rage as a man gets into no more than three times in his life." We see the implication here that in the *foyer* the father is usually calm and that there are certain aspects of him which are strange and unknown to the child; the attitude of awe and respect is striking. We doubt that we could find an American middle-class child who would say that he was "fascinated, marveling" at his father. The mother in this same story is presented in her typical role: the controlled mature woman who attempts to soothe her husband and curb his aggressive masculinity. "In vain did my mother tug at the sleeves of his jacket . . . ," she is trying to calm him but she cannot. It is also interesting to note that the villain in this story has an authoritarian conscience, whereas the father manifests a highly integral one. In another story dealing with a poor family, the mother is sick and the father's factory goes on strike so that he either must work as a "scab" or let his family starve. The wife is furious at him for not working, but "fearing no doubt that I might take her part against my father, she told me that she well knew that the poor man was not responsible for what had happened." Thus she is protecting the image of the father; he on the other hand is forced to destroy his own self-image and to act instead in terms of his primary role as provider for the *foyer*. When he decides to go to work the son says of him: "I think that he hated us at that moment, because we had obliged him to dishonor himself. Had he been alone in the world, he would gladly have let himself die, but that day we were his ignoble charges and his shameful duty." We must note also that the conflicts here described are much deeper and can more readily be identified as moral issues than the preoccupation with idleness in the McGuffey readers.

Of the seven animal stories used, five deal primarily with family relations and make a clear distinction between the complete and the incomplete *foyer*. One of the stories deals with the importance of finding a mother and father for some baby wolves who have lost their own, three deal with the "baby" who is lost and has ventured outside the safe and protective *foyer,* and one deals with the excitement of a mother bear as she tells father bear that the *foyer* is now complete and their roles fulfilled because they have children.

Of special significance too, are the stories which deal with dyadic relationships: in one story the relationship between mother and son is much as Mead and Métraux (1954) have described it: "The mother takes pride in her son's skills and successes . . . the mother may make something of a companion of her growing son" (p. 21). In our story the mother regards her son "with great pride" because he has just been made a schoolmaster; and indeed the relationship is so intense that to the American it would seem almost incestuous: "She took her son in her arms trembling with pride; and both stretched out, without speaking, without smiling, with a grave fervor and with eyes full of tears." Another story deals with the dyadic relationship between brother and sister, which is again much as Mead and Métraux (1954) have described it: "there is a mutual protectiveness between brother and sister, . . . If there is no actual 'foyer' to which the pair belong, as may happen in the case of orphans, a pseudo parent-child relationship may be deeply valued as a partial, but rather pathetic, substitute for a total 'foyer' " (pp. 25-26). In the story under consideration there is just such a situation and consequent relationship: the two are orphans and the brother has just passed his exams for entrance to the University; as soon as they heard this, the sister "took her brother by the hand, and led him to the photographs of their father and their mother, . . . she knelt, he in front of her, and they cried softly." And thus, "they passed the evening, Olivier at the knees of his sister, or on her knees, being cuddled like a small child." Again, this intensity of affect is never found in the American stories; perhaps it can occur only in the Lineal family system. It is interesting to note too that Mead and Métraux (1954) have pointed out that the French boy's first responsibility is for his sister's virginity, and this phenomenon is also true of the American South and upper class, both of which have a Lineal orientation.

Only two of the stories deal with peer-group relationships at all. In one the children merely take a walk together, the other is concerned with a deep friendship between two boys and their loyalty to each other. In contrast, eight of the present-day American stories were concerned with the importance of finding a friend, yet not a single story showed an intimate relationship between the friends. In France where "belonging" is not emphasized, most boys have a few intimate friendships which often last for a lifetime; in America the emphasis is not on friendship but on popularity, not on mutuality of interest but on casual acquaintance. Americans' fear of homosexuality in connection with their inability to make intimate friendships has been discussed too often for us to go into it here (e.g., Erikson, 1950), but we should like to add two observations. First, it is possible that in a Lineal family system where individuals are accustomed to deep and intimate relations within the family, there is little craving for the superficial acquaintance of many, but rather for a continuance of this intimacy with just a few; and second, the integral conscience type has a clear self-image so that it is not a threat for him to enter into close relationship with another, he need not feel that he will be swallowed whole. The other-directed person, however, has a very vague self-image and so he needs the opinion of many to reassure himself of who he is; if he were to enter into an intimate relationship, there is always the danger that his ego would be absorbed into the ego of the alter, since his own values and beliefs are so poorly internalized and quick to change.

Turning now to the valued Activity orientation, we see that twenty-four of the forty-five characters have the predicted Being-in-Becoming orientation. Six of these stories have as hero a character who is deeply concerned with understanding the nature of the world and men around him. One child is curious to know why it is that when he is moving it seems as though the trees are moving; another "meditates in his innocent soul the catastrophies which strike the big and the strong," and yet another child "wishes always to know the core of things." But it is not only the children who wonder, reflect, and observe; it is also the adults. From these stories one gets the impression that French children learn more just by observing the parents than by being told what to do. The children seem to be the passive audience to the parents, who act out the various emotions and approved behavior patterns. The French are deeply concerned with broad philosophical questions; they wish to know the core of things; their conversation and knowledge rarely turns to the superficial. Thus, we have four stories concerned with the implications of natural and social injustice. One of these is particularly worthy of our consideration; in the story one child is unjustly accused by the teacher of spilling ink, and is sent from the room; another child who is new in school that day sees the injustice of the teacher's accusation and walks out too. This is a highly integral, moral decision for a young child; he goes against the authority of the teacher and the approval of his peers, which to an American child would be vital particularly on his first day in a new school; moreover, he knows he will be punished, so there is no hedonism involved. Also, it is significant to note that whereas in the modern American readers there are many signs of early independence which lead to achievement—children babysitting, doing errands, and proving that they are not too young to do something after all—in the French readers there is no sign of this. On the contrary, in one story independence is explicitly discouraged: a boy tries to polish his shoes, does not do a very good job, and his mother immediately takes over. Thus, French children mature slowly and gain independence of judgment; whereas Americans are pushed to independence so quickly that they are never certain of their own judgments and so depend on others for guidance.

Of the twenty stories coded for the belief about human nature, we have nineteen showing a belief that human nature is a mixture of good and evil. This surprised us, because we stated earlier that it might be difficult to assess the "mixed" category. However, the "mixed" orientation comes out clearly here, and perhaps we can attribute the present-day American results to a tendency to see absolutes in ethics: where children were once seen as "bad," now a reaction formation has set in and they are "good" and ideally can do no wrong. Six of the French stories deal with the problem of control, of the necessity for the Golden Mean as a rule of action. In another context we have discussed two stories in which the child observes aggression in the father, a circumstance that makes the rest of the family uneasy. Verbal aggression is tolerated by the French, but there is always the fear that it may go further; when someone is aggressive they feel uneasy, and yet they can identify with the aggressor and get rid of some of their own: "We were all on the balcony, at the same time ravished by anguish and yet curiously *peaceful*." Control of aggression is highly emphasized among the French. Mead and Wolfenstein (1955) have pointed out that aggression among children is immediately prevented and that it is never seen as self-defense (Ch. XVIII).

Finally, seven of the stories deal with the necessity of forming and guiding the child; the implication is that only then will he be *bien élevé*. In one such story the mother who is proud of the man that her son has grown to be reflects: "She felt herself rewarded for her troubles. In doing her duty, she had prepared her happiness." Although not the sole master of his own fate and lacking the boundless American optimism, the Frenchman believes that man is in large part responsible for whether he will have *bonheur* or *malheur*. We see that the data and the individual stories bear out our hypothesis: the French believe that human nature is a mixture of good and evil, and that self-control for all and guidance for children is always necessary. When the child is very young, when the burden of self-control might be too great, the parents control him gently until he is able to inhibit his own actions in a socially acceptable fashion.

Turning now to the Nature orientation, we see that only nine of the forty-five characters are scored on this orientation, so that we cannot judge much from the results. We can say only that since six of those nine characters have a feeling of oneness with Nature, the results lie in the predicted direction. In one of these stories a peasant has worked hard to make the earth produce; when it does he is elated and yet there is no feeling in him that he has mastered Nature, rather we get the impression of humility and oneness with the earth. "He is standing in front of his fields. He has on his pantaloons of brown velour—he seems to be dressed in a piece of his labors—It is an earth of much good will." It is neither he nor the earth who are responsible for the crop, but rather both together. It is our impression that the integral type is most likely to view himself as a part of Nature, to be so aware of the universe around him that his egocentricity is diminished. At the present time we can do no more than speculate on this because the data are so meager.

In this section we have seen that it is possible to ascertain the values of a culture by close analysis of children's readers, and that there seem to be certain meaningful relationships between values and modal conscience. Tentatively we would like to suggest the following possible relationships between cultural values and modal conscience:

Time Orientation

First-Order Future Orientation: Here there will be a tendency toward an authoritarian or an other-directed conscience because, as we have seen in the two American groups, the parents encourage early independence so that the child will be socialized as quickly as possible. This means that the child is not allowed to be dependent long enough to form well-internalized principles. Also, in a Future-oriented society standards change frequently, and in order to keep up with the standards individuals must be ready to change their own. Thus, they need to refer to the opinions of others. Whether such a Future-oriented society will have an authoritarian or an other-directed modal conscience depends on whether, in the Relational orientation, Lineality or Collaterality is stressed.

First-Order Present Orientation: Although we have not yet studied a first-order Present-oriented society, we predict that the modal conscience of such a society will be either other-directed or hedonistic. The Present-oriented person is likely to look to his peers for guidance (rather than the parents who represent the past), hence the tendency toward other-direction. The Present-oriented person is also less likely to think of future consequences, hence the tendency toward hedonism. Whether the Present-oriented society will have an other-directed or a hedonistic modal conscience depends on whether the society has a Doing or a Being activity value. In the Doing-oriented society where achievement and early independence are stressed there is not time for the child to form well-internalized principles, so that he must look to others for aid and guidance. Since the peer group represents his Present orientation, he is most likely to conform to its demands. Furthermore, in the Present-Doing society the child would never be quite sure of the love of others: the Present orientation would tend to foster slow socialization and dependence, whereas the Doing orientation fosters an emphasis on independence. Hence these parents might be very permissive at the earlier stages, and then would suddenly begin to make high demands for independence and maturity. In meeting parental demands for independence, where dependency had been previously encouraged, the child might instead transfer this dependency onto his peers who would all be in the same situation. In the Present-Being-oriented society, however, we would expect a tendency toward permissive socialization and impulse gratification. Furthermore, if this Present Time orientation is combined with Individualism, we might predict the presence of a hedonistic modal conscience.

First-Order Past Orientation: The conscience type will be either authoritarian or integral. The outcome of this depends largely, we think, on whether the society is Doing or Being-in-Becoming oriented. A society which stresses achievement must value early independence, and in this case the parents will exercise strong control in order to inculcate their values quickly; also, a Past-oriented society tends to have much respect for the dicta of the older generation. On the other hand, in the society where Being-in-Becoming is highly valued, e.g., among the French, the emphasis is on slow and thorough development and parents emphasize this rather than obedience. Thus, this combination of values would tend to produce an integral modal conscience.

Relational Orientation

First-Order Individualism: As we have seen in the American groups, this would tend to produce an other-directed or authoritarian type conscience. The higher the degree of individualism, the greater the tendency to conformity, since in an individualistic society there are no broad standards for action. The individuals tend to seek a standard either among the authority figures or among their peers. Whether such a society becomes authoritarian or other-directed depends largely on whether the second-order orientation is Lineal or Collateral. If it is Lineal, the tendency is to seek the guidance of the parents or other authority figures; and if it is Collateral, the tendency is to seek the guidance of peers.

First-Order Lineality: Such a society will tend toward either an authoritarian or an integral modal conscience, since the parents are here the chief socializing figures. The outcome of this will again depend primarily on whether the society has a stronger Doing or Being-in-Becoming orientation. Whereas a first-order Individualism combined with a second-order Lineality tends to produce the authoritarian conscience, a first-order Lineality combined with a second-order Individualism would tend to produce an integral conscience structure, since the Lineal ties give the individual security and certain basic standards, while the emphasis on Individualism forces him to independence of thought and action.

First-Order Collaterality: Such a society will tend toward the hedonistic modal conscience; however, a second-order Collaterality when combined with first-order Individualism would tend to foster the other-directed conscience. In a culture whose first-order value in the Relational orientation is Collaterality, we can expect that the child will be socialized by several "mothers" and "fathers," so that the intensity of affect toward the biological parents will not be as great as in the small nuclear family. Thus, the intensity of the oedipus complex will be minimal and the child will not have as urgent a need to internalize the standards of the parent of the same sex. As part of a large extended family unit, he will receive love and attention from a variety of adults, siblings, and cousins so that their control of him will have to be external. The child who is not so very dependent on one set of parents for his emotional gratification will not be as likely to internalize parental injunctions, since the loss of their love is not as great a threat to him as it is to the child who has no one else on whom he can depend for gratification. In the culture where Individualism is the first-order value, and Collaterality the second, we can expect that the child will be socialized by the one set of parents on whom he is dependent for all gratification, but who insist on his independence; hence in his search for guidance and gratification he will turn to the peer group.

Activity Orientation

First-Order Being: Such a society will tend toward a hedonistic modal conscience, since strong emphasis is placed on impulse gratification, particularly if the values of Being and Present are combined. In the culture where both Being and Present are valued, socialization will be slow and impulse gratification will be high. The point to remember is that impulses of all sorts will be readily expressed by the parents, so that discipline will be fairly sporadic. One time a certain act will be punished, the second time it will go unnoticed by parents, since their awareness of it will depend primarily on the frustration that they themselves feel at a given moment. Without much emphasis on the precedent of the Past and with little push toward the Future, the child is given neither firm standards nor is he particularly anxious about conforming to them. We can expect that a Present-Being culture would have a long nursing, and in general a rather relaxed socialization period, so that the pleasure principle would be fostered. The child accustomed to much gratification has a low frustration tolerance, so that self-gratification is a much stronger motive to him than gratification of parents or others. And where these values are combined with a first-order Collaterality, the oedipal problem is minimal, so that there will be even less motivation for introjection of parental standards. In other words, gratification is high in the Present-Being-oriented society, which means that there is little motivation for the internalization of parental standards; when this is combined with Collaterality, there is even less motivation, since there is little of the guilt which arises as a result of the oedipus complex.

However, if this Being orientation should be combined with the belief that human nature is Evil, then there would be a strong tendency toward an authoritarian conscience structure, since in the Being culture there is emphasis on impulse gratification which would be intolerable for people who believed that such impulses are Evil. Hence, the bad "fit" between these two values would be a source of tension, and superego control would be highly rigid in order to counteract the Being tendencies. Furthermore, where the struggle between id and superego is intensified by the antithetical Being and Evil values, we could expect the ego to be quite weak.

First-Order Doing: Since such a society emphasizes success and achievement, there is again the emphasis on early independence. Thus, such a society would tend toward the authoritarian or other-directed modal conscience. The outcome of this depends on whether the emphasis in the Relational orientation is Lineal or Collateral.

First-Order Being-in-Becoming: As we have seen among the French, this orientation tends to give support to the integral conscience structure since the emphasis is on maturity, carefully integrated inner principles, and the development of a self-image which guides all action.

Human Nature Orientation

Evil: This conception will tend to foster the authoritarian modal conscience since it means that parents will be highly rigid in their demands and discipline will be stern. This will be the case particularly if the belief in Evil Human Nature is fused with Being, since these two values are antithetical in such a way as to create a demand for superego rigidity in order to cope with the Being value. Furthermore, if the belief in evil Human Nature is combined with Lineality, this will create a severe oedipal problem, since experimentation will not be allowed in adolescence. Hence, the guilt content will be so high that the authoritarian modal conscience will be fostered.

Mixed: This would tend to foster the integral, the other-directed, or the hedonistic modal conscience since discipline is more lax. The outcome will be integral in the Being-in-Becoming culture, other-directed in the Doing culture, and hedonism in the Being culture.

Good: Although such a society has never been found, we predict that it would foster a hedonistic modal conscience, since it would mean that parents would never discipline their children, and impulse gratification would be all important.

Relation to Nature

Harmony with Nature: This would tend to foster the integral conscience since it implies the tendency to see a unity of all things. The integral person has himself a highly integrated self-image, and so he tends to see the universe as being integrated also: since the microcosm senses its wholeness, it tends to project this feeling onto the macrocosm.

We do not think that knowing this orientation is enough to predict the presence of an integral modal conscience. In fact, we strongly suspect that this whole orientation is least useful in predicting modal conscience and are not at this time prepared to postulate any further relationships within this orientation.

*Predictions as to the Values or Value Combinations
Which Influence a Particular Modal Conscience Structure*

Hedonistic
  (1) Present—Individualism
  (2) Being—Collaterality
  (3) Present—Being
  (4) Collaterality
  (5) Good Human Nature
Authoritarian
  (1) Lineality (First or Second Order)—Future
  (2) Past—Doing
  (3) Individualism[1]—Lineality[2]
  (4) Lineality (First or Second Order)—Doing
  (5) Evil Human Nature
  (6) Lineality (First or Second Order)—Evil
  (7) Being—Evil
Other-Directed
  (1) Individualism[1]—Collaterality[2]
  (2) Future—Collaterality[2]
  (3) Present[2]—Doing
  (4) Doing—Collaterality[2]
  (5) Doing—Mixed Human Nature
Integral
  (1) Past—Being-in-Becoming
  (2) Lineality—Being-in-Becoming
  (3) Being-in-Becoming
  (4) Mixed Human Nature—Being-in-Becoming
  (5) Lineality[1]—Individualism[2]

IV

THE AUTHORITARIAN MODAL CONSCIENCE: IRELAND AND GERMANY

In this section we shall concern ourselves with testing some of the hypotheses about the authoritarian modal conscience that were presented at the end of Section III. In order to test our hypotheses about the particular value combinations which might lead to the authoritarian modal conscience we have chosen Ireland and Germany. In order to understand this choice we must return to our original definition of the authoritarian. "It is among this type that we can expect to find an explicit and fairly rigid moral code; the internalization of the code comes directly from the introjection of parental standards, and a transgression from the code implies the dreaded loss of love and retaliation by the father. . . . The dominant form of control in the authoritarian society is the internalized moral code, and a feeling of obligation to others. This moral code has an element of compulsion to it. . . ." We doubt seriously that any worker in the field would question that by this definition, in Ireland and Germany, we may postulate the presence of an authoritarian modal conscience. Although these two cultures differ greatly

TABLE 4

The Irish

Results of the Coding on a Basis of Twenty-One Stories

	Stories
Time Orientation	
Future	2
Present	4
Past	14
Total	20*
Relational Orientation	
Individualism	4
Lineality	11
Collaterality	6
Total	21
Activity Orientation	
Doing	4
Being	16
Being-in-Becoming	0
Total	20*
Human Nature Orientation	
Evil	14
Mixed	4
Good	2
Total	20*
Nature Orientation	
Mastery	2
Harmony	0
Subjugation	16
Total	18*

*It was not always possible to score all twenty-one stories.

—and we expect to deal with some of these differences—both have the emphasis on discipline and obedience to the father, the rigid moral code, and a sense of obligation toward others. Let us turn then to an analysis of the Irish stories, to see which values appear to be the dominant ones.

In the Time orientation we see that fourteen out of the twenty stories are scored in the Past time category. We must note at this point that only four of the twenty-one stories have any mention of children at all; of these only in one is a child the central character. Hence, these stories are not concerned with present-day life and activities of children; they draw on the tradition of the past: on the old folk tales and stories of the saints. Nine stories actually begin with "Once upon a time" or "Long, long ago," four more are about the saints or some fictional characters. One story, which is about a baker who used a horse for his work and then tried to become modern by using a truck, deals specifically with the value of the Past and resistance to change: "She [the horse] had been coming with the bread for *years and years* to the *same* houses. . . . The Baker was a cheerful man, having always a bright word or a merry whistle. He and his horse . . . had worked together for a *long, long time.*" When he began to use the truck, the "Baker became less and less cheerful," and when he reverted to the use of the horse he was back with his "merry old whistle and a cheerful knock. . . ." The emphasis on past time is here unmistakable; the past is reaffirmed, while the future and any value on "biggerism and betterism" is repudiated. We shall return to this particular aspect of conservatism after our discussion of the Relational orientation. Indeed, Arensberg and Kimball (1948) found that among the Irish discussion of the Past was a favorite topic: "The older men and women describe the 'old days' with enthusiasm and regret. The 'old times' are a ready topic among the country people, . . . many an evening an old person can be got to tell of the 'old times' . . . and the speakers throw a glow of courage and glamour round them. . . . Remembered necessities in the eyes of the old people who tell the tale are now feats of endurance and strength to which the new generation could never aspire. That is the point for those who tell and those who listen" (p. 170). We note how striking is Irish reverence for tradition when we contrast it with our own: Americans tend to think that the future will be the most glorious period of all, that progress is inevitable; for the Irish, however, "the past reflects their glories and is a convenient vehicle for the expression of their superiority, so the present can be measured against the past in the same terms, usually only to be found lacking" (p. 171). It is the old who are honored and respected, and when groups of men gather together in the pub "the enthralling game of presenting arguments, choosing sides, directing the flow of talk, belongs to the older men. The young men must listen in" (p. 177). It is significant that only one of our stories is really about children. Hence the stories reinforce the value placed on the spectatorship of the youthful audience while the older men do the acting. Children are to learn by observation rather than by action; the culture is adult-centered rather than child-centered.

This adult centeredness is further given support by the first-order Lineal Relational orientation. The results of our coding show that of our twenty-one stories eleven have a Lineal emphasis. In one story in which the father has just told his children about an episode in the life of one of the saints, he says at the end: ". . . it is an old, old story. My father told it to me when I was a boy, and he heard it from his own father. All these old stories have been handed down from father to son over the long years." Much of Arensberg's and Kimball's book is devoted to this Irish Lineality. Although there is much reciprocity and cooperation, authority lines are fairly distinct from father to son. "This paternal dominance continues as long as the father lives. Even though the major work of the farm devolves upon the sons, they have no control of the direction of farm activities nor of the disposal of farm income. Status in the family is highly important, the position of the parents is one of extreme super-ordination, that of the children of extreme sub-ordination" (p. 61).

In fact, the Irish family is a microcosm of the whole social order; authority is not simply delegated from parents to children; there is a hierarchical structure to this lineality. Authority goes from husband to wife to children: "the women and children do not eat until the men have finished. . . . The children may sometimes not come to the table but stay sitting upon the settee. . . . They are very silent children. They take little part in the family discussion between older members unless questioned directly" (pp. 37-38). Thus, we see how the combination of Past time and Lineality fosters this reverence for the old, and passive spectatorship on the part of the children. In many cases the paternal grandparents also live in the home so that there are often three generations in the household, which reinforces the hierarchical pattern. This pattern is curiously reflected in our readers: nine of the stories present the moral or the implicit assumption that "whatever is, is right," that it is not possible or actually not even right to attempt a change of status. Let us look closely at one story in which a doddering old Queen changes status positions with a young peasant girl. The young girl discovers, of course, that poor as she was, she was much happier when she could "laugh and sing," "see the flowers and the sunshine," and "dance like the leaves on the trees and run like the streams down the hillside." But the interesting thing to note is that the Queen discovers that she "cannot live without the homage of my courtiers and the grandeur of my throne." As a ninety-year-old Queen "she had very little hair and very few teeth. Her head trembled and she could not see well," she had "trembling hands," a "quavering voice," and had to "grope her way from chair to chair," yet she cannot psychically tolerate her change in status. The implication is then that each life position has its advantages and disadvantages; but these are not really important. What matters is that each individual has to live as he was born to live, and to attempt any change in the fixed order of things is futile.

In another story the father decides to better the family position by buying a horse; this effort is frustrated, however, by the fact that he spills the milk which he meant to exchange for the horse. The story of the Baker which we mentioned before is further indicative of the way in which Lineality and Past Time emphasis combine to create acceptance of things as they are. In another such story a shoemaker is made a rich man and immediately he becomes unhappy; the implication is again that he must remain a shoemaker and only in fulfilling his life's function can he be happy. The widely known story of the "Lion and the Mouse" falls into our sample; it is significant that the ultimate moral of this story is that there are advantages to being a mouse as well as to being a lion, that neither could exist without the other, and that although the lion is king, he *needs* his servants. All rungs in the status hierarchy must be filled if society is to function smoothly. The implication is that anything which exists must serve some purpose, and therefore it must be good. Irish Catholicism is in a sense then a religion of acquiescence, a doctrine which in no way advocates that men should revolt against existing social conditions. In so far as arrangements exist, they are God's handiwork and so must not be criticized; rather, a positive attitude must be taken toward them. Hence, the Queen must not deny her age and must look at the positive aspects of her status; the peasant girl must accept her poverty and rejoice in her youth. Because of the influence of the medieval doctrine of quietness and acquiescence, the problem was not to eradicate feudalism but rather to make it better. The popes themselves have been unalterably opposed to socialism, because the inequality among men, the hierarchical order, is seen to be beneficial to the welfare of society as a whole.

The hierarchy of the Catholic Church is, of course, both a support and a reflection of the Past Time-Lineal family system that we have been discussing. Just as the authority of God is absolute over all creation, so is the authority of the Pope to the rest of the Church hierarchy, and so is the authority of the father over his children. Morality and ethics would have no meaning without the existence of God, since God is the ultimate authority from Whom all Ethics are derived. The assumption is that without the authority of God, morality could not and would not exist. Hence, Irish Catholicism, which on the whole is the strictest Catholicism of any modern nation, is at least in part a reflection of the Past Time-Lineal values and the emphasis on a hierarchy of authority and of individuals, on a moral code which cannot exist except as it is derived from and sanctioned by authority. It is perhaps of interest to note that kings play a part in eight of our twenty-one stories.

Turning now to the results on the Activity orientation, we see that sixteen of the twenty stories coded for this orientation have a Being emphasis. This is in part a reflection of the notion of acquiescence which we have discussed above. A Doing orientation implies a certain militancy and desire to change the *status quo;* a Being-in-Becoming orientation also involves change or rather inward development. The Being orientation is most suited to the doctrine of quietness and acquiescence; the emphasis is on enjoying life as it comes along. In our two stories where a working man attempts to *do* something to make more money, he is made intensely unhappy. Value is placed rather on getting pleasure from the nature of the job itself. Before he decided to change things, the shoemaker "was as happy as a king, and quite content to sit in his little shop, working, and singing all day." Finally, when he can no longer "sleep," "nor work," "nor sing," he resumes his old rule. And the Baker revolts against the mechanization and depersonalization of his job which has been brought about in the interests of efficiency; he prefers instead to be the craftsman and to chat leisurely with his customers. He feels that the truck was a "strange, unfriendly thing, after Star's cheerful ways and friendly neighing." The horse was better to work with because "She knew the way so well, that if her master stood too long talking at the door of one house, she would amble on to the next." The Being aspects of work are certainly emphasized, and indeed Arensberg and Kimball (1948) point out that the Irish farmer is always ready to stop work in order to chat with a neighbor.

Before we take up the problem of the Human Nature orientation, we must first understand the life situation which is created for the child by this combination of Lineality, Past, and Being. As we have seen among the French, the combination of Past Time and Lineality tends to influence parental attitudes in such a way that socialization is not hurried. The value on Being tends to produce the same attitudes, so that until the age of about seven the Irish boy is not given much responsibility; at no time is independence encouraged. And in fact the Irish marry later and are dependent upon parents longer than the people of any other European nation: "the sons even though fully adult, work under their father's eye and refer necessary decisions to him" (p. 41). It is not at all unusual for a man of thirty-five or forty to be living at home under the rule of his father, and to be dependent on him for everything he needs. "If the son wants a half crown to go to a harley match or to take a drink on market day with friends, he must get it from his father. The authors have seen many sons, fully adult, come into shops to buy some farm requirement and say that the 'old fellow' will pay for it" (p. 55). "Even at forty-five and fifty, if the old couple have not yet made over the farm, the countryman remains a 'boy' in respect to farm work and in the rural vocabulary" (p. 56).

From our knowledge of clinical cases we could expect that such a long dependency period and submission to the father might lead to a very difficult oedipal adjustment. Until the boy is seven he remains always with his mother: "As the woman works in the house or fields, the child is kept by her side. In the house it usually sits in a crib by the fire or plays about on the floor, but always within sight and sound. It learns its speech from its mother, amid a flood of constant endearments, admonitions, and encouragements. The woman's work never separates her from the child" (p. 59). And then at the age of seven the son is put out to work in the fields, along with and under the authority of his father. We cannot expect that identification with the father will be simple when placement under his authority occurs at the same time as removal from the mother. Indeed, there is a great deal of evidence that the oedipal problem in Ireland is prominent. Father and son are never very close; their relationship is based on authority lines: "The barriers of authority, respect, extra household interests, and the imperatives of duty rather than of encouragement make it difficult for any intimacy to develop" (p. 59). The relationship to the mother is very different, however: "Throughout the years of the son's full activity in the farm economy under the father's headship, the mother still remains the source of comfort and the preparer of food and is still infinitely solicitous of his welfare. . . . When one goes home it is to see one's mother" (p. 60). In addition to this impressionistic analysis, there are certain startling facts which have a bearing on this problem. According to the 1926 census, "there was a larger proportion of unmarried persons of all ages than in any other country for which records are kept" (p. 103). In some very important ways, then, the Irish boy never loses the oedipal attachment to the mother, and the girl to her father.

We see then that the combination of Past, Lineality, and Being fosters a strong oedipal problem. It is in just this type of situation that we would expect the superego development which Freud described. If the son is taken after seven years of nurturance and dependency from the mother and put under the father's rule so that in every sphere the latter's authority is strongly in evidence, if the economy and life situation of these people demands close cooperation between father and son, then identification with the father is both mandatory and difficult. This closeness with and desire for the mother produces a high level of guilt so that the son identifies with the father and introjects his moral principles. Both the Heavenly Father and the earthly father, by their authoritarian rule, create intense guilt. The only way for the child to alleviate this guilt is through identification with and rigid adherence to paternal demands and imperatives.

TABLE 5

THE PERCENTAGE OF UNMARRIED PEOPLE AT A GIVEN AGE LEVEL*

Age	Percent of unmarried males	Percent of unmarried females
25-30	80%	62%
30-35	62%	42%
35-40	50%	32%
55-80	26%	24%

*This table was compiled by the author from data by Arensberg and Kimball (1948).

This problem of guilt brings us directly to the consideration of the Irish view about human nature. The analysis of our stories shows that of the twenty it was possible to score on this orientation, fourteen indicate the view that human nature is evil. Men are seen to be evil because they attempt to change their status, because they want money, because they take advantage of one another. The "good" persons are not those who are industrious and hardworking as in early America, but rather those who fulfill their obligations to others. In one story about a saint we note the contrast between the good and the bad: ". . . the country's people, over which Queen Y [the saint] reigned, were proud and haughty, . . . When Queen Y . . . learned that any of her people were poor or ill, she wished to attend to them herself. She carried food to the hungry. She washed the sores of those who were ill, and did everything she could to relieve pain and suffering." She even takes a little boy who has leprosy and puts him in her own bed. "The King's Mother was very angry." We note here the oedipal problem: the King's mother sets her son against his wife, but finally the Queen is rewarded because the leper turns out to be Christ. In another story another saint again recognizes his responsibility to others and is rewarded by God. "The winter had been very cold. All the land was covered with deep snow, and many people were suffering because they had no warm clothing. Food and fuel, too, were scarce." Only the saint gives his cloak to "an old man, poorly clad and shivering from the cold." The saint was at this time a soldier, but later he "became instead a soldier of God. He became a bishop. He lived to be an old man and did great things for God." Obligations to others and responsibility to the supreme authority, without whom there would be no ethics, is the ultimate in morality.

The Irish sense of sin and guilt about sexuality has been observed clinically, has been portrayed by novelists,[5] and is evidenced by their lack and delay of marriage. Relations with others seem to be primarily on the basis of degree of duty and obligation. The relationship between father and son is, as we have seen, based primarily on the imperatives of duty; when the collateral relatives cooperate with each other, this is because they "have right." "I have right to" means "the obligation is on me"; as Arensberg and Kimball (1948) have described it: "When asked especially why they were cooperating, the farmers' answer was that they 'had right to help' . . . Now the phrase 'have right' expresses an obligation, duty, or the traditional fitness of an act" (p. 75). Helping others, controlling impulses, and doing what is expected has an obligatory character to it and is made verbal in a highly explicit and rigid moral code. What the individual wishes to do must give way to what he should do; egocentricity is, in this culture, controlled by feelings of guilt and by rigid adherence to the imperatives of the moral code.

Antagonism between the sexes is traditionally strong; to be near women is first of all an unconscious disloyalty to the beloved mother, and secondly it constitutes a great threat since all impulses must be held under tight control. As Arensberg and Kimball (1948) have pointed out: "Men and women are much more often to be seen in the company of members of their own sex" (p. 203). There is of course no opportunity for adolescent sex play and experimentation. "The best evidence gives them a comparatively low illegitimacy rate, and the country people yield to no one in the strictness of their sexual morality" (p. 202). The unmarried person is definitely under a moral obligation to deny and repress his sexuality. "They equate any departure from the accepted norm as a sin, a lack of religion. They bring the whole weight of all their sanctions and values to bear upon it. They make the ultimate identification between their own norms and the only right conduct" (p. 210). Not only is man's sexual nature seen as evil, but also it is denied. The old are viewed as saintly, not only because this is a Lineally-oriented society, but also because old age brings freedom from lust and desire; sexuality for any but those who are married and of age to bear children is denied. "It is only with the married men and women who are still engaged

[5] See Sean O'Casey, *Mirror in My House* (1958), H. M. Robinson, *The Cardinal* (1950).

in producing offspring that any kind of sexual interest, officially at least, is permitted or *even deemed to exist*" (p. 208). This denial of sexuality becomes particularly significant when we contrast it to the French attitude of accepting the libidinal drive as a powerful and vital force. In France the full acknowledgment of one's sensuality is apparently a sign that one is "cultured" and belongs to the intelligentsia; in Ireland (and one might add to some extent in America) people "attribute sexual laxity to the classes of the population they consider below themselves" (p. 218).

The oedipal situation is further complicated by the combination of Lineality and the view that human nature is evil. Not only is the oedipus complex encouraged by the closeness of son and mother and the long protracted childhood, sometimes into the forties and fifties, but also by the rigid sex taboo. Since there is no sex play and experimentation in adolescence, the strong cathexis of the parent of the opposite sex never has a chance, until the very late marriage, to be displaced onto someone else. Furthermore, it seems to us that the combination of Evil Human Nature and Being is much more difficult than the combination of Evil Human Nature and Doing which we observed in pre-Civil War America. The American code was puritanical and sex was repudiated, but man was able and was encouraged to channel his libidinal and aggressive drives into an active mastery over things and nature; his drives were channeled, in effect, into doing. The Being value of the Irish, on the other hand, implies that man should not be militant against his instincts, but rather should allow them into play; the view that human nature is evil is of course directly antithetical to this attitude. In order to cope with this paradox the superego must become even more militant and authoritarian; if any leeway is given to man, even the good one, he must immediately become corrupted. Hence, in one of our stories a very kind woman gives her last bit of milk to a beggarman; she is rewarded for this kindness by the gift of a magic cow which gives her an unlimited supply. This kind model woman is corrupted by this ease and due to her own "pride" and "boasting" she milks the cow to death. Man's nature is so evil that the danger of regression, even in the very good, is always present.

If we turn now to man's place in Nature we see that in sixteen of the eighteen stories which it was possible to score on this orientation, the belief is that man is subjugated to Nature. Man is seen to be poor because Nature has been unbountiful; donkeys and camels run away when they are most needed, and a boy breaks his leg on some rocks. In one story the king has to enlist the aid of a group of fairies in order to clear his land of rocks, forests, and to harness the oxen; man alone, even a king, is incapable of this task. This belief that man is subjugated to Nature is, of course, part of the doctrine of acquiescence and hierarchy which we have discussed above. It is significant to note that poverty was a cardinal sin in the McGuffey readers because its presence implied that man had not worked hard enough, had not been industrious; in contrast, poverty, although it is dealt with in eight of our Irish stories, is never a sin. Rather, the chief sin in these stories is pride and any aspiration to rise in the hierarchy. The Protestant ethic that "God helps those who help themselves" is potent in the McGuffey readers; man is supposed to work and to *do* in order to combat poverty and misfortune. In the Irish stories people are rewarded magically by God for faith rather than for works, and for the fulfillment of their obligations to others rather than to themselves. Contrast the message of this quote from McGuffey: "... if you are not diligent it is one of the surest evidences that your heart is not right with God. You are placed in this world to improve your time. In Youth, you must be preparing for future usefulness. *And if you do not improve the advantages you enjoy, you sin against your Maker*" with the following Irish story: In brief, a little girl is orphaned and "sets out to find a new home. She had nothing but the clothes she wore and two slices of bread in her hand. As she walked along the road she met a poor old beggar who asked for food. The little girl gave him a slice of bread"; she continues to give her coat to a small boy, the last of her bread to another child. Finally, "Dusk fell and a chill night wind began to blow. The little girl had no money, no coat, and no home. . . . And then, as she stood there, a lot of stars fell in a shower at her feet and lay in a shining heap upon the ground . . . they were all changed into pure gold." Not by work and by industry, but through faith

TABLE 6

The Irish
Chi-Square Tests of Significance between First- and
Second-Order Values

A Chi-square of 3.84 or more indicates significance at the .05 level	
Time Orientation	
Past > Present	5.5
Relational Orientation	
Lineal > Collateral	1.4
Activity Orientation	
Being > Doing	7.2
Human Nature Orientation	
Evil > Mixed	5.5
Nature Orientation	
Subjugation > Mastery	12.2

and through kindness is this little girl rewarded; passivity and acceptance are in every way encouraged.

We have seen that the Irish meet our criteria for the authoritarian conscience, and Table 6 shows that they meet two of our predictions as to the possible value combinations which might produce the authoritarian modal conscience, whereas they meet none of our criteria for values which might foster any of the other three conscience types. The Evil Human Nature value is significant alone and in combination with the Being value; Lineality is not significant in relation to the second-order Collateral, but lies in the predicted direction. The value that human nature is evil fosters repression of sexuality and a stern moral code; the combined belief in Evil Human Nature and

TABLE 7

The Germans
Results of the Coding on a Basis of Twenty-One Stories

	Stories
Time Orientation	
Future	9
Present	3
Past	9
Total	21
Relational Orientation	
Individual	10
Lineal	10
Collateral	1
Total	21
Activity Orientation	
Doing	11
Being	10
Being-in-Becoming	0
Total	21
Human Nature Orientation	
Evil	9
Mixed	10
Good	2
Total	21
Nature Orientation	
Mastery	7
Harmony	0
Subjugation	4
Total	11*

*It was not possible to score all twenty-one stories.

Lineality creates a strong œdipal problem, so that there is a high content of guilt and consequent need to submit to and internalize the imperative commands of the father. Furthermore, we have seen that the combination of Being and Lineality fosters dependence and the willingness to submit to authority, while the value combination of Being and Evil Human Nature is so antithetical that impulses must be militantly fought against to counteract the Being tendencies.

Turning now to the Germans we shall attempt to point out some of the similarities and differences between Irish and German culture as they pertain to conscience formation. Though the value profile of the Germans is different, we shall see that they too meet our criteria for the authoritarian modal conscience. In speaking of the Germans we shall be concerned primarily with the middle class of West Germany, since our readers and most available material stem from this source.

Our results in the Time orientation do not show any difference between emphasis on Past and Future. The nine stories we have rated in the Past category all begin with "Once upon a time," or "Long, long ago," but other than this we see no special emphasis on the Past. There rather seems to be a certain ambivalence about the relationship between Past and Future. In one story about a cockchafer and a grub, the cockchafer is held in reverence because he can already fly and the grub longingly looks to the future; but then the cockchafer is seen to die soon after the once glorious future has become the present. Hence, in the beginning of the story the future is glorified and the past rejected; in the end it is the past which is glorified. When the grub reminds the cockchafer that once he too could not fly, "the beautiful chafer's face darkened; he did not like to be reminded of his dark past." The chafer dies soon afterwards and when the grub is puzzled by this a fellow grub tells him: "Oh, my son, it is a wonderful thing to be able to fly; but he who earnt it has to die soon after." Hence, it is perhaps better to be young after all. It seems that the German looks to the future, but is disappointed when it becomes the present. There seems to be a forward thrust toward a future which will be better than the past it is modeled on, yet which never seems as good as that past.

The German relation to the past and future is quite different from the French view of the past and the American view of the future. For the French the eighteenth century was the epiphany and the ideal time, and Frenchmen speak of it with pride and reverence; the Germans have never been as satisfied with their past. The Americans are optimistic about the future, they look to it with confidence; the Germans look to the future and plan for it, but at the same time there is a great deal of pessimism about that future.

That is, there is optimism about an ideal utopian future, and pessimism about the actual realizable future. The German emphasis is placed upon a tomorrow which seems to be a utopia, an ultimate destiny, rather than a reality. Rodnick (1948) found that on the whole Germans viewed the realizable future with pessimism and grave doubt (p. 173).

This ambivalence toward the Future is reflected also in German child training. Child training is geared toward the future, as is the American; but unlike the latter, the Germans fear that the future will not be rewarding: "most of the middle-class children have the feeling that they must be industrious and work hard so that they can become 'somebodies' in the future" (p. 48), and yet "adult life, from the German point of view, offers little gratification and little opportunity for self-expression" (p. 41). Adults train their children with a view toward their future, which stresses that the future will be so unorderly and complex that children need certain absolutes by which they are to be guided. Since it is believed that Germany's problem has been lack of unity and a too great diversity of foreign influences, the parents feel that the child, if it is to be the hope of the future, must have a unified well-structured moral code. It is this combination of hope for the future and yet pessimism about its outcome which is, at least in part, responsible for the expressed need of the parents to train children carefully. As the future generation, they are the hope of the parents; but the future is so unsure that German Destiny has a chance to be realized only if the children are endowed with certain very definite ideas and standards. Whenever a people hope for and are highly concerned with the future, but at the same time are anxious about its outcome, we can expect that their standards will be rigid, and that they will try to create order and unity out of chaos and multiplicity. Although there is no conclusive evidence, we would suggest that the Germans are Future-oriented, with the hope, and yet a grave doubt, that this future will be the fulfillment of a past which was never ideal. It is possible that the equality of Past and Future emphases in our stories is a reflection of this ambivalence; hope for a future which is to be modeled on an imperfect past and yet grave uncertainty as to the realizability of desired goals.

Turning now to the Relational orientation, we see that there are an equal number of Lineally and Individualistically oriented stories. The German son upon marriage is not expected to move his wife into the home of his parents; but the family and ties to parents play a great role. Métraux (in Mead and Wolfenstein, 1955) in her analysis of "The Family in German Juvenile Fiction" has said: ". . . the family as a whole consists of numerous households, each independent of the others and bound to the others only by ties of affection. . . . The separation of the household is symbolized by their being scattered not only in one city but quite regularly in different parts of Germany. . . . The child who, as an adult, does not move away has not achieved autonomy" (p. 260). In our sample we have eleven stories about children (human and animal); two are about ideal children and the rest are concerned with the need of parents to discipline, control, and comfort their children. All stories deal with the relationship between parent(s) and a single child, except one where the parents are dead. The most extreme of these stories has no parallel in any other country that we have studied.

The story under consideration is told by a boy: "My parents were extremely gentle and considerate with us children. But they made us feel their greatest anger whenever they caught us in an act of untruth." The story goes on to tell us that the boy stole a cherry branch and then lied to his mother about where he got it. He is caught in the lie and we are shown the reaction of mother and child: "I expected the worst, but my mother was silent. She was silent and went away; I followed her and found her crying bitterly." We are aware of the inculcation of guilt in the child by the use of love-oriented discipline, but we are not prepared for the very next sentence. "That is how a mother cries whose dearest son is led to prison." The association between one lie and the possibility of prison shows the need to keep children under tight control, the source of the rigidity of the moral code. We are reminded of Kant and his principle of universality: the basis for moral action rests on the principle that the individual must be ready to universalize his action, must be prepared to let it stand as an imperative for all people. We would like to suggest that this is a fantasy which could only emanate from a rigid and punitive superego; only the authoritarian superego and the guilt it fosters could create the association between prison and one lie. We note the need for the expiation of this guilt: "My eyes were opened—and were filling with tears. On my lips untruth, . . . I fell down upon my knees, owned up to everything and asked for forgiveness." But the mother does not offer forgiveness; instead she gives a command: "Get up . . . carry the branch to the neighbor and tell him what you have done!" Such an order can only be obeyed and the brevity of the next sentence is significant: "I did it."

Another of our stories is concerned with a mother who denies bread to her little girl until the latter has learned to say "please." Twice the mother *ignores* the childish demand and finally tells her a story which illustrates the need to say "please." Another story is about two elephants who are highly disappointed because their son does not conform to their pattern of desirable behavior: " 'How could we have such a son! It is so terrible to have a son who cannot keep anything in his mind!' You see elephants are very proud of their good memory." The implication is, of course, that because the elephant parents have a good memory they demand that the son have the same accomplishments and follow their pattern exactly; German parents tend to act as though, for each situation, there was only one possible form of behavior. As Métraux (in Mead and Wolfenstein, 1955) has said: "The intention of this education is not to prepare the individual to make choices but rather to know what is right and to have the strength and fortitude to do it" (p. 224).

The German ideal in child rearing fosters this unity of the moral code because in principle the parents are to present a united front to the child. Hence, the story of the cherry "thief" which we mentioned above begins with the fact that both parents disapprove of lying and almost imperceptibly "they" is transposed to "mother." "Good parents make decisions together behind closed doors: father calls mother aside, mother calls father aside, when there is news, when a decision is to be made. The decision, when it is announced, is one in which they concur. . . . The children enter the situation only when everything has been arranged for them" (p. 226). This "unity" of parents combined with the idea that children should be presented only with a definite solution rather than with the steps toward moral decision tends to create that absolute code by which the adult lives. As has been pointed out, he is not supposed to realize that there may be choice involved in a moral decision; rather there is always the known imperative to which the superego demands adherence. For the child who is involved in oedipal conflict this situation is particularly difficult. The parents are united at most times in their action toward him; this tends to increase his feelings of inadequacy and the hopelessness of displacing the parent of the same sex. When, however, he creates a rift between the parents over his own actions we would suspect that this creates much guilt. Not only does he fear paternal retaliation for the rift he has caused; the child will also, due to his autistic thinking, believe that by his omnipotence he has separated the parents and if this happens, he might be abandoned. The wish to replace the father has possibly come true, but this leads to intolerable guilt. Hence, for the child who is accustomed to unity in parental decision, any kind of disagreement or argument becomes a personal threat.

There is indeed much evidence that Germans cannot tolerate diversity of opinion. As Lewin (1948) has pointed out: "In Germany, for most persons, a political or even a scientific disagreement seems to be inseparable from moral disapproval. The congratulations that the defeated candidate for the [American] presidency sends to the elected, after a hard battle, would sound rather strange in Germany" (p. 13). And Schaffner (1949) speaks of the "inability of the German child to tolerate differences of opinion. . . . Un-accustomed to accept sincere disagreement as inevitable in an honest rela-tionship and finding it difficult to adopt a working compromise openly arrived at for the sake of group unity, the German prefers to eject the disagreeing elements. These elements naturally remain as rivals and com-petitors at a later time, and therefore every disagreement as to principles is seen as an unpleasant and potentially threatening situation" (p. 37). Furthermore, there is the German idea that only in unity can there be power. When the parents are united in front of the child they appear to be omnipotent and indestructible; when, however, the child is able through his own conduct to create a rift between them, it is he who is omnipotent and the parents are considerably weakened. Rodnick (1948) found that "most young people in all classes feel that the type of political democracy which exists in England and in the United States has no place in Germany. Political democracy, they believe, would be extremely harmful for Germany, since it would encourage political parties to spend their time attacking one another" (p. 90). The superego tolerates no diversity. There is only one proper way, only one right answer; if a choice presents itself anxiety will be intolerable unless a clear answer is already corporate in the moral code.

There has been a great deal of discussion in the literature as to whether or not the German father is the ruler of the household.[6] It seems to us that this must be the case, or else the threat in diversity would not be so great. However, the German woman is most probably not the helpless, frightened creature she has sometimes been made out to be. The German woman denies, in so far as this is possible, her femininity and identifies with the male. Her power in the home derives from the authority vested in her by her husband, and the further she is identified with him the greater is her strength. Hence, it seems that the father is indeed dominant, but the woman derives her strength from being in absolute unity with him. In this way she is given some of his power, and when there is this unity in all matters concerning children, he feels that he can trust her with their training since she is only a reflection of his person. It is through this unity and identification with her husband that the woman is given status and power; she may undermine him but never is he allowed to become aware of this. Hence any break in parental unity not only reactivates dangerous oedipal strivings and their resultant guilt feel-ings, but also constitutes a threat to the security position of the mother, which is seen as a threat to the child himself. In the home where there is any sort of equality in parental status we would expect that disagreement would not

[6] See Bychowski (1949), Erikson (1950), Rodnick (1948), and Schaffner (1949).

constitute a threat since it would be expected that two separate individuals might differ in their views on certain matters. In the German home, however, the father demands unity and the mother concurs because in identification with him lies her greatest potential for strength.

The German child has been observed to care very much about the approval of adults, and he strives to please them. He is encouraged to do only what the adults have outlined for him; their goals become his goals because he is taught obedience without knowing that he has ever been taught. Cooperation and loyalty are greatly stressed in the home, and the child's role in cooperation is to obey, to fulfill his obligations as a member of the family. Métraux (in Mead and Wolfenstein, 1955) quotes a story which is highly significant in this connection; the father is angry at his son for having disobeyed an order about playing the violin too much: "What do you think would happen if all you children did not obey, if everyone did as he thought best? That would be as if in an orchestra no one followed the director, . . . No, Frieder, my children must obey." When the child refuses to give up the violin the mother says: "Do you love the violin more than Father and Mother?" and the father says: "Then keep your violin . . . you can play as long as you like. But you will be our child only when you give it to us! . . . Go out, you strange child." After several hours the boy of course succumbs and the paternal reaction is: "Now everything is well, Frieder, and you are our child again. Frieder cried his pain away in his Father's arms" (p. 267). Now this is a devastating example of love-oriented techniques; it demonstrates clearly the need to realize that the German father does not beat his children into submission; rather the child is made to realize that the parent can only gratify his needs (parental obligation) if the child conforms to parental demands and thus fulfills his obligation within the family circle. Pressure is put upon the child by demonstrating that just as the orchestra cannot exist if everyone is not exactly in tune and ready to follow the conductor, so the family cannot survive if everyone does not fulfill his obligations. The analogy of the orchestra is a significant one: an orchestra really cannot function without a leader, so the family cannot function without the paternal leadership. In this same story the father tells his son of the sacrifices that everyone must make in communal living: "Do you think I would not rather go on playing than give a music lesson to Mrs. Verngelding when she comes? Do you think that mother would not rather go on reading her lovely books after supper than stop after half an hour and mend stockings? . . . and that the swallows would not rather get food for themselves than go out and get food for their nestlings, as God has ordered it?" (p. 268). We see then that the child is taught that every one has obligations, and that the child can shirk his only if he is willing to have mother and father withdraw their love and support. The child is even made to feel that he should be deeply grateful because the father is making a sacrifice of his own pleasure in order to care for the child: the swallow could be doing more enjoyable things then feeding his young. But if it is the father who orders the child, then it is God who orders the father. This gives special meaning to Lewin's (1948) statement that it is the "natural right of the adult to rule and the duty of the child to obey" (p. 7).

Hence, as Métraux (in Mead and Wolfenstein, 1955) has pointed out, the goal of training is the acceptance of "sacrifice for the sake of others, overcoming personal desire, mastering a weakness" (p. 269) so that harmonious unity can be achieved in the family. In one of our stories a little girl goes to get water for her sick mother, in a time of drought when everyone is dying of thirst. She is magically rewarded for this fulfillment of filial obligations: "She found none wherever she went. She lay down tired in the field, and went to sleep. When she woke and reached for the jug she almost spilt its contents. The jug was full of pure fresh water. The little girl was full of joy and at first wanted to drink from it herself, but she remembered there would then not be enough for her mother, and she hurried home." The mother on the other hand fulfills her obligation to the child: "I have to die anyhow. It is better for you to drink it!" In another of our stories a little boy is terrified of an object in the dark and longs to call his mother, but "he could not call his mother. She had been having a headache all day, she was not supposed to get frightened, no!" Even though he is "weak and tired from the fright," Peter manages to master his weakness, because the obligation to his mother is such that he should spare her.

Essentially, this view of cooperation and obligation is the same as the Irish hierarchical structuring of society. In German society, too, someone is always above and below; class lines are rigid and status is of vital importance. Ideally those above take care of those below, but in return they are owed obedience and loyalty. The swallow must feed his children, but for this they are to be grateful. As Schaffner (1949) has said: "In return for the position which he [the father] commands in the family, he has a number of definite responsibilities: he must provide food, shelter, clothing, and education for his children" (p. 16). In return, the children owe him *Ehrfurcht*. It is highly significant that Rodnick (1948) found that the German conception of democracy nearly always included a leader: "we must have a righteous, dear Führer, who does not think himself too big and who handles his people like a good father" (p. 50); "most German children consider a Führer necessary for Germany. There appears to be an identification in their minds between a Führer and a father: just as the father takes care of the needs of his children, so there must be a Führer to take care of the unfortunates who exist in German society. . . . Although these children came from anti-Nazi homes, they all felt that Germany needed another leader with the powers of Hitler. They could not envision a German government without a Führer: it was he, they said, who gave bread to people who were hungry" (p. 58). Without a conductor there can be no orchestra; no group, no matter how small, can function without a leader.

In one of our stories the parts of the body are disputing with each other as to which is the most important; each part emphasizes its vital function and contends that therefore it should be obeyed. At last the heart proves that since it is the source of all life it alone must be obeyed; but the leader is also the servant of the led and if everyone does not do his duty, anarchy is the inevitable result. "I am the *first* and noblest as you *all depend* on me. But I need you just as much as you need me to exist. I sustain you but at the same time I am your servant since eternity. Therefore, forget the quarrel, *everyone* should do his duty so that everyone may live." The principle here seems to be something like the underlying meaning of the Roman votive offering. In sacrificing to the Gods, the individual believes that he is giving the Gods power to help him: "I give you, in order that you may give me." The relationship between parents and children seems to have overtones of the votive offering. The heart says: "I sustain you but at the same time I am your servant since eternity." The parent is the source of life to the child, but if the child does not obey, the parent is somehow made helpless in his attempts to care for the child.

Individualism is highly valued, and the child is expected to have his own interests and friends; but there seems to be a strong underlying fear that unless this individualism is held in abeyance by family control the individual may become a dangerous member of society. In one of our stories a butcher is greatly mistreating his dog: "A butcher's wagon was driving along . . . abreast with it . . . panting and lolling out his tongue . . . was a dog running, running although the wagon was empty. . . . He was limping and tried hard to keep pace"; a stranger on the road is forced to curb this individualism. And in another story a bean, which refuses aid to and laughs when its fellow straw and coal are drowned, is punished for its egocentricity by drowning. The ultimate goal of German child rearing is to raise an individualistic child who may be the hope of the future only if he is in absolute control of his own egotistical impulses; the means to attain this goal is to make sure that all parental standards are fully internalized: the authoritarian conscience is the only way to attain this goal. As Rodnick (1948) has pointed out: "Children are made to feel that the most important goals for them are those which win the approval and affection of their parents" (p. 27). "German children begin early to learn from their parents which ideas and beliefs are considered 'right' and which 'wrong.' Conformity to parent's ideas is felt to be as much of an obligation as is adherence to their religion and class" (p. 30).

Turning now to the Activity orientation, we see that the results are again not significant. This is a reflection, at least in part, of German ambivalence on the subject. That the Germans are in some sense a Doing people is unquestionable: the reconstruction of their country, the fact that they are again the wealthiest nation in Western Europe is the best proof of this. But all workers in the field have concluded that the Germans do not encourage early independence in their children, and we know from McClelland's (1953) work that independence training is positively correlated with the achievement motive. The Germans are not interested in the sort of independence American children have, but there is strong desire to make the superego of the child function independently of the parental presence. The child is to learn very early in life how to control his impulses and to refrain from an action when the parents are absent, exactly as though they were present. Children are taught that if they ignore a certain sanction, their parents will undoubtedly find out about the misdeed. It is as though the parent had some magic apparatus in his own superego which can be tuned in to the child's. In the child's mind, due to the fact that the parents seem always to know what he is thinking, parental omnipotence is increased.

In the German child-care literature analyzed by Métraux (in Mead and Wolfenstein, 1955) we see that "the successful training of the child depends on the adult's being orderly, consistent. . . . repeating the same sequence until the child can take over and do what is required of its own accord" (p. 215). It is expected that by two years of age the child will understand, on his own, the difference between right and wrong. Parental demands are high, but their own superegos are so rigid that their actions toward the child are unusually consistent: "The parent must treat his own word 'like one of the commandments' or 'like a law of nature.' She must never break her word, change her mind, make an exception, or make a mistake which must be corrected by a change of orders" (p. 219). Authority is then absolute and impersonal. Hence, the child's greatest independence lies in his early internalization of parental demands; then he is to some extent permitted to command himself.

The child is not expected to spend a great deal of time in play or idleness; he is expected to perform certain tasks, but the point to remember is that these tasks are set and defined by the parents. Hence, Doing for the German is only possible in a context of guidance; they can rebuild and glorify Germany but only under the guidance of a Führer. The German values Doing almost as much as the American; in order to "do," however, he must have some guidance since independence in task-setting is never greatly encouraged. As Rodnick (1948) describes the Doing value of middle-class children: "To be looked up to by the rest of the population is a goal worth striving for. People are divided into two groups: those who are 'somebodies' and those who are 'nobodies'" (p. 33). The goal is of course to become a "somebody." These two statements are certainly indicative of a Doing orientation: "In school I make it my duty to be as industrious as I can, so that later on I can be whatever I want to be"; and "I should like very much to be a soldier, but I don't think that is possible now. The profession of doctor pleases me very much. . . . Then I shall earn a lot of money and be important" (p. 42). The Future and Doing orientation of these two eleven-year-olds is unmistakable; in fact they seem to have a better idea of what they want, and more realism about what they can do, than American children of the same age. Above all, this Doing orientation is almost always placed in a moral and obligatory context; one must strive to make parents happy, to rebuild Germany, to do one's duty. "Above all things, we must . . . be very industrious, so that we can get ahead when we grow up. Good-for-nothings aren't needed any more. . . . Those who . . . study hard will find that later on, by working industriously, they can be used in the reconstruction of Germany" (p. 51). The egocentric desire to "get ahead" is always controlled and rationalized by the belief that getting ahead means glory to Germany.

Children are the hope of the Future, and they are often told that Germany will be rebuilt only through their efforts. But because the future is so uncertain, parents must supervise, plan, and direct. Hence due to this particular future anxiety, Doing must be directed and the only way for the parent to make sure that his child will always be guided by parental injunctions is to see that they are internalized and given the status of absolute commands. Children are expected to "do" but only under parental guidance and only if the action can be construed to be fulfillment of an obligation; later, as an adult, he can "do," rebuild Germany, and prosper only under the guidance of a Führer. In our story of the quarrel among the parts of the body, we saw that each part is to strive and to work hard, but this must be under the direction of the heart. The contrast which Curtius (1932) has made between the Germans and the French is indicative of the essential value placed by Germans on Doing: "We Germans tend to value a man according to his achievement . . . The Frenchman estimates people less by their achievement than by what they are" (pp.11-12). But the German Doing differs from the American in that early independence is not encouraged and the Doing need always be seen in the context of the fulfillment of an obligation.

The German view of Human Nature seems to be that it contains potentialities for good or evil, but there is a tendency to assume that this potential evil energy can readily become kinetic. A striking example of this is of course the story of the lie and the immediate exaggeration and magnification of this childish act into a potential source of grave danger. The similarity to the following story taken from Abbott (1834), a pre-Civil War American children's book, is striking: the story is about a girl who had disobeyed her mother in chasing a butterfly on the way to school; when asked why she is late she says her mother needed her at home. "Thus she advanced rapidly in crime . . . Having thus become a truant and a deceiver she was prepared for any crime . . . The House of Correction became her ignominious home. And there she is now guilty and weakened and her poor mother in her solitary dwelling, is weeping . . . You see how very unhappy you can make your parents. After all they have done for you, in taking care of you when an infant, in watching over you when sick, in giving you clothes to wear, and food to eat, can you be so ungrateful as to make them unhappy" (pp. 11-12). The similarities are striking: emphasis on the danger of the superego becoming lax, children can make their parents unhappy, and they have an *obligation* not to do so since parents sacrifice so much for them.

Children are potentially sadistic and evil; in one of our stories a woman finds a kitten and her children wish to care for it; but "the kind woman did not give it to them, fearing they might hurt it. . . ." The contrast to present-day American children who are frequently given pets of their own is an interesting one. Domestic animals play a strange role in these stories: they appear in three others and are always associated with aggression. In one we have already mentioned, the butcher is cruel to his wounded dog and does not allow him into an empty wagon; in another the aggression of the child is projected onto a playful dog. Peter is flying his kite and is deriving pleasure from teasing the dog: "Peter nearly bursts with laughter; for whenever the dog wants to get hold of the tail, the kite flies high up. And the more the dog barks and rages, the more it amuses Peter." When the dog gets his revenge, however, for this sadistic teasing, by tearing up the kite, the father acts as though the dog were the original aggressor: "We shall . . . let it fly in the park. No *bad* dog will be able to get it there." In another story a judge is forced to reprimand a Duke for the cruel neglect of his horse: "Are you not ashamed, Duke, to let this horse, which has served you faithfully for so many years, run around thus starved?"

In addition, there seems to be an explicit idea that tolerance is not natural and must be taught; in no other culture do we have this preoccupation with the potential hostility of those who belong toward those who do not. Hence one story begins: "At one time, many foreign refugees entered our country. Once such a refugee had to remain behind in a nearby village, because his two sick children could not continue to go in the cold." This father attempts to get wood from a local peasant: "This is a foreign bird," thinks the peasant, "and looks pretty much frozen; I shall make him pay." In the end the law has to cope with the problem and the peasant is fined by a judge. In the story of the chafer and the grub the chafer says: "You'll get to the light without any effort, [i.e., you will succeed] if you are of the right *kind*." And in the story of the elephant, when the baby elephant proves it has something valuable to offer the father adequately sums up the moral: "Bobo has taught us something we shall not want to forget. 'In the big world there is room for everyone of us.' " It is interesting to note also that there are only three stories in which animals are given a family and made human: two of these stories are the chafer and the elephant ones. The need for distantiation is significant: the story of the "foreigner" is made distant in time, the other two are shifted to the animal world.

Rodnick (1948) points out that one German gynecologist has estimated that a great many middle-class husbands are impotent, while their wives are frigid. Also, "the German wife theoretically is not supposed to enjoy sexual relations but to find the real satisfactions of marriage in motherhood and in her children" (p. 112). The resemblance to the asexual Madonna, who fulfills herself with the infant but never with a man, is striking. Emotions are seen to be not quite safe; restraint is much more fitting. In Schaffner's (1949) study of attitudes toward open display of maternal affection, the general impression is that Germans are not quite comfortable in the face of emotion: "unpleasant to witness," "children have aversion to physical tenderness," "not to be encouraged to excess," "analogies in animal world," "should be held back," "an animal instinct," "should be restrained" (p. 26). It seems most probable that the woman who receives no sexual gratification from her husband is inclined to invest all libidinal energy in her son; the father cannot tolerate this because it threatens his supremacy and reactivates his own oedipal strivings; hence sexuality and display of affection are viewed as volatile and dangerous and must be strongly held under control. The son who is highly gratified by the mother might take the father's place; the German father accustomed to long years of submission to his own father and hence not quite sure of his own masculinity cannot tolerate this threatened displacement. Like his son, he was unable to get too close to his mother and now he will not tolerate a second rival for a woman's esteem.

The story of the chafer and the grub seems to be, in the last analysis, an expression and fulfillment of the death wish to the father. The distantiation is great: both are insects and they are only "relatives" not father and son. However, the chafer is elderly and already accomplished, the grub is young, naïve, and full of admiration: " 'You are a great fellow!' said the grub with a look of unconcealed admiration." The chafer is able to fly [sexual intercourse] and taunts the grub with " 'Can you do that too?' No, that he couldn't do, the grub had to admit, and his mouth was watering. Yet he felt a little offended at the chafer." The "father" has no right to make his "son" feel so inadequate. The "son" tries hard to think of a disadvantage the "father" might have; his hostility is manifest: "Don't you have any enemies?" The "son" is to receive no satisfaction though and right away he is threatened with retaliation for his hostile question because the answer makes the "father" seem even more powerful: ". . . the danger only increases the charm, I sat down on the neck of a young girl so that she screamed, and I flew into the middle of the judge's face so that he got frightened." The "son" is punished for his hostility, his sense of his own inadequacy has increased: "The grub looked respectfully at the chafer. He flew right into the face of the judge! But he himself trembled whenever he saw even a young goose." The "son's" position is hopeless; he fears the "father" and this dangerous and amazing being is even able to defy authority (the judge). The "father" leaves and "the grub looked after him with sad eyes. The years had yet to pass before he could be as far as the chafer. He *crept* sadly into the ground." The "son" cannot "fly," he has a long time to wait before he can be as potent and daring as the "father." This frustrating story ends, however, with the desired wish fulfillment. The chafer has been stepped on. "Deeply startled, the young grub stood beside the dead body of the once so *envied* chafer and he could not understand . . . why he had died." Already the death wish which has become gratified is a threat; it must be denied: the "son" cannot understand *why* the "father" had died, and hence refuses responsibility for the death.

German sexual taboos are not nearly as great as the Irish; experimentation is encouraged during adolescence. Most boys go to prostitutes or sleep with their steady girl friends. This lack of puritanism is reflected in our stories since the German ones have an equal proportion of mixed and evil human nature, whereas the Irish overwhelmingly present human nature as evil. However, the particular patterning of relations in the German family is such that emotions and sexuality are seen to be much safer outside the family; within the family restraint is safer and more fitting. The Irish code affords no outlet for volatile emotions, no opportunity for sexual gratification; the German code offers Doing as a substitute and prostitution as gratification.

We were able to score only eleven of our stories on the Relation to Nature orientation: of these, seven present man as able to master Nature. The Germans, like the Americans, have an exploitive attitude toward Nature; German science is oriented toward this for "science is power." In one of our stories an old man uses a stone to outwit a cook and to trick her into giving him some food; the stone is his chief means of attaining his goal. This is in striking contrast to the French story we discussed where an old man sees some stones which lead him to reflect on the wonder of the universe.

Our analysis of the German stories has presented us with several new aspects of the relationship between values and modal conscience. First of all we have seen that the German Past deeply influences a Future about which there is some anxiety; we would like to suggest then that there is a vital difference between "Future optimism" and "Future hope with anxiety." Although the Future orientation in general seems to lead to a tendency to conform to standards, we feel that anxiety about a future for which there are great hopes would tend to incline parents toward more rigid socialization, would bring out the need to see well internalized in their children the principles which the parents feel to be vital for future success and safety.

Furthermore, the near equal emphasis on Individualism and Lineality has suggested to us that the German first-order orientation is most probably Individualism, but Individualism which is well controlled by the sense of obligations to others that is so strongly emphasized in the home. The German attitude in this sphere is somewhat like this: men are fairly selfish beings who will overrun each other if their potential to work together is destroyed by lack of a leader. In other words, a group of such individualists can act in unison only if there is a strong leader who will aid them, and who will in turn demand their respect and obedience. These individualists have few collateral ties to each other; rather, each is related to and derives strength from the leader. He initiates interaction for them and guides them; only in this way is their individualism of use. This is quite different from the French concept of individuality and acting in unison with no one, and the American brand of individualism where interaction with the collateral peer group is much more important than interaction with the leader. There is also a subtle difference from the Irish among whom the individual is no one apart from his nuclear or extended family; the German individual is a definite someone apart from his paternal leadership, but a dangerous someone.

The German Doing orientation affords the individual an opportunity to release some of the tensions which arise from the tendency to view human nature as evil. The Irish Being orientation in combination with the view that man is evil only fosters further repression and conviction about the essential badness of man. Furthermore, the German because he has individualistic status can seek sexual gratification outside the home; the Irishman who has no status outside of the family has no such opportunity. The German since he has individualistic status can also express his aggression outside of the family; the Irishman is always within the confines of his family and hence he is more likely to turn his aggression inward: alcoholism. It is further possible that since the German can act outside of his family there is a greater need to impress upon him the absolute importance of his obligations to others. Hence, there is a greater element of compulsion to his obligations, so that if ever they are weakened we might expect that his aggression toward others will be greater than in the Irish case. There is some evidence for this hypothesis that the nature of German obligations to others is more rigid and more of an imposition on the individual than the Irish. German children are taught from infancy to be dutiful, obedient, and grateful, whereas Irish children are made little aware of duty until they are about seven.

We have seen then that our predictions about the relations between values and the authoritarian modal conscience have in part been verified and somewhat modified. It is important to note also that the value profiles of the Irish and the Germans in no way fit the predictions for any other conscience type, as they were given at the end of Section III. The picture is something like that shown in the following table.

Most probably we have here two forms of the authoritarian modal conscience. We have tried briefly to sketch some of the differences in Irish and German authoritarianism. We are aware, for instance, that the aggression of the Irish must be turned inward in the form of alcoholism, because the individual has no existence which is separate from the family, whereas the German is more in a position to externalize his aggression since his sphere of influence extends outside the confines of the family unit. Furthermore, these differences in the authoritarian conscience most probably affect the ego differently. We have suggested that the Irish combination of Being and Evil, the tension between the id and the superego, might greatly weaken the ego. This does not seem to be the case among the Germans; most psychoanalytic studies suggest a split rather than weakness in the German ego. These

TABLE 8

The German and Irish Forms of Authoritarianism

Predictions of Value Combinations for the Authoritarian Conscience	GERMAN			IRISH	
	Predicted First-Order Greater Than Second	Chi-Square	Qualification of the Non-significance of the Chi-Square	Predicted First-Order Greater Than Second	Chi-Square
1. Future & Lineality (1st or 2nd)	Future > Past; Lin.[2] > Coll.[3]	0; 7.3*	Future hope with anxiety Stress on Lin. rather than on Coll.		
2. Past & Doing	Past > Future; Doing > Being	0; 0.05	Emphasis on Past Glory. Doing without stress on independence, Lineal control.		
3. Individualism[1] & Lineality[2]	Indiv.[1] > Lin.[2]; Lin.[2] > Coll.[3]	0; 7.33*	Probably the case, but not verifiable from our data.		
4. Lineality (1st or 2nd) & Doing	Lin.[2] > Coll.[3]; Doing > Being	7.33*; 0.05	Stress on Lineality rather than on Coll. Doing without independence, Lineal control.		
5. Evil Human Nature				Evil > Mixed	5.5*
6. Lineality & Evil Human Nature				Lin. > Coll.; Evil > Mixed	1.4; 5.5*
7. Being & Evil Human Nature				Being > Doing; Evil > Mixed	7.2*; 5.5*

* A Chi-square of 3.84 or more indicates significance at the .05 level.

very important differences in ego structure and their relation to superego structure must be left until further study can be done. For the present we wish rather to point out that however great the differences between Irish and German modal personality, the fact remains that both are authoritarian and that neither of their value profiles is in any way such that it might lead to any other conscience structure.

Summary

Three problems have been raised during the course of this work: (1) the need for further research on superego theory; (2) the significance of the concept of modal conscience; and (3) the possibility of the relation between values and modal conscience. In recent years there has been much attention given to ego functioning: work has been done on the cognitive functions, the defenses, and the stages of ego growth.[7] Our knowledge of superego structure and functioning is, however, still scanty. We have merely touched on the problem of differential causation and outcome, and the need for further research of a clinical nature is evident.

The second problem, more general in its application, is vital for our understanding of international problems and the nature of ethical systems and ideologies. The application of information obtained through a further understanding of conscience structure is not limited to the consideration of individual motivation, but can be of universal scope. To consider an application which is broad yet still contained by conceptual boundaries, we would suggest that efforts at international stabilization should be tempered by a consideration of the protagonist's modal conscience.

Toward the problem of the relationship between values and modal conscience, we have advanced some hypotheses and partially demonstrated their validity. It has been our contention that a relationship between these two variables does exist, and that knowledge of such relationship would be valuable in the national character field. Further study is needed in three realms: (1) the use of other materials in deriving the value profile of a culture, (2) the actual testing of samples of the adult population in these countries for their conscience orientation, and (3) the study of cultures which present other value profiles, different social structures, and those which are not highly industrialized and organized into modern nation states.

[7] See Anna Freud (1936), Erik Erikson (1950), and Hartmann (1950).

BIBLIOGRAPHY

Abbott, J. (1834), *The Child at Home*. Boston: Cocker & Brewster.

Adorno, T. W. et al. (1950), *The Authoritarian Personality*. New York: Harper.

Arensberg, C. M. & Kimball, S. T. (1948), *Family and Community in Ireland*. Cambridge, Mass.: Harvard University Press.

Asch, S. E. (1952), Effects of Group Pressures upon the Modification and Distortion of Judgments. In: *Readings in Social Psychology*, ed. G. E. Swanson, T. M. Newcomb, & E. L. Hartley. New York: Holt.

Bateson, G. (1948), Some Systematic Approaches to the Study of Culture and Personality. In: *Personal Character and Cultural Milieu*, ed. D.G. Haring. Syracuse, N.Y.: Syracuse University Press.

Bettelheim, B. (1955), *Truants from Life*. Glencoe, Ill.: Free Press.

Brogan, D. (1944), *The American Character*. New York: Knopf.

Bychowski, G. (1949), *Dictators and Disciples: From Caesar to Stalin*. New York: International Universities Press.

Child, I. L., Potter, E. H., & Levine, E. M. (1954), Children's Textbooks and Personality Development. In: *Readings in Child Psychology*, ed. W. E. Martin & G. B. Stendler. New York: Harcourt Brace.

Curtius, E. R. (1932), *The Civilization of France*. New York: Macmillan.

De Tocqueville, A. (1945), *Democracy in America*. New York: Knopf.

Duncan, M. (1852), *America As I Found It*. New York: Carter.

Erikson, E. H. (1950), *Childhood and Society*. New York: W. W. Norton.

Fleming, S. (1933), *Children and Puritanism*. New Haven: Yale University Press.

Flugel, J. C. (1945), *Man, Morals, and Society*. New York: International Universities Press.

Freud, A. (1936), *The Ego and the Mechanisms of Defense*. New York: International Universities Press, 1946.

Freud, S. (1905), Three Contributions to the Theory of Sex. *The Basic Writings of Sigmund Freud*. New York: Modern Library, 1938.

―― (1917), Mourning and Melancholia. *Collected Papers, 4*:152-170. London: Hogarth Press, 1949.

―― (1920), *Beyond the Pleasure Principle*. London: Hogarth Press, 1922.

―― (1923), *The Ego and the Id*. London: Hogarth Press, 1940.

―― (1926), *The Problem of Anxiety*. New York: W. W. Norton, 1946.

Fromm, E. (1941), *Escape From Freedom*. New York: Farrar & Rinehart.

―― (1944), Individual and Social Origins of Neurosis. In: *Personality in Nature, Society, and Culture*, ed. C. Kluckhohn & H. Murray. New York: Knopf, 1953.

―― (1947), *Man For Himself*. New York: Rinehart.

Gorer, G. (1948), *The American People*. New York: W. W. Norton.

―― (1953), National Character: Theory and Practice. In: *The Study of Culture at a Distance*, ed. M. Mead & R. Métraux. Chicago: University of Chicago Press.

Hartmann, H. (1950), Comments on the Psychoanalytic Theory of the Ego. *The Psychoanalytic Study of the Child, 5*:74. New York: International Universities Press.

Inkeles, A. (1955), Social Change and Social Character: The Role of Parental Mediation. *Social Forces, 2*:12-24.

—— & Levinson, D. J. (1954), National Character: The Study of Modal Personality and Sociocultural Systems. In: *Handbook of Social Psychology*, ed. G. Lindzey. Cambridge, Mass.: Addison-Wesley Pub. Co.

Kiefer, M. (1948), *American Children Through Their Books*. Philadelphia: University of Pennsylvania Press.

Kluckhohn, C. (1951), Values and Value Orientations. In: *Toward a General Theory of Action*, ed. T. Parsons & E. Shils. Cambridge, Mass.: Harvard University Press.

Kluckhohn, F. (1950), Dominant and Variant Value Orientations. In: *Personality in Nature, Society, and Culture*, ed. C. Kluckhohn, H. Murray, & D. Schneider. New York: Knopf, 1956.

—— (1952), *The American Family: Past and Present*. Chicago: Delphian Society.

Leites, N. & Wolfenstein, M. (1950), *Movies: A Psychological Study*. Glencoe, Ill.: Free Press.

Levin, H., Sears, R. R., & Maccoby, E. E. (1957), *Patterns of Child Rearing*. New York: Row, Person.

Lewin, K. (1936), Some Socio-Psychological Differences Between the United States and Germany. *Character and Personality, 4*:265-293.

—— (1948), *Resolving Social Conflicts*. New York: Harper.

Maurois, A. (1936), *En Amérique*. New York: American Book Co.

McClelland, D. (1951), *Personality*. New York: Sloane.

—— (1953), *The Achievement Motive*. New York: Appleton.

—— (1955), *Studies in Motivation*. New York: Appleton.

McCranahan, D. V. (1946), A Comparison of Social Attitudes Among American and German Youth. *J. Abn. Soc. Psychol., 41*:245-297.

Mead, M. (1942), *And Keep Your Powder Dry*. New York: Morrow.

—— (1953), National Character. In: *Anthropology Today*, ed. A. L. Kroeber. Chicago: University of Chicago Press.

—— & Métraux, R. (1953), *The Study of Culture at a Distance*. Chicago: University of Chicago Press.

—— & —— (1954), *Themes in French Culture*. Hoover Institute and Library on War, Rev., and Peace, Stanford University, April, 1954. Series D: Comm. s., No. 1.

—— & Wolfenstein, M. (1955), *Childhood in Contemporary Cultures*. Chicago: University of Chicago Press.

O'Casey, S. (1958), *Mirror in My House*. New York: Macmillan.

Piaget, J. (1932), *The Moral Judgment of the Child*. New York: Harcourt Brace.

Reiwald, P. (1950), *Society and Its Criminals*. New York: International Universities Press.

Riesman, D. (1955), *The Lonely Crowd*. New York: Doubleday Anchor Books.

Robinson, H. M. (1950), *The Cardinal*. New York: Simon & Schuster.

Rodnick, D. (1948), *Post-War Germans*. New Haven: Yale University Press.

Schaefer, B. (1954), Cross-Cultural Experiments on Threat and Rejection. *Human Relations, 7*:403-440.

Schaffner, B. H. (1949), *Fatherland: A Study of Authoritarianism in the German Family*. New York: Columbia University Press.

Siegfried, A. (1940), *France: A Study in Nationality*. New Haven: Yale University Press.

—— (1952), *The Character of Peoples*. Oxford: Alden Press.

Vogt, E. Z. (1955), *Modern Homesteaders*. Cambridge, Mass.: Harvard University Press.

Weber, M. (1930), *The Protestant Ethic and the Spirit of Capitalism*. New York: Scribners.

Whyte, W. (1956), *The Organization Man*. New York: Simon & Schuster.

Wylie, L. (1957), *Village in the Vaucluse*. Cambridge, Mass.: Harvard University Press.

ETHNOPSYCHIATRY

PRIMITIVE THERAPY
A Cross-Cultural Study of the
Relationship between Child Training and
Therapeutic Practices Related to Illness

ARI KIEV, M.D.

Man in relation to other beings is unique in the sense that he is born into ongoing social systems whose general characteristics have been historically determined and to which he must adapt. Man not only adapts to his social group but actively participates in creating the conditions to which he must adapt. This adaptation of man to the prevailing patterns of his society and his development therein may be studied in several ways. One approach is to consider man as a product of his culture, as Mead (1928) has done in demonstrating how Samoan adolescent patterns are the direct outcome of the social and institutional forces present. In contrast to this is the view that certain aspects of culture are products of certain specific personality tendencies. Thus, for example, Benedict (1934) writes of some American Indians as being "passionately Dionysian" and describes certain institutionalized practices of self-abandonment as the product of these tendencies.

The present study has its origins in a third approach to the problem, that of investigating the reciprocal relationships of man and culture. In this approach, personality is seen as a link between two aspects of culture. Using this approach in his work on the Tanala and the Marquesans, Kardiner (1939, 1945) outlined his concept of basic personality structure. He considered certain primary institutions such as child-training techniques as the source of basic personality patterns common to all members of a society. These patterns then have important effects on what he calls secondary institutions such as religious and belief systems. Thus among the Tanala severe childhood discipline is seen to create certain need dispositions in the people which in turn influence the conceptualization of good and evil in the mythological and religious systems. This ontogenetic approach has its origins in psychoanalytic theory. As Erikson (1950) has pointed out:

The author is indebted to Dr. John W. M. Whiting of Harvard University for his advice and guidance in the preparation of this paper.

The oral stages then form in the infant the springs of the basic sense of trust and the basic sense of evil, which remains the source of primal anxiety and of primal hope throughout life . . . This point in an individual's early history is the origin of an evil dividedness where anger against the gnawing teeth and anger against the withdrawing mother and anger with one's impotent anger all lead to a forceful experience of sadistic and masochistic confusion leaving the general impression that once upon a time one destroyed one's unity with a maternal matrix. This is the origin of evil [p. 75].

Referring to the later development of character traits based on early childhood experiences, Erikson has pointed to the close relationship between the virtue of generosity among the Sioux Indians and its early foundation in the privilege of enjoying the nourishment and the reassurance emanating from unlimited breast feeding. In his observations Erikson is referring not simply to irreversible character traits which are the direct adult consequences of specific childhood experiences. Rather he is referring to a general system of goals and values formulated through child-training systems. These values persist from early childhood because they have become an essential part of the individual's sense of identity. In addition they persist because they work economically, psychologically, and spiritually, and are imbedded in a system of continued economic and cultural syntheses and in this way are related to the observed adult characteristics. As Hartmann, Kris, and Loewenstein (1951) have written:

We assume that in each environment certain predominant pathways of discharge, sublimation, etc., are more or less accessible, and therefore certain pathways of behavior facilitated and others impeded [p. 20].

The biological immaturity of the newborn child is the initial condition of human life. If the child is to survive certain primary or biological drives such as hunger and thirst, he must be cared for by an outside agency. Tension built up by various drives must be reduced. In 1895 Freud wrote:

This path of discharge thus acquires an extremely important secondary function—viz. of bringing about an understanding with other people; and the original helplessness of human beings is thus the primal source of all moral motives [p. 379].

This initial dependency of the child, which in a sense constitutes the beginning of communication and object relations, would seem to involve two factors—nurturance and deprivation. In so far as the primary drives are satisfied through parental care the child receives the necessary nurturance.

However, since the parents cannot be immediately available at all times, a certain degree of physiological tension is inevitable. The period between drive tension and drive satisfaction may be considered as a time of deprivation or frustration. Given a state of frustration, the child performs certain responses, which gradually become specific depending on which are more successful in gaining satisfaction of the primary drives. As Anna Freud (1936) has pointed out:

> The greater the importance of the outside world as a source of pleasure and interest, the more opportunity is there to experience pain from that quarter . . . in this period of immaturity and dependence the ego, besides making efforts to master instinctual stimuli, endeavors in all kinds of ways to defend itself against the objective pain and dangers which menace it [p. 74].

All behavior is learned by reinforcement. Those responses which in a given situation are accompanied by satisfaction to the child will in time become more strongly associated with the situation and hence will in the future be more likely to recur when the situation recurs. These responses are instrumental as performance of them brings about satisfaction or reduction of the drive. Such responses as crying, biting, and kicking may in a state of frustration enable the child to secure the nurturant behavior of the mother. When these responses are modified by physical maturation and learning experience one can distinguish between such patterns as dependence or "attention-seeking" behavior and aggressive or "intent-to-injure" behavior. These instrumental responses are reinforced in the sense that they permit the child to control his environment, thus leading to a satisfaction of his needs. As Spitz (1957) has shown, both the motor patterns involved and the need-gratificatory function are the product of inherited maturational processes. The development of these different patterns depends on the nature of interpersonal relations and the individual child's personal history. Developing this theme in terms of human communication and the development of the concept of self he has written:

> The use of head-shaking and head-nodding as semantic signals is widespread but not universal. What is universal is the road that leads to their development, even if the gesture which eventually emerges is different. Starting with the inborn motor patterns of rooting in the neonate, who is not conscious and for whom the "No" is nonexistent, this road leads ultimately to the concept of negation and to the conscious use of the semantic "No" for communication. This is the road to the humanization of man [p. 150].

Up to a certain point the child is in a somewhat commanding position, enabled by the performance of these responses to gain satisfaction of his primary drives. But from the vantage point of society, the initial condition of dependency is not to be tolerated. The child must outgrow this stage and learn to fulfill certain, more mature roles. Varying with the culture, environment, parents, and child, the time comes when cultural demands are mediated to the child. Certain stages of development and organ maturation offer themselves as suitable pivots for the instillation of societal demands. As Erikson (1950) has so pointedly written:

> There are stages . . . which are marked by such unavoidable development of rage and anger that mutual regulation by complementary behavior cannot be the pattern for meeting them. The rages of teething, the tantrums of muscular and anal impotence, the failures of falling, etc.—all are situations in which the intensity of the impulse leads to its own defeat. Parents and cultures use just these infantile encounters with inner gremlins for the reinforcement of their outer demands [p. 75].

In addition, certain instrumental responses previously successful must be altered for they are not desirable in terms of society. Aggression and dependent behavior present two such sets of responses which must be modified to fit the needs of the society. To secure the desired patterns parents generally institute a system of rewards and punishments, these being applied in varying degrees according to the importance of the demands. The reward-punishment system is analogous to the original nurturance-deprivation system. Parental reward for desirable behavior serves to reinforce certain responses. Punishment acts as a frustration serving to reduce undesirable behavior. The affective charge of frustration is such as to ensure permanent remembrance of the punishing situation. Dollard et al. (1939) have considered punishment as a stimulus adequate to motivate behavior. They state:

> When as the result of learning, previously neutral cues gain the capacity to play the same functional role in the learning and perceiving of new responses as do primary drives such as hunger and thirst, these cues are said to have learned drive value [p. 78].

Punishment or anticipation of punishment are capable of eliciting a tension state in the child which may be called anxiety, a feeling characterized by general unpleasantness, apprehensiveness, and physiological excitation. This anxiety, which is the learned drive, then serves to motivate the child to perform such behavior as will reduce the state of tension. Through repeated punishments the child learns to anticipate the painful consequences of performing the prohibited act. The most anxiety-reducing or anxiety-avoiding behavior would seem to be the culturally approved in so far as the additional reinforcing factor of parental approval or reward may increase the value of inhibiting the undesirable responses. For example, in describing the inhibition of aggressive behavior, Dollard et al. (1939) have said:

> There are two general methods for inhibiting aggression; one is to put the aggressive response into a response sequence that leads to non-reward. "If you strike your sister, you can't have any dessert." This mode of treating aggression is often expressed as withdrawal of "love" or "privilege." The other mode of dealing with the child's aggressive responses is to produce an inhibition of the aggressiveness by punishment. The theme here is: "If you strike your little sister, I will strike you" [p. 79].

The painful anxiety of the punishment becomes in time associated with the prohibited behavior, so that the performance of the undesirable behavior serves as a cue in later situations to elicit the unpleasant anxiety. In turn, this anxiety as an acquired drive will motivate the behavior which has proved to be rewarding or anxiety reducing. If a response is followed by reinforcement, the connections between the situational stimuli and this response are strengthened, so that the next time when the same drive and cues are present this response is more likely to occur. The propensity to perform certain rewarding responses in certain situations points to the presence of response potentials or habits in the personality of the individual.

That punishment is not completely a negative conditioned stimulus or negative reinforcement is not immediately apparent to the casual observer. However, psychoanalytic investigation has pointed to the addition of certain elemental concepts in viewing the punishment-reward situation. As Freud (1919) points out, the fantasy of a "child is being beaten" can be charged with a high degree of pleasure and may have its issue in an act of pleasurable autoerotic gratification. Emphasizing the intermediate phase of beating fantasies, Freud pointed out that in this case the fantasy of being beaten by the father was a direct expression of the sense of guilt, which had replaced the love for father. "My father loves me" was meant in a genital sense; owing to regression it turned into "My father is beating me." Thus:

> This being beaten is now a meeting-place between the sense of guilt and sexual love. *It is not only the punishment for the forbidden genital relation, but also the regressive substitute for it,* and from this

latter source it derives the libidinal excitation which is from this time
forward attached to it, and which finds its outlet in onanistic acts.
Here for the first time we have the essence of masochism [p. 184].

We are interested in this paper in providing evidence in support of
learning theory which stresses the importance of early life experiences on
the development of personality. Psychoanalytic theory has stressed the importance of early childhood experience in developing motivational patterns
which persist throughout life, and has advanced much clinical evidence for
this. It is our belief that early childhood experience exerts a major influence
on the development of personality. We are assuming this ontogenetic position and in the absence of evidence dealing directly with personality have
characterized personality processes in terms of their socialization antecedents.
Thus we expect that certain socialization experiences will lead to certain
types of response patterns in individuals which will be reflected in adult
behavior systems such as therapeutic practices.

Until recent times psychoanalytic theory has been predominantly a conflict psychology to the extent that the ego was seen to grow out of conflict
situations. However, we shall not restrict ourselves solely to the sphere of
conflict situations but shall follow the approach stressed by Hartmann, who
has stated that adaptation involves processes pertaining to the conflict-free
sphere as well. The early childhood training period aims primarily at adaptation and particularly at socialization of the child. Hartmann further (1939)
points out:

> But education actually goes beyond these aims and also instills certain
> ideals, which are usually, at least in part, fixed by tradition, but which
> may also become the means to change society. The adoption of pre-
> scribed forms and goals of behavior can, and certainly often does,
> facilitate adaptation, but it can also obstruct it [p. 82]. The social
> norms which the child adopts only partly coincide with the rewards
> and punishments he will actually receive from society in later life.
> Nevertheless, these value hierarchies may serve as switching-stations
> or crystallization points of human behavior; we have seen that action
> presupposes not only rational regulation but also goals set by the hier-
> archies of values [p. 76].

The application of these ideas to our study is further facilitated by
Hartmann's concept of "change of function": a behavioral pattern originating in a certain situation in early life may come to serve an entirely
different function in a later situation. Hartmann (1939) states:

An attitude which arose originally in the service of defense against an instinctual drive may, in the course of time, become an independent structure, in which case the instinctual drive merely triggers this automatized apparatus . . . , but, as long as the automatization is not controverted, does not determine the details of its action [p. 26].

Our second assumption involves consideration of therapeutic practices as indices of adult personality. For primitive man, illness can indeed be a perplexing situation, sometimes approaching catastrophic proportions. Given the threat to his existence and relative inability to cope with his environment, it seems likely that the primitive would be subject to anxieties more frequent and of greater magnitude than contemporary Western man. In addition, we should expect that the diffuse states of tension caused by a loss of regulation and a consequent upset in libidinal and aggressive controls would magnify and sometimes even create the illusion of an outer danger. Owing to his marked anxiety or fear the primitive would seem to be unable accurately to evaluate and objectify the external forces of disease. Accordingly we should expect primitive medicine to be more subject to the influence of personality factors than to the immediate realities of the illness situation. It is for this reason that we have utilized therapeutic practices as a source of projective evidence of basic personality patterns. The rationale for doing this is essentially the same as that of such clinical projective tests as the Rorschach and Thematic Apperception Tests. Here therapeutic practices are considered to reflect the anxieties and needs of the basic personality patterns of the primitive cultures being studied. As Whiting and Child (1953) have pointed out:

These customs are for the most part magical and unrealistic. By and large the beliefs with which we will be concerned do not accord with theories scientifically established by modern medicine and the therapeutic practices although they may be effective as psychotherapy generally do not have the physiological effects which are produced today by surgery or by the use of antiseptics and medicine. The magic medical theories and practices of primitive societies seem much more likely to be retained because of their compatibility with personality variables than because of their practical physiological utility [p. 120].

For our final theoretical assumption we turn to psychoanalytic theory which points to the relationship between the early childhood situation and the mastery of the environmental situation provoked by the forces of disease and by the fears generated within man himself. As we have seen, culture is mediated through the parents to the child by the use of a variety of child-training techniques which focus on certain instinctual bodily functions.

Around these drives are developed a variety of values and attitudes depending on the culture's emphasis. It is from these simple situations that man develops his ways of reacting to subsequent situations, real or imagined. As Erikson (1950) has written:

> Since his earlier sense of reality was learned by the painful testing of inner and outer goodnesses and badnesses man remains ready to expect from some enemy force or event in the outer world that which in fact endangers him from within [p. 362].

The first major attempt to employ therapeutic practices as indices of adult personality was made by Whiting and Child (1953). They assumed that in so far as therapeutic measures were intended to provide relief, they would be related to systems of behavior in childhood which were primarily areas of gratification. They predicted that strong and consistent gratification of a particular behavior system in childhood would give certain responses acquired reward value and that subsequent performance of them in therapeutic settings would provide security and pleasure. They found no significant evidence confirming this hypothesis.

Several alternative notions were then investigated. First, it was thought that therapeutic practices might be related to explanations of illness. If a society believed that illness was produced by ingestion of poisonous foods, it might prescribe vomiting as a means of purification. Eleven such possibilities were tested. All were in the predicted direction. Only two, however, were in the predicted direction and significantly related too. It was then considered that therapeutic practices might be direct outcomes of socialization anxieties in particular behavior systems. They considered therapeutic practices which indicated that the individuals were attempting to reduce anxieties in certain behavioral areas by undoing or by avoiding responses in that system. Out of ten relationships eight were in a positive direction, four of these eight being significant at the 5 per cent level of confidence. This evidence, although somewhat tentative, suggests that early anxieties may indeed be related to therapeutic practices.

The present study continues the investigation of therapeutic practices as a source of projective evidence for the study of personality. We have studied unexamined data, collected by Whiting and Child, dealing with the performance of certain therapeutic practices. These data included summaries of all therapeutic techniques employed in seventy-five primitive societies, determined from the existing literature and the Human Relations Area Files, Inc. We were interested (1) in obtaining evidence demonstrating the influence of early childhood experience on the development of adult personality patterns, and (2) in the relationship of these patterns to certain medical practices. The theoretical concept used in making a cross-cultural test of these hypotheses is Kardiner's concept of basic personality structure. From this concept we derived our third major assumption, namely, that the system of socialization techniques is related to the system of therapeutic techniques through a common personality pattern. Thus, child-training practices create certain basic patterns in personality which in turn influence the apparently unrelated behavior area of medical therapy. The patterns in the basic personality structure are accordingly viewed as intervening variables, unseen but functional in the sense that they permit us to make predictions about the relationship between child-training practices and therapeutic practices.

The feasibility of this approach has been attested to in other investigations. Friedman (1950) has presented evidence demonstrating the relationship of early independence training to the amount of need achievement present in the Coyote myths of several Indian tribes. Barry (1957) has produced evidence indicating the relationship of socialization anxiety to the complexity of design of primitive art. McAllester (1941) has shown that the use of water as a disciplinary agent in childhood was related to an institutionalized fear of water as was manifested in certain eating habits. Muensterberger (1955) similarly has pointed to the relationship between separation anxiety, fear of object loss, and lack of maternal care among the Mentaweians of remote Indonesia and certain myths of these people which deal with the same themes concerning the child's anxiety of being abandoned, starved, or roughly treated in a symbolic way. He concludes that an extremely traumatic experience of early infancy is retold in mythological form and reacted to in the ritual doctrine of these people.

METHODOLOGY

For the treatment of the material, the statistical-postulational method was used. Unlike the inductive method where general conclusions are drawn from examination of the data at hand, this approach involves the prediction from theory of certain relationships between the variables considered, prior to the actual testing of the evidence. Utilizing two by two contingency tables, we can compare the expected and observed association of variables in order to determine whether they are actually related. Thus if we postulate that a is related to b, we should expect to find that the societies high in a should be high in b, and conversely that societies low in a should be low in b. By means of the chi-square criterion we can then determine the relationship between the two variables and whether it is significant, i.e., what the probability is that the relationship found could have occurred by chance alone.

The scores for child-training practices were obtained from Whiting and Child. They have dealt with five systems of behavior: oral, anal, genital, dependence, and aggression. For each behavior system they have analyzed the conditions which would produce initial satisfaction of varying degrees, the age at which socialization begins, and the techniques of child training which would produce varying degrees of socialization anxiety. This measure of socialization anxiety refers to the total scores compiled dealing with those parental practices which are intended to establish inhibitory control of certain child responses by teaching the child to fear frustration and active punishment by the parents. There were four aspects of evidence which were considered in compiling these scores of socialization anxiety:

1. Brevity of the transition from freedom of indulgence of the initial habit to the requirement of complete acceptance of childhood or adult inhibitions. It was assumed that the briefer this transition, the stronger would be the anxiety required to achieve it.

2. The more severe the punishments used in imposing inhibiting control, the greater would be the strength of the subsequent anxiety.

3. The more frequently the child was punished for a given type of behavior, the greater would be the anxiety developed.

4. The severity of the emotional conflict actually produced in children in a given society by socialization in a particular system of behavior.

Judgments of the age of the beginning of socialization in a particular system of behavior were made by use of actual age estimates rather than by use of an arbitrary rating scale. In cases where the ethnographic literature did not clearly state these ages, the judges estimated them by making inferences from other portions of the literature and referring to age-developmental norms.

The scores for therapeutic practices were derived from the judges' reports which had not been analyzed by Whiting and Child. We felt that the amount of information was frequently inadequate for the testing of hypotheses. In many cases the judges' reports showed no rating for therapeutic practices. In these cases it was difficult to ascertain whether the practices were present or absent. One judge had rated the societies on a 1 to 6 scale as to the relative amount of information present in the literature and files pertaining to therapies. Only one society was given a rating of 6. Ten were given 5; twenty-seven were given 4; and thirty-seven were given 3 or lower including four zero cases. We decided to use only those societies with a score of four or more for the testing of our hypotheses. This division was somewhat arbitrary, but since it coincided with the median division, it provided us with a sample of thirty-eight societies which for the preliminary testing of certain hypotheses seemed an adequate amount.

In many of these thirty-eight societies the therapy scores to be tested were absent, making it difficult for us to determine quantitatively the degree of presence. We decided therefore to utilize the qualitative judgment of presence or absence in the testing of those variables which were scored inadequately. Fortunately in these cases the advantage of using quantitative measures has been somewhat achieved in that the divisions between presence and absence are close to equal, thus ensuring accurate comparisons.

The judges' reports presented us with data on several therapeutic practices which lent themselves quite readily to the testing of the general behavior theory outlined below. The performance of these therapeutic practices indicated certain instrumental responses most nearly corresponding to acquired drives learned in childhood. The range of responses to illness is enormous, varying with the severity of the sickness, the degree of technical competence, and the degree of emotional involvement. We elected to study four therapeutic techniques, the occurrence of which vary from one society to another.

Analysis of Therapeutic Practices Relating to Illness

Patient Activity

One crucial feature of serious illness situations is the patient's necessary reliance on others, whether parents, relatives or medical specialists. How the individual will respond to the circumstances of this dependency on others will vary with the motivational patterns present in the personality. We should expect that in different societies different patterns of response will develop in relation to this situation of dependency. Beatrice Whiting (1950), describing the formal setup between patient and doctor among the Paiutes, said:

> The Paiutes believe that only a doctor can diagnose and cure a major disease. Faced with the illness a person and his relatives depend upon these specialists. . . . If the pain continues for more than a day or two and increases in intensity or if there is high fever, delirium, unconsciousness or protracted vomiting, the individual sets a time and a place for the doctoring [p. 10].

It is clear from this account that among the Paiutes medical help is sought, and that doctoring plays a significant role in their community life.

This pattern contrasts sharply, however, with other societies. Evans-Pritchard (1937), reporting on Azande "leechcraft," writes:

When a Zande suffers from a mild ailment he doctors himself. There are always older men of his kin or vicinity who will tell him a suitable drug to take. If his ailment does not disappear he visits a witch doctor . . . But they do not like to send for a witch doctor unless sickness is diagnosed as serious because it is necessary to pay for his services. It is usually the presence of severe pain that persuades them to take that course . . . But plenty of people know of cures [p. 489].

This distinction between the Paiute and the Azande suggests that in one case the natural reaction is to call a doctor when ill, whereas in the other, the reaction is to treat oneself, seeking medical assistance only as a last resort to cure. We suspect that there are relative differences in the amount of patient motivation to depend on the assistance of a physician. Learning theory suggests that punishment for dependence behavior will lead to anxiety patterns which serving as acquired drives will, in dependence situations, motivate the individual to perform his own active responses as a means of allaying the anxiety created by dependence.

Several other investigations have gathered evidence along these same lines. Sears et al. (1953) have found that high maternal punitiveness not only reduces dependency behavior but produces generalized inhibition as well. Substantial correlations between independence behavior and punitiveness were also found. Spitz (1945) has reported that children raised in institutions where early mothering and affectionate nurturance were minimal developed apathetic, nondependent personalities in later childhood.

From these considerations we would predict that anxiety in the dependence system of behavior during socialization should be related to the relative amount of patient activity during illness. Thus societies which are high in dependence socialization anxiety should also be high in the relative amount of patient activity during illness; conversely, the societies low in dependence socialization anxiety should also be low in the relative amount of patient activity.

To test this hypothesis we needed a measure of the relative degree of patient activity. The data sheets presented us with scores for patient acts and doctor acts during therapy. From this we calculated the relative amount of patient activity by determining the percentage of patient acts to the total number of acts by patient and doctor. This percentage then is the relative amount of patient activity or independent activity, in therapy, reported by each judge. The index used for patient activity is the combined percentages of each judge. To calculate reliability we utilized a two by two contingency table and the following formula:

$$\% \text{ Agreement} = \frac{\text{No. of cases above and below the median agreed on by both judges}}{\text{Total number of cases}}$$

The per cent agreement of the judges was 72.

Our hypothesis that patient activity during illness should be related to dependence socialization anxiety is confirmed (Table 1). The chi-square value, however, is 3.35, which means that the result is significant at the 10 per cent level of confidence. In so far as the acceptable level of statistical findings is the 5 per cent level of confidence, we could not draw any definite conclusions from this result.

TABLE 1

RELATION BETWEEN PATIENT ACTIVITY DURING ILLNESS AND
DEPENDENCE SOCIALIZATION ANXIETY

	Societies below the median on dependence socialization anxiety		Societies above the median on dependence socialization anxiety	
Societies above the median on patient activity			1.05 Alor	15
			.95 Thonga	15
			.90 Kwoma	16
			.85 Azande	16
			.80 Navaho	15
	1.50 Chenchu	12	.75 Dusun	14
	.90 Lepcha	11	.73 Maori	15
	.90 Hopi	10	.70 Baiga	14
	.73 Chamorro	9	.66 Sanpoil	13
	.66 Slave	8	.63 Ifugao	13
	.50 Kurtachi	10	.50 Pukapukans	14
	.40 Witoto	12	.46 Chiricahua	14
Societies below the median on patient activity	.33 Palaung	11	.27 Rwala	16
	.24 Marshall	11	0 Lesu	15
	.20 Chagga	10	0 Malekula	14
	.16 Mauru	12		
	0 Teton	12		
	0 Ontong-Javanese	11		
	0 Yagua	10		

The name of each society is preceded by the value obtained for it on the index of patient activity, and followed by the value obtained for it on dependence socialization anxiety.

TABLE 2

RELATION BETWEEN PATIENT ACTIVITY DURING ILLNESS AND
ESTIMATED AGE AT ONSET OF INDEPENDENCE TRAINING

	Societies below the median on age at onset of independence training		Societies above the median on age at onset of independence training	
Societies above the median on patient activity	1.50 Chenchu	3.0		
	1.05 Alor	2.1		
	.95 Thonga	3.3		
	.90 Kwoma	2.8		
	.90 Hopi	2.7	.90 Lepcha	4.0
	.80 Navaho	2.2	.85 Azande	5.3
	.73 Maori	3.0	.75 Dusun	4.5
	.68 Kwakiutl	2.8	.73 Chamorro	3.7
Societies below the median on patient activity	.50 Pukapukans	2.1	.63 Ifugao	5.0
	0 Malekula	2.5	.50 Kurtachi	6.0
			.46 Chiricahua	4.0
			.20 Chagga	4.0
			0 Lesu	4.5
			0 Ontong-J.	4.0
			0 Teton	3.5

The name of each society is preceded by the value obtained for it on the index of patient activity, and followed by the estimated age at onset of independence training.

Sears has suggested that there is a curvilinear relation between the amount of frustration of a given drive and the occurrence of alternative instrumental activity for reducing it. This would mean that up to a point, punishment for dependence behavior would increase the strength of the drive for dependence on another. This then might account for the result obtained. To test a curvilinear relation requires trichotomization of the sample into three groups. Unfortunately the sample was too small to allow this.

Another source of support was available for testing. Due to the relative helplessness of the child at a young age it would seem that discipline should be a more effective measure in inducing desirable behavior at this point than at a time when the child is more able to cope with his environment. It would be expected that those societies which create anxieties in the dependence system of behavior would also be the ones which subject the child to early discipline or socialization in this particular system of behavior. To assure ourselves of the conclusiveness of the above finding we related our patient activity index to the age of onset of training in independence behavior. We hypothesized that early socialization of independence behavior should be directly related to the relative amount of patient activity.

Our result was found to be significant at the 5 per cent level of confidence. The argument might be posed that this result is not an independent finding, but is instead a consequence of the severity of socialization and our choice of samples. Whiting and Child (1953), however, have with forty-one societies shown that the correlation between age at beginning of training in independence and severity of socialization in the dependence system is only 0.11, a correlation which is not at all statistically significant. Thus we can conclude that our two results were independent of each other, and that we do have some evidence for the operation of dependence anxiety during illness. This result increases the reliability of the association of patient activity with dependence socialization anxiety.

Forcing the Agent of the Disease to Desist

Illness being painful, inconvenient, and often threatening to the total existence of the individual can rightfully be considered a frustrating experience. As such, we would expect that some degree of aggressive behavior would occur in reaction to illness and that this might be expressed in the therapeutic practices. Writing about Kwoma medical customs, J. Whiting (1941) observed:

> The Kwoma believe that all serious sickness is caused by sorcery . . . Whenever it is believed that a person is suffering from the result of sorcery the men of his hamlet immediately launch an anti-sorcery campaign . . . All the men of the subtribe, if they wish to be free of suspicion, visit the house of the sick person, pay their respects and drink water. Since a sorcerer cannot work his evil magic if he drinks water during the process, this is taken as proof of innocence . . . If the sick man does not show signs of recovery, some of his relatives will visit around the subtribe, going to the houses of those whom they suspect of sorcery and asking them to drink [p. 136].

As Whiting has noted, sorcery provides a means whereby persons can express their aggression against other members of society. The Kwoma, instead of resigning themselves to the forces of illness, invoke an institutionalized form of aggression to seek out the causative agent. Learning theory leads us to believe that the presence of this aggressive countersorcery therapy should vary from society to society depending on the relative degree of inhibition present with regard to the expression of aggression. We would expect that societies which employ "forcing the agent, believed to have caused the disease, to desist" as a therapeutic practice would also be the ones where there is relatively low aggression socialization anxiety. We hypothesized that this extrapunitive therapy would be more likely to occur in societies where the degree of punishment for aggression is low during socialization.

In only three cases did both our judges agree as to the presence of "forcing the agent to desist." However, there were sixteen cases where at least one judge scored it as present. The problem posed here was whether to consider the therapy as present or absent when only one judge scored it as present. Since thirty-seven cases had already been excluded, exclusion of the judge disagreements would have left us with a sample far too small to be useful for the testing of the hypothesis. We therefore decided that disagreements or cases where only one judge scored the presence of the particular therapy would be considered as either present or absent depending on which assignation would make the division between present and absent cases more nearly equal. Thus in the instance of this extrapunitive measure, judge disagreements were considered as present, giving us therefore nineteen present and nineteen absent cases. To calculate reliability the following formula was used:

$$\% \text{ Agreement} = \frac{N \text{ Agreements on Presence} + N \text{ Agreements on Absence}}{\text{Total Number of Cases considered}}$$

The per cent agreement of the judges with regard to extrapunitive therapy was 55.

The hypothesis was that societies in which aggression socialization anxiety was low would also be the societies using "forcing the agent to desist" as a therapeutic practice. The outcome of the test was in the predicted direction and was also significant. However, the chi-square value was 2.92, meeting only the 10 per cent level of confidence. This finding could only be considered as tentative evidence in support of the hypothesis. It seems possible that those societies with low aggression anxiety and absence of this therapy may utilize other forms of outward aggression in the therapeutic situation. This possibility suggests that further investigation of primitive medical practices may provide evidence in support of our finding. At this point, however, we can draw no definite conclusions (Table 3).

Sacrifice

In many primitive societies sacrifice is a therapeutic practice precipitated by death or by the occurrence of serious illness. It is considered to play a

significant part in the placation of the dead and of the spirits believed to
have caused illness. DuBois (1944), reporting the account of an Alorese
seeress named Kolmani, has offered an interesting description of sacrifice:

> Once I was sick and was sleeping. Then I dreamed that Atamo and
> Padaom divined to see what was making me sick. The divination
> pointed to a spirit bird. When I awoke I told my dream. I said they
> had better pound corn to feed a spirit bird because my elder brother
> died in Kalabahi. . . . I dreamed that my dead brother spoke to me.
> "Younger sister, you are sick and you have big troubles but I have
> come and your mother and father are following me. I cannot turn
> into a human being but your mother has planted beans and peas in
> your field for you. Your husband can fetch them" . . . I awoke in
> the morning and my abdomen was better. I could not walk so I crawled
> out and roasted beans and peas to feed my brother's soul. I said, "Oh,
> brother if you are making me sick, eat your beans and peas. You must
> not come near me any more and afflict me" . . . Later I was better
> and able to sit up [p. 508].

It can be seen from this brief account that sacrifice or the feeding of crops
to the dead spirits are attempts on the part of the ill person to stave off
his soul from death. The sick individual in performing these sacrificial rituals
attempts to make restitution for the behavior which seemingly aroused the
spirit. Giving up one's possessions in expiation of one's sins is here viewed
as self-punishing behavior. We would expect that the inhibition of aggression
and the redirecting of it toward the self have become instrumental in reducing the anxiety created by the punishing forces of illness. Since illness is here
considered as a situation similar to that in which the secondary drive of
anxiety was learned, we should expect that illness can elicit the anxiety drive,
and that the performance of self-punishing behavior—in this instance, sacrifice—will be instrumental in reducing the drive.

Behaviorist learning theory suggests that self-punishing behavior or aggression directed toward the self are alternative channels for the expression of
aggressive responses. In the face of punishing forces of childhood or in
illness, the individual inhibits the aggression and turns it on himself. As
Dollard et al. (1939) put it: "Other conditions being constant, self-aggression
should be a relatively non-preferred type of expression which will not occur
unless other forms of expression are even more strongly inhibited" (p. 48).

Our hypothesis was that sacrifice should be present as a therapeutic
practice in societies where aggression socialization anxiety is high, that is,
where punishment for aggression has led to inhibitions of aggression responses
and consequent intropunitive or self-aggression.

The association between punishment for aggression and inhibition of aggressive responses has been attested to in several other studies. Rosenzweig (1934), in characterizing types of reaction to frustration, has found that self-aggressive or intropunitive behavior follows in consequence of the inhibition of extrapunitive aggression. Doob and Sears (1939) have reported that the degree to which a given strength of instigation to aggression is actually translated into action of an aggressive nature is a function of the amount of punishment anticipated for such action. Sears et al. (1953) have produced evidence to show that the amount of aggression responses displaced from

TABLE 3

RELATION BETWEEN AGGRESSION SOCIALIZATION ANXIETY AND
THERAPEUTIC PRACTICE DIRECTED TOWARD THE AGENT BELIEVED
TO HAVE CAUSED THE ILLNESS

	Societies with agent-directed therapy absent	Societies with agent-directed therapy present
Societies above the median on aggression socialization anxiety	18 Chiricahua 18 Chamorro 18 Hopi 17 Palaung 17 Kiwai 16 Kwakiutl 16 Alor 15 Zuni 14 Slave 14 Teton 13 Omaha	17 Lepcha 17 Taos 16 Azande 14 Maori 14 Rwala 14 Sanpoil
Societies below the median on aggression socialization anxiety	12 Pukapukans 12 Ifugao 11 Navaho 11 Yagua 10 Kurtachi 9 Chenchu	12 Lamba 12 Chagga 12 Ontong-Javanese 12 Thonga 11 Yungar 111 Baiga 11 Kwoma 10 Lesu 9 Marshall 7 Murngin 5 Dusun

The name of each society is preceded by the value obtained for it on aggression socialization anxiety.

the original object of frustration to other objects is a positive function of the severity of punishment for direct overt aggression.

Turning to the data sheets, we found that there were twelve cases in which only one judge scored sacrifice as present. In keeping with the criterion formulated in the previous section we included these cases in the present category, giving us therefore twenty-two present cases and sixteen absent cases. The agreement between the judges was 68.5 per cent.

We tested the hypothesis (Table 4) and it was confirmed at the 5 per cent level of confidence. The chi-square value was 4.2. Thus the societies in which sacrifice is used as a therapeutic measure are also the ones in which the scores for aggression socialization anxiety are high.

TABLE 4

RELATION BETWEEN AGGRESSION SOCIALIZATION ANXIETY AND THE PERFORMANCE OF SACRIFICE AS A THERAPEUTIC MEASURE

	Societies with the therapeutic measure of sacrifice absent	Societies with the therapeutic measure of sacrifice present
Societies above the median on aggression socialization anxiety		18 Chiricahua
		18 Hopi
		18 Chamorro
		17 Lepcha
		17 Palaung
		17 Taos
		16 Alor
		16 Kwakiutl
		15 Zuni
	17 Kiwai	14 Maori
	16 Azande	14 Rwala
	14 Sanpoil	14 Teton
	14 Slave	13 Omaha
Societies below the median on aggression socialization anxiety	12 Lamba	12 Ifugao
	12 Ontong-J.	12 Chagga
	12 Pukapukans	12 Thonga
	11 Kwoma	11 Baiga
	11 Navaho	9 Chenchu
	11 Yungar	9 Marshall
	10 Kurtachi	5 Dusun
	11 Yagua	
	10 Lesu	
	7 Murngin	

The name of each society is preceded by the value obtained for it on aggression socialization anxiety.

Bloodletting

Bloodletting or phlebotomy is a therapeutic technique found frequently among primitive societies. Many moderns consider this as indicative of primitive mentality without realizing that it was not until the seventeenth century that the Western world learned of the circulatory function of the blood. The practice of bloodletting is often accompanied by explanations which clarify the purpose behind its use. Among the Kwoma, for example, boys are taught that growth to adulthood depends upon the continual flow of fresh blood through the body. They believe that if the blood remains in the system for some time, it becomes stale and rotten. In so far as worn-out blood is believed to lead to cessation of growth, a common practice is reported to be the scraping of penises to permit the bad blood to escape from the system. In describing the medical customs of the Kwoma, J. Whiting (1941) has said:

> Sickness is the chief source of anxiety for a Kwoma infant. The mother successful in bringing about the reduction of other discomforts knows no efficient means of coping with most of the diseases which her child contracts. Indeed one method, employed to cure minor ills, increases the infant's pain instead of reducing it. If he complains of a headache or stomach ache, the mother cuts the skin on his temple or belly and allows blood to flow from the wound. In this sphere, an infant experiences pain without anticipation and possibility of its reduction except by slow and natural means [p. 136].

In so far as bloodletting is a painful procedure and is directed toward the patient, we considered it to be a form of self-aggression. Our discussion of learning theory in relation to sacrifice applies equally well to bloodletting since both are considered to be self-punishing responses. Thus we predicted that bloodletting as a therapeutic practice would be present in societies where aggression socialization anxiety was high.

Our judges reported on two therapeutic practices which seemed to indicate bloodletting, cutting or pricking and loss of blood. Since the two seemed interchangeable we considered a score on either one as indicating the presence of bloodletting. Both judges agreed on the presence of this therapy in twenty cases, so that we included the ten disagreements in the absence category. The reliability was determined in the same way as in the previous tests. The percentage of judge agreement was 75.

Our hypothesis was confirmed at the 5 per cent level of confidence (Table 5). The chi-square value obtained was 4.2. Thus the societies in which bloodletting is used as a therapy are the ones with high scores for aggression socialization anxiety. It seems possible that the presence of bloodletting might more directly be an outcome of beliefs dealing with the symbolic and ritualistic significance of blood. Thus among the Kwoma, a belief about "bad blood" may lead to the practice of bloodletting. Concern with blood might also arise from observation of the menstrual cycle. In the absence of data bearing directly on such problems we were unable to test these possibilities.

TABLE 5

RELATION BETWEEN AGGRESSION SOCIALIZATION ANXIETY AND THE
PERFORMANCE OF BLOODLETTING AS A THERAPEUTIC MEASURE

	Societies with the therapeutic measure of bloodletting absent	Societies with the therapeutic measure of bloodletting present
Societies above the median on aggression socialization anxiety		18 Hopi
		18 Chiricahua
		17 Kiwai
		17 Lepcha
		16 Azande
		16 Kwakiutl
		15 Zuni
	18 Chamorro	15 Maori
	17 Palaung	14 Rwala
	17 Taos	14 Sanpoil
	16 Alor	14 Slave
	14 Teton	13 Omaha
Societies below the median on socialization anxiety	12 Lamba	12 Thonga
	12 Ontong-J.	12 Pukapukans
	12 Ifugao	12 Chagga
	11 Baiga	11 Kwoma
	11 Navaho	9 Marshall
	11 Yungar	7 Murngin
	11 Yagua	
	10 Lesu	
	10 Kurtachi	
	9 Chenchu	
	5 Dusun	

The name of each society is preceded by the value obtained for it on aggression socialization anxiety.

Therapeutic Practices as Guilt Behavior

The fact that the measures of bloodletting and sacrifice related significantly to the socialization anxiety established during childhood in the aggression system of behavior suggested the possibility that they might be related to the potential for guilt present in various societies. In so far as bloodletting and sacrifice were considered intropunitive, we expected their presence to be related to the degree of superego formation in these societies with a potential for guilt. The learning theorists view the enforcement of cultural rules as a function of the amount of punishment or fear of punishment instituted in a society. In accounting for the persistence of desirable behavior patterns, psychoanalytic theory describes a process that goes beyond simple fear. In resolving the oedipal complex through the mechanism of identification the child internalizes the standards of the parents, i.e., the child learns a system of self-reward and self-punishment modeled on that of its parents. Henceforth the performance of socially prescribed behavior is guided by this internal authority or superego. From then on the child inhibits undesirable responses in fear not of the external punishing authority but in fear of its own internalized authority or conscience. This form of anxiety is generated whenever the standards of conscience are transgressed, and is considered to be different from the initial objective fear of external authority. It is this anxiety which is responsible for motivating the behavior which is called guilt behavior.[1]

Psychoanalytic theory specifies that one of the associated responses to these feelings of guilt is the performance of self-aggressive responses. In the discussion of superego formation, Freud (1930) pointed out that the conscience-ridden individual in an effort to relieve the guilt anxiety exposes himself to self-punishment.

> By the process of identification it [the child] absorbs into itself the invulnerable authority, which then becomes the super-ego and comes

[1] That the mechanism of identification does not function solely at this stage has been amply demonstrated by Spitz (1957) in his studies of children and the development of language function. "Imitation of and identification with the gesture are one of the child's major contributions to the formation of object relations. The first identifications with parental gestures appear in the third and fourth quarter of the first year and are echo-like reproductions of the adult's gestures . . . That identification proper is at work in this performance is evident; the infant has incorporated into the memory system of his ego actions observed in the libidinal object, and as a result a modification of the ego's structure has taken place . . . On the age level of nine to twelve months at which primitive gesture identification develops, the child also acquires the first understanding of commands and prohibitions" (pp. 42-43).

into possession of all the aggressiveness which the child would gladly have exercised against it . . . [p. 115]. The tension between the strict super-ego and the subordinate ego we call the sense of guilt; it manifests itself as the need for punishment . . . [p. 105]. Hence we know of two sources for feelings of guilt: that arising from the dread of authority and the later one from the dread of the super-ego. The first one compels us to renounce instinctual gratification; the other presses over and above this towards punishment . . . [p. 111]. The effect of instinctual renunciation on conscience then operates as follows: every impulse of aggression which we omit to gratify is taken over by the super-ego and goes to heighten its aggressiveness (against the ego) [p. 117].

In accord with this formulation of the origins of self-punishing or intropunitive behavior we expected that our measures of sacrifice and bloodletting would be directly related to the strength of superego formation.

This problem has been investigated by several other studies which are worth mentioning. Investigating the effects of guilt on memory, MacKinnon (1938) set up a situation which permitted violation of a prohibition imposed on the subjects by the experimenter. The nonviolators were found to engage in more oral activity, e.g., nail biting, thumb sucking, nose picking, which was regarded as masochistic or self-punishing. They also were less outwardly aggressive, more self-blaming, and in normal life tended to feel guilty more often than the violators. This evidence is somewhat suggestive of the association between guilt and intropunitive aggression. Heinicke (1953), in studying the differences between "guilt" and "fear" children, has found evidence to indicate that high guilt children inhibited aggression in the classroom but displayed more of it in fantasy tests. This finding has been confirmed by Levin (1953) who has found that children with high superego formation displayed more fantasy aggression in doll play.

Patient Responsibility

Whiting and Child (1953) have provided us with an index of the tendency for individuals in particular cultures to feel guilty. In order to study the origins of guilt they designed an index of patient responsibility based on the degree to which illness in a particular society is attributed to the actions of the patient. That is, in the absence of direct evidence of the degree of guilt potential present in the personalities of primitive peoples, they utilized an indirect measure based on various explanations of illness which seemed to imply self-blame.

In accordance with psychoanalytic theory, we tested our scores for self-punishing therapies with this measure of patient responsibility. Our results

(Tables 6 and 7) show no relationship to the index of guilt. The chi-square values obtained were .045 and 0.0 for bloodletting and sacrifice respectively. Since the number of cases tested (eighteen) was small, this finding cannot be considered conclusive.

TABLE 6

RELATION BETWEEN PATIENT RESPONSIBILITY FOR ILLNESS AND THE PERFORMANCE OF BLOODLETTING AS A THERAPEUTIC MEASURE

	Societies with bloodletting absent	Societies with bloodletting present
Societies above the median on patient responsibility	17 Navaho 16 Alor 13 Chamorro	21 Maori 18 Pukapukans 15 Hopi 14 Kwoma 11 Chiricahua 10 Lepcha
Societies below the median on patient responsibility	9 Teton 6 Kurtachi 5 Lesu 1 Chenchu	9 Azande 8 Kwakiutl 4 Rwala 4 Thonga 2 Chagga

The name of each society is preceded by the value obtained for it on the index of patient responsibility.

TABLE 7

RELATION BETWEEN PATIENT RESPONSIBILITY FOR ILLNESS AND THE PERFORMANCE OF SACRIFICE AS A THERAPEUTIC MEASURE

	Societies with sacrifice absent	Societies with sacrifice present
Societies above the median on patient responsibility	18 Pukapukans 17 Navaho 14 Kwoma	21 Maori 16 Alor 15 Hopi 13 Chamorro 11 Chiricahua 10 Lepcha
Societies below the median on patient responsibility	9 Azande 6 Kurtachi 5 Lesu	9 Teton 8 Kwakiutl 4 Rwala 4 Thonga 2 Chagga 1 Chenchu

The name of each society is preceded by the value obtained for it on the index of patient responsibility.

Child-Training Antecedents

We next correlated our therapeutic practices with the antecedent conditions of guilt, which are certain child-training practices suggested by psychoanalytic theory and modified in the hypotheses used by Whiting and Child. It was assumed that any evidence here might clarify the result found with patient responsibility. The child-training antecedents considered were:

a. Initial indulgence of the child's drive for dependence on the mother.
b. Relative importance of love-oriented techniques of punishment.
c. Relative importance of parents, in comparison with other persons, as agents of socialization.
d. Relative importance of relatives, in comparison with unrelated persons, as agents of socialization.

Our results (Tables 8 and 9) show no relationship between our indices of intropunitive therapy and the child-training antecedents of guilt. It is for this reason that we have not elaborated the reasons advanced for considering these socialization techniques as antecedents of guilt. The chi-square values obtained for these results are presented in the tables. It will be seen that in one instance, the associations are in a direction opposite to the predicted one. Thus bloodletting and sacrifice are negatively related to the scores for initial indulgence of dependence, the chi-square values for sacrifice meeting the 5 per cent level of confidence. Here again we may only speculate as to the significance of this result since the number of cases was small. It is possible that this result may be due to the association of low nurturance or indulgence with high aggression anxiety, and in this sense the result may be considered as valid. Whiting and Child have pointed out that this variable of initial indulgence, which indicates the amount of nurturance given to the child, may not be a valid index of the strength of the dependence drive of the child on the parent. They point out that inconsistency of nurturance rather than degree of nurturance may be the antecedent variable relevant to the strength of the acquired drive for dependence.

The over-all findings with patient responsibility and the child-training antecedents tend to indicate that no relationship exists with our measure of intropunitiveness. However, due to the limited number of cases and in the absence of further evidence, no definite conclusions can be made about the relationship between superego formation and the performance of self-punishing therapeutic techniques.

TABLE 8

RELATION BETWEEN THE CHILD-TRAINING ANTECEDENTS OF GUILT
AND THE PERFORMANCE OF BLOODLETTING AS A THERAPEUTIC
MEASURE

Child-Training Practices		Bloodletting Absent	Present	
a. Initial indulgence of	High	7	4	x2=2.2
dependence	Low	2	5	
b. Relative importance of	High	6	5	
love-oriented tech-				x2=.008
niques of punishment	Low	4	3	
c. Relative importance of	High	7	4	
parents as agents of				x2=.08
socialization	Low	4	3	
d. Relative importance of	High	7	4	
relatives as agents of				x2=.08
socialization	Low	4	3	

The entries in this table refer to the number of societies in which bloodletting
is present or absent, and in which the score for child-training antecedents place
them above or below the median division.

TABLE 9

RELATION BETWEEN THE CHILD-TRAINING ANTECEDENTS OF GUILT AND
THE PERFORMANCE OF SACRIFICE AS A THERAPEUTIC MEASURE

Child-Training Practices		Absent	Present	
a. Initial indulgence of	High	8	4	x2=3.98
dependence	Low	1	5	
b. Relative importance	High	6	5	
of love-oriented tech-				x2=.34
niques of punishment	Low	4	2	
c. Relative importance	High	8	4	
of parents as agents				x2=.009
of socialization	Low	3	3	
d. Relative importance	High	6	6	
of relatives as agents				x2=1.76
of socialization	Low	5	1	

The entries in this table refer to the number of societies in which sacrifice is
present or absent and in which the scores for child-training antecedents place them
above or below the median division.

DISCUSSION AND CONCLUSIONS

We have been interested in this paper in assessing the influence of early childhood experience on the development of subsequent personality patterns. We have produced significant evidence to show that certain anxieties acquired during childhood persist as secondary drives and subsequently motivate certain rewarding responses in other situations. We have shown that child-training institutions utilize certain instinctual forces such as aggressive and sexual drives, which are highly mobile and plastic, for purposes of developing action patterns of behavior and patterns of inhibition. And we have seen how these very patterns appear in a totally different sphere of adult life, that of medicine. As Hartmann (1939) has written:

> The child, by accepting these [socially determined hierarchies of] values, may find an appropriate way to cope with his libidinal and aggressive impulses, and his acceptance thus may amount to a synthetic achievement. But, of course, not all elements of the social value hierarchy will lend themselves equally to this use. The superindividual nature of such value systems and ideals facilitates cooperation with other people and thus adaptation also. Social value systems are just like other conventions . . . though they often hinder adaptation, under certain conditions they can also facilitate it [p. 75].

We have also been interested in assessing the influence of these acquired drives on the therapeutic practices performed during illness. These findings are inextricably associated with the evidence regarding the formation of these personality patterns. Thus the results indicate that certain therapies are related to certain motivational patterns present in the basic personality structure of the members of various primitive societies. Such findings are important, for psychoanalytic theory has only in recent decades concerned itself with the conflict-free sphere of ego development and the problems of adaptation. The subject of primitive therapy is a useful area for studies of the problem of adaptation because it not only is concerned with a realistic threatening set of events but also is an area on which are projected the most basic human emotions and fears. The patterns of adaptation to these situations are laid down early in the life of the individual in the setting of his family. I refer again to Hartmann (1939) who says:

> Though the newborn human child is not devoid of all "instinct equipment" (for instance, sucking, swallowing, eye closure on light stimulation, crying), nor of additional inborn equipment (instinctual drives

and ego apparatuses) much of which matures only later, the fact
remains that in comparison to other animals the "instinct equipment"
the newborn human has ready for use is extremely meager. In his prolonged helplessness the human child is dependent on the family, that
is, on a social structure which fulfills here—as elsewhere— "biological"
functions also [p. 29].

It is during this period of ontogenesis, as Spitz (1957) has shown, that
adaptive processes ensure autoplastic modifications performed by the individual himself. With the help of adaptive processes the individual adjusts to the
ensuing autoplastic changes. It is during this same period that thought
processes and the reasoning faculty are developed through "learning" by
individual experience and through the transmission of parental experience.
In tracing the development of the concept of self, Spitz (1957) gives an excellent demonstration of this learning process:

> The child's congenital equipment is the focus of a field of forces
> created by shifting object relations. These object relations produce
> reverberations in the child's endopsychic processes leading to shifts
> of cathexis, to the formation of psychic structures, which in their turn
> interact in a circular process with the force field of ever-changing
> object relations. In short, the achievement of negation is the result
> of an interaction between the child's object relations and his endo-
> psychic processes. The child's use of "No" in gesture or word indi-
> cates that this has been accomplished . . . [pp. 130-131].
>   The acquisition of the "No" is the indicator of a new level of
> autonomy, of the awareness of the "other" and of the awareness of
> the self; it is the beginning of a restructuration of mentation on a
> higher level of complexity; it initiates an extensive ego development,
> in the framework of which the dominance of the reality principle
> over the pleasure principle becomes increasingly established [p. 129].

Our study derives from a theoretical orientation which considers different cultural areas to be integrated through certain personality mechanisms.
We have postulated that certain socialization experiences lead to the learning
of certain acquired drives which become component parts of the basic personality structure. These acquired drives then play a major part in determining the therapeutic techniques of the society. These drives are seen as
intervening variables mediating between the child-training practices and the
therapeutic practices. By application of this integration construct we were
able to produce evidence bearing on two distinct problems. Thus we have
seen that certain instrumental responses learned during socialization are
subsequently utilized as reactions to illness. For example, punishment for
aggression in childhood establishes certain anxieties about the expression of

aggressive responses. Given the frustrating and oftentimes punitive circumstances of illness, we have seen that this anxiety still persists in so far as the responses learned in association with childhood frustrations are reactivated to reduce the anxiety. Indeed many authors have linked the entire developmental process to a succession of frustrations. Spitz has pointed to the physical frustration of birth, the psychological frustration of weaning and of other developmental steps, each stage imposing on the individual a progressively increasing need for compliance with the reality principle. It is through learning to cope with these frustrations, through the differentiation of the I from the non-I, and through the acquisition of such patterns as negation, that the child develops the autonomy and maturation which it will need and use in the adult situations of life and in particular such situations as illness.

In so far as the child-training practices relate significantly to the therapeutic practices we may conclude that the intervening personality factors influence the performance of these therapies. Accordingly, anxiety about expression of aggression will lead to therapeutic practices which in the instance of aggression-provoking circumstances are such as to alleviate this anxiety. Thus bloodletting may not only have some therapeutic value, but lends itself as well to the expression of aggressive responses which reduce anxiety.

The theoretical orientation we have used in this investigation has provided us with an adequate approach in ascertaining certain empirical relationships. However, it does not permit us to determine definitely the causal sequence operating. We cannot conclude that therapeutic practices are a direct outcome of certain personality factors or that child-training practices directly influence the formation of adult personality. It is possible that the similarities present in child-training practices and therapeutic practices may be due to the direct influence of adult attitudes and behavior in the societies studied. Thus, adults who are anxious about the expression of aggression might be more likely to inhibit aggressive behavior during illness, and might also treat aggressive behavior more severely in children. In the absence of direct evidence on the adult personalities of the societies studied we were not able to explore this possibility. In so far as our view of adult personality patterns as intervening variables which enabled us to relate areas of child-training practices and medical therapies has been somewhat confirmed by our evidence, it is sufficient to accept this approach until further evidence indicating otherwise is advanced.

Hartmann, Kris, and Loewenstein (1951) have written an extremely provocative paper, the thesis of which is in essential agreement with the approach used here. That is, they feel that certain types of behavior shared by individuals in a given group may be related to common practices in child care and education. However, they develop an interesting hypothesis for subsequent research:

> We assume that not only with mothers in any one of the Western sub-cultures, but probably also with mothers in "preliterate" societies the problem of a gradation in devotion to the child exists; that even there a child may represent the self, the sibling, the own mother, etc., and mobilize unconscious impulses of various kinds. We therefore suggest the formulation that noninstutionalized behavior may serve an important function of discharge. In the examples given what is discharged are unconscious tendencies. . . . Anthropologists . . . tend to draw conclusions from observed behavior to underlying motivations and neglect frequently, paradoxically enough, to take into account that in different environments similar impulses may find different expressions [pp. 27-28].

We were unable to produce any evidence confirming the psychoanalytic notions regarding self-punishment. Since the number of cases was limiting we could not consider our result to be conclusive. Our study of guilt, although it provides no significant evidence, opens the way for speculations which apply as well to the general study of therapy. Examination of the correlations of our indices of bloodletting and sacrifice with patient responsibility (Tables 6 and 7) suggests a possible explanation of the insignificant relationships. It is seen that several societies, e.g., Pukapukans, Kwoma, are considered both present and absent with regard to intropunitiveness, depending on which variable, sacrifice or bloodletting, was being considered. Possibly more than one response may serve the needs of the self-punishing individual. This suggests that a more successful association with superego antecedents could be achieved if we were able to characterize primitive societies in terms of the relative degree of intropunitiveness. Thus other therapeutic practices, such as sweating, vomiting, washing, might be intropunitive responses. The fact that the directions of extrapunitive ("forcing the agent to desist") therapy and intropunitive therapy were in opposite directions in their relations with aggression socialization anxiety lends credence to this belief. By considering all such intropunitive and extrapunitive therapies we might be able to distinguish the relative amounts of patient-directed therapy and agent-directed therapy. Further investigation may clarify the result we obtained. Thus if this speculative statement were to be confirmed, we might discover that patient responsibility and intropunitive therapy are alternative responses to the illness situation.

In line with this reasoning, Piers and Singer (1953) have offered a pertinent, though somewhat indirect thought. Considering the shame impulse as rage turned against the self, they point out that self-punishing behavior is associated with the emotion of shame.

> The moral masochist, haunted by a deep-rooted and all-pervading sense of guilt, continuously attempts to buy off his sadistic superego by enduring shameful humiliation. . . . Shame for him is evidently easier to bear than the primary guilt and experiencing humiliation he achieves temporary surcease from his conscience [p. 20].

Viewing this statement in terms of our result, we are led to conclude that the individual may experience more than one emotional response to the illness situation. It is possible that the incidence of patient responsibility explanations, and self-punishing therapeutic practices might depend on other emotional factors present in the illness situation. Unfortunately the evidence on shame is considered at present to be insufficient, but it may prove to have some important bearing on the processes considered here.

One other consideration seems relevant here. It was seen that bloodletting was a therapeutic technique used in Kwoma and it was shown that it was in part due to the beliefs prevalent in that society about "bad blood." That this is of influence cannot be determined here, but it would seem that beliefs play some part in accounting for the presence of bloodletting. Sacrifice is another therapeutic practice which might be subject to prevailing beliefs, particularly those dealing with the religious systems of a society.

Lastly, we cannot deny the influence of realistic factors. Primitive people survive to the extent that by chance or otherwise they hit on techniques which work. A whole field of pharmacopoeia has developed in this light to investigate certain primitive herbs and medicines with wonder drug powers. In fact, bloodletting has been accepted by modern medical practitioners in certain specific cases.

BIBLIOGRAPHY

Ackerknecht, E. H. (1942), Problems of Primitive Medicine. *Bull. Hist. Med.*, *12*:503-21.
—— (1942), Primitive Medicine and Culture Pattern. *Bull. Hist. Med.*, *12*:545-574.
—— (1943), Psychopathology, Primitive Medicine and Primitive Culture. *Bull. Hist. Med.*, *14*:30-67.
Barry, H. III. (1957), Relationships Between Child Training and the Pictorial Arts. *J. Abn. Soc. Psychol.*, *54*:380-383.

Benedict, R. (1934), *Patterns of Culture*. Boston: Houghton Mifflin.

Dollard, J., Doob, L. W., Miller, N. E., Mowrer, O. H., & Sears, R. R. (1939), *Frustration and Aggression*. New Haven: Yale University Press.

Doob, L. W. & Sears, R. R. (1939), Factors Determining Substitute Behavior and the Overt Expression of Aggression. *J. Abn. Soc. Psychol., 34*: 293-313.

DuBois, C. (1944), *The People of Alor*. Minneapolis: University of Minnesota Press.

Erikson, E. H. (1950), *Childhood and Society*. New York: W. W. Norton.

Evans-Pritchard, E. E. (1937), *Witchcraft among the Azande*. Oxford: Clarendon Press.

Faigin, H. (1935), Child-rearing in the Rimrock Community with Special Reference to the Development of Guilt. Unpublished doctoral thesis. Cambridge: Harvard University.

Fenichel, O. (1945), *The Psychoanalytic Theory of Neurosis*. New York: W. W. Norton.

Freud, A. (1936), *The Ego and Mechanisms of Defense*. New York: International Universities Press, 1946.

Freud, S. (1895), Project for a Scientific Psychology. *The Origins of Psychoanalysis*. New York: Basic Books, 1954.

—— (1919), 'A Child Is Being Beaten': a Contribution to the Study of the Origin of Sexual Perversion. *Collected Papers, 2*:172-201. London: Hogarth Press, 1924.

—— (1930), *Civilization and Its Discontents*. London: Hogarth Press, 1946.

Friedman, G. A. (1950), A Cross-cultural Study of the Relationship between Independence Training and Achievement as Revealed by Mythology. Unpublished Honors Thesis. Cambridge: Harvard University.

Garrett, H. E. (1947), *Statistics in Psychology and Education*. New York: Longmans, Green.

Goldfarb, W. (1945), Psychological Privation in Infancy and Subsequent Adjustment. *Amer. J. Orthopsychiat., 15*:247-255.

Hartmann, H. (1939), *Ego Psychology and the Problem of Adaptation*. New York: International Universities Press, 1958.

—— & Kris, E., Loewenstein, R. M. (1951), Some Psychoanalytic Comments on "Culture and Personality." In: *Psychoanalysis and Culture*, ed. G. B. Wilbur & W. Muensterberger. New York: International Universities Press.

Heinicke, C. (1953), Some Antecedents and Correlates of Guilt-Fear in Young Boys. Unpublished doctoral thesis.

Hilgard, E. R. & Marquis, D. G. (1940), *Conditioning and Learning*. New York: Appleton-Century.

Kardiner, A. (1939), *The Individual and His Society*. New York: Columbia University Press.

—— (1945), *The Psychological Frontiers of Society*. New York: Columbia University Press.

Levin, H. (1953), Effects of Parental Punishment on Fantasy Aggression. Paper delivered at the meetings of the American Psychological Association, Cleveland, Ohio, September 5.

MacKinnon, D. W. (1938), Violation of Prohibitions. In: *Explorations in Personality*, ed. H. A. Murray et al. New York: Oxford University Press.

McAllester, D. P. (1941), Water as a Disciplinary Agent Among the Crow and Blackfoot. *Amer. Anthropol.*, *42*:593-604.

Mead, M. (1928), *Coming of Age in Samoa*. New York: Murrow.

Mowrer, O. H. (1950), *Learning Theory and Personality Dynamics*. New York: Ronald Press.

Muensterberger, W. (1955), On the Biopsychological Determinants of Social Life. *Psychoanalysis and the Social Sciences*, *4*:7-25. New York: International Universities Press.

Piers, G. & Singer, M. B. (1953), *Shame and Guilt; a Psychoanalytic and a Cultural Study*. Springfield, Ill.: Charles Thomas.

Rosenzweig, S. (1934), Types of Reaction to Frustration: a Heuristic Classification. *J. Abn. Soc. Psychol.*, *29*:298-300.

Sears, R. R., et al., (1953), Some Child-rearing Antecedents of Aggression and Dependency in Young Children. *Genet. Psychol. Mon.*, *47*:135-234.

Spitz, R. A. (1945), Hospitalism: an Inquiry into the Genesis of Psychiatric Conditions in Early Childhood. *The Psychoanalytic Study of the Child*, *1*:53-74. New York: International Universities Press.

—— (1957), *No and Yes*. New York: International Universities Press.

Whiting, B. B. (1950), *Paiute Sorcery*. New York: Viking Fund Publications in Anthropology, No. 15.

Whiting, J. W. M. (1941), *Becoming a Kwoma*. New Haven: Yale University Press.

—— & Child, I. L. (1953), *Child Training and Personality*. New Haven: Yale University Press.

PIBLOKTOQ (HYSTERIA) AMONG THE POLAR ESKIMO

An Ethnopsychiatric Study

ZACHARY GUSSOW, Ph.D.

The cross-fertilization of the sciences of culture and psychiatry has, in recent years, led to significant modifications of thinking concerning the relative nature of mental illness. Recent studies in culture and psychopathology negate the view that there are "bizarre native psychoses," that mental illnesses are "unique" to the society in which they occur, and emphasize instead cross-cultural parallelism in the structure and process of mental disorders.[1] It is the specific content of mental disorders which is held to be related to a given society at a given time, a factor which accounts for the variety of detailed symptomatology from one culture to another, reflecting differences in prevailing beliefs, customs, traditions, interests and conflicts.

The present paper is a contribution to the field of ethnopsychiatry. It presents data on a mental disorder found among, though not confined to, the Polar Eskimo of Northwestern Greenland, and referred to in the literature as *pibloktoq*.[2] In 1913, when A. A. Brill published the first account of this disorder in the psychiatric literature, drawing on the works of Admiral

An earlier version of this paper was read at the Annual Meeting of the American Anthropological Association, 1958. Materials for this paper were gathered by the author while assisting Dr. George Devereux on a study of mental disorder in primitive society. Funds for research, granted to Dr. Devereux, were supplied, in part, by the National Institute of Mental Health (M-1669), and the Society for the Investigation of Human Ecology. The author is deeply indebted to Dr. Devereux for his guidance and constructive criticism of the research and for his clarification of a number of methodological and diagnostic problems.

Credit is also due Mrs. Gitel P. Steed for allowing the author access to her unpublished interviews with Niels Rasmussen, and to Mr. Samuel Moskowitz for valuable criticism.

[1] Yap (1951, 1952), Joseph and Murray (1951), Teicher (1954), Devereux (1956). Among earlier writers, see Seligman (1932), Zilboorg (1938).

[2] *Pibloktoq*, as described in this paper, bears a striking, if not identical, resemblance to one form of the so-called "arctic hysterias," found among a number of Paleo-Siberian peoples, and referred to in the literature as *menerik* (Czaplicka, 1914). Scattered references to *pibloktoq*-like performances have also been reported for a number of Indian groups in the Yukon-Mackenzie area of Alaska (Aronson, 1940, p. 33; Dall, 1870, pp. 171-172; Honigmann, 1949, pp. 239-240), and in Korea (May, 1956, p. 82).

Robert E. Peary and conversations with Donald B. Macmillan for his material, he drew attention to the underlying similarities between this native Eskimo illness and certain psychiatric manifestations present in modern Western society.

The present paper extends the efforts of Brill. It brings to the study of this ethnic disorder a considerable body of new data. This material will be used to provide a clinical-anthropological picture of *pibloktoq,* and will relate this disorder to concrete situations in the lives of the Polar Eskimo. Data on the precipitating causes of this condition will be used to criticize the common and labored view that *pibloktoq* and other Eskimo and arctic mental derangements are brought on by the "depressing," "melancholy," "monotonous," etc., effects of the arctic winter climate on the Eskimo mind. And finally, an exploratory section on the psychodynamics of this disorder will be offered.

The *Pibloktoq* Syndrome

In the literature the term *pibloktoq* (arctic hysteria, polar hysteria, transitional madness, etc.) has become the designation for a group of "hysterical" symptoms which may afflict adult Eskimo men and women at any time.

In *pibloktoq* there are no single and recurring symptoms to be found in each case. The syndrome is composed of a series of reactive patterns, any number of which may combine with other symptoms in each seizure performance. Thus, features found in case A may be totally reproduced in case B, but only partially present in case C. B may then share features of its own with C, but not with A, and so on. In other words, the total repertoire of symptoms does not necessarily appear in each instance, but each seizure will, as it were, draw its symptoms from among the "pool" of reactive patterns.

Case Material

It is the purpose of this section to present the available case material and to draw up an inventory of symptoms for the attack proper. Prodromal and terminal symptoms will be listed separately. Some of these data—the personal observations and comments of Niels Rasmussen—are new, never having been published before.[3] The material is organized into (1) discrete cases, (2) composite cases, general ideas or comments about *pibloktoq* and (3) one story or tale of a past occurrence of this disorder.

[3] Steed's interviews with Niels Rasmussen, son of the famed arctic explorer, Knud Rasmussen. Niels Rasmussen was in Greenland from 1939 to 1945. Three years of this period were spent among the Polar Eskimo near Etah. The Rasmussen inter-

Discrete Cases

(1) "Tukshu began suddenly to rave upon leaving the boat. He tore off every stitch of clothing he had on, and would have thrown himself into the water of the Sound but for the restraint of the Eskimos. He seemed possessed of supernatural strength, and it was all four men could do to hold him" (Whitney, 1911, p. 67).

(2) "We were on the threshold of the long dismal night at last. They [Eskimo women] were affected not only by the natural depression that impresses itself upon all with the vanishing of the day, but an increasing apprehension had sprung up for the safety of the hunters. A rapid driving of the ice pack . . . had raised a fear that the men had gone adrift on it. . . . I dropped into [one of the igloos] one evening and amused the woman . . . presently Kudlar's kooner [wife] came in and the two women began to cry and moan . . . (Give me my man! Give me my man!). At half-past one that [same] night I was awakened . . . by a woman shouting at the top of her voice—shrill and startling, like one gone mad. I knew at once what it meant—someone had gone problocto. Far away on the driving ice of the Sound a lone figure was running and raving. The boatswain and Billy joined me, and as fast as we could struggle through three feet of snow, with drifts often to the waist, we gave pursuit. At length I reached her, and to my astonishment discovered it was Tongwe [Kudlar's wife]. She struggled desperately, and it required the combined strength of the three of us to get her back to the shack, where she was found to be in bad shape—one hand was slightly frozen, and part of one breast. After a half hour of quiet she became rational again, but the attack left her very weak" (Whitney, 1911, pp. 82-84).

(3) "On the evening after the hunters returned . . . Tongwe [see case 2] was again attacked by problocto. She rushed out of the igloo, tore her clothing off and threw herself into a snow-drift. I ran to [her husband's] assistance, but the woman was as strong as a lion, and we had all we could do to hold her. A strong north wind was blowing, with a temperature eight degrees below zero, and I thought she would surely be severely frozen . . . but in some miraculous manner she escaped even the slightest frost-bite. After getting her into the igloo she grew weak as a kitten, and it was several hours before she became quite herself. In connection with this woman's case, it is . . . interesting to note that, previous to the attack which she had suffered the day before the return of the hunting party, she had never shown any symptoms of problokto" (Whitney, 1911, pp. 87-88).

views were taken in 1947-48 as part of a larger study, *Directed Culture Change in the Far North;* Gitel P. Steed, Director. Interviews consist of data on Rasmussen's own observations and personal experience, his knowledge of his father's life among the Eskimo, and his critical comments and discussion of the available arctic literature. In this paper, materials from the Rasmussen interviews are quoted verbatim.

(4) "In July 1909 I was witness of such an attack in the woman Inadtliak. It lasted 25 minutes. She sat on the ground with the legs stretched out, swaying her body to and fro, sometimes rapidly sometimes more slowly, from side to side and tortuously, whilst she kept her hands comparatively still and only now and then moved her elbows in to her sides. She stared out in front of her quite regardless of the surroundings, and sang and screamed occasionally, changing the tone, iah-iah-iaha-ha . . . , now and then she interjected a sentence, e.g., that the Danish had at last come to them, and again the great happiness this gave her now in the glad summer-time and so on. Her two small children sat and played about her, whilst the members of the tribe scarcely looked at her during the attacks; they seemed to be very well acquainted with such things. She recovered quite suddenly and only some hectic, red spots on her cheeks indicated anything unusual. Without so much as looking about her or betraying a sign of anything unusual she began, literally with the same movement, to give her youngest child milk and then went quickly on to chew a skin" (Steensby, 1910, pp. 377-378).

(5) "In one case NR [Niels Rasmussen] was a passenger on a sled driven by a very simple, friendly not too bright young man; always friendly, untalkative, but reliable fellow. They had had some trouble on the land before they got to the ice cap, very tough going, no snow and very tough work. Finally reached the ice cap which meant safety and then they had some smooth going of course, and they would be home in a day or two. NR thought that everything was all right with him. Had his back towards him; he was standing in front of the sled and disentangling the dogs. He heard him talk very strangely; didn't understand a word of it.[4] Suddenly he began to kick the dogs, one or two of them. Then systematically he started to kick them all, talking louder and louder until he was screaming unintelligibly. He warmed up for about a minute or so that way and after about a minute or so he was in full swing screaming all the time. He tore all the stuff off the sleds, skins, boxes, stoves, and hurled them at the dogs. It lasted about ten minutes. . . . It didn't do much harm to the dogs, in fact nothing at all, couldn't hit them actually. All of a sudden it was over. He sat down on the sled completely exhausted. A short attack. Later, days later when they got back to the village, he had a lot of fun about it. The other companions on the trip kidded the fellow about his behavior and the young boy himself always asked NR whether he had been scared; it is not disgrace that these things happen. It can happen to anybody. It's a natural incident. Usually turns it into a funny story . . ." (Steed, 1947-48, pp. 205-206).

(6) "NR has seen another 'bird' [man] rolling in the snow without any clothes on, completely naked, for about a half hour. That is what

---

[4] According to Steed, Niels Rasmussen understood enough of the Eskimo language at this time to know that the individual in question was not speaking "ordinary" Eskimo.

usually happens: KR [Knud Rasmussen] described it that way too, they tear off all their clothes. NR saw only one instance of this; but it's supposed to be a common characteristic" (Steed, 1947-48, p. 207).

(7) "One was a girl who suddenly decided she wanted a piece of sea-weed and without a stitch waded into the sea; still open water and it was bitter cold, way below freezing point. She waded out dangerously—she had hardly any foothold she was out so far; got the sea-weed, came back triumphantly and with great dignity and with the same dignity she suddenly threw it away again. All of a sudden her dignity broke—completely—she started screaming and made a continual somersault. Could not have done that in a sober state. Must have been a couple of hundred feet. She was so exhausted that she slept for 15 hours or so" (Steed, 1947-48, pp. 207-208).

(8) "Knud Rasmussen tells an incident, reported by NR, of a man who had had more than one [inebriation]. He suddenly climbed up a steep cliff; bluffs outside the village; completely vertical. Climbed up to top of those although obviously humanly impossible to do it; but he did it somehow. There is no doubt . . . that he could not have possibly done it under normal circumstances. Then he grabbed the knife and went into a tent where three little children were sleeping; they were alone there but the father of the children followed the man, quietly took the knife out of the hand and at that moment the man collapsed" (Steed, 1947-48, p. 208).

(9) "In 1898 while the Windward was in winter quarters off Cape D'Urville, a married woman was taken with one of these fits in the middle of the night. In a state of perfect nudity she walked the deck of the ship; then, seeking still greater freedom, jumped the rail, on to the frozen snow and ice. It was some time before we missed her, and when she was finally discovered, it was at a distance of half-a-mile, where she was still pawing, and shouting to the best of her abilities. She was captured and brought back to the ship; and then there commenced a wonderful performance of mimicry in which every conceivable cry of local bird and mammal was reproduced in the throat of Inahloo.

"This same woman at other times attempts to walk the ceiling of her igloo . . ." (Peary, 1907, p. 384).

Macmillan (Brill, 1913, pp. 515-516) also describes the attacks of this woman: "Inahloo, a woman of 45 years, was very violent during her attacks. She did not know what she was doing, she appeared crazy and demented, and would bite when an attempt was made to restrain her. Her specialty was to imitate the call of birds and to try to walk on the ceiling. She also put ice on her chest. Her face was very congested, her eyes were bloodshot during the attack, and . . . she foamed at the mouth."

(10) "Whenever Elkiahsha, nicknamed Bill, had an attack she would walk around the deck of the Roosevelt and pick up everything lying loose and throw it up in the air. She also climbed up the rigging

and foresheet and stuck her head under the sail" (Brill, 1913, pp. 515-516).

(11) "Inahwaho showed her attacks by walking on the ice, singing and beating her hands together."

According to Macmillan, this woman also feigned attacks. Macmillan was told that "Inawaho was running around on the ice having an attack. He got his camera and went out to take some pictures of her while in this state. He saw her running on the ice and beating her hands, but as soon as she noticed him her whole attitude changed, she became very excited, grabbed big chunks of ice and hurled them at him. The following day she told him that she did not have piblokto, that she was only shamming, and asked him not to use her pictures because she was naked. Whether or not she was fully conscious during the attack is difficult to say" (Brill, 1913, p. 516).

(12) "Alnaha, nicknamed Buster, 25 years old, was the only woman who jumped into the water during her attacks." She "was the only unmarried woman in the north." No one wanted her "not because she had no charms but because she was a very poor seamstress. She had more attacks than any one else" (Brill, 1913, pp. 515-516, 518).

(13) "Macmillan also witnessed an attack of piblokto in an Eskimo woman immediately following a rebuff by a White man who just showed her some favor" (Brill, 1913, p. 518).

Composite Cases, General Ideas, Comments

(14) *Niels Rasmussen:* "Certain things are common to all people as NR has observed it; they are always completely oblivious to their surroundings; they are always . . . strongly agitated, have a feverish light in their eyes, talk very fast but completely unintelligibly; and their speech makes no sense, 'speaking in tongues' so to say, just jabbering away but not in the Eskimo language. There is no way of telling where and when it may come. Some people can feel it coming. In . . . severe cases, they become completely exhausted and go to sleep for 12 hours; completely drained of all strength. Do most fantastic things, completely idiotic. Picking up all kinds of junk outside the house, carrying it into the house as if they had found some great treasure. Or the person in question may decide that he wants a little stone that he sees way up on top of the mountain. He will go and get it naked sometimes. Nudity won't keep him or her from running way up on top of the mountain. Women don't behave differently from men. Eskimos believe it is an absolutely natural phenomenon. They don't fear it" (Steed, 1947-48, pp. 204-205, 207, 209).

(15) *Peary:* ". . . women, more frequently than men, are afflicted. During these spells, the maniac removes all clothing and prances about like a broncho. A case of piblocto lasts from five minutes to half-an-hour or more. When it occurs under cover of a hut,

no apparent concern is felt by other inmates, nor is any attention paid
to the antics of the mad one. It is only when an attempt is made to
run abroad, that the cords of restraint are felt" (Peary, 1907, pp.
384-385).

"I have never known a child to have piblokto; but some one
among the adult Eskimos would have an attack every day or two, and
one day there were five cases. The immediate cause of this affection
is hard to trace, though sometimes it seems to be the result of a brooding over absent or dead relatives, or a fear of the future. The patient,
usually a woman, begins to scream and tear off and destroy her
clothing. If on the ship, she will walk up and down the deck, screaming and gesticulating, and generally in a state of nudity, though the
thermometer may be in the minus forties. As the intensity of the attack
increases, she will sometimes leap over the rail upon the ice, running
perhaps a half a mile. The attack may last from a few minutes, an
hour, or even more, and some sufferers become so wild that they
would continue running about on the ice perfectly naked until they
freeze to death, if they were not forcibly brought back . . . nobody
pays much attention, unless the sufferer should reach for a knife or
attempt to injure someone. The attack usually ends in a fit of weeping,
and when the patient quiets down, the eyes are bloodshot, the pulse
high, and the whole body trembles for an hour or so afterward"
(Peary, 1910, pp. 166-167).

(16) *Macmillan:* "A woman will be heard softly singing and accompanying herself by striking the fist of one hand with the palm of
the second, making three sounds, one long followed by two short ones.
The rhythm and motion continues to increase for some time, during
which she usually tears off her clothing, and ends in a fit of crying or
screaming in which the woman may imitate the cry of some familiar
animal or bird. No two women act alike; there is a certain individuality to every attack. Some drop down on their hands and knees and
crawl around barking like a dog. One woman used to lie on her back
on the snow and place some ice on her breasts. Some jump into the
water and wade among the ice cakes, all the time singing and yelling.
Others wander away from the houses into the hills, beating their
hands as if demented." According to Brill, "Macmillan was certain
that all of them showed a loss of consciousness; he thought they
were all in a confused state. I asked Professor Macmillan whether
he formed any idea as to the causation of this malady, and his answer
was as follows: 'I believe that the attacks are caused by abuse. Most
of the Eskimo women who had this disease were of a jealous disposition. They either imagined themselves ill treated or they actually
suffered abuse at the hands of their husbands, who often beat them
with their fists' " (Brill, 1913, pp. 515-517).

(17) *A Tale:* "This is a 'very old story.' It must have happened
about November . . . A whole family had met to pass the winter.
. . . Everything appeared all right—good hunting during the summer. In August the sky had been full of birds. . . . There had been

so many . . . [seakings] that they had caught hundreds and hundreds. A little before September the streams . . . were boiling with salmon. Foxes, good gracious, they were everywhere not to mention walruses and seals. 'We're rich,' said the father. But with the winter misfortune was to fall on them. For some days, now that the sun was low on the horizon, the mother had changed. She who used to work from morning till evening, who could be heard laughing from the time she got up, now remained for hours doing nothing in the igloo, silent, her expression vague. They weren't worried because . . . [they] know that people are generally a little out of sorts at this time. Once or twice, however, she had said strange things. One evening when the father and one of his sons went to eat seal with some neighbours, the mother remained lying down, saying that she was tired. Suddenly, towards midnight, they heard the dogs howl. 'Let's go back,' said the father. 'Something is wrong over there. I feel it here,' and he pointed to his skull. They could see the igloo light, which seemed to shine and then go out. One would have said that somebody was passing backwards and forwards ceaselessly. . . . When the father and son opened the door they saw a horrible sight. The house was upside-down. Torn caribou skins were strewn on the floor in the midst of seal-meat and streams of blood. The mother, her face black and congested, was running backwards and forwards, with her clothes in disorder, and an *oulou* (round woman's knife) in her hand. The children were trembling in the corner. The sound of the door made her jump. Suddenly she leapt, but the father was on her before she had taken three steps. The unhappy woman broke free and ran off, with hardly any clothes, towards the sea-ice in spite of the cold. She still held her knife, and without stopping picked up everything that seemed solid—pebbles, wood and so on. When she felt the men coming too close she threw everything at them over her shoulder. If she saw dog's droppings she smelt at them, rubbed her face with them and then gluttonously devoured the rest. The men pursued her to an iceberg. She tried to haul herself up, but she was badly shod and slid down. But she hung on to a spur, and finally managed to sit astride an ice-ridge. From here she managed to get away. Running toward the sea-ice . . . she leapt from ice-floe to ice-floe and defied her pursuers. Her situation was terrible. Every moment she almost fell into the water. Fortunately her strength suddenly failed, and the *Inouit* managed to reach her not far from the camp. The woman was exhausted by then. They tied her on the sledge, and, trembling with fever, she was taken back to the . . . igloo. Her face was pale. She had lost consciousness and rapidly fell into a heavy agitated sleep. When she woke some hours later she remembered nothing.

"The cases of *piblocta* (hysteria) were frequent among women, said the Eskimo. But one no longer saw such serious ones. And these hysterias have never killed anybody as far as I know" (Malaurie, 1956, pp. 75, 78-80).

Symptomatology

Loss or disturbance of consciousness during the seizure and amnesia for the attack appear as the central clinical features in the *pibloktoq* performance. Attacks are short-lived episodes, lasting from a few minutes to, in a few cases, a little over an hour, and terminate in complete remission afterwards.

Behavioral symptoms—motor and verbal—present in the *pibloktoq* seizures are listed below, roughly, in order of their frequency of appearance. These symptom categories have been delineated on the basis of fourteen seizure performances (discrete cases and one tale; data from composite cases, general ideas and comments re *pibloktoq* have been omitted from this frequency count).

(A) Tearing off of clothing; achieving partial or complete nudity. This is frequently one of the first behavioral signs of an attack. Niels Rasmussen speaks of it as a "common characteristic," as does Peary. *References:* 7: 5 women (cases 3, 7, 9, 11, 17); 2 men (cases 1, 6).

(B) Glossolalia and related phenomena. Two types appear here: *phonations frustes* (a miscellaneous group describing mutterings that vary from gurglings to meaningless syllables; *see* Carlyle May, 1956, p. 79), which forms our main group; and animal language. *References*: 7: 5 women (*phonations frustes*: cases 2, 4, 7, 11; animal language: case 9); 2 men (*phonations frustes*: cases 1, 5).

(C) Fleeing, nude or clothed. Running across ice or snow. Wandering into hills or mountains. If indoors, afflicted persons may run back and forth in an agitated state. If aboard ship, they may pace the deck ceaselessly, climb the rigging, and so forth. *References*: 6: 5 women (cases 2, 9, 10, 11, 17); 1 man (case 8).

(D) Rolling in snow. Jumping into water. Throwing self into snow drift. Placing ice on exposed breasts. These actions may be performed either in a clothed or nude state. *References*: 5: 3 women (cases 3, 9, 12); 2 men (cases 1, 6).

(E) Performing acts of slightly bizarre but harmless nature, viz., attempting to walk on ceiling, picking up and cherishing all sorts of odd objects, etc. *References*: 3: 3 women (cases 7, 9, 10); no men.

(F) Throwing everything handy around, creating disordered scene. *References:* 3: 2 women (cases 10, 17); 1 man (case 5).

(G) Performing mimetic acts, engaging in choreiform movements, accompanied by vocalization. *References:* 2: 2 women (cases 4, 9); no men.

(H) Coprophagia (feces eating). *References*: 1 woman (case 17).

Supernatural Strength, Restraint and Capture

During attacks *pibloktoq* individuals are possessed of supernatural strength which (1) enables them to perform the difficult and exhausting feats described above, and (2) abets them in forcibly resisting restraint and capture. We suggest, however, that the *pibloktoq's* desire for escape is not altogether a genuine one, but rather represents a dramatic invitation to be pursued and overtaken. This point will be discussed more fully later.

Prodromal and Terminal Symptoms

Prodromal symptoms—tiredness, depressive silences, vagueness of expression, confusion—have been reported. These symptoms may precede the attack by several days.

Weeping, body tremors, feverishness, bloodshot eyes, high pulse are frequent terminal symptoms.

Invariably, individuals are thoroughly exhausted after an attack and may, in some instances, sleep for as long as fifteen hours. Rational behavior is resumed immediately once an attack has terminated.

Sex and Age Factors

Previous writers have characterized *pibloktoq* principally as a female disorder. Peary (Brill, 1913, p. 517) is quoted as saying that in twenty years he saw only one man who had what was thought to be *pibloktoq*. According to our data, on the basis of 14 seizures (discrete cases and one tale), we observe ten instances in women and four in men. This sample suggests that although occurring predominantly in women, *pibloktoq* is also far from infrequent among men.

Although reliable testimony (Niels Rasmussen) states there are no sex differences in symptomatology, our data suggest that *pibloktoq* is more florid in women: for example, no instances of symptoms E (slightly bizarre, harmless acts), G (mimetic acts, choreiform movements, etc.) or H (feces eating) appear in men. Symptom C (fleeing, nude or clothed) is represented by only one male example (case 8)—and that, a doubtful one.

No instances of *pibloktoq* have been reported for children. Age and marital status data are too incomplete for generalization. All persons, however, are described as adult; the youngest age mentioned is twenty-five, the oldest forty-five. Four women are mentioned as married, one unmarried. For four other women and the four men no data are available.

Alleged Harmfulness of *Pibloktoq*

Various writers (Knud Rasmussen in Steensby, 1910, pp. 377-378; Kloss, 1923, p. 254; Ackerknecht, 1948, p. 917; Mowat, 1952, pp. 189-190; among others) refer to the potential harmfulness of *pibloktoq*, while others (see cases 8, 17) cite instances of acts which appear to be the beginnings of real violence, but which, significantly, are never carried through. We have already cited Malaurie's informant to this effect. According to the available evidence, there are no recorded instances of afflicted individuals ever causing harm to others. Personal injury, with the exception of occasional frostbite, is also unknown; this despite the terrifying risks undertaken. Damage to property, yes; to persons, no. Thus, Ackerknecht's (1948, p. 917) and Kloss's (1923, p. 254) comparison of *pibloktoq* with amok is not affirmed by our examination of the data. Unlike true amok, the *pseudo*-amoklike behavior present in some of the *pibloktoq* cases, with no aggressive, harmful intentions, is a well-known feature of agitated hysteria and has been reported by Dembovitz (1945) to occur among West African troops and by Dobrizhoffer (1822) for the primitive Abipones of Paraguay. According to Dembovitz (p. 73):

> *Running amok* is a popularly known form of abnormal behavior. The picture is one of a man suddenly seizing a hatchet or a tommy-gun or a rifle and rushing around slaying all he meets. These cases usually have a rapid and fatal ending. . . . Pseudo running amok is seen in excited hysterics. They are always careful not to injure anybody and, when cornered, they go quietly, in sharp distinction to the true berserk who fights to the end.

Among the Abipones, according to Dobrizhoffer (1822), the agitated *Loaparaika*—men as well as women—"rave and storm like madmen," threaten the villagers with armed violence, "strike the roof and mats of every tent again and again with their sticks," etc., but do not actually cause injury to any of the inhabitants (p. 233ff.).

In this connection, it is important to distinguish *pibloktoq*, as described in this paper, from "psychotic" episodes which terminate in maniacal, murderous acts. Such acts are not uncommon among the Eskimo. However, there is no evidence of similarity in symptomatology or behavior between these two manifestations. They appear as distinct phenomena. The confusion seems to stem from the term "arctic hysteria," which has been used as if it were a unit phenomenon, a rubric under which every form of mental disorder observed in the arctic has been subsumed (Czaplicka, 1914, pp. 307-325: Aberle, 1952, pp. 294-295).

The calmness with which Eskimo culture receives *pibloktoq* is further evidence of its nondangerous nature. The Eskimo accept *pibloktoq* as a natural phenomenon, as something that can happen to anyone. This suggests that the *pibloktoq* reaction does not arise from any special difficulties of adjustment to particular situations on the part of abnormal individuals, but rather that it is a manifestation of aspects of the personality and ego organization common to the individuals comprising the group. Yap (1952, p. 552) reaches the same conclusion with respect to the *latah* reaction among Malays. The tolerant attitude displayed by the Polar Eskimo toward *pibloktoq*, combined with their failure to view *pibloktoq* as a "disease," supports the inference that we are dealing more with an aspect of the basic ethnic personality than, strictly speaking, with a mental illness.

It is important, at this point, to note that Eskimo culture institutionalizes "hysteroid" behavior that is directly related to those events, happenings, anxieties, etc., perceived as ego and culturally dystonic. Briefly, at the onset of winter, women, singly and in small groups, weep disconsolately, wail, cry and groan. Some frantically writhe to and fro in expressions of mournful anguish. At other moments they dance about with "emotions of madness." The men take part in similar, though separate, displays. In emotive dances and chants which terminate in bouts of uncontrollable weeping and "hysterical laughter" the men give vent to their emotionality. When these "mourning" rites, which may last a number of days, are over, the Eskimo lapse into a brief period of lethargy and melancholy from which they soon recover (Cook, 1911, pp. 92-97).

A careful examination of this group "hysteroid" behavior—which represents a memorialization of all misfortunes and hardships of the past year, but at which time individuals also express their grief for events which transpired many years ago—reveals the major axes of stress and trauma embedded in Eskimo culture: threat of starvation, insufficiencies of food, loss of members through hunting and other accidents, as well as the physical discomforts and dangers ever present in their lives. In a later section, we will see that these identical anxieties recur as precipitating causes of *pibloktoq*.

Climate as Cause of *Pibloktoq*

The arctic winter climate has frequently been cited as a cause of Eskimo mental derangements (Steensby, 1910, pp. 377-378; Novakovsky, 1924, pp. 113-127; Jenness, 1928, p. 52; Weyer, 1932, p. 386; Birket-Smith, 1936, pp.

54-55; etc.). The Polar winter, which lasts from about the beginning of November to the middle of February, has been termed "depressing," "monotonous," "melancholy," and for these reasons seen as productive of morbid reactions on the part of the Eskimo.

The deficiencies of the climatological point of view as causation of mental disorder are considerable, and in this connection Aberle's (1952, p. 295) findings of the negative relationship between Siberian *latah* and the arctic winter are pertinent. The writings of long-experienced arctic explorers offer telling evidence that the Eskimo are not morosely affected by the arctic winter climate as such, that they do not, as a group, become depressed and morbid once winter sets in. According to Knud Rasmussen (1908, pp. 79-80):

> The first dark evenings are hailed with the same glee as the first daylight, after the Polar night. Up there, as here, people like change. When, a whole summer through, your eyes have been bathed in light, day and night, you long to see the land vanish softly into the darkness again. . . . And with the idea of change they associate the thought of all the good things the winter will bring with it: the frozen sea, and the hunting on the ice, and the swift sledge-drives, far from the sweltering houses, after bears.

Stefansson (1922), writing of the Mackenzie Delta Eskimo, says:

> In the books I had read about the Eskimos I had always been impressed with how lonesome and depressing it must be to spend the several weeks of midwinter without one ray of sunlight. This had been worrying me a great deal even before the sun disappeared, but Roxy [an Eskimo] had told me that he had never heard of any Eskimos who minded the absence of the sun, and had added that all white men got used to it after a year or two. Sten had confirmed this and, altogether, I had gathered from him and the Eskimo that in the Arctic the period of the sun's absence is looked forward to by everybody and is the jolliest time of the year [p. 130].

Niels Rasmussen (Steed, 1947-48) states:

> Dark time for whites is depressing, irritating more than in other times. But Eskimos have a gay time during that period. Not so for the whites. There are other whites who get very temperamental about it. Trader and parsons don't have this trouble. When one knows what to expect of the dark time, it is not a strain, especially if one has work. NR didn't feel it the first two years because he had plenty of work; but the third year when he was a weather observer, felt excessively sleepy, depressive, no interest in the future; lived alone and if he had had a companion he would have acted quite irritably he believes [p. 209].

Bertelsen (1929) sums up the effect of the arctic winter on Europeans:

Of the greatest importance in respect of health, is, however, the influence of the country on the nervous system of those who come to live here. The long distance from the Mother-country, the forced association with the same people or the absolute loneliness, the lack of suitable variety, the comparative inactivity, the monotony which often makes life feel curiously unreal and shadowy, an existence essentially limited to the daily metabolic process, the journeys, frequently with a distinct element of danger, the close contact with the forces of nature, the illimitable space, the stillness and the darkness, operate strongly on the mind. During the first part of the stay all of these factors not infrequently result in an increased irritability and a morbid distrust of the surroundings; later on a certain dulling of the initiative and a coarsening of the whole mental life are the most conspicuous symptoms. In certain cases, with special mental predispositions, the reaction may set in far more strongly, terminating in pronounced insanity [p. 382].

On the basis of the above, and other similar statements, we suggest, therefore, that the theory of the arctic winter climate as a cause of *pibloktoq* or other Eskimo or Siberian mental derangements represents nothing more than a projection of what the European in the Arctic may experience, and in no way accounts for Eskimo psychopathology.

Precipitating Causes of *Pibloktoq*

Our data show little that is specific about the precipitating causes of *pibloktoq*. *Pibloktoq* may occur at any time of the year and may be precipitated by a sudden fright, unusual mental shock, brooding over absent or dead relatives, fear of the future, imagined or actual abuse, and so forth. Earlier, we suggested that *pibloktoq* did not arise from the difficulties of adjustment on the part of abnormal persons to specific situations, but rather that such reactions were a manifestation of the basic Eskimo personality. To this will now be added the fact that *pibloktoq* represents reactions of the Polar Eskimo to situations of unusually intense, but culturally typical, stress. Certain "triggering situations" are generally recognized as traumatic. The knowledge that Eskimos are prone[5] to panic when out of sight of land and in unfamiliar waters was, according to Frederick Cook[6] (1911, pp. 11-12)

[5] Panic and desertion by Eskimo from the ships of European exploring parties was not an uncommon occurrence. For some accounts, see Melville (1896, p. 464).

[6] The merits of the Cook-Peary controversy have no bearing upon the validity of Cook's Eskimo observations.

among them the delusion that the mirages and low-lying clouds they saw used by him to *prevent* panic among his Eskimo by deliberately creating from his ship were signs of land. The abnormally high rate of *pibloktoq* among the Eskimo accompanying Peary—"some one among the adult Eskimos would have an attack every day or two, and one day there were five cases" (Peary, 1910, pp. 166-167, 230)—may, we suggest, be attributed to panic at being so far from home, in unfamiliar surroundings and fearful of whether they would, in fact, ever return. Peary's Eskimo, unlike Cook's, became *pibloktoq,* we suggest, because no defenses against this trauma were provided. Cook supported his Eskimo into believing what they could not help knowing to be false; they were willing to be deceived as a defense against panic.[7] Peary, on the other hand, employed no such therapeutic measures, and in fact did the opposite, forcibly encouraging them to accept reality, thus "feeding" their panic (Peary, 1910, p. 230; Cook, 1911, pp. 11-12).

Writers stressing climatological factors in the etiology of *pibloktoq* point to its prevalence in winter. We have already noted that consciously the Eskimo look forward to winter as a relatively happy time of year. We suggest, however, that *unconsciously* winter is perceived by the Eskimo traumatically, not for reasons of darkness, oppressiveness of environment, etc., but rather that winter, more than other seasons, intensifies Eskimo insecurity and hence their proneness to derangement, because increased threats of starvation, high accident rates, etc., are inherent, though perhaps psychologically denied, features of the Polar winter. Case 17, a legend, and therefore a culturally selected synthesis, dramatically calls attention to the close relationship between *pibloktoq* and repressed winter starvation anxieties by overemphasizing the amount of food on hand *prior* to winter.

CULTURAL MATRICES AND *Pibloktoq*

The *pibloktoq* syndrome, bizarre and incomprehensible as it may appear at first glance, is nevertheless composed of elements, many of which appear regularly in Eskimo culture but in a variety of different matrices.[8] In the *pibloktoq* performance these behaviors are lifted out of their cultural context and fitted into new patterns.

Nudity, one of the more statistically prevalent symptoms and often one of the first to appear in an attack, is not an uncommon feature among Es-

---

[7] I am indebted to Dr. George Devereux for this insight.

[8] For a discussion of matrices in anthropology and psychoanalysis, see Devereux (1957).

kimos. Partial or complete nudity is a frequent state of dress indoors. Following a sweat-bath, Eskimos will emerge and roll naked in snowbanks or have snow thrown on them. Glossolalia and mimetic animal behavior are well-known standard features of Eskimo medicoreligious functionaries. Shouting and singing are features which also appear in verbal duels (drum fights). A number of the "mourning"-rite features described above—weeping, wailing, crying, groaning, etc.—are also repeated in *pibloktoq*. In another part of the world, Korea, behavior in exact duplication of Eskimo *pibloktoq* is found in connection with the initiation rites of sorcerers (May, 1956, p. 82).

The "individuality" of *pibloktoq* would seem to stem from a fusion of culturally linked symptoms either with idiosyncratic features (representations of the individual unconscious), or else with subjectivized elaborations or modifications of cultural behavior. We suggest, further, that there exists a "fitting" of the individual ethnic neurosis pattern to particular situations; that is, there is an unconscious relationship between precipitating contexts and the specific symptoms chosen. Unfortunately, there are at present insufficient data upon which to test this assumption.

PSYCHODYNAMICS

The principal psychopathological element in *pibloktoq* is some basic underlying anxiety, "triggered off" by severe, culturally typical, stress: fear of certain concrete or impending situations; fear of, or experience of, loss, especially of emotional support, including the sense of being within safe, solid, familiar land, etc. The *pibloktoq* performance represents a culturally patterned panic reaction to such trauma. It is apparent that afflicted persons face a double danger: a threatening real world and unconscious material stirred up by the traumatic experience. The *pibloktoq* seizure aims at restoring the ego balance through the instrumentation of various defense mechanisms.

Regressive features play an important role in *pibloktoq*. Such features dramatize the underlying psychodynamic element, namely the *infantile* need for love and emotional support in the disturbed individual. One of the chief characteristics of *pibloktoq* is the childlike and naïve quality of the performance. This quality did not escape the perceptive eye of Macmillan: "It [*pibloktoq*] reminded me of a little child discouraged and unhappy because it imagines that no one loves it or cares for it and therefore runs away" (Brill, 1913, p. 517).

Earlier we cast doubt upon the genuineness of the *pibloktoq's* desire for escape. We suggest that the flight reaction represents a regressive act, a dramatic, though thoroughly unconscious, invitation to be pursued, i.e., to be attended to, taken care of. It is noteworthy that attacks tend to occur under favorable circumstances,[9] at times when their occurrence will not put into jeopardy the lives of other members of the group and when other persons are available to render assistance. Furthermore, there is no evidence that attacks ever take place while an individual is alone. The dread of attacks occurring under unfavorable conditions probably lies behind the fact that seizures may be delayed until it is safe to have one (see case 5). Whitney (1911, p. 67) commenting on Tukshu's attack (case 1) remarks that it "would have been a very serious matter . . . had Tukshu been attacked while in the boat." As it was, he had his attack while *leaving* the boat.

Furthermore, *pibloktoq* demonstrates important denial and compensatory features. The individual experiencing deep anxiety and fear attempts via *pibloktoq* to deny these feelings and compensate for these emotions by dramatically engaging in antithetical behavior which stresses mobility, dangerous and strenuous feats, etc. In other words, *pibloktoq* represents an expression of control over, denial of, and compensation for, feelings of helplessness and deep anxiety.

To sum up: it would appear that afflicted individuals experience acute helplessness and deep anxiety. In *pibloktoq* the traumatized ego reacts in a psychologically primitive and infantile, but characteristically Eskimo, manner. In other words, though the psychological mode is ontogenetically primitive, much of the behavior is congruent with adult Eskimo ethnic personality.

The interpretation of helplessness may, in part, help explain why women are both more prone to *pibloktoq* and why their symptomatology tends to be more florid. The dependence of Eskimo women on the male hunters for food and, more particularly, their added helplessness in the face of culturally typical traumatic experiences increases their vulnerability. In cases 2 and 3, for example, Tongwe had no alternative but to sit and await the return of the hunters.

Diagnosis

Finally, we come to the question of diagnosis. Forty-six years ago, upon reviewing the Peary and Macmillan material, Brill (1913) wrote:

And yet is there really so much difference between the hysterical mechanisms as evidenced in piblokto and the grande hysterie or

[9] Whitney (1911, p. 67) mentions that attacks may also take place under unfavorable conditions, but cites no cases.

other modern hysterical manifestations? We may assume unhesitatingly that the difference is more apparent than real. The deeper determinants as we have seen are the same in both. With due apologies to Mr. Kipling we may say that the modern lady and Eskimo Julia O'Grady are the same under the skin [p. 520].

Nothing in the cases cited in this paper seems to warrant any substantial change in Brill's original diagnosis of hysteria. Certainly, schizophrenia is ruled out, despite feces eating in one case, on the grounds of the brevity of attacks and their complete remission afterwards.

BIBLIOGRAPHY

Aberle, D. F. (1952), Arctic Hysteria and Latah in Mongolia. *Trans. N. Y. Acad. Sci.*, Series II, *14*:291-297.

Ackerknecht, E. H. (1948), Medicine and Disease among Eskimos. *Ciba Symposia, 10*:916-921.

Aronson, J. D. (1940), The History of Disease among the Natives of Alaska. *Transactions and Studies of the College of Physicians of Philadelphia*, 4th Series, Vol. 8.

Bertelsen, A. (1929), Sanitation and Health Conditions in Greenland. In: *Greenland*, *3*:363-386. London: Humphrey Milford.

Birket-Smith, K. (1936), *The Eskimos*, tr. W. E. Calvert. London: Methuen.

Brill, A. A. (1913), Pibloktoq or Hysteria among Peary's Eskimos. *J. Nerv. & Ment. Dis.*, *40*:514-520.

Cook, F. A. (1911), *My Attainment of the Pole.* New York: Polar Publishing Co.

Czaplicka, M. A. (1914), *Aboriginal Siberia.* Oxford: Clarendon Press.

Dall, W. H. (1870), *Alaska and Its Resources.* Boston: Lee & Shepard.

Dembovitz, N. (1945), Psychiatry amongst West African Troops. *J. Roy. Army Med. Corps, 84*:70-74.

Devereux, G. (1956), Normal and Abnormal: The Key Problem of Psychiatric Anthropology. In: *Some Uses of Anthropology: Theoretical and Applied.* Washington, D.C.: Anthropological Society of Washington.

—— (1957), Psychoanalysis as Anthropological Field Work: Data and Theoretical Implications. *Trans. N. Y. Acad. Sci.*, Series II, *19*:457-472.

Dobrizhoffer, M. (1822), *An Account of the Abipones*, 2. London: John Murray.

Honigmann, J. J. (1949), Culture and Ethos of Kaska Society. *Yale University Publications in Anthropology*, No. 40.

Jenness, D. (1928), *The People of the Twilight.* New York: Macmillan.

Joseph, A. & Murray, V. F. (1951), *Chamorros and Carolinians of Saipan.* Cambridge, Mass.: Harvard University Press.

Kloss, C. B. (1923), Arctic Amok. *J. Roy. Asiat. Soc., Malayan Branch, 1*:254.

Malaurie, J. (1956), *The Last Kings of Thule: A Year among the Polar Eskimos of Greenland*, tr. G. Freeman. London: George Allen & Unwin.

May, L. C. (1956), A Survey of Glossolalia and Related Phenomena in Non-Christian Religions. *Amer. Anthropologist, 58*:75-96.

Melville, G. W. (1896), *In the Lena Delta*. Boston: Houghton, Mifflin.

Mowat, F. (1952), *People of the Deer*. Boston: Little, Brown.

Novakovsky, S. (1924), Arctic or Siberian Hysteria as a Reflex of the Geographic Environment. *Ecology, 5*:113-127.

Peary, R. E. (1907), *Nearest the Pole*. New York: Doubleday, Page.

—— (1910), *The North Pole*. New York: Frederick A. Stokes.

Rasmussen, K. (1908), *The People of the Polar North*, ed. G. Herring. London: Kegan Paul, Trench, Trubner.

Seligman, C. G. (1932), Anthropological Perspective and Psychological Theory. *J. Roy. Anthropol. Inst., 62*:193-228.

Steed, G. P. (1947-48), Unpublished Interviews with Niels Rasmussen.

Steensby, H. P. (1910), Contributions to the Ethnology and Anthropogeography of the Polar Eskimo. *Meddelelser om Gronland, 54.*

Stefansson, V. (1922), *Hunters of the Great North*. New York: Harcourt, Brace.

Teicher, M. I. (1954), Three Cases of Psychoses among the Eskimos. *J. Ment. Sci., 100*:527-535.

Weyer, E. M. (1932), *The Eskimos: Their Environment and Folkways*. New Haven: Yale University Press.

Whitney, H. (1911), *Hunting with Eskimos*. New York: Century Co.

Yap, P. M. (1951), Mental Diseases Peculiar to Certain Cultures: A Survey of Comparative Psychiatry. *J. Ment. Sci., 97*:313-327.

—— (1952), The Latah Reaction: Its Pathodynamics and Nosological Position. *J. Ment. Sci., 98*:515-564.

Zilboorg, G. (1938), Critique: Section Meeting on Culture and Personality. *Amer. J. Orthopsychiat., 8*:596-601.

THE EVOLUTION OF AN ACTIVE ANTI-NEGRO RACIST

TERRY C. RODGERS, M.D.

Members of hate groups are not prone to subject themselves to psychological investigation. Therefore, any observation of such individuals, no matter how brief and incomplete, deserves to be communicated.

While in practice in the South I had the opportunity to witness the transformation of one admittedly prejudiced individual from a passive, pacifistic, severely inhibited and obsessional state into an active, rabid hater of Negroes. This transformation took place during a five-month period and while undergoing psychoanalytic therapy. It is not suggested that the pathological mechanisms observable in this case account in full for the phenomena of prejudice and discrimination—phenomena which are undoubtedly multidetermined. They do, however, throw some light on how psychological and social factors contribute to the development and expression of such phenomena, particularly those that predispose to overt acts of aggression.

The body of this paper will consist of two parts. Part I will be a case presentation with discussion. Part II will contain a brief selective discussion of the literature together with some comments on certain psychological and sociological influences peculiar to the South.

I

A forty-three-year-old single white male sought analysis following its recommendation by the staff of a major medical center where he had gone for a comprehensive medical investigation. His presenting complaints of fatigue, lassitude and constipation were of twelve years' duration beginning approximately one year after his father's death from a degenerative neurological disease.

An abbreviated version of the preamble and Part I of this paper was read before The Association for Psychoanalytic Medicine, New York, April 7, 1959 and the Brief Communications Section at the Annual Meeting of The American Psychoanalytic Association in Philadelphia, April 24, 1959 under the title: "From Reformer to Persecutor—A Case Report." I am indebted to the following discussants for their insightful and thought-provoking comments: Dr. B. Ruth Easser (New York), Dr. James C. Skinner (Boston), and Dr. Charles W. Socarides (New York).

Psychiatric examination revealed a markedly obsessional individual with a plethora of obsessive rituals, doubts, and fears dating back to early adolescence. Poorly integrated reaction formations abounded along with increasing ego restrictions as the former proved insufficient to protect against his sadistic impulses. Such was the power of this man's unconscious aggression that though a registered member of the Bar, he had given up the practice of law ten years previously for the following reason: He might be appointed by the Court to defend a client charged with a capital crime. In his defense he might make some technical error as a result of which his client would be convicted and executed, thereby, in effect, making him a murderer. A most revealing example, of how the overdetermination of his reaction formations led back to killing and death in symbolic form, was in his expression of regret that he had not become a professor of Latin. As a dead language it was the only place in this world where certainty was possible. Since giving up his law practice he had been an active worker in an organization devoted to the abolition of capital punishment. So great was his preoccupation with capital punishment that he had read "in the interest of justice" the court transcripts, appeals, and judicial reviews of every individual that had been executed in his state for the past fifty years. He expressed opposition to military service, and was an exponent of pacifistic religious and philosophical systems. He was, in short, a professional pacifist.

In typical obsessive fashion his whole world was divided into good and bad, pure and impure, clean and dirty, acceptable and unacceptable. This splitting was most manifest in his sexual life. Though he had since college days been sexually active, his relations had been limited to "degraded" objects. The following categories of women were taboo: virgins, wives, and widows. He was especially vehement in his insistence that widows should remain faithful to their deceased husbands.

He was the only child of upper-middle-class parents who resided in a small town. His father was an attorney who, in addition, owned and operated a cotton plantation. At the age of fifty-three his father was afflicted with the aforementioned neurological disorder and died from this condition at the age of sixty. His mother was living, in good physical health, and he lived alone with her in the house where he was reared. Both parents were rigid obsessional characters, preoccupied with health, cleanliness and "proper" behavior. He was said to have been completely toilet trained at the age of two. One of his few childhood memories was his mother's careful attention to his bowel habits and her insistence that he wash his hands after urination. Except for this supervision he was cared for by a Negro nurse who was still employed by his mother as cook and maid. It is of interest that while he was most insistent that his mother abide by the compulsive systems that he had devised, he did not demand this of his old nurse. He was remarkably tolerant of her.[1]

He occupied the parental bedroom until the middle of his third year but had no memory of this. Infantile masturbation was not recalled and he denied even sexual curiosity prior to puberty. The only sexual prohibition that he could recall was a warning from his father when he was seventeen to stay away from the girls in "nigger town" lest he catch a venereal disease. He claims this was his first knowledge of the existence of venereal diseases. The facts of reproduction were learned sometime during adolescence, but he could recall no affective response to this. Adolescent masturbation was also denied. He states that he masturbated once at the age of twenty, out of curiosity and without fantasy. He found it only mildly pleasurable and did not repeat it because it was "unhealthy and wrong." His first heterosexual experience was a year later with the daughter of his landlady, an experience in which he was essentially passive. Following this he led a very active sexual life with "easy" women. He had, however, a compulsion to have them tell him in minute detail and repeatedly of their other sexual experiences, thereby, through identification, vicariously enjoying the sexual experience of the female. He called it his "painful pleasure." He denied ever having been in love.

His physical appearance and manner were most striking. He displayed a degree of hypotonicity so pronounced that he reminded one of an overheated wax figure. For the first four months of his analysis he lay on the couch with his hands tucked under his head, his legs crossed at the ankles and absolutely immobile. His speech was measured, pedantic, and professorial. His productions were typically obsessional in that they dealt with detailed recitations of life experiences, past and present, but without affect. Interspersed with these were abstract philosophical digressions and obsessive ruminations.

Gradually he was able to see in an intellectual way that the common denominator running through all his obsessive symptoms was a struggle with authority (conscience or external representations of his conscience). Feelings toward or concerning me were denied for the first three months. I then noticed that he had acquired the habit of looking at the couch for several seconds at the termination of each session. When I called this to his attention he replied that it was to see if any coins had fallen from his pockets during

---

[1] This dual relationship with two mothers, one white and one colored, one "fitten" and one "not fitten," one rigid and proper and one permissive and indulgent, was a common experience for the Southern white child of the upper and upper-middle classes a generation ago. It provided ready-made the concept of a "degraded" and a "tabooed" love object. See Smith (1949).

the session. A few sessions later, with some show of affect, he volunteered the information that his looking at the couch was really motivated by a fear that some of the mineral oil that he habitually took had leaked from his anus and soiled my couch. Though he rationalized his fear with a statement that he often soiled his underwear in this manner, it clearly revealed not only his hostility but his fear of anal rape. Approximately one month later he reported his first dream.

> I am walking on ———— Street in my home town. It is late at night. A group of teen-agers are doing "rock and roll" in the street. I stop to watch them, feeling a mixture of pleasure and envy that they are so vigorous, carefree and joyous. I then notice Mr. X., a colleague and contemporary of my father's standing beside me. He appears very old and emaciated like my father before his death. He is also carrying a black cane like the one my father carried. He berates me for being out so late at night and for associating with delinquents. Before I can explain he begins to beat me with his cane. I try to raise my arms to protect myself but I am paralyzed. I feel ashamed and humiliated—then I awoke.

To the "rock and roll" he associated the purported sexual freedom of present-day adolescents. Perhaps it also refers to masturbation. Mr. X. is obviously his father. Perhaps he took his father's warning to stay away from "nigger town" more seriously than he thought. The black cane might refer to Negroes—Negroes were like animals about sex. The shame and humiliation he felt reminded him of an incident at the age of eight. He wonders why he hadn't thought to tell me of it before. He had never forgotten it and considered it the most painful experience of his childhood. One day in school he had impulsively pulled the pony tail of a young girl sitting in front of him. He had pulled it with all his might and she had cried. There was no reason for this; it was done on impulse and was as inexplicable to him as it was to the teacher who had witnessed it. He was severely reprimanded and was overcome with shame and humiliation. At this point he blocked. I inquired as to his thoughts. He replied that he was thinking of ———— Street but could not tell me what. (Why?). The name of the street reminded him of a lady. (What about this lady?). That was what he couldn't tell me. (The rule of free association is explained again.) Then with considerable trepidation and protestation that it was not gentlemanly to reveal such information about someone else he related the following story: Some three weeks before he had met a lady. Her husband had died two years previously and she had a ten-year-old son. She was intellectually stimulating and to relieve his loneliness during his four-day stay in town each week he had spent several evenings with her.

He had no sexual interest in her since he considered her to be a married woman. The preceding evening he had had dinner at her house and after her son had retired she had literally seduced him. However, he was unable to perform, suffering from ejaculatio ante portas. His first reaction was one of relief that intercourse had not taken place. He sought and received reassurance from her that she had not already been unfaithful to her deceased husband. Could he be sure? Had she told him the truth? If she was so willing with him how could he believe her? It really didn't matter. To be willing was the equivalent of the act anyway. Certainly she would sooner or later. Nevertheless he didn't want to be the culprit. He had told her he couldn't see her again. Still she might be telling the truth. That was why it was wrong for him to tell me of the incident. He was caught between his obligation to her and his obligation to me. He was sure it would lower my opinion of her regardless of what I might say.

During this recitation he abandoned his usual immobile position on the couch and became increasingly hyperactive. He left the session somewhat agitated and for the first time in weeks did not look back at the couch. The following day he was somewhat calmer but repeated his obsessive doubts about the virtue of the lady in question. Because of increasing guilt about revealing her name to me he had telephoned the evening before to confess his confession to me. She had assumed he would and seemed unconcerned about it. This only increased his doubts about her. Was it really true that seemingly respectable people could be so casual about sex? Of course the Negroes were, but no one expected any more of them. Was I as tolerant as I seemed? Perhaps, but he found it hard to believe.

Following a week-end break he began to talk of the integration-segregation issue—a theme which he never abandoned during the remaining weeks of his treatment. Though he would never associate with a Negro, he had not until now felt personally affected by desegregation. But now he could see it was not going to stop with the schools. Public transportation was being desegregated. Before long you could not find a place to eat without having to risk sitting beside a Negro. What he found incomprehensible were the "nigger-loving" white Southerners—the traitors to their heritage. Would I permit my children to go to school with Negroes? Interpretations to the effect that he was still concerned with my attitude toward sex—that he saw me as a seducer and feared becoming like me were rejected. This was another matter. He reversed his position on capital punishment, saying it had to be retained as the only means of keeping the Negroes in line.[2] He expressed

[2] This was at a time when the Emmett Till murder was still headline news. He declared his approval of this killing. See Huie (1956).

concern about leaving his mother alone during his visits to me lest some Negro assault her. With increasing insistence he demanded to know where I stood on this issue. If he were to judge from the contents of the magazines I kept in my waiting room he would have to conclude that I was an integrationist, but he didn't want to believe it. Three weeks later, near the end of the last session of the week, he reported a second dream.

> My mother is lying on the ground about to be gored by a huge bull with black horns. I feel momentarily paralyzed as in the other dream, but by an enormous act of will I overcome it. Then with a feeling of almost unlimited strength I leap at the bull and rip its horns off with my bare hands. I feel an indescribable sense of triumph and exhilaration.

His associations dealt with his recent anxiety about leaving his mother alone during the greater part of each week. The black horns were associated with Negroes, his father's black cane and my black horn-rimmed glasses. Perhaps he was afraid of me and had been of his father, but this was just an idea. . . . His fear for his mother was real; the danger was real. . . . When the castration theme was pointed out he expressed the idea that it would be a good thing if all Negroes were castrated. His ability to act in the dream pleased him immensely and the session was terminated on this note.

Two days later I received a special-delivery letter from him stating that some unexpected difficulties on the farm demanded his immediate attention and that he would have to discontinue treatment for a few weeks at least. I did not hear from him again until approximately six months later when I received from him some propaganda leaflets prepared by the White Citizens Council together with information indicating that he had assumed a role of leadership in this organization. This performance was repeated several times during the next eighteen months. The theme of all these leaflets was that integration would lead to miscegenation, intermarriage and " mongrelization" of the races.

Thus by the wholesale use of the defense mechanisms of projection and identification with the aggressor, he protects himself against eruption into awareness of (a) his unconscious homosexual wishes, (b) his incestuous desires, and (c) his patricidal impulses—and in so doing wards off a potential psychotic breakdown. Instead of being the white female who will be attacked by the Negro male (father, analyst) or the Negro male who commits the unpardonable crime of sexual union with the white female (mother), he becomes the powerful white male who protects the white female from the fantasied lust and aggression of the Negro male.

It is of interest to compare and contrast his reactions in the analytic situation, when under the impact of the transference his ego-alien impulses threatened to overwhelm the ego defenses, with his reactions at the time of his father's death. In each instance we are able to see both the original impulses and the defenses mobilized against them.

The death of his father removed the external inhibitory force acting against his sexual and aggressive drives, particularly his incestuous desires. This inhibitor he attempted to regain by ego restrictions, various neurotic symptoms, and extensive reaction formations on both a psychic and somatic level. This allowed him to live close to his mother and permitted a very restricted sexuality with degraded love objects. His ardent crusading against capital punishment demonstrates both his aggressivity and the defense against it. By identifying with his dead father and by abandoning his law practice, he both denies and atones for his patricidal wishes.

The developing transference revived these original impulses, which once again threatened to overwhelm his ego defenses. His feared loss of control is clearly revealed in his concern with loss of coins and feces. The gradual breakdown of his reaction formations against aggression was first met with an exacerbation of his positive feelings for the analyst (father) which was experienced as the wish and dread of anal rape. In an attempt to protect himself against these impulses he took a precipitous flight into heterosexuality. He attempted intercourse with the widow—for him a tabooed incestuous object—but his castration anxiety was too great to permit its consummation. Then in a near panic he projects his incestuous desires onto the Negro male and becomes acutely anxious about a possible sexual assault upon his mother. By assuming the role of protector of his mother he achieves an ego-acceptable outlet for his aggression and can return to her in a disguised incestuous relationship. In the last dream there is a triumphant frenzied celebration of the recapture of his "Southern manhood" reminiscent of the murder of the primal father by the sons (Freud, 1913, 1921). Its primal-scene quality is self-evident, and as a "rescue dream" it is incestuous (Freud, 1910). He kills the father (analyst) and becomes the "father of himself."

Such a resolution of his conflicts was undoubtedly aided and abetted by the fact that his culture not only condoned it but supplied him with all the necessary rationalizations.

II

No attempt will be made to review in detail the not inconsiderable amount of literature dealing with racial prejudice and discrimination. The greater part of it tends to focus on one particular form of it, namely, anti-Semitism (Ackerman and Jahoda, 1948, 1950; Loewenstein, 1951; Simmel, 1946). Granting the obvious psychodynamic similarities between anti-Semitism and anti-Negro prejudice, there are, I believe, also basic differences— and these differences are based on the unconscious meaning of color. Furthermore, there is a deplorable tendency, both in the scientific and popular literature (and in the minds of many of our public officials), to treat the phenomena of prejudice and discrimination as being, if not one and the same thing, so closely allied that there is no practical advantage in differentiating between the two. Happy exceptions to this tendency are Brian Bird's (1957) "A Consideration of the Etiology of Prejudice" and Richard Sterba's (1947) "Some Psychological Factors in Negro Race Hatred and in Anti-Negro Riots." Bird's article is such a thorough and lucid consideration of the etiology and psychodynamics of prejudice both from the viewpoint of the individual and the group that the reader is referred to it for a discussion of this phenomenon. Sterba's paper is a more specific one, limiting itself to a consideration of anti-Negro prejudice and overt acts of violence against the Negro. His findings are, therefore, particularly applicable to the case presented in Part I of this paper.

From the clinical material obtained from patients in analysis during the Detroit race riots in June 1943 he concludes "that the negative attitude toward Negroes has a twofold origin, and that it manifests itself in two different forms of hatred and aggression. The first form is the constant and general antagonism against the Negroes, and includes all members of the race. It is expressed in the general trend of many white people to 'draw the color line.' . . . Negroes are considered, or better, experienced emotionally, as unwelcome intruders" (p. 412). This reaction is based on repressed sibling rivalry and in the unconscious of such people the Negro represents unwanted younger siblings. The second form of Negro hatred and aggression is directed against male Negroes only, manifests itself in race riots and lynchings, and, according to Sterba, has as its unconscious motive repressed hostility toward the father. The case just described fully justifies this hypothesis.

This hostility is derived largely from the negative feelings of the child for the father during the oedipal phase of psychosexual development, is repressed in the interest of preserving the positive feelings for the father, and subsequently projected onto the Negro male. White children who are brought up by Negro "mammies" have not only two mothers but by extension two fathers and with the development of the oedipus complex quite naturally bring the Negro male into the position of the hated father. In the unconscious of white people the Negro male represents the hated father, particularly the father at night.[3] To quote Sterba again: "The fact that the Negro riot regularly breaks out through the rumor that a Negro has raped a white woman confirms our opinion about its patricidal origin" (p. 419). The killing of the Negro male is thus a repetition of the killing of the primal father by the group of sons.

Two other important points are made by Sterba to which I can add nothing except their special applicability to the South. The first of these is that in our monotheistic system of religion,

> . . . our negative feelings against God the Father have to be displaced onto a substitute figure which is created for this purpose, and that is the devil. Psychologically God and Satan were originally one and the same. The myth of the Fall of the Angels betrays that originally the two belonged to the same locality; Satan wears horns,[4] which are the attributes of gods in many other religions. . . . Satan is therefore the substitute for God as the object of our negative feelings, which derive from our original ambivalence toward our father in childhood. The devil has one significant feature in common with the Negro: both are black. In the unconscious of many people the two are identical, both being substitutes for the father insofar as he is hated and feared [p. 417].

The South makes up the greater part of what is commonly referred to as the Bible belt. The clergy of this region not only make extensive use of color as a moral indicator, but they preach a religion that is intensely personal, narcissistic, puritanical, and devil centered. In psychoanalytic terms it is an id-archaic superego religion, actively hostile to the introduction of any ego (rational) elements into its doctrine. Lillian Smith (1949) in her incomparable *Killers of the Dream* has this to say on the southern revivalist:

[3] Herein, I believe, lies the deep-seated equation in the unconscious of darkness, black, sin, evil, etc. It has a biological basis in the cycle of day and night and is therefore not a purely cultural phenomenon. It is, I suspect, a universal equation. If this is true, it neither supports nor contradicts the theory of phylogenetic inheritance. The cycle of day and night is a part of the ontogeny of everyone and, as Feldman (1947) has pointed out, "as far as instinctual needs are concerned there is no difference between the human being in primeval and in present times; and furthermore there is no difference in the tools the ego uses when dealing with instinctual drives" (p. 173).

[4] Note the second dream.

They preached on the sins that tough frontiersmen committed: drinking, fighting to kill, fornication, self-abuse, gambling and stealing. And because they made these sins of heroic size by a passionate eloquence no other sins have ever seemed real to the southern imagination but merely vexatious problems that do not belong in church. . . . Guilt was then and is today the biggest crop raised in Dixie, harvested each summer just before cotton is picked. . . . Like the child in love with his own image and the invalid in love with his own disease, these men of God were in love with Sin that had come from such depths within that they believed they had created it themselves. This belief in the immaculate conception of Sin they defended with a furious energy and stubbornly refused to assent to the possibility that culture had had any role in its creation [pp. 96, 97, 99-100].

These intensely ambivalent men are almost as eloquent (and here I speak with the authority of a native of the rural South) in portraying the attractiveness of the Dark Gentleman with Horns as in describing the terrors that will befall should one succumb to his blandishments. Unconsciously they cultivate envy to only a slightly lesser degree than guilt and fear and in so doing create the constellation of emotions that is pathognomic of prejudice (Bird, 1957). This, together with all the aforementioned factors, makes the Negro an especially vulnerable target for the projections of the white man's, and especially the white Southerner's, repressed impulses.

Sterba's second important point is that hunting and Negro rioting (man hunting) have the same unconscious origin in patricidal impulses and represent repetitions of father murder as it occurred among archaic tribes. Based on personal observation from having lived in almost every section of these United States I am of the distinct opinion—and I believe it could be statistically validated—that fanatical devotion to hunting as a sport is so much greater in the South than elsewhere that it might properly be considered a regional character trait.

BIBLIOGRAPHY

Ackerman, N. W. & Jahoda, M. (1948), The Dynamic Basis of Anti-Semitic Attitudes. *Psychoanal. Quart.*, *17*:240-260.

—— & —— (1950), *Anti-Semitism and Emotional Disorder*. New York: Harper.

Bird, B. (1957), A Consideration of the Etiology of Prejudice. *J. Amer. Psychoanal. Assn.*, *5*:490-513.

Feldman, S. S. (1947), Notes on the Primal Horde. *Psychoanalysis and the Social Sciences*, *1*:171-193. New York: International Universities Press.

Freud, S. (1910), Contributions to the Psychology of Love: A Special Type of Choice of Object Made by Men. *Collected Papers*, *4*:192-202. London: Hogarth Press, 1948.

—— (1913), Totem and Taboo. *The Basic Writings of Sigmund Freud.* New York: Modern Library, 1938.

—— (1921), *Group Psychology and the Analysis of the Ego.* London: Hogarth Press, 1948.

Huie, W. B. (1956), The Shocking Story of Approved Killing in Mississippi. *Look* magazine, Jan. 24.

Loewenstein, R. M. (1951), *Christians and Jews.* New York: International Universities Press.

Simmel, E. (1946), *Anti-Semitism: A Social Disease.* New York: International Universities Press.

Smith, L. (1949), *Killers of the Dream.* New York: W. W. Norton.

Sterba, R. (1947), Some Psychological Factors in Negro Race Hatred and in Anti-Negro Riots. *Psychoanalysis and the Social Sciences, 1*:411-427. New York: International Universities Press.

CREATIVITY

THE CREATIVE IMPULSE—
BIOLOGIC AND ARTISTIC ASPECTS

Report of a Case

BERNARD C. MEYER, M.D. AND RICHARD S. BLACHER, M.D.

And the Lord God formed man of the dust of the ground, and breathed into his nostrils the breath of life; and man became a living soul.   Gen., 2:7

Psychoanalysts have long recognized the intimate psychic connection between artistic production and the act of parturition. Kris (1953) and others have emphasized that the artist's attitude to his product mirrors the relationship between parent and child, and that by virtue of the inevitable analogy to the Supreme Creator the artist partakes of divine attributes. Though much work has been devoted to both creativity and childbirth, we were unable to find in the psychoanalytic literature an example discussing the interrelationship of these two functions. This finding may in part be due to the fact that accounts of female artists are comparatively rare in psychoanalytic writings. In this paper we shall present the case of a woman whose history demonstrates a common origin of artistic creation and procreation.

CASE PRESENTATION

A few years ago, a thirty-nine-year-old Negro woman, in the eighth month of an out-of-wedlock but planned pregnancy was admitted to the psychiatric ward of the Mount Sinai Hospital because of an increasing depression. In her diary, maintained over a period of nearly twenty years, she wrote: "I think this will begin the last lap of my journey," a figure of speech which is of more than passing interest for it recalls the title of a short story,

---

Read before The New York Psychoanalytic Society, October 15, 1957 and The American Psychoanalytic Association, May 10, 1958.
From the Mount Sinai Hospital, New York City.

The Long Journey, sketched out some years before but never completed by this gifted, restless, and troubled woman.

The Long Journey relates the story of a lonely young woman, who in a melancholy mood determined to end her life. Not quite prepared to take this fateful step, however, she thought of postponing it until she had completed the construction of her own coffin. To her surprise she discovered that she possessed an unusual skill in working with wood, affording her a satisfaction which further served to delay her suicide. Carving the exterior of her sarcophagus brought the realization that she was a gifted sculptor. Her coffin nearly finished, enriched with beautiful carvings, she turned to other subjects and within the space of some months had turned out a large number of sculptured works of singular beauty. "Years flowed by as she studied and perfected herself in wood sculpture, adding a touch to the nearly finished coffin now and then as a gesture to the dormant determination to keep her word." Filled with enthusiasm over her new-found gift— her death thoughts now set aside—she left her lonely dwelling and ventured to a big city to show her work to critics and connoisseurs of art. Filled with admiration they arranged for an exhibition of her work. At first she had thought to withhold her sarcophagus from the exhibit, but realizing that the latter would be incomplete without it, she rushed from the gallery on the eve of the "opening" to make arrangements for the inclusion of her first and greatest work. In her excitement, alas, she ran heedlessly into the street where she was struck down by a passing vehicle which killed her instantly.

This story, to which we shall have occasion to return later, is but one of the many diversified artistic activities that Elsa—as we shall call our subject—engaged in. Its incompleteness as well as its content seems to us most characteristic of this woman, about whom we learned much from her verbal account, her diary and other writings, and finally from our own clinical observation.

Upon her admission to the hospital, Elsa was in a mood of elation, which, however, soon gave way to tears. She ascribed her depression not to her pregnant state, but rather to a troubled relationship with her brother, who with his white common-law wife and an infant son had lately moved next door. Four years her senior, he had caused her much concern over the years. Once he had served a prison sentence for stealing. Not long ago he had abandoned his lawful wife and three children, of which the youngest, a girl of fifteen, was now pregnant.

The mood of depression soon abated as Elsa settled into the comfortable ward environment, proving herself a cheerful and uncomplaining patient, somewhat garrulous and eager, and in no way ashamed of her pregnancy.

Indeed, she allowed her bathrobe to separate as she strolled about the ward, proudly exposing her ample abdomen. "This is the way I'd like to be forever," she averred, leading us to conclude that it was the state of pregnancy rather than the prospects of maternity which she sought. Consequently, we anticipated with some alarm the date of delivery, for it seemed likely that Elsa was destined to experience this as a termination rather than as a beginning. Such conjectures were not unfounded, for a few days after her admission Elsa began to have pains to which she reacted with frantic excitement, screaming as she was being prepared for transfer to the obstetrical service, "It's too soon; it's too soon! I'll be empty!" Fortunately this proved to be a false labor. She was returned to the psychiatric ward where she settled back into a peaceful and relatively untroubled existence. During the ensuing period we attempted to reconcile her to the inevitable termination of her pregnancy.

This was her first experience in psychotherapy. Quickly she correlated her current experience with events in her past. She related that after her own birth her mother had become blind for some six months, a circumstance which Elsa now regarded as an expression of her mother's distaste for her scrawny infant. Elsa feared that she too might reject her child—persistently referred to as *him*—and that "he" too might be scrawny and undersized. She asked whether past homosexual experiences might contribute to her producing a hermaphrodite. To reassure her about the normal size of her baby she was shown an X-ray of her abdomen. Pointing to the coccyx, she asked whether this was the baby's head. When corrected she was momentarily relieved, saying that now the baby seemed real for the first time. Suddenly she became sad again and complained, "But this is only another nail in my coffin." When asked what she meant by this, she related the story of the postponed suicide mentioned above: *The Long Journey.*

During this same period she recounted some details of her life experiences, describing a restless pursuit of various artistic interests, embracing virtually all fields and forms of art. She had been a singer in church choirs and had entertained plans to embark on a concert career. For a number of years she had been a professional actress. She had written stories, poetry, and newspaper copy. Like the subject of her short story, she had been a sculptress and had painted as well. For several years she had been a model and had taught painting and sculpture. When she gave up the stage she had become a professional photographer. Clearly she had stuck to nothing, completed nothing, and had never been satisfied. It was evident that she regarded being a mere mother and housewife as an admission of failure.

Presented at staff conference before a considerable number of strangers, she spoke unabashedly of many intimate things, disclosing the same lack of modesty manifested in her dress. "When I was a little girl" she said, "I used to talk to my mother about my penis. Mother repeatedly reminded me that I didn't have one. I told her, 'I know it, mother, but I like to pretend.' "

As her expected date of confinement approached she became determined to have "natural childbirth" and tried to persuade a friend to photograph the entire procedure. At times, however, she expressed some fear of dying during delivery. Significantly the expected date came and went, and four more weeks elapsed without any sign of labor. On New Year's Eve some mild pains began but these stopped soon and nothing further happened for another two days, when she finally went into true labor and under minimal sedation and pudenal block was delivered of a girl. Her reaction was a strange repeated laughing chant: "I got a baby; I got a baby." Then she wept and repeated the same words, adding, "I don't know what, but I've proved something—I got a baby!" For the next twenty-four hours she was virtually psychotic, manifesting a marked state of panic and tenuous hold on reality. She insisted upon being in someone's arms; she demanded to be fed milk through a straw. "For awhile I was my baby," she later declared, "and I wanted to be held like my baby because I never had been, and I remember it. . . . I got them to feed me milk with a tube; I wanted my mother to hold me in her arms." Soon she quieted down, became rational, and within a week she took her baby and went home. Thus ended a phase of her life which had caused no little concern to those whose task it had been to steer her through it without a major psychiatric upheaval.

During her hospital stay it had been our impression that Elsa was the younger of two children; it was only after reading a dream recorded in her diary that we began to suspect that there had been additional siblings. Meeting with her a full year later we learned for the first time that actually she had been one of nine children of whom her brother had been the sixth and she the eighth. According to her sketchy information the first five and the seventh died of "diphtheria." When she was eight years old a ninth child was born soon after the family migrated from the South to New England, a move which so grieved her homesick mother that this new baby was alleged to have died of neglect. Of interest was Elsa's insistence that the entire account of this ninth child was a matter of hearsay and that she herself could recall nothing of it, despite her age at the time and the acuteness of her recollection of other contemporaneous events.

Her father, a hard-working man, had died of "enlargement of the aorta" some ten years before Elsa's confinement. He had at one time been to sea, where like his daughter he had kept a journal. One gains an impression of a man who moved from place to place and from one type of work to another. He presents a picture, moreover, of sharp contrasts, especially in his attitude toward his children. The household was organized upon a strict, routinized, and duty-bound basis. "Buzzie" and Elsa were assigned to unvarying chores. They were not permitted to lie about in bed after awakening and they were held accountable for every hour of the day. Yet despite this apparent severity Elsa's father was often openly seductive to her. Surreptitiously he would kiss her upon the mouth and as she approached puberty he invited her to come to him if she should "develop any unusual feelings." On another occasion he urged her to join him while watching animals in coitus. Not infrequently he exposed himself to her while getting into bed. He gave her a hunting knife which she wore dangling from the waist while following him about the farm helping him with the chores. He whipped his son, and the latter more than once ran away from home. Elsa assumed a protective attitude toward Buzzie, who related to her his own sexual experiences including those attempted with farm animals. In recent years he had made frank sexual advances to her, and on one occasion, while drunk, proposed intercourse. She declared that in her home men were "gods," "in the upper echelons," and that both her father and brother openly opposed her "dating." In her journal she mentioned playing with dolls until the age of fourteen or fifteen, adding that she did not go out with boys until considerably later. Not long after entering high school, however, she began a close relationship with a girl, Evelyn, which lasted some twelve years.

An interest in music began with choir singing in high school. In rapid succession she took up one artistic endeavor after another. At twenty-eight, having already been an actress, painter, sculptor, singer, and model, she took a six weeks' summer job in the art department of a prominent women's college and was able to remain for two years. Here she felt happy and relaxed for the first time, declaring that her life there was like a "green womb with no tensions and no pressures." Finally, after two years she felt constrained to leave, complaining that it was "all too comfortable." Now, at thirty years of age, she returned to the theater, playing a leading role in the road company of a successful Broadway play. Toward the beginning of this year too she fell in love with a young white soldier, with whom she experienced her first coitus. Although this relationship continued for a number of years, it consisted mainly in the exchange of poetic love letters containing vague and unrealistic plans for the future. Almost at the same time she began an intimate relationship with a member of the cast, a man twelve years her senior, a husband and father. Toward the end of the first year of this affair she became pregnant and underwent an abortion. Not long thereafter the relationship ended. Elsa quit the show and turned to photography as a source of livelihood, numbering among her clients several adoption agencies. Now she darted from one man to another, engaging in a number of bizarre and short-lived liaisons.

As the years rolled by her interests in work and in art proved to be as capricious and inconstant as was her love life. On the heels of another unhappy love affair she began to toy with the idea of an out-of-wedlock pregnancy which she openly discussed with several of her lovers. When finally she found herself pregnant she tried to persuade one of them to marry her, while frankly admitting to him that the child might not be his. It was this pregnancy which brought her to the hospital.

This concludes a brief outline of her history as it was gathered during her hospital stay, subsequent to which the patient permitted us to read her diary and some sketches for a projected novel, both of which furnish important insights into our problem.

The Keepsake

The novel, entitled *The Keepsake,* concerns a widower and father of grown daughters, a man named Isaiah, who is torn between an infatuation with a high-spirited restless girl, Lily, and a more sober attachment to a selfless, church-going maternal woman named Phyllis. When the latter is injured in a street accident, Isaiah nurses her back to health and finally marries her. Lily, desperate, takes to drinking and driving her horses through the streets at unseemly hours of the night—conduct which results in her expulsion from the church. However, she has become pregnant by Isaiah and gives birth to his son, while Phyllis remains sterile and dies young. Just before leaving town to have her baby, Lily presents an earring she had received from Isaiah to one of his daughters, a gesture which determines the title of the story. Although neither the plot nor the writing have much to commend in them, the story contains some features which reflect upon Elsa herself. The patent oedipal theme is resolved through a compromise; one woman loses the father but gets his child; the other wins the father but remains sterile. The bestowal of the earring upon the true daughter, furthermore, only serves to reinforce the oedipal theme. Of interest too is the reference to a street accident, recalling the death of the sculptress in the story, *The Long Journey.* Horses, moreover, occupy an important role in the patient's history and imagery as will be seen in her diary. Finally, attention should be drawn to the strong religious element as manifested in the names of the protagonists and the general setting. It attests to Elsa's own obsessional preoccupation with religion, God, inspiration, and the creative act.

The Diary

Begun at the age of twenty-one her journal comprises eighteen books of closely written material, and possibly some additional volumes not available to us. The first seven books, covering the years twenty-one to twenty-five, reveal a deep and devoted preoccupation with Evelyn, a girl of her own age with whom the patient experienced a painful love relationship which lasted at least twelve years. The physical manifestations of this love affair are not disclosed: indeed, in approaching any hint of intimacy the writer suddenly employs a code. At other times she writes of Evelyn in French, calling her "ma petite" while sighing out her miseries on nearly every page. For Elsa suffered all manner of torment at the hands of her friend, who evidently held Elsa in virtual thralldom. In the midst of her masochistic suffering Elsa alternately vows that she will free herself, upbraids herself for being selfish, begs her lover for small crumbs of affection, pleads with her for forgiveness, and finally enslaved surrenders once again to her hapless infatuation. A few men are mentioned, but they are lightly dismissed, often with some comment upon their lack of masculinity. Aside from Evelyn the only affectionate relationship which engages her consistently is her diary. Addressed in familiar, confidential, and often loving tones, the diary is clearly a representative of a love object to whom she turns for consolation in her distress. Actually when she feels loved by Evelyn she is prone to neglect the "reader." In her melancholic moods she addresses the diary in religious terms, indicating at such moments an identity between her journal and God, to whom she confesses, declares her love, and describes her abiding faith.

Throughout the writing there runs a somber note of melancholy and despair which she is at pains to drown out. Sudden bursts of enthusiasm or a renewed expression of her faith in God's love serve to raise her flagging spirits, frequently to a degree of virtual hypomania. At such times, her writing, obviously directed to an audience and edited at some later time, assumes a quality of purple grandiosity. Following the extraction of a tooth, to which she made a number of references, she lamented, "I wish they (anyone) would write to me. I guess Evelyn is lost to me. She refused to write. . . . The face hurts still." Within one day, however, she exults, "It was destined from the beginning—my seeing under the masks of others—my eventual understanding of God and the great scheme of things. There is something eternal in this *small brown column of flesh* [italics ours]—a thing detached, observing with knifelike definite clearness. . . . To live is to be a creature, creative. . . . There is a great responsibility growing within me for something I have not yet seen or heard. I was not meant for mental things

alone. I must create as God has done. It is only in league with Him that I
shall succeed." Now her pace accelerates; she breaks into poetry, makes
references to Christ and closes with "God, please help, help. Good night
God." The next entry, two days later, returns to a mundane recital of how
she ironed her dress after breakfast. She is obviously full of schemes and plans
which engage vast quantities of enthusiasm but always die before they have
begun. One such item involved opening a snack bar in order to earn some
money during the summer vacation. She invited five girls to meet with her
to talk it over, although it was quite clear that none of them were to have
any role in the venture. This meeting is described in terms more appropriate
to a prophet surrounded by his disciples. She instructed each one to pray
before the meeting broke up "that God would help them find themselves—
that they would keep their confidence in and love for me—that I could help
them a little. We six pledged ourselves with the Bible afterwards." The hint
of an identification with Jesus is inescapable. Of interest too is the fact that
all this ceremony and prayer was directed to the success of a projected eating
establishment. Characteristically, this was the first and last time that the
snack bar was mentioned in her diary.

The religious note, wherein she alternately seeks for a god and identifies
with him, bursts into full volume upon her first opportunity of hearing the
Negro singer, Marian Anderson. Adoringly the latter is described as the
"magnificent goddess. She closes her eyes when she sings, but, oh, when she
finishes, they open and it's like looking into dark honey. Serenity and the
laughing animated peace of damp green woods are there. They have a
strange deep-seeing that grips the spine of you. . . . and holds you open-
mouthed silly looking slave to whatever she commands. . . . She is an
amber fountain, geyser, jet-of-flame sound." She claims that she could be a
fitting friend for the great singer. "I would sense her weariness, or her moments of exaltation. . . . her desire for tenderness, her objection to being
touched—anything about her as I do Evelyn—only Evelyn is mine." A few
days later we learn that she has started to do a sculpture of her "goddess, the
Instrument of God." "The woman possesses me! she is so unspeaking powerful. . . . so much a mixture of lace and steel." Not long thereafter she is
sculpting a baby, from which subject she turns in her journal to Evelyn,
whose material needs she describes with maternal solicitude. Soon she was
boasting, "I am broad-earth broad and deeper than anything on earth or
earth itself, and tall, standing high on a peak of infinity looking where God's
finger points into men and women at himself! I am Ceres, mother of earth.
I am mother of all whom I meet. I take them into my wide open eyes and
suck in their souls, their unseen selves. [Compare her previous remarks about

the eyes of Marian Anderson.] I feel them, hold them. . . . sucking their substance into me, exulting in the sight of their nakedness and comprehending all that they feel and think." Despite the fact that these are men of whom she is speaking she frankly expresses her fear of a relationship with one. "I have defenses against falling into the vat with a man of my own," she writes. "It frightens me. God and I, you God, are tremendous enough for me. We'll be together, not some man and I. Evelyn? Evelyn doesn't disturb my relationship with you. A man? Well, no chances taken." One of the men, however, dropped a hint about homosexuality, prompting her to deny to her diary that there was anything "lesbian" about her relationship with Evelyn. Nevertheless within a few days she was writing about the possibility of having a sexual experience with a man, in the nature of an experiment. Nothing came of this idea, however, and she continued to suffer in her frustrating love for Evelyn. To help finance the latter's college expenses Elsa now gave a song recital and turned over all the proceeds save the expenses to her friend, who seemingly accepted this generosity as a matter of course and even berated Elsa for borrowing sixty-five cents of the proceeds for herself. Not long after the concert she wondered what it would be like to have a baby in her arms —"one out of me. I thought early this morning what it would be like with me singing on the concert stage and the milk wetting my dress a little. Then how it would be to go into the anteroom and get my baby and nurse it as I sang—what people would think." And, yet in the next paragraph she could add, "I think often now of being caressed and kissed and I don't see the person doing it. The face doesn't matter so much; it's the being adored by some wonderful person that matters." Consciously the latter was not her mother, for Elsa writes full of bitterness about both her parents, and especially when she saw her mother handling her brother's child. When Elsa criticized her mother for not feeding the child properly, she received a sharp slap across the mouth.

At the age of twenty-five, Elsa apparently abandoned her diary for four years. It was during these years that she retired from the city and from the stage and lived at the women's college where she modeled and taught art. During this same interval she broke off her relationship with Evelyn and had her first heterosexual experience.

Some changes are discernible in the new diary begun at the age of twenty-nine. It is written in larger books, contains fewer daily events, and includes a number of dreams recounted in considerable detail. A curious feature is the fact that these dreams tend to appear within the last few pages of each volume, reminiscent of those analytic patients who react to imminent separation from the analyst with a particularly vivid dream. Later on she acknowl-

edged that as she approached the end of each volume, she experienced a
sense of regret—"a kind of good-by." In other respects too the diary suggests
a "psychoanalysis." Interspersed with random thoughts addressed to a silent
reader are frequent references to the distant past. She even wonders about
the meaning of the slips of her pen.

Significantly, her first entry opens with a reference to creation:

> This day I have learned a new thing that helps make clear an
> old idea. It is about the necessity or the usefulness of the creator's
> being both male and female, because he produces out of himself and
> cannot otherwise. [This is followed by some remarks about human
> relationships.] When I become fond of [someone] it seems to me that
> we must exchange something of our personalities, our invisible selves.
> When I see him I am glad because then I am more complete—that is,
> part of my integrity, my wholeness has extended (as an amoeba ex-
> tends) into him. . . . moreover, if we break from each other we
> leave part of ourselves in the other, and we feel in varying degrees,
> the bruise, the severing when we hear his name or see him. But those
> whom we keep extend us, increase our invisible size. . . . and one
> blood flows between us. . . . Often it breaks off but always with
> leaving a bit of each in the other willy nilly. That makes memory.
> Maybe there is [but] one self with everyone sharing in it and until
> they realize it they will try to protect what they think is theirs, private
> and only.

And now without the slightest interruption she describes that when she
was a child a horse ran away and broke her father's legs, how sorry she felt
for the horse, desiring to pet him, while her brother wanted to kill the animal,
a memory which is striking in view of the frequent appearance of this animal
both in her dreams and in her writings.

At the time of these entries in her diary she was having an affair with an
older and married man in the cast of the play in which she was acting. Although evidently strongly attracted to him, she insisted upon remaining in
control: "I had him tossing about like a leaf," she boasted, "and he weighs
230 pounds. . . . it would preen his vanity if I were to fall in love with
him. . . . with him I would have to be a thrall as I was with Evelyn. . . . I
was in love with her as I will never be again. I was too lost, too overwhelmed,
too glutted with her. . . . He thinks to hog-tie me with his penis but he
can't." After biting him on the lip she accused herself of being "a kind of
witch," admitting to her diary that she was quite detached from him and
was using him as "material" for her literary efforts.

Not long thereafter she learned that her brother's wife was again pregnant. This was followed by a dream of anal parturition; a dog squatted in

front of her excreting egglike substances which turned into little dogs. There were nine of them and the last one had to struggle against being suffocated by the surrounding membrane; then it floated out of sight. In retrospect she declared that the dog giving birth reminded her of her brother. That the creative urge was strongly upon her was evident from a subsequent slip of the pen after reading Thomas Wolfe's *God's Lonely Man,* about which she wrote: "It is the least painful of his expressions that I've *written.*" Referring then to an outline of a story of her own, she added, "It caused much of the bruising bursting agony that comes with the beginning of a thing." Soon she found herself pregnant by her lover and she left the play to have an abortion. In language which recalls her grandiose prose following the tooth extraction she wrote during her lonely convalescence: "Slowly I am coming alive again. . . . Suddenly it came clear—the meaning of the experience, the significance of it all—that I was like one possessed with fire and ecstasy." Curiously the overwhelming psychic experience to which she refers has no stated connection with her recent pregnancy nor its rude and lonely termination. Apparently it is about her book: "I crawled out of bed to tell mother about it. I cried with relief at the solution I had been looking for in the book and with the beauty of the meaning of the pain, with the depth of the maturity that was being wrought in me, I reached for paper and pencil and this is what I wrote: 'By the hand of my mind I am clutching a great idea—many great ideas about me, about the pain I have just endured and the book.' " Now she indicates that she has solved the problem of the style she is to use in her book, *The Keepsake.* Suddenly, and as if she were momentarily unable to distinguish between reality and fiction, she begins to excoriate her character Isaiah for marrying Phyllis and thus neglecting his daughters: "By this deep and fibroid love which you cover with the increased, the thus artificially increased discharge of your devotion to God and Church, what do you make of the house in which your daughters grow?" In sentences replete with religious references, play on words and utter grandiosity, she writes,

I find, bless the dear Lord, my God, that I am able to use the mosaic approach to the revelation of ideas by juxtaposing events and characters in such a way, etc. . . . Suddenly I see deep verdant loamy valleys and bold mountains and great wide skies inside myself. I am a tremendous giant with a huge kind laughter sitting sadly in me, next to love. I used to be Mother of the World. . . . I laugh inside to see how voluble I am this sore-wombed beautifully quiet sunny morning. I am a little weak with discovery and pain and ecstasy and suffering and loneliness. [Now she arranges that one of her characters will have an abortion. Her apostrophe to God continues with a valiant effort to assert her creative omnipotence:] Oh dearest God,

in the vice [sic] of your mind, you take an idea and stubbornly cling
to the chromium thing through all satans and demons and climates
of emotion—and make of the sterile seeming metal smoothness a seed
of yielding fertile, fecund seed, blossoming and blooming and fruiting,
on that great day, until there is hardly place to be its produce. . . .
another   inescapable proof that one lives in spite of himself—is surrounded by the myriad of *stampeding horses* [italics ours] of events
which can make feasible to one's self through meditation which develops to open the psychic eyes—thus seeing the grasping of the *reins*
[italics ours] and better to guide them for the creative sowing and
plowing—the creative cultivation of one's own individual porch of
the vast Overlife and as not one part of it where so many parts are
sick there is well being it is a boon, an assurance, an insurance, dear
God, against the death of the creative progress of humanity. . . .
suffering is no good unless something comes of it. One must use it,
and all of it familiar, even the writing it down. The crowded pregnant page. . . . and I no longer pregnant except in my head.

Poor girl! How desperately she attempts to deny by wild and angry
thrusts issuing from her "pregnant head" the crushing effect of the abortion,
the interruption of her biological creative achievement. Both the richness of
the religious language and reference to stampeding horses are noteworthy,
prompting the suspicion that her loss of the child is historically linked with an
earlier disappointment.

Now she flitted from one man to another, from one idea to another; she
planned to identify herself for the first time actively with her race: "It is
a gigantic task I am setting myself—to encompass and digest Harlem and the
Negro people—my discovery of them. . . . I suddenly about two weeks ago
became a Negro." Like all her schemes, however, this one was short-lived.
Within the space of two weeks she described plans to work on her novel,
spend all her time on photography, to go to Italy to make a movie about
herself, to compose a weekly news sheet and do sculpture.

Another serious love affair occurred and like all its predecessors came to
grief. In words reminiscent of her affair with Evelyn she wrote,

I need his love, his expressed articulate love so badly. I am thread-
bare in a cold wind without it. . . . I believe that love should line
and decorate about a third of life and be at the elbow of the rest. I
think it is an invisible and iridescent bag like the womb we lived in
earlier. I think it should feed what we do altogether. . . . like warm
close cuddled puppies. [At times she confesses thoughts of suicide, especially before her menstrual periods.] I get wild notions like cutting
my wrists or killing someone—I long to be free of this prison. God!
life seems so barren and fruitless the way I'm living it.

Within a short time and after learning that her brother's wife was pregnant once more, she began to plan to have a child out of wedlock. When she thought herself pregnant three weeks later, although unable to identify which of three men might be the father, she began to discern the "drama" of it all, made plans to write her experiences as a serial novel which she would sell to the movies and which would serve as a pattern for the "countless women who have longed for children but who are too intelligent for marriage." Despite these enthusiasms for eugenic children, artificial insemination, etc., she tried to persuade one of the putative fathers to marry her. That night she dreamed she was at a ball where she sat with her head in a man's lap; then she heard a phonograph record of herself singing the Ave Maria. Later she saw a stout white man wrapping up grapefruits and puddings in a napkin, which reminded her of how her father used to display his genitals as he got into bed. "I used to hate father for doing that and yet I found it hard not to watch and see if he would do it each time." In the last part of the dream she went out to get her horse which had been trampling on some children. The allusions to fellatio, oral impregnation, and the oedipal attachment are self-evident. The singing of the Ave Maria, moreover, suggests an identification with the Virgin Mary and divine impregnation by God the Father. The reappearance of the familiar horse and its obvious role as an expression of murderous impulses toward other children led us to ask her about the number of children her mother had borne, revealing for the first time that there had been nine in all, not two as originally understood.

Elsa now desperately searched for a husband. Despite her childlike pleadings, her insistence that she really had a husband who had simply not yet made his appearance, no one came forward. As time went on her loneliness increased. She began to suffer from recurrent sore throats and colds. Because of an apparent elated mood observed on one of her clinic visits, admission to the hospital psychiatric ward was recommended.

In the hospital she continued her diary in which she confessed, "I guess I have always worshipped and wanted to be a male person. I have pretended to myself way underneath all along that I am a boy, not a man, a boy. I suppose I have felt anger and contempt toward men because they were supposed to be—maybe I felt that they betrayed me. . . . I think I was frightened when I first saw Father's penis. . . . I thought of it as a club." She expressed a wish for a "permanent relationship" with her therapist, and typically she saw herself as his colleague: "Blacher and I." Then she confessed an idea of becoming a psychiatrist. She began to make attempts at denying the impending delivery, dismissing the foetal movements as "gas or some phenomenon of my own that has developed, like a third finger or something." Then began obsessive ruminations concerning "a fear or a wish" that she might kill her baby, for example, by its dropping out of her in the bathroom. Quickly she rescued herself by ascribing such murderous impulses to her mother, and to her brother, who would be hostile to her child, she felt, especially if it were a boy. As the time of expected delivery approached she appeared to become more and more concerned with recollections of her brother. After recounting a dream about him she confided that she had often wanted intercourse with him and that she had always been jealous of his sexual activities with other girls. Then she described how he had come to her drunk a year before and had proposed they have a child together. (It is noteworthy that her two pregnancies followed reports of pregnancies of her brother's wife.)

The events surrounding her actual delivery have already been recounted. In her diary she drew a picture of the erection of her nipple as little Nancy was being nursed adding the following lines:

This is the thing I long have sought
And mourned because I found it nought.

The remainder of the diary consists of highly obsessional thoughts concerning the care of her baby. Despite Elsa's compulsive caution, her refusal to allow her mother to hold the baby lest she drop her, Nancy managed to sustain at least three falls from considerable heights within the first few months of her life. The diary during this phase reflects a state of vast tension and suppressed impatience. Moreover, the return of her menses found her as depressed as ever. "I realize that I used to have this footless, unmoored feeling as a child. It seems somehow connected with the vagueness, the disorganizedness of Mother. She used to offer me things. . . . and what she offered was always bland, tasteless." These complaints were followed at once by the recording of a dream in which men were laughing and having a good time sitting at a bar. Then an older woman came in and treated the dreamer with cavalier neglect: "as though I were nonexistent. . . . I had a rejected feeling, depressed, counted for nothing, disappointed—but it was a familiar feeling."

DISCUSSION

The spectacle of this unhappy creature, struggling to free herself by random and promiscuous thrusts of creative energy from a net of dark purposes within her, cannot fail to evoke both our compassion and our curiosity. Wherein lies the origin of this insistent creative urge? What is it that she hopes to create? Why do her manifold efforts terminate in consistent failure or frustration?

Psychoanalytic literature contains several papers (A. Freud, 1923; Kris, 1952, 1953; Sachs, 1942) in which the authors view an artistic product as a later elaboration of a childhood fantasy. Our patient reported a fantasy which we believe to have undergone a similar development: the game in which Elsa pretended to possess a penis. Elsa contended that her mother's "blindness" represented an aversion to the sight of her newborn daughter, the patient, and that in her home only males enjoyed status. These assertions imply that Elsa felt rejected by her mother because of the lack of a penis. Equipped with a fantasied phallus Elsa might acquire a passport to her mother's unquestioned acceptance. This is undoubtedly the major meaning of Elsa's post-partum psychotic state during which she insisted that she was the baby who was being held and nursed by her mother for the first time. Endowed with a singularly un-green thumb, Elsa's mother had apparently allowed seven of her nine children to wither away like plants in an untended garden, a circumstance which permits us to question as well her adequacy as a mother to her two surviving children. It is our view that the establishment of a blissful union with an idealized mother, endowed with an inexhaustible abundance of nourishing love, constitutes the deepest longing of our subject: "This is the thing I long have sought and mourned because I found it nought."

As an elaboration of the early penis fantasy her creative efforts and their accompanying elations must represent temporary denials of her castration through a vigorous affirmation of her fictitious phallic endowment. Such outbursts seem to occur typically in an atmosphere of depression, hopelessness, and failure. This sequence is epitomized in a remarkable passage in her short story when the melancholy girl, preparing for her suicide, surveyed her half-finished coffin: "a faint breath of pride stirred within her. She did not know that her head had ceased to bobble. Suddenly she stood up. 'Carving!', she ejaculated, in a burst of wonder. . . . She went upstairs cautiously, so as not to spill any of the wonder of the ideas that had come to her." Here we are presented with a vehement and ecstatic denial of castration wherein every image and virtually every second word contains a phallic allusion. Noteworthy too is the aura of inspiration attending this scene, recalling similar bursts of grandiose inspirational outpourings contained in Elsa's diary. Seen in their most flamboyant form they follow some renewed and painful reminder of mutilation: after the removal of a tooth she declares, "There is something eternal in this small brown column of flesh. . . . I must create as God has done." Again after her abortion she plunges into wild and hypomanic assertions, proclaiming that she is a "tremendous giant." At such moments words tumble forth from her in gushing profusion, her creative potential becomes limitless, and she is the phallic mother of the world, Ceres, and God Himself.

Failure in her creative efforts from whatever source, on the other hand, must be construed as a realistic recognition of her castration, a recognition which is accompanied by thoughts of suicide. A literary expression of this depressive preoccupation with her castration is again recorded in her short story, when the unhappy girl gazes out of the window and notices a fat robin picking at worms. "Once her brother shot a robin with a gun; she recalled the limp warm body, the dangling head with the drop of red in its bill, and the dusty odor of the feathers as she laid her sad cheek against their smoothness. She wondered with a deep longing about the difference between the two birds. What is it? The strong invisible Thing that could never re-enter the limp quiet bird, that throbbed in the one singing in the tree. Baffling, baffling. But without it no living thing is made." Elsa's identification with the dead—castrated—bird is self-evident. Indeed, the entire tone of these sentences is strongly reminiscent of her own premenstrual lamentations.

Even in her high-school years Elsa had had thoughts of suicide by means of asphyxiation in a small curtained room, a foretaste of the claustrophilia implicit in her fascination with perpetual pregnancy and in its fictional counterpart, *The Long Journey.* Yet in its deepest sense, this claustrophilia fantasy is but another expression in an altered form of her intense longings for fusion with the mother, a fusion attained by being devoured. This idea is indeed spelled out in the short story, when upon deciding to construct her own sarcophagus (literally: eating flesh), the girl refers to it as "an evening tray with a tidbit for Death's supper." Thus both in her hypomanic, phallic, creative state as well as in her depressed and castrated mood the object of her longings appears to be the same. The difference lies merely in the means of achieving this union. In her phallic state the unity is attained seemingly through a process of introjection of the idealized object with a resulting identification. Nowhere is this more clearly depicted than in those pages of her journal which relate the successive stages of her interaction with the singer, Marian Anderson: first, there is a slavelike idolization—"she holds you open-mouthed silly-looking slave to whatever she commands"; this is followed by thoughts of being the singer's companion and a decision to cast her image in sculpture; finally, there is a complete identification: "I am Ceres mother of earth. I am mother of all whom I meet." Having at the outset described her "goddess" as an "amber fountain, geyser, jet of flame sound," once the incorporation has been completed Elsa too gives a song recital and indulges in a fantasy of nursing her baby before an entire audience which witnesses the leaking of milk through her dress. This progression is reminiscent of one described by Kris and Pappenheim (1946) in a psychotic artist who was first God's apprentice, then His helper, and finally the Master Himself. Typically in our patient, however, there is no stability to these identifications; indeed, there is the same unremitting oscillation between them as can be discerned in the shifting fluctuations of her mood, the alterations between eating and being eaten, between active and passive incorporation, as well as in her vacillating pursuit of life or death. The broad clinical picture readily suggests the oral triad described by Lewin (1950): the wish to eat, the wish to be eaten, and the wish to sleep (die), whose derivations attain especial prominence in marked disturbances of mood, that is, in those feeling states characterized by hypo- or hyperactivity of the superego. It is to the role of this mental agency that we must turn therefore in our endeavor to account for the restless instability of our subject's life.

In the story, *The Long Journey,* the writer leaves no doubt that her heroine was destined to die. "Faced with freedom," she wrote, "the girl was impotent before it. She was foresworn; her word had been given and she could not recant." Although she can postpone her death as long as she maintains an isolated life-in-death existence, somehow the impression is created that as soon as she strives to join the busy vibrant world about her, the axe of fate will put her down: she resembles a condemned prisoner enjoying a modicum of parole. What was her crime? Contemplating her past, the girl recalls how she had always felt apart, an eccentric, who peered through the windows of drug stores watching happy children enjoying ice-cream sodas, a picture suggesting a primal scene of either nursing or coitus, and a strong hint of jealousy toward a favored sibling. This assumption is reinforced by a further detail in her story: we hear that the girl had been obliged to forego her education because of "sickness in the family." Yet this sickness turns out to be nothing graver than the miscarriage of her brother's wife, itself a most implausible reason for so great a sacrifice. When it is recalled, however, that Elsa's two pregnancies occurred shortly after she had learned that *her* brother's wife was pregnant, and when it is further recollected that Elsa had freely acknowledged incestuous desires toward her brother whose early sexual experiences aroused both her fascination and her jealousy, the magnitude of the "sacrifice" assumes a more logical position.

Unlike her story, *The Long Journey,* which was written, incidentally, during the "green womb" years at the women's college, the sketch of her novel, *The Keepsake,* is a frankly sexual romance containing a manifest oedipal theme: a woman, who is clearly a substitute for a daughter, obtains a child from a father; the child, by the way, possesses the same first name as that of the patient's own father. It is plausible to assume that this plot is a derivative of an oedipal childhood fantasy involving both Elsa's father and brother. Moreover, if her mother's pregnancy when Elsa was eight years of age was subjected to complete repression—as her failure to recollect suggests —it must have been a most unwelcome event. In this scheme of things, the subsequent death of the infant must have created a profound emotional disturbance in this young child, setting the stage for the later preoccupation with injured and dead children, a preoccupation which appears both in her dreams (e.g., horses trampling on children) and in her severe obsessional conflict concerning the safety of her own child. A more careful scrutiny of her incestuous conflict, however, indicates that it is not as two-dimensional as might be inferred from its literary rendition. It is also apparent that its pathogenic potential is greatly influenced by preoedipal factors. It should be recalled, for example, that until her eighth year Elsa was the youngest child in a family in which six out of eight children had died. The subsequent birth and death of a ninth child can only have added to the sense of precariousness and uncertainty to which Elsa was exposed.[1] The advent of a ninth child therefore might have been doubly repugnant to her: as a frustration of an oedipal wish and, more important in our estimation, as a threatening rival. The convergence of these elements may well have created a psychological fusion between oedipal-sexual and sadomasochistic-infanticidal impulses.

A further characteristic of the oedipal pattern in our subject lies in the relative unimportance of the male as an object to be cherished in undisputed possession. His very identity in fact would appear to be a matter of near indifference: his role is to impregnate and disappear forthwith. Indeed the virtually anonymous paternity of Elsa's second pregnancy bears an unmistakable stamp of parthenogenesis, a phenomenon which Helene Deutsch (1944- 45) described as: "I have a child born of me alone; I am its mother and its father; I do not need a man for the begetting of a child." The parthenogenetic illusion is further suggested by her dream of singing the Ave Maria, with its implications of Immaculate Conception and divine impregnation.

---

[1] This family pattern is reminiscent of the case of Frau Emmy von N. reported by Freud in the *Studies on Hysteria.* Of interest too in this connection is the comparable role played by runaway horses in Freud's patient. See the discussion of I. Peter Glauber's paper, "Freud on Stuttering" (Meyer, 1956).

Finally the oedipal aim is less to have a baby than to achieve eternal pregnancy, that is, to achieve the perception of something growing inside. Thus Elsa was able to speak of the foetal movements as "some phenomenon of my own that has developed, like a third finger or something," and she viewed with alarm the termination of her pregnancy, crying, "It's too soon!"

Like her other creative efforts, therefore, the attainment of pregnancy had predominantly a phallic significance. Hence the role of the male is essentially ancillary—by bestowing the pregnancy-phallus upon Elsa the man becomes the tool or vehicle through which she will find her way back to mother. Both her artistic and her biologic creative efforts therefore have the same goal—the acquisition of a phallic omnipotence capable of enabling her to establish contact with an object or objects. The driving force propelling her to the achievement of this goal assumes particularly powerful proportions in the face of self-destructive impulses and tendencies. Seen in this light, the formulation corresponds to those of Kris (1953) and others (Rickman, 1940; Sharpe, 1930; Tarachow, 1949) who view the artistic efforts of psychotics (and perhaps of normal subjects as well) as phenomena of restitution. Unfortunately in seeking to attain these goals our patient is as thwarted in acquiring a real penis by considerations of reality as she is prevented from gaining an illusory one by powerful inner psychic forces.

To the painter Degas, Thomas Mann (1945) attributed the statement that the artist must approach his work in the same frame of mind in which the criminal commits his deed. In actuality this is only partly true for it implies a freedom from conflict over criminal impulses, for which the history of art provides little evidence. On the contrary, a relative detachment from areas of conflict and a firmly established autonomy of the creative process appear to constitute an essential element in artistic achievement. Psychoanalysts are all too familiar with instances of failure in this process of detachment, with instances in which malfunctioning in the artistic sphere reflects a persistence of psychic connections between creative efforts and primitive instinctual qualities. Such a failure in neutralization is manifested in the restless and promiscuous creative thrusts of our patient, who moves from art form to art form, from object to object, and from aim to aim, like a fugitive seeking a transient haven from the remorseless constable within: a relentless superego which perceives in her every phallic striving the shadow of a hidden infanticidal impulse. For the God she would become, alas, is not alone the Supreme Creator: He is as well the God of Vengeance.

Follow-Up

Elsa has recently asked for an interview in order to discuss a problem she was encountering with her daughter Nancy, now almost five years old. Nancy was beginning to show interest in the boys in her nursery school, and expressed a wish to have a penis, suggesting to her mother that they make one. Together they fashioned a penis out of a coil of paper, affixing it to Nancy with "scotch tape." The child was delighted and tried to urinate through it, while Elsa kept repeating that it was all make-believe, emphasizing the advantages of being a girl, and secretly reassuring herself that Nancy would soon tire of the game. The child then told her mother of performing fellatio, evoking the anxious reply that this was a dirty thing to do, and that the penis was for urinating, not for licking. Finally she admonished Nancy not to talk about these matters with anyone except herself.

The entire episode strikingly recalls Elsa's own childhood. Now she repeats the "penis game" with her daughter much as she tried to play it with her mother. Unlike the latter, however, Elsa cooperates with Nancy's wish to create a penis, while allaying her own anxiety by repeating, like her mother, "Of course it's all make-believe." At the same time Elsa is clearly identifying herself with her father, who, when she was eleven years old, invited her to come to him if she should develop "any unusual feelings." (Without any awareness of the similarity between these two conversations, Elsa recalled this talk with her father during this recent interview.)

Three different identifications can be discerned here: (1) with her daughter Nancy who acquires a toy penis; (2) with the "giving" mother who bestows it; and (3) with the seductive father who promises her a real one some day.

BIBLIOGRAPHY

Deutsch, H. (1944-45), *The Psychology of Women*, 2 Vols. New York: Grune & Stratton.

Freud, A. (1923), The Relation of Beating Phantasies to a Daydream. *Int. J. Psychoanal.*, 4:89-102.

Kris, E. (1952), *Psychoanalytic Explorations in Art*. New York: International Universities Press.

—— (1953), Psychoanalysis and the Study of Creative Imagination. *Bull. N.Y. Acad. Med.*, 29:334.

—— & Pappenheim, E. (1946), The Function of Drawings and the Meaning of the "Creative Spell" in a Schizophrenic Artist. *Psychoanal. Quart.*, 15:6-31.

Lewin, B. D. (1950), *The Psychoanalysis of Elation*. New York: W. W. Norton.
Mann, T. (1945), Introduction to *The Short Novels of Dostoievsky*. New York: Dial Press.
Meyer, B. C. (1956), Discussion of paper "Freud on Stuttering" by Dr. I. Peter Glauber, presented at the New York Psychoanalytic Society, October 16.
Rickman, J. (1940), On the Nature of Ugliness and the Creative Impulse. *Int. J. Psychoanal., 21*:294-313.
Sachs, H. (1942), *The Creative Unconscious*. Cambridge, Mass.: Sci-Art Publishers.
Sharpe, E. F. (1930), Certain Aspects of Sublimation and Delusion. *Int. J. Psychoanal., 11*:12-23.
Tarachow, S. (1949), Remarks on the Comic Process and Beauty. *Psychoanal. Quart., 18*:215-226.

THE ORIGINS OF CULTURE: COOPER AND FREUD

WILLIAM WASSERSTROM, Ph.D.

We must undertake to give James Fenimore Cooper special credit for high accomplishment within one extraordinary realm of thought. At his worst he was, as Mark Twain knew, an artificer without cunning. But at his best, we begin to understand, he was a mythmaker, a purveyor of legend, a fabulist of unusual talent. Assuming this role, he became nearly as inventive as the Indians and frontiersmen whom he prized, as quick as they to infer a thing in the thicket from the lightest quiver of a twig. The work in which this gift is most fully realized is *The Prairie,* his own favorite fiction in the Natty Bumppo series, and the only one of his novels which is both programmatic and emblematic but not a tract or an allegory. It is also the sole work in which his ideas are argued by characters whose lives are formed according to an accurate psychology. And though the novel is nowadays much admired, no one has recognized that its strength is rooted in what we must call a striking achievement of Cooper's unconscious imagination. Even D. H. Lawrence (1930) who called *The Prairie* a "strange, splendid book," full of the "shadow of violence and dark cruelty"—even he was unable to say exactly why it filled him with "the sense of doom." Lawrence believed that the novel harbored, at its core, "the aboriginal demon," but he did not realize that Cooper's demon was precisely the one which was to preoccupy Freud throughout his life and which Freud described first in *Totem and Taboo,* (1913), next in "Psycho-Analysis and Religious Origins" (1919), again in *Group Psychology and the Analysis of the Ego* (1921), and finally in that vexing little book, *Moses and Monotheism* (1939).

At first gasp this does indeed seem an odd, even factitious notion—Cooper and Freud under a common yoke. And though they do make an extraordinary pair, the two men did in fact share certain intellectual traditions, some aims. The issue examined in Freud's essays did not after all concern theory or therapy alone but applied some implications of these to still larger matters—to the problem of reconstructing those events which underlay the creation of social order during a remote time. In that day men lived dangerous but more or less untrammeled lives, which later in history they ex-

From the Department of English, Syracuse University, Syracuse, N.Y.

changed for safer and more orderly forms. Anarchic freedom, however in-
spiriting in some ways, provided little protection against all the forces of destruction, which in fantasy and in fact men saw threatening them. Cooper,
too, admired the frontiersman's freedom but recognized some limitations,
foresaw its inhibition by the unremitting forces of civilization. And both men
were saddened by the very high price mankind is forced to pay for the com-
forts and solace of culture. Freud is after all, we are now accustomed to say,
the apogee of all the natural philosophers who flourished during the Enlight-
enment. And Cooper, who came to maturity under its guidance, would have
had no difficulty understanding either Freud's vocabulary or his explanation
of the way union developed among primitive men as a "sort of social contract" which established an organization based on "a renunciation of instinctual gratification. . . ." Both men participated in a tradition of thought
which claims that the discontents of civilization occur because culture defiles
or distorts human nature.

On a still deeper level of communion, each would have respected the
other's reliance on a unique theory of evolution, the phylogenic. Freud required this principle, "phylogenic inheritance," in order to explain the recur-
rence of certain phenomena within man's unconscious life. He argued—
against the opinion of colleagues—that "the mental residue" of primeval
times is "a heritage which, with each new generation, needs only to be reawakened." Then men recall ancient, barbarous crimes and feel anew a sense
of guilt. Cooper borrowed, from eighteenth-century cyclists of history and of
culture, theorists who are, as David Riesman (1954) remarks, like Freud in
that their thought is "phylogenic and teleological"—from Condorcet and
Turgot, Cooper borrowed some early versions of this principle and applied it
quite precisely to American society. According to its description of social
evolution, all human societies pass through a series of fixed stages, "from that
of the hunter in the forest through the patriarchal stage of migratory pas-
toral tribes," Henry Nash Smith says, "and so on through ever more complex
and stable forms of organization. . . ."

This is the theory Cooper introduced in *The Prairie* where "the march
of civilization" is located at "those distant and ever-receding borders which
mark the skirts and announce the approach of the nation. . . ." In the
course of its development, American civilization was to pass through all the
stages of culture, Cooper believed, much as ontogeny was thought to reca-
pitulate phylogeny. He was convinced, therefore, that social conditions at the
frontier resembled a situation "as near barbarity" as that under which men
lived in the prehistoric past. And in order to portray the conditions of the
migratory, patriarchal phase, he created the tribe of Ishmael Bush.

It is at this point that a casual interplay of the intelligence—a mere circumstance of history, notable because two men of vastly different times and places see eye to eye—at this point, interplay is not casual but turns schematic. Freud drew on information available in biological, Biblical, archaeological, and anthropological studies, then composed a hypothesis which described how men lived originally in a primal horde, itself disciplined by a severely patriarchal code. And Cooper removed the Bush family from settlements to prairie, to that remote frontier where he hoped to represent the stages and to penetrate the mystery of culture. There alone, he remarked in an essay on American literature (1828)—written one year after *The Prairie* appeared—an American writer could find "subjects to be treated with the freedom that the imagination absolutely requires." Unfolding the theme which Henry Bamford Parkes (1957) calls an expression of the "embryonic beginnings, in patriarchal form, of organized law and order"; reproducing the experience of this tribe; undertaking to define what deep impulse and dark desire underlay the creation of human culture, Cooper allowed his imagination to range and he conceived what Freud was to call the most barbarous of all acts, the mythic primal crime.

II

We meet the Bush clan at the moment when the novel opens and immediately we realize that its experience signifies the central matter of the fiction as a whole. Ordinarily, this fact is overlooked, and the Trapper is regarded as the novel's main personage; the special quality of his beautiful human nature is thought to be its principal subject. The Trapper, however, dies in a work originally designed less to lament his passing than to say what must succeed him in the wilderness. We do indeed suffer a loss. But Cooper reminds us that civilization is ceaseless and does in fact confer some advantages. A community of honest men, purged of evil, vitalized as a result of exposure to the teachings of the Trapper, to nature's own agriculture of the spirit—this community might well establish on the American continent a new Eden.

What the tribe does, therefore, is crucial; what each of its chief persons learns about himself, about the others, about property and passion and honor; about Indians, the Old Trapper, the Prairie, Mother Nature—all this informs its body and members and will inform the still larger community of Americans in later and higher stages of culture. Its leader, Ishmael, is a figure of legend, a man of "vast and . . . prodigious power" who marched at some "distance in front of the whole," followed by "a group of youths very similarly attired, and bearing sufficient resemblance to each other, and to their leader, to distinguish them as the children of one family." Thus Cooper introduces the primal horde. In his mind, as in Freud's, it is a self-contained and self-supporting unit ruled by the father. It is composed of seven sons and numberless daughters; Ishmael's wife Esther; his brother-in-law Abiram; his wife's orphaned niece Ellen: "including both sexes and every age, the number of the party exceeded twenty." There are two outsiders, both of whom are included in order that the various segments of Cooper's program may be represented. The scientist, Dr. Bat, is a man whose natural intelligence has been corrupted by cyclopedic but inapt learning. And Inez embodies the highest achievement of an old and supremely refined aristocracy—Creole New Orleans'. Her marriage with a natural nobleman, Duncan Uncas Middleton, represents an amalgam of old and new, a blend of the best virtues in each.

These persons perform certain obvious tasks within the formal plot. Inez's abduction by Bush and his brother-in-law, for example, expresses their lawlessness, their disavowal of the usual rules of conduct, of property and indeed of paternity. It is a lawlessness which must be overcome else none of the members of the clan will be properly equipped to assume their high duties, to compose what Whitman was to call the great national *en masse*. Of course the abduction is also a prototype of the chase required in all Westerns, and allows Cooper to show off his buffalo, his Indians and the rest. What is considerably less familiar and far more subtle is the way Inez links all elements of plot.

Quite as the experience of the Bush family provides the center of interest in the novel as a whole, so Inez's abduction helps to clarify the meaning of the most telling events enacted within the inner life of the tribe itself. In "a weak moment," urged by Abiram White, the Patriarch had kidnapped this woman and brought her into his "peaceable and well-governed family." Ostensibly, his aim was to receive high ransom for her return. Actually, the abduction serves another purpose: it enables Cooper to portray a clash between generations, a rebellion of the sons against the father. For Ishmael, "grave in exterior, saturnine by temperament, formidable in his physical means, and dangerous from his lawless obstinacy," wields what Cooper calls a peculiar "species of patriarchal power." And this power is threatened when his eldest son, Asa, revolts.

The revolt develops when Ellen disobeys Ishmael's order to stay far from the secret place where Inez is hidden. Shamed by his evil deed, fearful that the rest of the family will discover his guilt, Ishmael had hidden her in a wagon "covered with a top of cloth so tightly drawn as to conceal its contents with the nicest care." The others are told that the wagon holds a dangerous beast brought out by Abiram into the wilderness to serve as a decoy should they be forced to use that device. Ellen disregards the standing order to stay clear of Inez's hiding place. Ishmael commands her not to open the flap, but she is less docile than Ishmael's own children and she disobeys. He fires his rifle; she shrieks and disappears inside. It is this act which precipitates the quarrels that follow—between son and uncle, between uncle and father, between sons and father.

For the first time in their lives, Ishmael's sons are outraged by a display of their father's autocratic rule. They "manifested, in an unequivocal manner, the temper with which they witnessed the desperate measure. Angry, fierce glances were interchanged, and a murmur of disapprobation was uttered by the whole in common." Their response is extraordinary, Cooper says, and cannot be attributed to sudden gallantry. It is at this point, then, that Cooper introduced the Freudian matter. Asa, the eldest son, speaks for the others:

> "What has Ellen done, Father," said Asa, with a degree of spirit which was the more striking from being unusual . . .
> "Mischief . . . boy; mischief! take you heed that the disorder don't spread."

Keep your place, Asa, Ishmael answers, and control your brothers. But Asa is enraged, disdainful; he forgets his first purpose, to defend Ellen and seems to want to provoke a battle, man to man. Ishmael senses his mood and reminds him, "I am your father, and your better." "I know it well; and what sort of father?" Ishmael again warns that disobedience will bring severe punishment. But Asa is ready to provoke a crisis in the rule of the tribe because he has arrived at a critical moment in his own life. He is no longer willing to remain inside the "web of authority within which Ishmael had been able to envelope his children." Ellen is forgotten. And we realize that the scene is composed less to portray a debate on the propriety of firing bullets at young women than to represent the psychology and consequence of rebellion, during the patriarchal stage of civilization, within the tribal horde. In the final exchange between the two men, therefore, we see how far behind they have left its original cause. "I'll stay no longer," Asa says, "to be hectored like a child in petticoats. You . . . keep me down as though I had not life and wants of my own." And there we have Asa's main grievance: he is ready to risk his father's wrath in contention over the only nubile women available in their private world.

Asa's ripening adulthood, his assertion of sexual needs no less valid than his father's, is symbolized in the very next occurrence when Inez materializes and stands at some distance from the assembled company. Seeing her, Asa turns to his uncle and remarks, "This then is the beast . . . I know you to be . . . a dealer in black flesh," but not till now had he realized that "you drove the trade into white families" too. Abiram answers, "Look to your own family"; that Ishmael and the sons are not renowned for their honesty. And Asa's accumulated fury is loosed. He hits Abiram a "back-handed but violent blow on the mouth that caused him to totter. . . ."It is a fateful act, directed against a surrogate but in fact meant for the father himself, as everyone but Abiram is aware. And because Ellen's disobedience and Asa's blow are traceable to Inez's presence, we realize that this genteel lady of high station and Roman Catholic breeding is, in quite another sense than the irony reports, indeed a "ravenous, dangerous beast."

Inez is a fragile woman of iron virtue but her "sylph-like form," which Cooper calls the "beau ideal of female loveliness," is lush: "long, flowing and curling tresses of hair, still blacker and more shining than her robe, fell at times about her shoulders, completely enveloping the whole of her delicate bust in ringlets. . . ." Seeing this vision, all the men are stirred. The young Pawnee chief "riveted his eyes on Inez" and immediately his head is turned. "He had the air of one who maintained a warm struggle . . . in the recesses of his own thoughts." Even his sense of direction is lost. Although he is absolutely at home on the prairie, his return to his village is delayed when, setting off, "he rode for a moment . . . in circles, as if uncertain of his course." Middleton, a gentleman, is no less moved but is better at disguising his passion. Indeed, we do no violence to the text if we read the novel as a kind of teaser in which this young man chases his lady all over the prairie in order to get her back where she belongs: in bed. For Ishmael and Abiram had kidnapped Inez as she returned home from her prayers, during the short time between her wedding and its consummation. She had disappeared while Middleton—"the lover, the husband, the bridegroom"—impatiently waited.

Asa's accusation is wrong: neither Abiram nor Ishmael had planned to sell her into sexual bondage. But his error is consistent with his mood and his mood is provoked by the odor of passion which Inez exudes. She is a genteel female of Cooper's usual sort, and simultaneously she is a woman of peculiar erotic power. She is therefore ideally suited to play the role Cooper reserved for her, to take her place at the center of a plot encircled by crimes of passion.

When Cooper removed Inez from the darkness of her prison-tent and, at a critical moment in the argument between Ishmael and Asa, placed her high on a windy hill, dress fluttering "like gossamer around her form"—in this image, we recognize his way of exposing to the light of day what it is that animates Asa's rebellion. The young man is ready to assume the responsibilities and enjoy the prerequisites of adult manhood. And these are unavailable so long as Ellen Wade, who provokes the crisis, and Inez, who symbolizes its essential meaning, are held within his father's heavy hand. In the instant before he hits Abiram, Asa has two choices: he can somehow overmaster his father and put himself in the older man's place; or he can leave. Before Inez's appearance, he had threatened to leave and, with deadly playfulness, his father had replied, "the world is wide, my gallant boy . . . Go. . . ." When he strikes the blow, however, we understand that he has undertaken to follow the first course. We realize, too, that Cooper has conceived what Freud later was to call the "crime of liberation," a version of the oedipal drama, and that this now will be enacted, ritualistically, to its inexorable close.

It is unnecessary to reconstruct the whole of Freud's argument. We require merely its substance and this is given succinctly in *Moses and Monotheism,* where Freud maintained that "all primeval men, including, therefore, our ancestors," underwent the fate which Cooper's fiction unfolds. The parallel is not merely striking: it is extraordinary. "The strong male was the master and father of the whole horde, unlimited in his power, which he used brutally. All the females were his property, the wives and daughters of his own horde as well as perhaps also those stolen from other hordes. The fate of the sons was a hard one; if they excited the father's jealousy they were killed or castrated or driven out." There is an echo of the "expulsion of the eldest son," Freud observed, "in many myths and fairy-tales." Its echo in *The Prairie* is quiet, however, because Cooper decided on one of the alternate choices. When Asa refuses his father's invitation to leave and instead commits an act which threatens the Patriarch's rule, he is exposed, vulnerable. And his hopes for survival—in a story which recapitulates what Freud called the myth of the tribal horde—are modest indeed.

Abiram kills Asa, in hate, revenging himself for the insult. Cooper's readers long have accepted this as a valid motive because Abiram is a demonstrably vicious man. But they have accepted it on less persuasive grounds too. Cooper is a notoriously careless writer, quick to sacrifice the world of fact in favor of the larger universe of fancy. Comprehending the essence of an idea or an experience, he was impatient or neglectful when he set out to describe its surface. In this instance, Asa's death at Abiram's hand is true to the spirit of the whole situation but inappropriate, unbelievable when presented as a result of the sheer incident, the mere insult, alone.

The necessary reasons for murder transpire once we realize that Abiram has a dual role even in the explicit plot. He serves as Ishmael's evil genius, a tempter whose "voice is like a raven in my ears," and simultaneously he serves as the instrument of Ishmael's will. Murdering Asa, he accomplishes Ishmael's design: it is Abiram's gun that shoots, but it is Ishmael's bullet that kills the son. This is not Cooper's figure of speech, but one evoked by Ishmael's ruminations in the scene where Asa's body is discovered and buried. Ishmael tries to dissociate himself from the crime, but he shares the murderer's guilt if only because he feels relieved to learn that his eldest son is dead. Asa had not followed his father's command to keep the disorder from spreading; on the contrary, "the spirit of insubordination, which emanated from the unfortunate Asa, had spread among his juniors" and had threatened the father's rule. Freud would have said that it threatened the father's life— that one of the sons sooner or later would have murdered Ishmael. That Cooper shared this opinion too is indicated by Ishmael's recollection of his own past, of the time when "in the wantonness of his youth and vigor, he had . . . cast off his own aged and failing parents, to enter into the world unshackled and free." The fear of being similarly cast off—killed—crosses Ishmael's mind but is immediately replaced by a more comforting thought. With Asa's death, "the danger had abated, for a time at least": that is to say, until the time when another son grew rebellious. And he is pleased. thinking that although his "authority was not restored with all its former influence," nevertheless it maintained "its ascendency a little longer."

In order to underscore Ishmael's sense of his own danger, of temporary reprieve, Cooper diverts our attention to the private thoughts of the mother and the remaining sons. And we learn that the latter "had glimmerings of terrible distrust as to the manner in which their elder brother had met his death." These glimmerings are the more remarkable, Cooper observes, because usually the young men are dull. Even their mother, a most loyal wife, suspects her husband, as Ishmael later remarks. Neither mother nor sons have as yet any reason to accuse Ishmael, not the least clue confirming his guilt or innocence. Nevertheless, each of the sons fears for his life: their thick minds grow suddenly supple, prescient. And they wonder if Ishmael is ready to "imitate the example of Abraham, without the justification of the sacred authority which commanded the holy man to attempt the revolting office." Invoking the Biblical story, Cooper causes the figures of Abiram—Abraham —and Ishmael to merge and become one. The horde of restless sons recognizes in this person an absolute ruler who killed their brother though he had no sanction higher than that dictated by his own nature and by his tribal rank; who is ready to deal with each of them in a similar fashion. And the main result of this awareness, Cooper notes, is "to strengthen . . . the authority of Ishmael." His reign is assured because he, the man whose own rebellion had succeeded, has overridden the challenge of his eldest son and in consequence has kept the disorder from spreading. Primal justice has triumphed and a primitive culture—having suffered neither social revolution nor anarchy—has survived.

III

These are the events and the issues that occur in two pivotal scenes, extraordinary because both accord, in outline and in detail, with those described in the Freudian hypothesis. "The story is told in a very condensed way," Freud said, "as if what in reality took centuries to achieve . . . had happened only once." This remark of course describes Cooper's method too. And a story with which initially Cooper hoped to symbolize primeval experience in the life of the nation came somehow to comprehend what Freud later was to call the paradigm of man's racial experience, the origin of civilization itself.

But we have not even yet fully described all the ways in which Cooper anticipated and applied these intricate ideas. Freud contended that the desire to kill a tribal leader—fulfilled in the case of Moses or forestalled as in the case of Ishmael—is itself the source of the idea of original sin. And this idea, in turn, distinguishes Hebrew from Christian organization. "Paul, a Roman Jew from Tarsus, seized upon this feeling of guilt and correctly traced it back to its primeval source . . . it was a crime against God that could be expiated only through death." This is Ishmael's opinion too when, later in the novel, he does finally recognize an authority higher than his own. "Abiram White," he says, at the moment when Abiram's crime is discovered, "you have slain my first born and according to the laws of God and man you must die." The Patriarch is no longer a kind of Hebrew nomad chieftain; instead he speaks as a Christian who has received God's Word and knows what he must do in order to gain salvation. In the period preceding that moment in which he pronounced sentence, he had searched the Bible to find those "rules of conduct which have been received among all Christian nations as the direct mandates of the Creator." Asa's murder, a crime committed without God's sanction, had abrogated God's law. Originally the crime had pleased Ishmael, but now he regards it as the work of "the devil incarnate," inflicted as a "terrible retribution from Heaven." In the idiom and form of the novel the event does indeed carry the whole weight of original sin. And if Ishmael is to be purged of guilt, he himself must suffer and must somehow die.

Cooper solves this problem not only by causing Ishmael to sentence Abiram, the actual criminal, to death but also by intimating that both men share one soul and a common fate. Abiram stumbles as he moves toward his "last agony," and appears to totter "beneath a load of . . . guilt." Ishmael, though implacable, is moved, for he feels as if he "had been suddenly and violently separated from a recent confederate forever." We realize that this unaccustomed emotion does not represent a sudden affection for his brother-in-law. Rather Ishmael feels that he is about to be rid of nothing less than his own concupiscence, malice, envy. This is why, in the next instant, Abiram's death cry "seemed to have been uttered at the very portals of [Ishmael's] . . . ears." Suddenly, feeling his own blood gush "from every pore in his body," he is amazed to hear "a sort of echo burst . . . from his own lips . . ." Having offered in sacrifice that part of himself, as we may say, which is culpable, Ishmael assumes his own share of guilt, participates in Abiram's agony, achieves expiation and is reborn.

In these transmutations of plot we recognize a transformation of its religious tone. What Freud would have called the Mosaic order has been replaced by "the new religion founded by Paul," based in the twin principles of "original sin and salvation through sacrificial death." In the action of Cooper's novel, transformation occurs when the remaining members of the family depart from the primitive West and return to "the confines of society," where their "train was blended among a thousand others" and where their descendents—good Christians—are forever "reclaimed from . . . lawless and semi-barbarous lives. . . ."

It is ironic indeed that Freud's distaste for American life forced him to remain ignorant of American letters, of Cooper's novel where his own speculation would have been supported by the kind of testimony he was delighted to receive—by that found in the arts. And his theory would have been granted a form of attestation got nowhere else despite lifelong and comprehensive research. The only idea which Cooper does not anticipate and exploit is the one suggestion which remains unconvincing even today, Freud's Lamarckian notion that each of us inherits and retains a memory trace of the primal event. Its absence from Cooper's imagination implies that it is one of the least reliable contrivances of Freud's prodigious mind. Cooper's opinion on this matter is the more creditable—and the more amazing—when we remark, finally, how completely his work incorporates every other element in Freud's argument, even some suggestions Freud (1921) attributed to Otto Rank concerning the origins of art and the nature of myth. These emerge, Freud and Rank agree, when some one man, moved by the aspiration to replace a tribal father, chooses to invent a story in which this accomplishment is described as actually having occurred though in fact it has not happened. In "the exigency of his longing," Freud says, he is "moved to free himself from the group and take over the Father's part. He who did this was the first epic poet. . . . He invented the heroic myth."

When we recall that the five Leatherstocking novels compose a series which has precisely this effect, we realize how fully Cooper's attitude and effort simulates and encompasses Freud's. For it is well known—though in a far less discrete way than I have hoped to show—that the novels establish what Richard Chase (1957) calls "a myth of culture," in which the leading "episodes in the life of the hero are those which universally involve the life of society. . . ." It is less well known how fully the facts of Cooper's own life—his replacement of his father, Judge Cooper as Lord Temporal over thousands of acres in Cooperstown, New York—accord with motives presented in his fiction. But surely we can see that experience in the one realm is inextricable from experience in the other. Concerning Freud, too, Erich Fromm (1959) has demonstrated how the events of professional life represent a personal sense of rivalry, and with no less a personage than the greatest of culture heroes, Moses himself. For Freud did indeed see himself as a kind of lawgiver, a spokesman of new and somehow ineffable knowledge, a creator of "the last word in man's understanding of himself and of the world." Some fascinating similarities in the inner lives of both men, therefore, allow us to speculate why each man hoped to conceive and to recreate the beginnings of human society.

Unlike Freud, however, Cooper identified the origins of society with the earliest stages of American civilization. Interlocking these, he introduced the traditional stuff of the American dream and then incorporated the whole matter in a line of action that concerned the public and the private life of a single family. Thereby he fulfilled his own mission as a novelist, a creator of a quite new kind, a fabulist of America who assisted at the birth of the Nation and who served it by imagining a legend which portrayed how the New Society, purified, might lead the way for all mankind. For Cooper, like Freud, realized that the forces which animate the life of this tribe are the same forces which, suitably ordered, compel men and nations to fulfill their highest destiny.

BIBLIOGRAPHY

Chase, R. (1957), *The American Novel and Its Tradition*. New York: Doubleday.

Cooper, J. F. (1827), *The Prairie: a Tale*. New York: Rinehart, 1950.

—— (1828), *Notions of the Americans*. Philadelphia: Carey, Lea & Carey.

Feldman, S. S. (1947), Notes on the "Primal Horde," *Psychoanalysis and the Social Sciences, 1*:171-193. New York: International Universities Press.

Freud, S. (1913), Totem and Taboo. *Standard Edition, 13*:1-161. London: Hogarth Press, 1955.

—— (1919), Psychoanalysis and Religious Origins. *Collected Papers, 5*:92-97. London: Hogarth Press, 1953.

—— (1921), *Group Psychology and the Analysis of the Ego*. London: Hogarth Press, 1948.

—— (1939), *Moses and Monotheism*. New York: Knopf.

Fromm, E. (1959), *Sigmund Freud's Mission*. New York: Harper.

Jones, E. (1957), *The Life and Work of Sigmund Freud, 3*. New York: Basic Books.

Lawrence, D. H. (1930), *Studies in Classic American Literature*. New York: A. and C. Boni.

McCall, L. B. (1958), Freud and Scientific Truth. *Commentary, 25*:343-349.

Parkes, H. B. (1957), Metamorphosis of Leatherstocking. *Literature in America*. New York: Meridian, pp. 431-445.

Riesman, D. (1954), *Selected Essays from Individualism Reconsidered*. New York: Doubleday.

RELIGION

THE ROLE OF THE MOTHER IN THE DEVELOPMENT OF HEBRAIC MONOTHEISM

As Exemplified in the Life of Abraham

DOROTHY F. ZELIGS, Ed.D.

The basic contribution which psychoanalysis has made to the understanding of religious phenomena is the demonstration that religion grows out of man's psychological needs and is shaped by his early experiences in the family group. In the development of Hebraic monotheism the relationship between father and son is more readily apparent than the role of the mother. In an earlier study (1954) I have dealt with the problem of ambivalence in the life of Abraham and tried to show how this factor affected his attitudes toward God as well as toward father and son imagos. The present study will attempt to see the role played by the mother figure in Abraham's new concepts of religion and of life. It will deal with this role both on the preoedipal and oedipal levels of functioning and with some of the consequent defenses and sublimations. This relationship cannot of course be understood apart from the larger Gestalt of the whole familial group.

Whether he was a historical personality or not, Abraham, as the traditional founder of the Jewish religion, represents psychically, as in a myth, the basic determinants that helped the Hebrews reach out for a different kind of relatedness to the Deity and to the group. In fact, the patriarchal period of Biblical history has been more solidly substantiated in the past few decades than ever before. While archeology has dug up no evidence for the specific heroes of this epoch in Hebrew life, the historicity of the period itself, as described in the vivid details of the Biblical narrative, becomes very convincing (Albright, 1954, p. 236; Baron, 1952, p. 34). Conjecturally speaking, Abraham may be partly historical, partly myth. But the psychological forces he represents must be wholly valid or his story would have losts its meaning for humanity a long time ago.

The material on which this analysis is based comes from two sources. One is *The Holy Scriptures, According to the Masoretic Text;* the other is the authoritative compendium of post-Biblical stories, legends, and commentary contained in *The Legends of the Jews* by Louis Ginzberg (1909-1938). The latter draws most heavily upon the Talmudic-Midrashic literature, covering the period from the second to the fourteenth century. This material can be understood as a response to the Biblical narratives, reflecting both the popular fancy and the homiletic frame of reference. It attempts to fill in what the highly condensed style of the Biblical story omits. We thus have a continuous stream of Jewish thought and tradition in regard to the Biblical writings. In a sense, the extra-Biblical material can be viewed as the *associations* of the people to the stories of the Bible.

Returning to our theme of Abraham, we will try to reconstruct a picture of his family group. Abraham's mother is not mentioned in the Bible. Even in this literature, where genealogy is usually reckoned through the father, it seems a somewhat conspicuous omission not to refer to the mother of so important a personage as Abraham. Extra-Biblical legendary sources have been more generous in this direction. The Talmud has a number of references to the mother of Abraham. She is called *Emtelai,* the etymology of which is *either mother or servant* (Ginzberg, Vol. V, p. 208). Psychoanalytically, this uncertainty may be an expression indicating ambivalence toward the mother on the part of Abraham, and also perhaps on the part of Terah, her husband. The need of the child to denigrate the mother because she is the sexual partner of the father is well known.

The name of Abraham's father, *Terah,* also offers some material for consideration. It probably comes from the Aramaic word meaning *was emaciated* (Ginzberg, Vol. V, p. 208). Legend says that Terah and his immediate predecessors lived at a time when wickedness was widespread. It seems that when Terah was born, the leader of evil spirits, Mastema (Satan), sent ravens to eat up the seeds planted in the furrows and thus rob the earth of its produce. So the father of Abraham was named *Terah,* descriptive of the fact that he was *emaciated* because men were so destitute in his time (Ginzberg, Vol. I, p. 186).

Since Abraham is the hero of the Biblical story, legends must be viewed as fantasies in relation to him. The fact that Terah was emaciated would have no particular significance in the development of the Biblical theme. If, however, Terah is here a substitute figure for Abraham himself, then we get another confirmation of his ambivalence toward the nursing mother. That this attitude was projected onto Terah indicates identification and reversibility in the father-son roles, a mechanism characteristic of Abraham's personality. It should be noted, however, that actually it is the evil father who prevents the mother from producing the nourishment needed by the children.

The theme of ravens who devour the seeds scattered in the fields occurs again in another legend, this time in regard to Abraham himself. The story is that when Abraham was fourteen, he left his father so that he would not be forced to worship idols. Abraham went among the people and taught them how to save the seeds strewn upon the furrows, so that the devouring birds could not destroy them. The legend states that it is not known what *tool* Abraham invented to achieve this purpose (Ginzberg, Vol. V, p. 217). The myth can be understood as the fantasy of a boy at puberty who fears that his own seed may be destroyed by the punitive preoedipal parent as punishment for the revival of oedipal wishes. Abraham, in revolt against this infantile destructive imago, "discovers an instrument" to bring about the fertilization of the earth and thus makes it possible for his own seed to inherit the land, a sublimated and symbolic expression of those same oedipal wishes. The two legends described above form a continuity. The preoedipal fears of early childhood, expressed in the fantasy of the devouring ravens associated with Terah's childhood, return in later maturational stages. In the second myth Abraham takes an active role toward the solution of the problem. He parts with both parents and he himself becomes a father to the people, setting them an example of fruitful impregnation of the earth. In this myth we see a counterphobic attitude to the feared oedipal father, who also takes on the characteristics of the devouring preoedipal imago. The raven can be understood as a combined parental figure, starting from the frustrations of the nursing period and later modified through displacement to the father. Abraham's mode of solution, the unconscious identification with the father as the possessor of the instrument and his symbolic impregnation of the woman, is thus characteristic of the universal human pattern.

The fact that Abraham's wishes were displaced and sublimated to serve the needs of the people is perhaps the most important aspect of his development. One must assume that there were positive elements in Abraham's relationship to both parents or this constructive solution would not have been possible.

Other legendary material corroborates Abraham's ambivalent feelings toward a frustrating preoedipal mother and shows his wish to be independent of her. At the time of his birth a royal edict was issued to the effect that all male infants were to be destroyed. This precautionary measure was the result of predictions by soothsayers that a boy would be born who would displace the king himself. When the time for Emtelai's delivery came, she left the city and wandered in the desert until she found refuge in a cave, where the baby was born. However, she soon abandoned him and returned to her home, declaring that it was better for him to perish alone in the cave than that her eyes should behold him dead at her breast. So she evoked God's blessing upon him and departed.

God sends Gabriel down to help the infant. The angel causes milk to flow from the little finger of the child's right hand so that he can feed himself. In another legend, Abraham can also draw honey from another spout. Like the Promised Land of his later life, Abraham flows with milk and honey (Ginzberg, Vol. I, pp. 186-189; Vol. V, p. 210). He thus gives up the frustrating object and identifies with her instead, incorporating her nurturing qualities.

The failure of the Biblical narrative to mention Abraham's mother can be regarded as a form of repression, with the purpose of defense against the wishes and fears associated with preoedipal affects. At the time when the story in Genesis begins, Abraham presumably has already lost his mother. It is reasonable to assume that if she had still been living at this time, Terah would have taken her along on the migration to Haran. It is curious that the death of Terah's youngest son, also named Haran, is specifically mentioned as having occurred while the family still lived in Ur. This fact makes the lack of reference to the mother, either in life or death, even more striking.

There are indications, to be noted later, that in leaving his home and his native city in Babylonia, Abraham must have gone through an experience of separation anxiety although he was already a grown man and married. The symbolic value of *city* and *land* as representative of the mother seems to have had more than usual significance for the early Hebrews. One wonders why this was so. In Ur, where Abraham grew up, the most imposing building was a temple to the moon-god, the *ziggarut,* which dominated the town not only architecturally but through its impressive cultic ceremonies which attracted large assemblies of people. Moreover, this temple was the center of a busy life of trade and services needed to keep such a large institution functioning. Thus it dominated the city and the surrounding region economically as well. In addition to this main place of worship, almost every street intersection in Ur had a shrine dedicated to some lesser deity, where passers-by were accustomed to stop for worship several times a day (Bailey, 1943, pp. 30-33). One could say that the town was almost literally possessed by the gods, a situation which must have found a responsive representation in the unconscious life of the people.

A fuller understanding of Abraham's relationship toward the mother is bound up with a view of his feelings toward siblings. Are there any indications in the Bible about Abraham's attitudes in this respect? We have the factual statement that Terah had three sons, Abram, Nahor, and Haran.

Abram is evidently the eldest. We are then informed that Haran died in Ur. It is Haran's son, Lot, who accompanies Abraham, first to the town of Haran and later to Canaan.

These facts must have some psychological meaning, some bearing upon the life of Abraham. Was he here expressing ambivalence toward a rival sibling? Haran conveniently dies. Abraham sublimates his feelings of guilt by caring for the son of his brother, but at the same time replaces the latter as a father figure and takes away his heir. Later on, his ambivalence is transferred from father to son and he finds a way of parting with Lot also. These interpretations will receive more substantiation later on in this study.

Legend gives a further corroboration of the rivalry between Abraham and Haran. When the former was tossed into the fiery furnace by the king as a punishment for his denouncement of idol worship, he was saved by God. Seeing this miracle, Haran also declared his belief in Abraham's God. But when he too was thrown into the fire, he perished, for his faith had not been sincere (Ginzberg, Vol. I, pp. 198-203). We have here a contrast between the loyal and faithful Abraham and his unworthy brother.

Legend states further that Sarah, the wife of Abraham, was really the daughter of Haran, referred to in the Biblical text by the name of *Iscah,* descriptive of her prophetic gifts (Ginzberg, Vol. I, p. 202; Vol. V, p. 214). In this context, Abraham would then have taken away both of Haran's children, Sarah and Lot, while their father suffers a premature death in Ur.

According to one commentary, Haran's death was a punishment for an "incestuous crime." The logic for this thinking is that Lot, his son, did unwittingly commit such a misdeed, and he must therefore have been following in the footsteps of his father. Another view is that Haran was punished for the anticipated crime of his son (Ginzberg, Vol. V, p. 214). Projection and the law of talion are prominent here. What emerges clearly is a highly disguised sibling rivalry on the part of Abraham toward his younger brother.

This rivalry must have had its first roots in relation to the mother. As the youngest of the three brothers, Haran may have occupied a special position in her affections and thus stimulated Abraham's feelings of jealousy and abandonment. Both she and Haran suffer death in Ur, and her name and memory are so repressed that they are never mentioned.

It might be well as this point to discuss more fully Sarah's relationship to Abraham. This important personality is somewhat of a mystery as far as her origin is concerned. In Genesis, 11:29 the statement is made: "And Abram and Nahor took them wives: the name of Abram's wife was Sarai;

and the name of Nahor's wife, Milcah, the daughter of Haran, the father of Milcah, and the father of Iscah." Thus we are clearly told the parentage of Nahor's wife, but this information is omitted in the case of Sarah. It is only much later in the story that Abraham gives some information about this matter. In Genesis, 20:12, he says, " 'And moreover, she is indeed my sister, the daughter of my father, but not of my mother; and so she became my wife.' " This explanation was made in self-extenuation for posing as Sarah's brother rather than her husband during their sojourn in Egypt and Gerar.

The rabbis, uneasy about the incestuous aspect of his relationship, point out that the word, *daughter* in the Bible was also used to describe the relationship of *granddaughter*, so that Sarah may have been Abraham's niece. Abraham's statement, however, seems a clear and forthright one.

The fact that he made it for defensive purposes may point to a *reluctance* to reveal this information rather than to any ambiguity in the statement itself. The feeling of obscurity that is created about Sarah's parentage may reflect Abraham's own unconscious confusion about her real role and identity in their relationship. If she was indeed a half sister, the strength of Abraham's unconscious incestuous attachment to her, a situation that will become apparent later, would have some basis in reality.

There is no indication in the Biblical narrative that Abraham left Ur on his own initiative for the migration to Haran. On the contrary, we are clearly informed that *Terah took his family,* including Abraham and Sarah, and departed from Ur. They settled in the town of Haran, which lay to the northwest, along the edge of the Fertile Crescent. Abraham is therefore taken away from his motherland by his father, a separation which followed the earlier loss of his real mother.

The fact that Abraham remained in Haran until Terah's death may indicate a rather close attachment to the father, for Abraham was already seventy-five years old when he began his new life at God's behest. Even then he was able to assume an independent role only by turning for guidance to a greater Father.

In order to understand the early influence in Abraham's life, it was necessary, as it were, to read between the lines of the scanty material that related indirectly to this area. However, the most important evidence for any theory of personality that could be formulated would have to involve the main body of the Biblical account concerning the patriarch. This material deals largely with Abraham's relationship with God. We may assume that a psychoanalytic study of this relationship should reveal elements of Abraham's early experiences with his earthly parents and, in a circular process, help us understand the roles that their images played in his development of religious concepts and attitudes.

Perhaps the most clear-cut approach to an analysis of how Abraham related to God is to view the situations in which communication took place between them. There were an impressive number of such events throughout the patriarch's life, eight in all. Although these happenings seemed to be initiated by God Himself, and the immediate setting was not always marked by apparent crisis, we shall assume that it was indeed Abraham who called upon God at such times and that in each instance some special tension must have existed within Abraham. A study of these episodes of communication between God and Abraham justifies this assumption. In seven out of the eight times, the situation is one in which *the element of separation,* of one kind or another, is clearly involved. In the eighth, it can be inferred. Other common factors will emerge as these situations are described more specifically.

It is in the twelfth chapter of Genesis that Abraham hears the voice of God for the first time. This event takes place after the death of Terah.

> Now the Lord said unto Abram: "Get thee out of thy country, and from thy kindred, and from thy father's house, unto the land that I will show thee. And I will make of thee a great nation, and I will bless thee, and make thy name great; and be thou a blessing."

Abraham's response is one of unquestioning obedience. "So Abram went, as the Lord had spoken unto him; . . . ."

Abraham may have needed the stimulus of such a command in order to accept his new status as head of the tribe. The fact that it had to come from God indicates that a conflict must have been involved. It was not easy for Abraham to take his father's place. The grandiose nature of God's promise suggests that Abraham harbored opposite feelings, for which he needed compensation. Moreover, only by "being a blessing" to others could he feel justified in assuming the role of leadership in Terah's stead.

The move to another land may have been an effort to transfer his libido from the object which he had shared with his father, their common homeland in Haran, reminiscent of Ur and symbolic of the mother. This effort may have been necessary to free himself psychologically from his attachment to Terah. This first communication with God thus involved a separation from parental figures. Leaving Haran signified a move toward independence and greater emotional maturity.

God next reveals himself to Abraham in the one situation referred to earlier where the concept of separation does not seem to be directly related to the content. Abraham has passed through a large part of the land and is now at Shechem, in the central portion of Canaan. "And the Lord appeared unto Abraham and said: 'Unto thy seed will I give this land.' " This is indeed a brief communication. Abraham responds, not verbally, but by building an altar to God and, presumably, offering a sacrifice there. One wonders why the patriarch needed a confirmation of God's promise at this time. He had made his way for a considerable distance through a strange land. It was a peaceful penetration that utilized sparsely populated regions where the Hebrews could maintain their seminomadic existence. Interestingly, in the sentence immediately preceding the announcement of God's appearance to Abraham, we are told: "And the Canaanites were then in the land." It was well known that the Canaanites were in the land through which Abraham was passing. Why then this laconic statement, seemingly unrelated to the context? If we put in the causal connections which seem to be left out here, the text tells us that Abraham, after he had *walked through* the land, became uneasy when he reached the hostile town of Shechem. He had taken possession of territory in which the Canaanites were still the masters. He therefore needed God's reassurance that it was all right for him to be in Canaan. This assurance must have been greatly desired because God not only *speaks* to Abraham but also *appears* to him.

Shechem has certain specific associations in early Biblical history. It was here that several generations later Dinah, the daughter of Jacob, was violated by the prince of Shechem. For this deed, a heavy punishment was exacted from all the men of the town at the hands of Dinah's brothers. Legend says that the inhabitants of this locality sought to do the same injury to Sarah and Rebecca in earlier times. It declares that the Shemites persecuted Abraham when he was a stranger and that they *vexed his flocks when they were big with young*. They were known for taking away people's wives by force (Ginzberg, Vol. I, p. 403). All these stories probably have their source in the Biblical narrative of Dinah's shameful experience in this town. However, the underlying theme is that the stranger who invades the land is subject to having his women attacked and, no doubt, himself castrated, a projection of oedipal dangers. Alone in this unfamiliar territory, Abraham must have suffered from separation anxiety in addition to his other fears.

Shortly after the experience at Shechem, in terms of narrative sequence, there is a famine in Canaan. Abraham seeks refuge in Egypt. One wonders why he fled so quickly from the country to which God had directed him. The Bible does not enlighten us regarding this situation. It merely makes a factual statement: "And there was a famine in the land; and Abraham went down into Egypt to sojourn there; for the famine was sore in the land."

Abraham's flight from Canaan may have been precipitated by unconscious feelings of guilt stimulated by the reality factor of the famine. It was customary in those days to view drought as a sign of God's displeasure. Abraham may have felt that God was punishing him for taking possession of the "land," symbolic of the woman. Evidently the conflict was so great that the earlier reassurance of God, evoked by Abraham's anxiety, was not sufficient to allay it. If only the realistic situation had been involved, Abraham might have relied more on his faith in God and remained in the land to which he had been directed. We may also see in Abraham's precipitate flight from Canaan a reactivated fear of the childhood threat of starvation. *The father will take away the nourishing mother.*

However, Abraham experiences some uneasiness about entering Egypt too. His conscious fear is that his wife Sarah, because of her great beauty, would be appropriated for the Pharaoh's harem. The impression is clearly given that his own life would then be in danger, a sequence of events that is puzzling on a reality level. He pleads with her to pose as his sister so his own safety would be insured.

The same weakening of his defenses and sublimations that caused Abraham to abandon the "Promised Land" may have been the basis of his anxiety on entering Egypt, the territory of a powerful father-king. In both situations, the identification of the land with the woman must have strengthened Abraham's unconscious feelings toward Sarah as a mother surrogate. Abraham is now ready to surrender Sarah too, in order to save himself from death, a derivative here of the castration fears. Thus he reveals his guilt and anxiety in regard to the possession of the forbidden woman. This situation also involved a reversal and projection of the usual oedipal fantasy. It is the father who takes away the son's wife and threatens to kill the son.

Abraham's third communication with God occurs on the occasion when the patriarch parts from Lot. The immediate stimulus for this separation is the strife between the herdsmen of Lot and the herdsmen of Abraham. The patriarch's purpose in suggesting this parting of the ways between himself and his nephew was ostensibly the laudable one of maintaining peace. He suggests that Lot choose the territory in which he would like to dwell and he himself would then go in another direction. Lot chooses the area of Sodom. The full import of this episode and the underlying ambivalence involved is brought out in the earlier study already referred to (Zeligs, 1954).

One wonders if there is any significance to the fact that just before God speaks to Abraham, the following statement is made: "Now the men of Sodom were wicked and sinners against the Lord exceedingly." Then the text continues,

And the Lord said unto Abram, *after that Lot was separated from him:* "Lift up now thine eyes and look from the place where thou art, northward and southward and eastward and westward; for all the land that thou seest, to thee will I give it, and to thy seed for ever . . . Arise, walk through the land in the length of it and in the breadth of it; for unto thee will I give it.

The preceding reference to the wickedness of the men of Sodom must also apply to Lot, who is now among them. The last time God spoke to Abraham, the event was preceded by a reference to the fact that the Canaanite was then in the land. God's reassurance at that time clearly implied that in spite of the presence of the hostile rival, the land would belong to Abraham. Now, once more, a potential rival is removed, and an association is established between him and the wicked men of Sodom among whom he chose to reside. By implication, he too is now unworthy. The whole difficult problem of an heir, longed-for and yet feared as a dispossessor, is projected safely into the future. In the meantime, Abraham is permitted and encouraged to "walk through the length and breadth of the land," that is, to take undisputed possession of the mother. Again he shows his gratitude and submission to God by building an altar to Him at Hebron, a locality far to the south.

This departure of Lot, Abraham's closest potential heir at this time, may have served to arouse anxiety in the patriarch on several levels. First, there must have been guilt in thus abandoning his nephew. The earlier pattern of separation anxiety may have been reactivated here. Parting from Lot may unconsciously have been a re-enactment of Abraham's own separation from his mother. He wishes to get rid of Lot, representative of the younger sibling who took the mother away from him. But he also identifies with Lot as the abandoned one, who lost the mother. For in sending Lot away from the patriarchal household, Abraham was also separating the younger man from Sarah, a mother figure for the entire clan. Moreover, this preoedipal trauma must have been colored by later stages of development. Abraham may have felt that it was he himself who was being left to the unbridled impulses of the wicked men of Sodom, known for their sexual aberrations, chiefly homosexuality. The mother serves as a protection against the dangerous seductiveness of the father. Thus, in identification with Lot, as well as on his own account, Abraham must have suffered anxiety and guilt.

In addition to these other aspects, Abraham was giving up a possible heir, the transmitter of his physical and spiritual heritage to his people. Unconsciously, this son imago would be equivalent to the phallus. The parting with Lot must therefore have been an emotional crisis during which Abraham needed help and reassurance from God.

It must be evident by this time that one of the constant and characteristic features relating to Abraham's communications with God is "a passage through the land." We might review this factor in our study thus far. Abraham's first move is with his father Terah, who brings him from Ur to Haran. Abraham then assumes the initiative, upon God's command, and migrates from Haran into the Promised Land. It is after he has "walked through the land," that God appears to him again at Shechem. The third communication with the Deity involves the *removal* of Lot from the Promised Land and God's injunction to Abraham to walk through the length and breadth of it. The identification of *land* and *woman,* particularly mother, receives continuous emphasis.

The fourth time God makes Himself known to Abraham is again in connection with Lot. It occurs immediately after Abraham has gone to the rescue of his nephew, who has been taken as a prisoner in the war between Sodom and the kingdoms to the north. Abraham succeeds in his courageous mission, freeing not only Lot but the other captives of war and recovering the very considerable spoils taken by the enemy. The grateful king of Sodom wishes to reward the patriarch, but Abraham refuses to take "even so much as a shoe-latchet," for he had acted only on behalf of God and conscience.

It is after he separates from Lot once more, with a possible renewal of all the implications of such a parting, that Abraham has his fourth visitation with God. He now openly expresses doubt and ambivalence toward the Deity, demanding proof that God would really give him a son of his own. God responds to this challenge by instructing Abraham to prepare for the ritual known as the "covenant of the pieces." I have discussed this experience, as a study in ambivalence, in a separate paper (1960). In essence, God again promises Abraham that his seed would inherit the land. He declares, however, that the people of Israel would first have to go through a period of slavery in Egypt. Thus again ambivalence is expressed. The people must be punished, undergoing submission and atonement before they have the right to enjoy their own land. Interestingly, this period of penance is projected onto Abraham's heirs, taking place in the future. The patriarch himself is to be spared this trial and is to live until a ripe old age.

The fifth time God appears to Abraham, He renews His covenant with the patriarch. On this occasion, the important rite of circumcision is made the symbol of their pact. Significantly, at the same time, God predicts the birth of Isaac. Thus we have the familiar psychoanalytic connotation of this ceremony as a symbolic partial castration, the price of submission for the privilege of fatherhood. This communication is unusually lengthy. It occupies twenty-one verses of Chapter 17 of Genesis. The account of the visitation is preceded by an announcement that Hagar, the Egyptian handmaid, whom Sarah had offered Abraham as a substitute for her own barrenness, had indeed borne him a son, whom he named Ishmael. This momentous event had occurred when the patriarch was eighty-six years old.

We are then informed, in the following verse, that Abraham was ninety-nine years old at the time of this particular visit made by the Deity. The thirteen intervening years between the birth of Ishmael and this communication with God evidently did not contain anything of sufficient significance to record in the Biblical narrative. It is not difficult to see that the main theme in Abraham's history is the story of his relationship to God, to sons, and to the land of Israel.

God begins His communication this time with the impressive words,

"I am God Almighty; walk before Me and be thou whole-hearted. And I will make My covenant between Me and thee, and will multiply thee exceedingly." And Abraham fell on his face; and God talked with him, saying, "As for Me, behold, My covenant is with thee, and thou shalt be the father of a multitude of nations. Neither shall thy name any more be called Abram, but thy name shall be Abraham; for the father of a multitude of nations have I made thee."

God follows these words with the commandment regarding circumcision and immediately afterwards announces that Sarah shall bear a son.

If we proceed upon our assumption that God communicated with Abraham at times of special stress, then one wonders where the crisis was in the present situation. What special need for reassurance or support did Abraham require at this time? Ishmael, his son, was then thirteen years old, the age of puberty. In the covenant of the pieces, referred to earlier, God had promised Abraham that a son of his own loins would be his heir. Ishmael fulfilled this description. But he could not fulfill Abraham's deepest need. Ishmael would always be a source of dissension and of reproach between him and his beloved Sarah. Moreover, this son was not the oedipal child of his unconscious fantasy.

As Ishmael approached the age of thirteen and his father ninety-nine, the patriarch must have tried to come to terms with the situation but seemed unable to do so. God's introductory words at this time, therefore, have a special significance. They are an exhortation to Abraham to have faith, to be wholehearted in his belief in God.

In the course of this visitation, Abraham falls upon his face twice before the Presence of God. This act of adoration and submission occurs the first time when God promises to make a covenant with him and to multiply him exceedingly. It happens the second time when he is told that Sarah will bear him a son and that she will be a mother of nations.

> Then Abraham fell upon his face, and laughed and said in his heart: "Shall a child be born unto him that is a hundred years old? and shall Sarah, that is ninety years old, bear?" And Abraham said unto God: "Oh that Ishmael might live before Thee!"

God, however, repeats His promise that Sarah would have a son. The reaction of laughter in Abraham, his lack of frankness with God, reveals his doubt and ambivalence. Yet this very doubt must also be seen as a sign of his strong sense of reality. It would indeed be unusual for people of such advanced age to have a child. In spite of his doubt, however, Abraham tries to maintain his faith. He fulfills the rite of circumcision upon himself and upon all the male members of his household.

Seen as a projection of Abraham's fantasy, the appearance of God at this time can be understood as an effort on the part of the patriarch to deal once more with the problem of an heir. There was evidently a reluctance to accept Ishmael in this role. His hesitancy may have had a further unconscious content in addition to those mentioned before. Abraham's anxiety about being displaced by a son may have increased when Ishmael reached the age of puberty. If the patriarch could still cling to the hope that Sarah herself would bear a child, this feared displacement would once more be safely put off to the future.

It is significant that the rite of circumcision was not required of Abraham before the birth of Ishmael, but came before the birth of Isaac. Greater submission and sacrifice is involved in a relationship which contains unconscious elements of an incestuous nature, as must have existed between Abraham and Sarah. The birth of Isaac represented the overcoming of such a conflict.

Of interest also is the fact that Abraham and his son Ishmael were circumcised at the same time. Psychologically, this can be seen as a sign of identification between father and son. And indeed Abraham seemed to alternate uneasily between these two roles.

It might be observed that in this fifth visit, the usual characteristic of a "passage through the land" is absent. Perhaps its place is taken by the prediction of the birth of Isaac, a "passage through the mother," in a more realistic connotation. Whether we accept literally or not the ages of

Isaac's parents, the long time it took Abraham to realize his wish for a son from Sarah may be symbolic of his psychic struggle in this area.

The sixth visit which God makes to Abraham is characterized both by length and complexity. It contains an unusual degree of action. This event is concerned with the story of Abraham's hospitality to the three strangers. One of the peculiar features of this narrative is the presentation of God as *three men* and as *God Himself,* alternately, the two methods being used almost interchangeably for the most part. This procedure comes out clearly at the very beginning of the episode.

> And the Lord appeared unto him by the terebinths of Mamre, as he sat in the tent door in the heat of the day; and he lifted up his eyes and looked, and, lo, three men stood over against him; and when he saw them, he ran to meet them from the tent door, and bowed down to the earth, and said: "My Lord, if now I have found favour in thy sight, pass not away, I pray thee, from thy servant. Let now a little water be fetched, and wash your feet, and recline yourselves under the tree. . . ."

There seems to be some confusion here on the part of Abraham about the nature of his guest. First the story clearly states that it is the Lord. But Abraham projects this vision onto a more earthly scene. He *looks* before him and sees *three strangers.* His hospitality has a kind of urgency about it that betokens anxiety. He does not seem to know whether he is addressing *one* or *three,* speaking first to *my lord,* and then suggesting, "recline *yourselves* under the tree." This projection from God to three men is also suggested in the conflicting picture of the statement, "lo, three men *stood over against him,*" and in the next instant they *are before him on the road,* for he runs to meet them.

The content of the communication which God makes to Abraham at this time consists of two seemingly separate parts. After the duties of hospitality have been eagerly performed by Abraham, God again makes a pronouncement about the coming birth of Isaac. This time it is Sarah, modestly hiding behind the curtains of the tent door, who overhears and laughs at this unlikely prospect. It is not without interest that God rebukes Sarah for this demonstration of her disbelief, yet He had ignored similar behavior in Abraham on an earlier occasion, when the patriarch had also laughed at the prediction of Isaac's birth. It seems that God tended to be protective of Abraham.

As the visit draws to an end, a curious division takes place. We are now told that *two* of the men went in the direction of Sodom, ostensibly to carry out the punishment of that city and of Gomorrah. God Himself, however, tarries and has a rather remarkable conversation with Abraham. It is on this occasion that Abraham makes his eloquent plea that God should spare the cities of Sodom and Gomorrah, provided a certain number of righteous men are found there.

Both of these two seemingly disparate parts of the visit deal with sons of Abraham. The patriarch's interest in the fate of two wicked cities must have been largely in terms of what would happen to Lot, who lived in one of them. The predicted birth of Isaac must have evoked once more feelings of guilt in regard to Lot, whom the patriarch had rejected as an heir. Abraham therefore tries to make reparation by pleading for Lot's life in the coming destruction of the city.

The *three* men who visit Abraham on this occasion may symbolize the phallic father, who thus announces the birth of Isaac; the *One* figure, God, is the strict superego that will investigate and determine whether *Lot* deserves punishment. Lot here may represent a projected aspect of Abraham himself. Lot within the wicked city of Sodom may symbolize the wicked son in a fantasied incestuous relationship with the mother. If Lot is punished for this crime, then Abraham can have a son with Sarah—the deed will have been "paid for." But the "injustice" of this makes Abraham plead with God to save Sodom, or rather Lot. In the narrative that follows, the city is destroyed, but Lot is saved. Lot's wife, also symbol of the mother, meets with a cruel punishment too, being turned into a pillar of salt. Abraham's ambivalence toward the oedipal mother, especially the unfaithful one who harbors a rival, may be expressed here.

In the seventh communication, Abraham hears the voice of God at a time when the patriarch's distress is quite apparent. He must make a decision about his son Ishmael and the boy's mother, Hagar. Sarah had come to him in bitterness of spirit and demanded, " 'Cast out this bondwoman and her son; for the son of this bondwoman shall not be heir with my son, even with Isaac.' " As a rationalization for this wish, Sarah declared that the young Ishmael had "made sport" of her on the occasion of the feast when Isaac was weaned.

The text tells us that Abraham was very grieved about this situation. It is then that God speaks to him comfortingly, saying,

"Let it not be grievous in thy sight because of the lad, and because of thy bondwoman; in all that Sarah saith unto thee, hearken unto her voice; for in Isaac shall seed be called to thee. And also of the son of the bondwoman will I make a nation, because he is thy seed."

It is then that Abraham supplies Hagar and Ishmael with some food and water and sends them out of the encampment, into the desert. They are subsequently rescued by an angel of God. But Ishmael remains in the desert and grows into manhood there. He has indeed been cast out by Abraham.

We see here how a conflict in regard to a son is again acted out by sending away the son. Sarah's influence has an important part in Abraham's behavior, but his own ambivalence toward Ishmael must also have played a large role. Abraham has to vindicate his conscience by projecting the decision for his act upon God.

At the same time, sending Ishmael away was also a form of renunciation, a masochistic act of self-sacrifice. He may have sent Ishmael away as a form of atonement, in order to retain the love of Sarah. For the youth was, in a sense, the symbol of his infidelity to his wife. Perhaps Abraham unconsciously was trying to appease his feelings of guilt toward her.

There are some men who feel that they owe all their loyalty to the mother figure and that they have no right to any other woman. Sarah may have occupied such a role in Abraham's fantasy. He may then have felt that he had no right to the son who was born of another woman. It might be appropriate to mention here what happened many years later in regard to other sons. After the death of Sarah, Abraham took another wife, Keturah, who also bore him sons, quite a number of them. But the text says, immediately after enumerating these progeny,

> And Abraham gave all that he had unto Isaac. But unto the sons of the concubines, that Abraham had, Abraham gave gifts; and he sent them away from Isaac his son, while he yet lived, eastward into the east country.

It seems that Abraham has a tendency to part with his sons. Even though he took Keturah as a wife, he must still have regarded her as a concubine. Thus, he disavows his real relationship with her and with the children she bore him. Abraham's behavior in this respect is strikingly different from that of Jacob. The latter kept all his sons with him, those of his concubines as well as those of his two wives, and there is little indication that he made much distinction between them. However, Jacob did, of course, have a favorite son, his beloved Joseph.

The last communication between God and Abraham is in connection with the near-sacrifice of Isaac. Again, this dramatic and poignant experience will only be touched upon briefly here, since it has been dealt with in another context (Zeligs, 1954). It might be of interest to observe that while Abraham feels that this nearly overwhelming sacrifice is demanded by God Himself, in a direct communication, the rescue of Isaac at the critical moment is effected by the *voice of an angel*. Does Abraham at this point lose direct contact with God? Has God become so fearful and so remote that Abraham can only communicate with Him through an intermediary? Or, along more positive lines, does this differentiation express a stronger sense of reality on the part of Abraham? It is a more realistic and mature Abraham who suddenly, in a blinding flash of *self-revelation,* no longer needs to believe that God wants child sacrifice. He withdraws momentarily from the God who had commanded him to such an act. He becomes less Godlike himself in his power of life and death, and thus is content to communicate with the Deity in a more remote relationship. In this last communication too, the aspect of a "passage through the land" is involved. For Abraham is directed to take Isaac to the land of Moriah, probably *Mount Moriah,* which later became the site of the Temple, as the place where the offering was to be made. A journey of several days was involved to bring them to this place.

Basic to understanding the psychodynamics of any personality is not only his relationship to the individual parental imagos but his perception of the ways in which these two figures relate to each other. The importance of this form of Gestalt is receiving increasing recognition in psychoanalytic thought. How could this concept apply in regard to Abraham? The answer is not difficult. *The mother belongs to the father.* In the social and historical setting of his time, under the influence of the patriarchal form of family life, this idea was the prevailing one. However, such a formulation seems native to the unconscious even in more sophisticated times, because it is influenced both by social factors and the biological relationship between sexuality and aggression.

It follows then that the mother can be shared and enjoyed by the children only under the conditions stipulated by the father and with his consent.

Abraham works out a beautiful and unique solution to both oedipal and preoedipal problems with the parental imagos. The land belongs to God but is given to the patriarch and his heirs under certain conditions. The fact that these conditions came more and more to involve moral concepts and social responsibilities imparted to the Biblical literature its special character and to the Jewish people the specific nature of its collective images of good and evil.

God controlled the fruitfulness of the land by the amount and timing of the rainfall. This concept was particularly meaningful in a land like Canaan, with its dry and rainy seasons. Drought always brought the danger of famine, thus stimulating the primary fear of starvation set in motion by the talio principle of the infantile unconscious. The father uses the mother as the instrument for punishment, a situation which can be seen as a regression from oedipal to preoedipal levels.

Much of Biblical life and thought acquires a deeper and richer meaning when the words of the Psalmist, "The earth is the Lord's, and the fulness thereof," expressing the attitude of God to the land, is understood as having vitality both on a real and symbolic level.

The concept of the mother as belonging to the father must have been a vital one with Abraham, both in regard to the land and to the woman.

If, as we assume, *the land is the mother*, then the common element of "passage through the land," as a feature in Abraham's periods of crisis, can be clearly understood. To pass through the land is to take possession of the woman. This process evokes fear of punishment from the jealous Father-God. Thus the effort to resolve the separation anxiety by reunion with the mother stimulates castration anxiety. Such situations then required reassuring communications on the part of God and acts of submission and homage on the part of Abraham.

This projected image of the Jealous God seems to have been quite strong in Abraham. It must have been associated with his own jealous concentration of feelings upon the person of Sarah. If he suffered from separation anxiety at an early age, as his later character structure suggests, then this fixation of libido upon Sarah can be readily understood. Karl Abraham (1909, p. 25) calls attention to the monogamous trait in certain types of men whose libido becomes strongly attached to a mother surrogate.

Abraham's attachment to Sarah showed strongly monogamous traits. Although childless for many years, he did not follow the usual custom of those days and take a concubine until Sarah herself proposed this solution. That this gesture on Sarah's part represented a tremendous effort is apparent by her subsequent attitudes toward both Hagar and Ishmael. Sarah, too, had the need for exclusive possession of the love object, a factor which must have strengthened Abraham's tendencies in this direction and helped to create a kind of symbiotic relationship between the two. Thus, when circumstances forced him from his position, Abraham must have suffered considerably from anxiety and guilt.

That Abraham's feelings of possessiveness for his beautiful wife were compounded with guilt and fear is brought out in his sudden willingness to give her up, first to the Pharaoh of Egypt, and later, to the king of Gerar. The fear of death at the hands of the powerful rulers prompted this action, which can be understood as fear of castration from the angry father, to whom the woman belongs.

The patriarch's ambivalence in father-son relationships must have been in proportion to his need for the sole possession of the mother figure as well as to his guilt and fear relating to these wishes.

Abraham's tendency to monogamy and his monotheistic views in religion bear further exploration. The man who wants to have exclusive possession of the mother also wants to be the exclusive object of love. This need to be *the only one,* when projected onto a Deity, leads to monotheism. "Thou shalt have no other gods before Me."

It is interesting that Akhnaton, the Egyptian Pharaoh of the fourteenth century, B.C., showed certain similarities to Abraham in character traits. Akhnaton had a strong mother fixation and an equally strong monogamous attachment to his wife, Nefertete, to whom he was married before he was ten years old. It was this monarch who became famous for his revolutionary monotheistic tendencies (Abraham, 1912, p. 268).

Abraham's intolerance of a rival makes it understandable why the periods of crisis in his life are associated either with his own fear of taking possession of the land and thus of facing the danger of an equally intolerant father figure, or the prospect of being displaced by a son. Yet, on the other hand, his deepest wishes are related to these very two situations. They are involved in God's promise to make of him a great nation. The fulfillment of this promise would necessitate a given territory and an heir. These wishes must indeed have been strong in the patriarch. He wanted to be a great father, whose name would mean "father of multitudes." He wanted to possess the motherland. Interestingly, however, even in God's assurances to him about the Promised Land, the wording is always in terms of Abraham's *seed* possessing the land, an ambiguous expression in which his unconscious fantasy finds sexual fulfillment but at the same time postpones the reality of an heir to the future. There is also the implication that Abraham does not dare to ask this privilege for himself but only for his descendants.

It is not surprising at this point to note that out of the eight times God communicates with the patriarch, six are concerned with the subject of a son and heir. Three of these situations are associated with separation from Lot, either directly, symbolically, or by implication in terms of the sequence of events. In all these episodes the promise of an heir and a multitude of descendents is made at the same time. Thus there is a process of doing and undoing. Abraham parts with a present, potential heir and God promises him another one, a better one, in the future. A further visitation has to do with the covenant of circumcision and the prediction of the birth of Isaac. Another communication concerns the parting with Ishmael, also compensated for by the reminder about Isaac, who is to be the real heir. The final episode of these six father-son themes deals with the sacrifice of Isaac.

The element of sacrifice is associated both with each "passage through the land" and with the promise of an heir or its fruition. The latter situations seem to call for the greater sacrifices. As the intensity of the father-son ambivalence increases, the quality of the sacrifice does too, until it culminates in the episode at Mount Moriah. Abraham is indeed in painful conflict between his wish to be a father and his fear of thus usurping a Godlike privilege; on the other hand, he also has to struggle with jealousy toward the son who would take his place. However, as we have seen, ego strength wins out in the end.

The Deity of early Hebraic monotheism seems, on one level, not only to allow but even to encourage sexuality. "Be fruitful and multiply," is His exhortation. But beneath this conscious permissiveness the unconscious resistance of the father-son ambivalence remains and has to be "worked through" in the long process of civilization. The God of Abraham is still a fiercely jealous God, Who declares, "Whatever openeth the womb is Mine," thus demanding sacrifice and submission for the right of sexual privilege with the woman.

It has been pointed out in a number of studies that the first-born evokes the special jealousy of the father—and of the Father-God—for this child is the first to pass through the genitals of the mother, although in the reverse direction, after the father's relationship with her. The Hebraic laws of sacrifice demand the first-born of all animals produced in the flocks and herds and the first fruits of every season. The first-born sons owe special obligations of service to God, from which they are freed in infancy through a ceremonial of redemption.

Róheim (1955) interprets the Biblical injunction referred to above as really meaning, "Whatever openeth the womb *from the outside* is Mine." The threat of castration is therefore implied to anyone who approaches a woman sexually (p. 193).

The basic anxiety in the emotional life of the human being is fear of separation from the mother, as Freud (1926) explains. This form of anxiety becomes the prototype for the later experiences of castration anxiety, super-ego anxiety, and the fear of death.

Géza Róheim puts even greater emphasis on the importance of the early mother-child relationship, the "dual unity." Any form of separation brings back the anxiety of the first departure from this early symbiosis. He traces all aggressive impulses and the reactive defenses against them to the oral destructive feelings of the infant at the breast. Róheim (1955) regards primitive orality as the basic force underlying the sublimations and defensive processes involved in religion.

The longing for the mother and the wish to reunite with her is certainly an important aspect of unconscious life. Where separation anxiety is particularly intense, this drive toward reunion will have strong oral qualities and considerable ambivalence.

The fact that the element of separation was involved in all the periods of crisis in Abraham's life seems convincing evidence that separation anxiety, originally developed in regard to the mother figure, had important consequences for his later development. Accompanying such a constellation would be a closer attachment to the father imago as displacement for the mother. However, such a substitute figure, with its associative dangers of feminization, would mobilize strong reactive measures.

How does Abraham deal with these conflicts which involve, at the same time, a strong wish for independence and maturity? He separates himself from his earthly parents and projects their imagos upon cosmic forces. The role of the father is taken over by God. *The Promised Land takes the place of the mother.*

The symbolism of *mother earth* is a familiar one. There are deep, unconscious ties between a people and the particular part of the physical world that they inhabit. In a wider sense, Bychowski (1958) calls our attention to the affinity between certain species of animals and the terrain they cling to, especially for purposes of mating and rearing their young. In regard to human beings he concludes from both biological and sociological implications that they introject aspects of space and territory, both as individuals and as groups, endowing these factors with mythological and ideological significance.

How profoundly the unconscious fantasy of *earth* as *mother* can affect the lives of men is brought out in the study, "Mother-Country and Fatherland" (Feldman, 1955). More specific is the analysis by Ernest Jones (1923) of "The Island of Ireland," indicating the psychological implications for the people of this country that their homeland is an island.

The particularly involved and emotional tie between the people of Israel and the land of Israel is one of the unique features of Jewish history. Meaningful aspects of this relationship from a psychoanalytic viewpoint have been noted in other studies (Rosenzweig, 1940; Brenner, 1952). But the full extent of this significance and the highly specific role it played both in the Biblical history of the early Hebrews and in the culture and continuity of Jewish life to the present must still be more fully explored. The story of Abraham seems to exemplify this connection between the people and their land as a kind of model for the rest of Jewish history. It seems to answer the intriguing question put by Barag (1946): "What is the role of the mother goddess in the development of Jewish monotheism?" The answer, as I see it, is this: *The land became the symbolic mother imago.* Yet it differed from most symbols in that it offered vital and varied avenues for reality satisfactions. It was therefore not only a symbol, but to use Seche-haye's expression, *symbolic realization* (1951).

We have noted three common elements in the situations involving Abraham's communications with God. These were: (1) a state of anxiety caused by some form of separation; (2) a passage through the land; (3) some form of sacrifice. The relationships concerning these three features have been brought out in the body of this study. Briefly, separation anxiety colored the preoedipal and oedipal wishes for reunion with the mother, influencing other forms of anxiety on various levels, particularly when the problem of an heir was involved. These conflicts stimulated efforts at new kinds of relationships with the father, in which the element of sacrifice played an important role.

It must have taken a special set of fortuitous circumstances that enabled Abraham, or someone like him, to pattern his conflicts in a way that strengthened inner capacities for integration. If we regard Abraham in a more mythical sense, as representing the psychic forces of the group, the same observation still holds. The highly personalized relationship with One God instead of many—moreover, with a moral, responsible, covenanting God—and the sublimation of the longing for the mother into the wish to possess the land made possible constructive strivings toward both realistic and moral goals.

The tendency of gifted individuals to project their conflicts upon cosmic forces and to sublimate their impulses through artistic, religious, and social endeavors is discussed in a study by Greenacre (1958).

Abraham's life story is of social and historical importance because of the ways in which he tried to cope with his problems. His attempted solutions were pathways for the group. The patriarch's *life motif* is summed up in the very first communication God makes to him. It contains the complete directive for his existence—to go to a new land, to become the father of a new nation, and *to be a blessing*. Abraham thus saw his mission as having social significance. God became the Moral Law, and the life task of his people was to work out their destiny in accordance with that Law. Thus the model for the collective ego ideal of the Hebrew nation was formulated and expressed in the life of Abraham.

Modern Biblical criticism has long considered the patriarchal heroes of the Bible as purely mythical figures, representatives of various tribal groups rather than as individuals. However, many of the formerly widely accepted theories of this school have, in recent decades, either been abandoned or revised, and the whole field of Biblical research is in a state of considerable fluidity (Rowley, 1951). It is not the task of this particular study to attempt an explanation of how the Bible came to be what it now is. The purpose rather has been to understand the material before us, a literature that has influenced a large part of the world for many centuries. Abraham is completely understandable as an individual, or a real person, from a psychoanalytic point of view. At the same time, he is truly an exponent of the Hebrew people, expressing in his own life the psychodynamics that became the pattern for the group.

BIBLIOGRAPHY

Abraham, K. (1909), The Significance of Intermarriage between Close Relatives in the Psychology of the Neuroses. *Clinical Papers and Essays on Psychoanalysis*, 2:21-28. New York: Basic Books, 1955.

—— (1912), Amenhotep IV: A Psychoanalytical Contribution towards the Understanding of His Personality and of the Monotheistic Cult of Aton. *Clinical Papers and Essays on Psychoanalysis*, 2:262-290. New York: Basic Books, 1955.

Albright, W. F. (1954), *The Archeology of Palestine*. London: Penguin Books.

Bailey, A. (1943), *Daily Life in Bible Times*. New York: Scribner.

Barag, G. G. (1946), The Mother in the Religious Concepts of Judaism. *Amer. Imago*, 6:32-53.

Baron, S. (1952), *A Social and Religious History of the Jews*, Vol. I. Philadelphia: Jewish Publication Society of America.

Brenner, A. B. (1952), The Covenant with Abraham. *Psychoanal. Rev.*, 39:34-52.

Bychowski, G. (1958), Ego and Introjects. *Psychoanalysis and the Social Sciences*, 5:246-279. New York: International Universities Press.

Feldman, B. A. (1955), Mother-Country and Fatherland. *Psychoanalysis*, 2:27-45.

Freud, S. (1926), *The Problem of Anxiety*. New York: W. W. Norton, 1936.

Ginzberg, L. (1909-1938), *The Legends of the Jews*, Vols. I-VII. Philadelphia: Jewish Publication Society of America.

Greenacre, P. (1958), The Family Romance of the Artist. *The Psychoanalytic Study of the Child*, 13:9-36. New York: International Universities Press.

The Holy Scriptures. Philadelphia: Jewish Publication Society of America, 1917.

Jones, E. (1923), The Island of Ireland: A Psychoanalytical Contribution to Political Psychology. *Essays in Applied Psychoanalysis*, 1:95-112. London: Hogarth Press, 1951.

Róheim, G. (1955), Some Aspects of Semitic Monotheism. *Psychoanalysis and the Social Sciences*, 4:169-222. New York: International Universities Press.

Rosenzweig, E. M. (1940), Some Notes, Historical and Psychoanalytical, on the People of Israel and the Land of Israel, with Special Reference to Deuteronomy. *Amer. Imago, 1*(4):50-64.

Rowley, H. H. (1951), *The Old Testament and Modern Study.* London: Oxford University Press.

Sechehaye, M. A. (1951), *Symbolic Realization.* New York: International Universities Press.

Zeligs, D. F. (1954), Abraham and Monotheism. *Amer. Imago, 2*:293-316.

—— (1960), Abraham and the Covenant of the Pieces: A Study in Ambivalence. *Amer. Imago* (in press).

THE DEVELOPMENT OF ETHICAL MONOTHEISM

ANDREW PETO, M.D.

The aim in this study is an investigation, by the psychoanalytic method, of the early development of a religion, namely, the monotheism of the Old Testament, which sprang from one people (called "Israel" in the Bible) and gave rise to what is now called "Judaism."

I shall trace the processes whereby, in a peculiar and specific way, the unconscious fantasies of the nomadic Bedouins (who gradually united to form the people of Israel) became the decisive factor in the growth of this religion.

The period of development of ethical monotheism covers almost one thousand years, the beginnings of which are lost in the haze of nomad desert life, while the end is marked by the prophets Jeremiah and Ezekiel. The last great prophet, Deutero-Isaiah, represents an entirely new period. The psychological history of this monotheistic attitude may be divided into three phases of thought development. These phases, however, are not sharply separated but merge into one another.

The first period is that of nomadic life in the desert. Its beginnings are vague, but its end is marked by the settlement in Canaan. This period embraces those events that are related in the Bible in the histories of the forefathers of the people, the period in Egypt, and the adventures in the desert.

A peculiar relationship to God developed during this period, which displayed several characteristic features. One of them was the tendency to eliminate the Goddess from the manifest religion. Along with this trend, an extremely close and ambivalent relationship arose between the people-son and the God-father. This relationship shows several phases in its development, the most striking being that finally a single demon, Yahweh, gained complete ascendancy. The political and social struggle between the representatives of the different deities is vividly described in the Bible. The later priestly editors endowed this struggle with moral notions, which appeared only at the end of the whole religious development. An unusual aspect of this development is that in the struggle between father and son, which is present in every

From the Department of Psychiatry, Albert Einstein College of Medicine, New York.

mythology, the father in the Bible version conquers the son, and then special psychological and consequently ritual measures have to be taken to allay the arising anxiety of the succumbed people. I refer here to the final role of Israel as the bride of her single god and bridegroom, Yahweh.

I shall attempt to support the assumptions that this development was the result of a particular fantasy involving the mother, and that the aroused castration anxiety led to the complete suppression of the mother. This repression was supported by a strong homosexual trend, and finally established an extremely close and ambivalent bond between the father-God and the son-people.

The second period, the period in Canaan, embraces the organization of the tribes into a people and ends with the fall of the state in the year 586. This stage offers a striking reversal of the previous developments. The people return to their polytheism, and in addition accept the colorful deities of Canaan. Thus they take the usual course of religious development in which an anthropomorphic phase follows the demonic phase. This I attempt to interpret as the manifestation of the usual oedipal conflict with its ramified relationships and its sense of guilt related to both parental figures. In the course of its history this second period is often under the spiritual influence of the third period, that of the prophetic movement, the development of which is chronologically parallel with the previous one. This third period is marked by the development of the prophethood and its ideology, extending from the ninth century to the sixth century B.C. It represents the climax of the ethical monotheism of the Old Testament. The manifest religion shows the beginnings of a meticulous elaboration of ritual, the return of Yahweh's predominance, and his final complete rule. This return to the "nomadic ideal" unfolds on a more and more sublimated level until in the course of about three hundred years the final stage of the monotheistic God concept is attained.

I want to show that the psychoanalysis of this phase displays a sublimated oscillation between closeness to Yahweh and an effort to escape from the God Who still possesses, mingled with the features of the bridegroom, the dangerous qualities of the demon in the desert.

YAHWEH IN THE DESERT

Historical Survey of the Desert Period

The study of the desert period may be approached from the archeological discoveries and from the Old Testament. Documents bearing on the political relations of the great Powers (Babylon, Egypt, and the Hittite Empire) and their Canaanite vassals with the nomadic tribes are few. They refer to the period 1500-1200 B.C. Reliable sources of major importance are the Amarna letters and the Merneptah inscription.

At Tell-el-Amarna letters were discovered addressed by the local princes of Canaan to the Pharaoh Amenophis III and Ikhnaton IV (first half of the 14th century). In some of these letters Abdi-Hiba, the prince of Urusalim (Jerusalem), complains of the Habiru, whose marauding expeditions endangered his authority.

The Pharaoh Merneptah (1225-1198), son of the great Ramses II, was frequently compelled to "appease" his Near-Eastern vassal lands (Canaan and Syria). In his stele of victory (about 1200) he mentions, among Palestinian townships, the people of Irisail (Israel), "Israel is desolated, her seed is not (existing)."

The Hittite text of Boghazkoi (14th century) shows that the name Habiru covered a group of nomadic robber tribes.

Our other source is the Old Testament from which modern Biblical criticism has established the following authoritative conclusions.

The first six books (Genesis, Exodus, Leviticus, Numbers, Deuteronomy, Joshua) present in their final form the results of four different works originating from four different schools.

1. The Yahwist school (Y) which flourished in the Southern State, Judah. Its followers assumed that God was called Yahweh from the very beginning. Time: 10th century.

2. The Elohistic school (E) in the Northern State. The scholars of this school referred to God as Elohim until the scene where he allows Moses to called him Yahweh (Exod. 3:14). Time: 9th century.

3. The Deuteronomists (D) were the representatives of the reformist movement under King Josiah (622). The greater part of the Fifth Book is their work.

4. The authors of the priestly codices (P) in exilic and postexilic times (6th to 5th centuries). This school finally collated a substantial portion of the ritual.

Later writers revised the work of their predecessors in the light of their own religious views. On the basis of the critical study of the Bible and comparative archeology, the following rough outline of the early political history of Israel may be established.

The conquest of Canaan took place most probably from two directions, from the South and from the East. The tribes which pressed up from the South came from the desert regions of Arabia. At some time and in some way they were in contact with Egypt. Whether the connection was merely cultural or one of political dependence remains uncertain. Whether they were robbers, mercenary soldiers, or slaves is unknown.

The extent to which the religious influence of Egypt was felt may be summed up by saying that the formal elements of Egyptian religion undoubtedly exercised an influence on the Bedouins' relation to God. The figure of Moses has the unmistakable features of an Egyptian sorcerer-priest-king.

The possible effect of Ikhnaton IV's (1375-1358) monotheism on the Bedouins of Mount Sinai is referred to in Freud's ingenious hypothesis on Moses. Furthermore, reference is usually made to Psalm 104 with its really striking resemblance to Ikhnaton's Hymn to the Sun; the text is, in some parts, identical word for word.

Yet other tribes appeared from the East, springing from the flourishing culture of the Sumerian and Akkadian peoples of Mesopotamia. Ur, the home of Abraham, was one of the main cultural centers, and was the focal point of Babylonian moon worship. The fate of these tribes is told in the stories of Abraham, Isaac, and Jacob, whose hero name, Israel, finally embraced the whole people.

The influence of Babylon on Israel is significant. The religion of these tribes, however, put new meaning into the cultural framework which they brought with them. The ethical ideas were most probably developed by the Southern tribes, presumably by communities which had hardly come into contact with Babylon.

The Jewish religion evolved from its own internal psychological motivations. The two great cultures of Egypt and Babylon influenced its initial stages in so far as any cultural creation exhibits *some* foreign origins and takes over some formal elements.

The Religion of the Desert

The difficulties which beset research into political history are multiplied in the study of religion. With religion as well as with national pride there arises the problem of morals, and Israel's history is composed of unique religious feelings which later distinguished the Jewish people from other peoples of the ancient East. In the Exile and afterwards the relationship to God was the sole spiritual support of the people. The later editors of the Books interpolated their own religious outlook into the account of relations to God in the desert.

An example: The Decalogue cannot have reached its final form earlier than the end of the seventh century. The text of the Decalogue, its moral and social outlook place it within the prophetic movement and the Deuteronomic reform of the year 622; e.g., all carved cult images are forbidden on principle (Exod. 20:4). This means that a custom is forbidden which flourished in Israel and Judah and which was attacked neither by the prophet Elijah (9th century) nor by Amos (8th century); the Yahwists and the prophet Hosea (8th century) condemned only those luxury statues that represented animals. Nevertheless the final editors alleged that the whole Decalogue was conceived already in the desert and antedated it—in the interests of religious and national pride—by about six hundred years.

Despite these editorial corrections we are able to distinguish some elements of the nomadic religion. In the following pages an attempt is made to present such elements in the religion of the desert phase.

Totemism

At the beginning of historical times the social organization of the Israelites was based on the clan, the *mispaha*. There are traces showing that the *mispaha* originated in a totemistic organization.

The remnants of some totem cults appear quite clearly connected with a definite tribe. Thus the Lea tribes carry the name of antelope, the Rachel tribes that of lamb. The ass seems to have been the totem of the tribe Manasseh (Judg. 10:4).

The calf was the principal god of the Northern tribes until the destruction of the Northern Kingdom (722). The horn is repeatedly used as a symbol of divine power (e.g., Deut. 33:17).

Certain animals were credited with supernatural powers. The snake knew the magic power of the tree before man did (Gen. 3:5). The worship of the snake can be traced back to Moses himself (II Kings 2:18). The she-ass of the seer Baalam, a man of magic power, noticed Yahweh's angel earlier than he himself did (Num. 22:24-35).

The special position of the ass is also proved by the fact that alone among other animals its first-born was not inevitably sacrificed, but could be redeemed, like the first-born among humans (Exod. 34:19-20).

The Demon and the Taboos

In the religion of the Semites evil beings prowling by night hold a prominent place. Such beings frequent desolate places, where in the guise of various animals they lie in wait for their victims. These bloodthirsty demons are the "Jinns" of the people of Arabia. Robertson Smith (1889) holds that the demons developed out of the totem animals and that they expressed in the animistic religion the malignant aspect of the totem father.

The qualities and actions of the various demons were ascribed by editors of subsequent epochs to Yahweh, the One and Only God. Yahweh's demonic nature is revealed by the danger involved in being close to him or seeing him. The danger of proximity is obvious in the first meeting of Moses with Yahweh, who said: "Draw not nigh hither. . . . And Moses hid his face; for he was afraid to look upon God" (Exod. 3:5-6). The danger of touch is well exemplified when David brings the Ark of the Covenant into Jerusalem. One of the men grabs it in order to prevent it from falling from the cart. "The anger of the Lord was kindled . . . and God smote him there for his error, and there he died" (II Sam. 6:6-7).

Taking the census of the people was considered as extremely dangerous. The reason may have been that Yahweh was regarded as the tribal father, and the census was obviously felt therefore to be a sinful investigation into Yahweh's procreative capacity. The census was an intrusion into the primal scene and implied the sharing of the father's potency by his children, the people (Exod. 30:12; II Sam. 24:1-10).

Fear of the demonic qualities of the God may have been one of the reasons why the line of march was so arranged that Yahweh and the people had to be separated by several miles (Num. 10:33).

Perhaps the most threatening quality of the demon was his desire to castrate his victims. Such an attempted, though foiled, castration is at the root of the most important tenets of this religion: the blessing. This seems to be an elaborate countermeasure to ward off the demon-father's castrative desires against his Son-people. When Jacob, alone and in fear of Esau, spent the night at Jabbok: "there wrestled a man with him . . . and when he saw that he prevailed not against him, he touched the hollow of his thigh; and the hollow of Jacob's thigh was out of joint, as he wrestled with him" (Gen. 32:24-29). Then Jacob did not let the demon go before he blessed Jacob. All translations use the word "thigh"; in the original text, however, the word is *"jarech,"* which is also used for the "region of shame"—the genitals. The nocturnal demon strove, since he could not kill Jacob, at least to injure his masculinity.

In this scene Jacob also inquires though in vain the name of the captured demon. It is of interest to note that the taboo of the name was so effective that by the eighth century B.C. the name of the god was no longer known.

Another aspect of the demon's castrative desire was his thirsting for the blood of the first-born, which aimed at taking away from the people-son the most valuable signs of its potency, its offspring (Num. 3:11, and many other passages). Later on he allowed himself to be appeased with animal sacrifice and ransom, paid in substitution for the offering of sons. In the Priestly Codex

(6th to 5th century B.C.) one passage reveals the existence of human sacrifice: "None devoted, which shall be devoted of men, shall be redeemed but shall surely be put to death" (Lev. 27:29).

Originally the taboos were openly referred to as measures of protection against the dangerous malignity of Yahweh. It is only later that they develop into a minutely detailed, sacred ritual and assume a moral significance.

There are definite signs of a higher stage of development in the desert. Most prominent is the Volcano God on Sinai, who punishes with fire and leads the wandering people through fire and smoke.

Magic

Magic thinking plays an important part in every religion. It is expressed in magic rites and magic phrases. The fate, the action, and the whole history of an individual or of a group can be directed by the thoughts and psychological influence of an individual who possesses magic power. The effect is produced by ceremonies. This magic power is vested by God in the magician or seer, and by means of specific rites handed on to new disciples. This select group then holds a privileged position in the cultural circle, and its influence can infiltrate into public and private life.

The covenant, the taboo prescriptions, the circumcision mean a magic protection against evil whether caused by foreign Gods or by their own God, the latter the most dangerous of all because of his proximity. We thus see the dual aspect of the divine power which is also expressed in the ambiguous meaning of many primitive words. Sacred-accursed, blessing-destructive, procreating-destroying are attributes of the selfsame God. All this gradually unfolds in the Bible.

The examples that follow were prevalent among the Nomads of the desert period.

Magic omnipotence derived from Yahweh is displayed in the magic actions of the man of God, Moses. The rod changes into a serpent, the healthy hand into that of a leper, and water into blood (Exod. 4:2-9).

Invested with divine-magic power, Moses is the carrier and possessor of Yahweh's omnipotence, an omnipotence which he exercises through gestures and words, and by which he causes the Ten Plagues (Exod. 6-10).

The victory over the Amalekites was secured with the aid of Yahweh's rod in Moses' hand (Exod. 17:11-12).

In times of drought water was charmed out of the rock by Yahweh's rod (Exod. 20).

Again in one of the many mutinies of the people against Yahweh he sent fiery serpents (Num. 21:5-6).

The worship of the serpent flourished in Judea (II Kings, 18:4), and its inauguration was attributed to Moses.

There are numerous examples in the Bible of magic by word, in the form of utterances of blessing and curse. Before they entered Canaan the people were gathered on two opposite mountains. Both halves of the people were allotted the duty of pronouncing blessings and curses respectively for the good and evil of the whole people. This was meant as a magic procedure the effect of which would endure for all time (Deut. 27).

The fall of Jericho was brought about by magic processions and the sounding of trumpets (Josh. 6).

The great importance of the spoken word is apparent in the story of Jacob, in which the fate of the two brothers and of the two tribes descended from them, Israel and Edom, was predetermined by Isaac's blessing. This story illustrates how the effect of the word essentially and exclusively depends on its having been spoken, quite irrespective of the intention of the speaker. Isaac, weak of age, and blind, wants to bless his elder son, Esau, before his death. Jacob deceives him with his mother's help and Isaac gives him paternal blessing in spite of his doubt (Gen. 27). The discovery of Jacob's trick is of no avail; the blessing so treacherously obtained has full validity.

The magic mark betokens the adherence to a particular God, whose protection and power were transmitted and intensified by it. In the same way as the covenant, the mark symbolizes unity within the clan, security and blood relationship within the community. It bespeaks a physical communion even though the bearer of the mark be alone and at a distance. The distinguishing mark might be a tattooing, or a special cut of hair and beard.

The mark of Cain was a tattooed protective marking; "And the Lord set a mark upon Cain, lest any finding him should kill him" (Gen. 4:15).

The meticulous prohibition of these signs at the time when the Priestly Codices were being edited (6th and 5th century B.C.) proves that they were widespread even after the Exile (Lev. 21:5; Lev. 19:27-28; Deut. 14:1).

These magic insignia and tattooings seem to have been applied by the prophets and seers as special marks of their standing (I Kings 20:38-41). One passage in Deutero-Isaiah (about the end of the 6th century) seems to indicate magic signs on the hand of the chosen ones (Isa. 44:5). The prophet Zechariah (519-517) of the postexilic period speaks of the prophets who had wounds on their hands (Zech. 13:6).

The Psychology of the Religion in the Desert

In the previous section we have briefly sketched the religious outlook of the tribes during their desert life. Stress was laid upon the fact that there were diverse stages in the development, a diversity intensified by the various religions of the tribes which only gradually merged into the Jewish religion. Some stages in the religious development, such as totemism, are traceable only in their rudiments: others, like demonism, are clearly observable toward the end of the desert period. Higher concepts, such as that of the Volcano God of Sinai, are also permeated with demonic qualities.

According to Meyer (1906), Yahweh was the Volcano-God of the tribes residing at Kadesh. Here, in this oasis of the desert, is the background of the organized worship of God among the Israelites. The Levites, who were a tribe or a class of priests, gradually transplanted this cult into Canaan and created a significant position for themselves. Meyer ascribes great significance to the fact that this Volcano God in spite of his distant residence became so prominent, and attributes this development to the special influence of the Southern tribes. Robertson Smith considered the God's far-away residence as instrumental in the development of a concept of a God imperceptible to the senses.

It seems, however, that this Volcano God had no dynamic influence on the psychological development of this religion. Robertson Smith has stressed the demonic attributes of Yahweh. He lived on Sinai or Horeb, but not only there. He was in the Ark of the Covenant, in the midst of his people, and later in Canaan in the midst of his land.

There are two outstanding features of the desert period which must be regarded as characteristic of it—the unsuccessful revolts and the absence of any female deity.

The Failure of the Revolts

Revolts are mentioned in great number and actually had taken place at every opportunity whenever things had gone wrong. Risings against Yahweh and Moses are mentioned so frequently and recorded with such detail and follow such a uniform pattern that we must conclude that the events are historical.

The motives no doubt were not as naïve as they were represented. We may safely assume that they were caused by political and religious conflicts.

These revolts are directed against Yahweh and against his representative and prophet, Moses. It is contended here that—psychologically considered —Yahweh and Moses are one. From the people's point of view Moses' thoughts, feelings, and actions are those of God. He took over the role of the father in his people's oedipus conflict. Love and hate are directed toward both. Whether the Moses figure represents one person or is the merger of several leaders is psychologically of little importance.

Yahweh tells Moses all his plans and decisions, the latter is the only person who is not destroyed by Yahweh's demonic power while contacting the God. Moses can and may associate physically with Yahweh. "And Moses went into the midst of the cloud [of Yahweh] and gat him up into the mount: and Moses was in the mount forty days and forty nights" (Exod. 24:18).

In the story of the Golden Calf Aaron speaks to Moses as if he were Yahweh. Then Moses rages like the demon Yahweh, the punishment is meted out by Moses, though Yahweh has forgiven his people (Exod. 32).

The Ten Commandments were written down by Yahweh in the first meeting between Yahweh and Moses, in the second place by Moses himself. On return from the second meeting with Yahweh the divine magic power that had been imparted to Moses was so terrifying that the people fled before him, and he had to cover his face so that the people should not be destroyed (Exod. 34).

Another example of the Yahweh-Moses unity: "And the Lord said unto Moses, See, I have made thee a god to Pharaoh: and Aaron thy brother shall be thy prophet" (Exod. 7:1).

Centuries of editing and working over could not erase the demonic features of Yahweh's bloodthirstiness.

The case so far presented does not appear unique. Similar demonic features are to be found in any religion. The Demon God everywhere embodies the aggressive impulses of the people, originally directed against the father representative and then projected upon it.

What is peculiar to Israel is revealed in the desperate revolts and their failure. The groups or group leaders, represented by Yahweh, tried to force their demon upon all other tribes and thereby to revolutionize the existing social and religious order, an order which prevailed among the rest of the Bedouins right up to Mohammed's time. They were extremely tolerant; each tribe had its own God who did not worry himself at all about others. This brutal tendency of the Yahweh faction to enforce conformity was nothing but a monodemonism. It provoked the revolts, forced the people by a series of traumas to adopt and develop a particular oedipus situation, namely, that of the Yahweh group, which we are going to discuss in what follows.

The revolts and their failure, as narrated in the Bible, have to be considered the same way as we assess a clinical symptom. It is the manifest end result of a conflict series. Its function is the warding off of anxiety. Since it never operates in a perfect way, i.e., it never represses completely the anxiety, we will always find inconsistencies and contradiction in the structure of a symptom.

Clinical experience has taught us that these "weak" points provide an inroad to the underlying conflicts. It is at these weak points of the defense measures against anxiety that the repressed tries to break through and gives some hint of the past mental struggle for solution.

Similarly we always find contradiction and inconsistencies in religious tenets, rituals, and stories. We also find in every religious structure the ever-present operation of some form of anxiety, e.g., sense of guilt, fear of punishment, etc. Thus I shall approach the revolts and every following religious manifestation as a symptom. First I shall describe it, then point out the "weak" points in the structure, and then attempt to find the original psychological conflicts which had to be overcome because they aroused anxiety and guilt.

The revolts assume various forms in the later re-editing. They are directed against Yahweh—against the ritual and the taboo regulations; they demand back their own gods; and finally they attack Moses. The latter revolts are so realistically described that they seem to have suffered least at the hands of tendentious priestly editors, and may be claimed to have been factual.

The intolerance of the Yahweh tribes prevented any intercourse with the other Bedouin tribes, and branded it as adultery (Num. 25). Some tribes which were closely related to the Yahweh tribes revolted against the ritual and against certain taboo regulations concerning meat. Two sons of Aaron were killed, the other two escaped by the skin of their teeth (Lev. 10). Miriam, Moses' sister, was punished with plague (Num. 12).

Corah's large-scale movement was directed against the leader or leaders. Many of the nobility took part in it and many tribes must have been involved (Num. 16).

The statement, that as a punishment none of the nomads (except two tribes) might enter Canaan but must die in the desert, seems to camouflage the fact that in the perpetual intertribal fighting a high proportion of the men were killed. Sellin's view that Moses himself died in one of the uprisings —as quoted by Freud (1939)—is of relevance in this respect.

These stories received their final and tendentious form in the postexilic period, and they were intended to serve as traditional examples against the religious and ethnic communications of the chosen people with Samaritans, Edomites, etc. Nevertheless the themes reveal the historical kernel of truth. The most telling item is to be found in the book of Joshua:

The Lord said unto Joshua, Make thee sharp knives, and circumcise again the children of Israel the second time . . . and this is the cause why Joshua did circumcise. . . . Now all the people that came out were circumcised: but all the people that were born in the wilderness

by the way as they came forth out of Egypt, them they had not circumcised—For the children of Israel walked forty years in the wilderness, till all the people that were men of war were consumed, because
they obeyed not the voice of the Lord [Josh. 5:2-6].

This passage shows how intense was their objection to the claims of
Yahweh. An old custom which was introduced as long ago as the stone age
(still carried out with a stone knife in the bronze age) had been rejected.

Constant reference is made to the "fleshpots of Egypt," to the hardships
and probations of the desert, and to other gods, e.g., the Golden Calf. A
typical revolt is the occasion when all but two of the tribes "murmured"
against the raid into Canaan (Num. 13-14). It appears odd for Bedouins to
protest against a raid. Nevertheless the revolt is there, and it can be very
probably interpreted as psychic opposition against Yahweh-Moses.

It sounds strange that nomadic Bedouins should be so sensitive to the
hardships of their own native land. This incongruity becomes more evident
when it is recalled that these languishing weaklings are so ready for war,
murder, and plunder. (An example: the havoc on Sichem, Gen. 34.) The
obvious inconsistency is heightened by the fact that some of the revolts had
been stirred up by the refusal of these tribes to settle down in Canaan to give
up the nomadic life for an agricultural one.

The revolts suggest the general impression that the nomadic tribes succumbed after desperate and prolonged struggles. They also suffered near
extinction by the hand of the Yahweh tribes or as it is narrated in the Bible
by the hand of Yahweh and his representative, Moses. The usual form of
historical or religious tradition of a people reveals a similar course so that
the struggle of the people against the oppressor or oppressors is glorified, and
in addition a strong moralistic coloring is attributed to the struggle. The general folkloristic or mythological elaboration of struggles and rebellions in the
past of a people is traditionally formalized in such a way that the people
which is involved in this struggle first succumbs to an oppressor or conqueror
but then succeeds without fail and thrives in great glory.

This traditional elaboration of a people's past is a repetition of individual
development in the human race. The growing and at first helpless child gradually recognizes his increasing power and makes repeated attempts of liberation from parental authority and discipline. These attempts are doomed to
failure because of the slow development of the human being physically, intellectually, and emotionally. From this point of view the developing human
child is involved in a constant struggle with his parents for the first two
decades of his life in almost every known culture. Then, gradually, he is able
to turn the scales. He becomes the more powerful in this struggle and his

final victory is reached with the death of the parents. This course is reflected in some form in every people's mythology.

The mythology of Israel offers a strikingly different version. Here the people succumb to the father; Yahweh maintains his supremacy "forever." At the same time this struggle, the outcome of which is so strikingly peculiar, is considered by the priestly editors of the Bible as something crucial and decisive which determines the fate of Israel for eternity. The sojourn in the desert constitutes for the editors and for the great prophets the central point from which they interpret the meaning of their people's very existence. Yahweh and Israel bound their lives together in the desert forever. This is the dominant idea of the Old Testament. The nomadic ideal, that is what the prophets yearn for; they believe in a return to the nomadic way of life as a panacea for all evil.

This belief emphasizes the significance of the failure of the revolts, whether they actually occurred or were dominant elements of a built-up mythology. Their preservation and underscored importance point to their extreme psychological significance. Clinical experience shows that a failure of the growing child's revolt against his parents may be determined by several factors, which in individual cases combine in varying proportions. It almost never occurs that only one factor is present. In what follows I shall refer to those factors which, in my opinion, are significant for the case of Israel.

1. The father is extremely powerful and ruthlessly aggressive in reality. He constantly forces his son into submission, punishes and humiliates him at every opportunity. Moses, who must be considered as psychologically identical with Yahweh, as discussed earlier, was a particularly oppressive personality. Few other "heroes" could be mentioned who display such a variety and vehemence of emotions. His unlimited courage against both Yahweh and his people is evident in the story of the Golden Calf. He destroys Yahweh's Commandments and desires to annihilate his people (Exod. 32). He wipes out his closest relatives (Lev. 10); whole generations are killed ruthlessly (Num. 16); his sudden anger frequently rouses Yahweh's wrath (Num. 20:11-12).

I assume that this extremely aggressive figure, whether he represents one person or several historical personalities, or a ruling class, was the one cause of the failure of the revolts. Historical events, traumata suffered at the hands of aggressive leaders or enemies might have been partly responsible for the psychological establishment of this invincible father.

2. If a child is permanently frustrated in the expression of his aggression, and constantly experiences ruthless oppression, he may take a particular path of defense measures, to allay his anxieties and to control his hate and aggres-

sion. In the course of his superego development he not only introjects the existing threatening qualities of his father but projects onto him his own aggression, which makes the father even more dangerous. Then the ensuing introjection of these additional cruel aspects of the father enhances the severity of his superego. Thus an extremely oppressive and crushing sense of guilt may develop. Though this briefly outlined development occurs to some extent in every child's development, in some cases of extreme severity it may lead to a permanently submissive and passive attitude of the child. We can often observe such a moral-masochistic course in cases where an originally extremely aggressive child adopts this solution in order to overcome his aggression which leads him into crippling clashes with the parents. He takes this course to allay his fear of retaliation, of fantasied castration. It goes without saying that these developments of the oedipal conflict unfold themselves unconsciously.

Applying such an interpretation to the sadistic features of Yahweh and to the acceptance and glorification of the failure of the people to succeed against Yahweh-Moses, we assume that these tribes originally had very strong aggressive drives, drives which were directed against the God-leader, but could not find an outlet. These impulses were projected onto Yahweh and added to the concept of a terrifying and ruthlessly powerful leader.

3. A further step in such a father-son relationship may develop as follows: However threatening the father is, tender feelings enter into the relationship, because of the bisexual constitution of man, and also because almost every father offers, irrespective of his other traits, protection and support. Furthermore, one aspect of a tyrannical father may be extreme possessiveness, a kind of jealous despotism, which binds the boy with exclusive ties to the father. Any protection or love the father gives is given under the condition of absolute and exclusive loyalty to him. This ambivalent attitude of a father, which may be conditioned by strong latent homosexuality of both father and son, brings the child to a point at which in order to survive and to overcome an extreme fear of castration, he is forced to give up all other objects, first of all the mother, and to remain bound only to the father with both feelings, love and hate. Every rebellion against this ambivalent relationship runs two risks: on the one hand, provoking the father's annihilating, castrating anger; on the other hand, losing his love, which has been the child's only existing tie and support.

The Bible shows and the great prophets taught that Yahweh desired not only unconditional, undivided power, but also love which he demanded exclusively for himself. Rivals were branded as "lovers." The libidinous and aggressive drives were directed into one and the same channel and greatly contributed to the development of the sense of guilt. Guilt was felt for hating a father, the relationship with whom was so full of love. It is evident that the pressure of the sense of guilt assisted essentially in the perpetuation of the father's dictatorship and in the breaking down of resistance. The people bowed beneath the burden of guilt they felt for hating a loving father.

The ambivalence of love and hate maintained a high level of tension between the people and Yahweh-Moses. It led to discharges which could not produce any real relief. The success of any of the revolts would have been made intolerable by the increased pressure of guilt that would have occurred subsequently. Victory was the father's, who conquered his son by his son's ambivalence. By the use of harshness and love he spurred the son to fresh aggressions and so the play of ambivalence began all over again.

4. These sadomasochistic vicissitudes of the son-father relationship, which are in my opinion assumedly responsible for the peculiar development of the relationship to God, indicate that apart from traumatic experiences, latent homosexuality may have played an important role in these developments. A further support for this assumption is offered by the explicit statement of the prophets that Yahweh and Israel are bound forever as bride and bridegroom. Whenever they refer to the desert period as the time of happiness between god and people they stress that this relationship is the basis and essence of the Yahweh worship. They state that Israel's life and future depend on the strict maintenance of this relationship of the devoted bride to her loving bridegroom. They try to prove that disasters of the past were caused by the abandonment of this bridal attitude, and that "unfaithfulness" is bound to cause the extinction of the nation.

Again our clinical experience shows us that such a development may be the outcome of a father-son relationship, in addition to the previously discussed factors, if the son feels that the only way to escape the father's wrath and destroying power is the complete abandonment of the male role. Then a feminine identification enables the son to turn from a rival into a desired love partner, who is wooed and accepted by the father. This also allays the sense of guilt which is felt for challenging the father's power. This identification with the mother, so apparent in Israel's role as Yahweh's bride, leads to the discussion of a conflict which may be even more important than the previous ones for the peculiar relationship to God. This identification with the mother as a means to avoid the father's wrath is a plausible measure to avoid castration and to allay the sense of guilt in the developing conflict with the father. Still, if it plays such a central role as in the Bible, and if it leads finally to the complete elimination of the Goddess from the religion, then we must agree with the prophets that it has an unusual significance. Then we must assume that the most archaic human relationship, that of the son (child) to his mother, must have had particularly significant features. Then the vicissitudes of this son-mother conflict were of basic and causative importance in the development of the son-father relationship, and must have primarily contributed to the elimination of the mother from the religion, and helped to establish secondarily the peculiarities of the son-father relationship.

The Ruthless Mother

The peculiarly close bond with Yahweh was greatly intensified by the repression of the mother, a process which led eventually to the complete elimination of the female deity.

What psychical events can be elucidated behind the fact of the missing mother? There is one passage which appears to be "meaningless," and set there out of all context, but it is just its very meaninglessness which attracts the attention of the psychoanalyst. The episode is that of the circumcision performed by Zipporah, Moses' wife, on her son.

> And it came to pass by the way in the inn, that the Lord met him [Moses], and sought to kill him.—Then Zipporah took a sharp stone, and cut off the foreskin of her son, and cast it at his feet, and said, Surely a bloody husband art thou to me.—So he let him go; then she said, A bloody husband thou art, because of the circumcision [Exod. 4:24-26].

In dreams and symptoms it is such odd patches which betray the existence of important conflicts whose impact prevents them from being completely warded off. The "meaninglessness" arises from the unsuccessful compromise of the drives with the defense measures. Encouraged by this commonplace experience in psychoanalysis one is emboldened to consider the episode concerning Zipporah as important from the psychological point of view. The episode is arbitrarily chosen, but its apt application to the goddess relation of this religion justifies its use in illustration.

The first circumcision is presented in the Yahwistic (which is the oldest) version as having been performed by a mother. The castration has two aims, first to appease the attacking Yahweh-father; secondly to preserve the Moses-father. The father, Yahweh, is supported in his aggression by the mother or, according to the other interpretation, the mother redeems the father by the castration of the son. Biblical scholars generally take the phrase "feet touched by the foreskin" to mean the genitals. It is not clear, however, whether the phrase means that Yahweh's or Moses' genitals were touched with the foreskin, i.e., with the youth's castrated organs. It is also doubtful whether the "bloody husband" is Yahweh or Moses.

This is of no importance from the point of view of the son. The important point is that the mother castrates him; it is *she* who carries out the aggression for the father's sake; and after the act is accomplished the union of father and mother is emphasized: "bloody husband thou art." Their unification follows the castration and becomes possible only by the removal of the son.

As a matter of fact, this is a fantasy found in addition to numerous other oedipal fantasies in the history of mankind and of the individual. However, real importance must be assigned to the fact that the most ancient recorded presentation of circumcision is the expression of this particular fantasy. A spotlight is thrown on the unconscious fantasy life of these Bedouins who pressed up from the south. The destroying, castrating, malignant mother was apparently predominant over all other mother fantasies, and the released castration anxiety could be overcome only by the complete repression of the mother.

It never reached the stage of being the center of a fluctuating ambivalence in the manifest religion of the desert, as far as it was recorded. Sadistic mother fantasies were so overpowering that no other defense than total repression was effective.

There is no historical source indicating the occurrence of a series of traumas which might point to this development of the oedipus conflict.

The difference between the struggle of Jacob (Gen. 32:27-30) and that of Moses (Exod. 4:24-26) is striking. In the former there is a normal oedipus fantasy—the son struggles with the father who tried to castrate him. The latter is finally foiled and therefore must pass his strength on to his son. In the case of Moses the mother cooperates with the father and castrates the son, and no blessing of the son follows. The first fantasy was worked out within the framework of the legendary history of those tribes who came from Mesopotamia and formed the Northern State. They never were real Yahweh worshipers but venerated many deities. Their main god was the Golden Calf. They followed the ordinary solution of the oedipus conflict of this stage of cultural development.

The second (Moses) fantasy, however, represents the psychic structure and dynamics of the tribes which formed the Southern State where the Jewish religion gradually developed.

Two main mechanisms are traceable which point to the subsequent vicissitudes of the fantasies about the mother imago: identification and projection. The former is a process which we can observe in our male homosexual patients. In order to escape the castrative threat of the mother, identifications are set in motion, and the son identifies himself with his mother. This detaches him from the mother as a heterosexual partner, on the one hand; on the other hand, it enriches him with highly esteemed female qualities. The bride role of Zipporah (Moses' wife) was taken over by her son—the people —in the course of its development. This annulled the threat of castration and put the people into the role of a partner with the father-God Yahweh.

This role of the bride plays a prominent part in the prophetic writings and is expressed in an all too realistic symbolism of a passionate love affair. For example, "Therefore, behold, I [Yahweh] will allure her [Israel], and bring her into the wilderness . . . and she shall sing there, as in the days of her youth, and as in the day when she came up out of the land of Egypt.—And it shall be at that day, says the Lord, that thou shalt call me Ishi [my husband]" (Hos. 2:14-16).

This feminine identification largely contributed to the failure of the revolts. To succumb to the mighty partner, Yahweh, meant not only failure but also the establishment of an unconscious homosexual relationship with a much desired partner. Yahweh no longer considered Israel as a dangerous rival, as in the episode concerning Zipporah, but as the wooed bride. As already mentioned, prophets later expressed this thought explicitly when they warned Israel that the only way to happiness and life was to take the role of the bride who is loved and protected by her bridegroom, Yahweh.

The results of projection are clearly discernible in Yahweh who often displays tenderly loving characteristics which strikingly contrast with his demonic features. After identification with the mother, her tender qualities were projected onto Yahweh, and thus the libidinal ties with him were increased.

On the other hand, the projection of the previously introjected ruthless mother onto Yahweh added to his demonic features and accentuated his threatening characteristics.

These considerations imply that the whole ambivalence which originally related to the mother imago, was shifted also to Yahweh. It goes without saying that the inevitable step that followed in these dynamics was a tremendous increase of the sense of guilt again concentrated on Yahweh though originally related to the mother, who was loved and hated at the same time.

This introjection-projection series caused "return of the repressed" in the guise of Yahweh. Love for Yahweh meant love for the mother who was (in the way described) represented in Yahweh. Events in Canaan in the course of later psychological developments proved that the above-described repression was far from successful. Astarte, the mother imago, returned, and it required further defense measures and manly sublimations until the mother could be finally relegated into oblivion.

Although no further data are obtainable from the Bible, it is supposed here that—apart from the motives already discussed in reference to the father —the revolts also represent the external symptoms of resistance against the total repression of the mother ("the fleshpots of Egypt"). They expressed the longing and fight to recover the benign, fertile mother, worshiped all over the Ancient Orient as the source of all blessing, joy, and love. The revolts could express the yearning of every child for its loving mother in the bitter struggle of the oedipus conflict, the yearning for which there was no place in the Yahweh cult.

Thus two fantasy series prevailed and proved decisive: (1) the brutally aggressive and invincible father who eternally subdues his son; (2) the dangerous mother who displays mainly castrating tendencies.

These dynamics saved the son from annihilation at the hands of the mother. They turned the father into a lover instead of a dangerous rival. Yahweh, who was the mother's partner in love and her accomplice in the son's annihilation in the episode concerning Zipporah, became the previously threatened son's bridegroom.

Being Chosen

The historical development of the God-father most likely occurred in two stages: the first within the "Yahweh tribes" where it probably developed from internal causes; the second stage, the external pressure on the other tribes, when the Yahweh tribes tried to force the other tribes into a coherent religious and social pattern.

Aggression and sadomasochistic homosexuality determined the development of a passive homosexual solution. Yahweh is the "bridegroom" and Israel the "bride" as a final elaboration of the ambivalence of the negative oedipus conflict. The projection of the people's aggression was formulated by Amos already in the eighth century as the relation of an animal of prey and its victim: "Can two walk together except they be agreed? Will a lion roar in the forest, when he hath no prey?" (Amos 3:3-4). Thus already at this stage of monotheistic development the God-people relation was formulated in terms of hopeless annihilation.

This unusual development resulted partly because on deeper levels the mother representation had to be repressed. Of the various mother fantasies one became dominant, namely, that of the castrating, son-hating mother. To overcome the anxiety caused by this situation, complete repression ensued. The mother disappeared, relevant traits were projected onto the father and contributed partly to his demonic bloodthirstiness, partly to his lovable and loving characteristics.

Both processes encountered desperate opposition—as expressed in the desert revolts, which were doomed to failure because of the internal and external phenomena with which we have dealt.

The way in which this people tried to cope with Yahweh, in the initial stages of the struggle, may be symbolized in the key word "chosen." The castration anxiety was warded off by this measure and the ever-revolting, ever-suppressed and humiliated son changed himself into the favorite son, the "chosen" child of the dangerous father. Circumcision and ensuing blessing are the attenuation of Yahweh's original murderous attempt. The Zipporah scene is, in a way, the unsuccessful condensation of the process from the bloodthirsty demon-god and goddess to circumcision as a symbol of blessing.

Here it may be objected that the concept of the "chosen" people developed much later, coming to maturity only with the prophets, and therefore it can hardly be assumed that this concept was current to the extent described among the Bedouins in the desert. There are two answers to this objection. In the first place, the earliest Yahwistic accounts refer quite explicitly to this idea which reached its completed form about the year 900 B.C.; it must therefore have had a long spiritual evolution. Secondly the idea of being chosen is closely connected with the "nomadic ideal" of the prophets. There was the contention that the bond between Yahweh and Israel began in the desert. That this was not a mere retrospective idealization of the past is substantially borne out by references to the clan of the Rechabites (II Kings 10:15; Jer. 35). They seem to have followed a Bedouin life even in the sixth century and were considered the most ardent adherents of Yahweh.

The ritualistically established symbols of "being chosen" are the circumcision and the ensuing blessing. The episode concerning Zipporah indicates that the earliest (Yahwistic) recorded meaning of circumcision was the sacrifice of the son by the mother for the sake of the father. The bond of love between Yahweh-Moses and Zipporah is established with the son's blood. The castration anxiety thus aroused compelled the son-people to take the next step in defense. The relevant and later-edited (Elohistic) circumcision stories of Abraham (Gen. 17:9-10 and Gen. 22:1-19), Jacob (Gen. 32:27-30), Joshua (5:2-6) show that the very act of circumcision was converted into the father's blessing. These solutions of the usual oedipus conflict secure the son's potency—thus he can continue his fight against the father.

After the elimination of the mother, the evil, castrating father changes, by blessing, into the good father promoting virility. The magic symbol of the son's annihilation, the circumcision, turns into a symbol of manhood and protection. Nevertheless this reacquired manliness arouses feelings of guilt in the son. Therefore Yahweh's terrible demands prevail: denial of manhood (Israel is his bride) absolute devotion of the subdued son, and abandonment of the mother.

This conflict between the people and their superego, Yahweh, is well illustrated by later developments of the relationship to God. In the course of the centuries which followed the settlement in Canaan the solution of the oedipus conflict in the desert broke down transitorily. The mother, Astarte, returned from repression and Yahweh became a heterosexual Baal. Thus the blessing of being chosen worked in the heterosexual direction.

This set into motion such a sense of guilt and such defensive measures as we find them in the usual course of religious developments. These defensive measures took the form of an elaborate ritual, the sanctuary, the priesthood and the Levites. I intend to discuss these institutions in the analysis of the second stage.

The Canaan Period (Fifteenth Century to 586)

Historical Survey

The conquest of Canaan was a very slow process, and was never completed. For about a thousand years (16th to 6th centuries) Syria was a political jumping-off board to the West and to the East, a military operational base for the two great powers, Assyria-Babylon and Egypt. For a short period the New Hittite Empire also occupied the political stage of the Near East (1500-1200). From the fifteenth century there followed a period of about two hundred years of political and military weakness for both the great powers. The Amarna letters (first half of the 14th century) show that an infiltration by pilfering groups of Bedouins began at about that time. The cities were more or less in the hands of native vassal princes under Egyptian suzerainty, but Egypt's political influence on Asia Minor was lost under the reign of Ikhnaton IV. These events were followed by the disintegration of the Hittite Empire on the northern border and with the inertia of Assyria in the last centuries of the second millennium. The remaining minor states, however, did not have the power to defeat the infiltrating Bedouins.

These tribes formed loose entities and undertook their incursions for booty or conquest, sometimes alone and sometimes with alliances specially

formed for the purpose. True Nomads, they changed their place of abode
frequently and only gradually settled down in the cities they conquered and
plundered. It was long before they finally stayed in Syria instead of returning
to the desert. Separate tribes settled in partly separated regions. Some tribes
disappeared; whether they were annihilated or disappeared through assimi-
lation cannot be determined. The small numbers of these tribes, their lack of
political organization, and their slow progress in adapting themselves to the
more civilized life of city dwelling and to agriculture caused that Syria's
higher culture exercised decisive influence on the invading conquerors. It
was then, in Canaan, under more settled living conditions that the cultural
centers of Mesopotamia and Egypt exercised any real influence on the infiltrating tribes.

The books Joshua and Judges describe this stage. Tendentious re-editing
has, of course, tried to prove a united political and religious development.
Fortunately, however, the real state of affairs has not been completely ob-
scured. The separate tribes led a seminomadic existence throughout the
changing political situation. Energetic leaders, the so-called Judges, from
time to time took power into their hands and carried out successful minor
wars, the gains from which were soon dissipated and forced various Jewish
tribes into their former dependent position. The most dangerous opponents
were the Philistines of the coast whom they were never able to subdue, and
who barred the tribes and later the weak Jewish states from the coast. Gradually, however, there came about a unification, the effect of which was
mainly in the religious sphere.

Attempts were made to build up city kingdoms, as in the case of Abimelek
(Judg. 9), always within a single tribe. The attempted formation of a kingship over several tribes is embodied in the story of Saul. This kingdom was
only consolidated within one tribe, Benjamin; the other tribes were loosely
coordinated with it and fell away from the organization at the first opportunity. The kingdom lacked authority and power. David was the first, and the
last, to achieve a unified and independent kingdom. His figure, though over-
loaded with mythological features, is one of the most exciting in the Bible.
He, the leader of a robber band, by means of cunning, violence, and assistance from women, sets himself up as a brutal, selfish leader, slaughtering
friend and foe alike. Despotically he establishes his autocratic rule, but finally,
enfeebled by battle and his advanced years, retires to the relaxation of an
extensive harem. Whether he is the embodiment of one or more historical
figures is debatable.

A period of decadence immediately follows David's rule. The glamorous,
inflated accounts of Solomon cannot conceal the facts of military impotence,

political dependence on Tyre and Egypt. Jorobeam leads a movement of separation in Solomon's lifetime and unites after the king's death the tribes settled in the North. This is the kingdom of Israel. The tribes of Judah and Benjamin form the puny southern kingdom of Judah, powerless and doomed to vassalage.

The internal political history of Israel is a series of bloody palace revolutions continually leading to extermination of a dynasty. Its external situation and its final tragic fate were determined by the reawakening of the Assyrian Empire, reappearing in Syria in the tenth century B.C. In 200 years of continuous fighting the states of Syria were either conquered, destroyed, or reduced to vassalage. The history is full of these battles. Israel's part in them is constantly changing: now it enters into an alliance with the other minor states and attacks Damascus, hard pressed by Assyria; then it unites, frequently under pressure, with Damascus against Assyria. Sometimes the foreign policy is dictated by prudent expediency, at other times by narrow-minded chauvinism. The little Jewish states often attack each other. Judah is for long Israel's vassal. Finally Damascus is subdued, and neither the payment of tribute nor desperate revolts are of any avail against Assyria. In the year 722 the state, partially disrupted eleven years earlier, was destroyed, plundered, and the ruling classes were carried off. Ten tribes disappear from history forever.

The affairs of the small southern state of Judah were during its whole history mixed with the politics of Assyria just as much as those of the larger state of Israel. There was internal unrest and the palace conspiracies, but the same dynasty lasted to the end. Short periods of pseudo independence alternated with periods when it was vassal and tributary to Tyre, Israel, Egypt or Assyria. After the fall of the major states Judah became the strategic jumping board for Assyrian expeditions against Egypt and Tyre. In these large-scale expeditions Jewish soldiers took part as members of a tributary state. The collapse of Assyria brought about by Babylon raised new hopes of freedom, which were, however, disappointed by the new active Babylonian dynasty. Syria was conquered, Egypt beaten, and the Jewish kings imprisoned by Nebuchadnezzar. The last revolt ended in 586 with the conquest and despoiling of Jerusalem, when the Temple was destroyed, the state wiped out, and the ruling classes deported to Babylon.

The political history of this people did not produce outstanding political personalities. Weakness and insecurity as external factors contributed one further step to the development of monotheism. This may have been the third trauma which impelled them along their road of sublimation, the first two having been the dangerous mother and the failure of the desert revolts.

Religion in Canaan

The Yahweh religion of the desert underwent far-reaching changes in Canaan. To speak of the "God relation of Canaan," and then of the "prophetic God relation" is to make an arbitrary division, since the activities of the prophets had a marked influence on the official religion of their time and certainly on the belief of the masses. The Deuteronomic reform of King Josiah in 622 is inexplicable without the preceding activity of Amos, Hosea, and Isaiah. Nevertheless they represent successive stages of a psychological development.

Gods and Goddesses

The bloodthirsty demon Yahweh who in the desert sought to destroy the other demons and who made his excursions from his dwelling place on Sinai or Horeb was in Canaan relegated to the background by the varied pantheon of gods. In accepting city culture and adopting the agricultural way of life the Israelites also accepted the local native Gods, the Baals. The editors of the Bible have of course attempted to superimpose a uniform pattern of Yahweh worship and to treat Baal worship as disloyalty. Actually Yahweh was only one God among many.

The numerous names under which God is referred to in connection with different places of worship, whether on a primitive or more highly organized level, point to a variety of gods worshiped by tribes, regions, communities. The cult centers were partly those of the Canaanites, partly new ones founded by the immigrants. In the Genesis the Deity is referred to at different places by different names. *"El eljon"*—"Possessor of Heaven and Earth" (Gen. 14:22); *"El roj"*—"the God Who appears" (Gen. 16:13); *"El saddaj"*—"the God Who is my Rock" (Gen. 17:11); *"El olam"*—"the God of the World" (Gen. 21:33); *"El brith"*—"the God of the Covenant" (Gen. 33:20).

Cult centers were to be found in Hebron, Bethel, Beersheba, Shilo, and many other places to which mythological stories were attached. There are many examples in the Book of Judges. Horeb and Sinai were already important in the desert. In Canaan the Gods lived, worked, and enjoyed happiness everywhere; in the mountains, in groves, in rivers and in all deserted places where nature appeared in all her fertility and splendor.

In the Book of Kings (II Kings 23) there is a summary of the actual religious practices. When the scroll that is now known as Deuteronomy was allegedly found in the Temple, it was read out to King Josiah who tore his clothes repentantly and ordered the introduction of this code. There is, fortunately, preserved a complete list of all rites that were abolished by the king in order to reintroduce the "true" Yahweh cult.

Baal is mentioned first; he was the most important god of the Semites in Canaan. Baal was the owner of the soil which was taken on loan and rented from him (Lev. 25:23). The king himself was only lessee of the land. When new land was conquered, its Baal was brought into the conqueror's pantheon. The fertility of the soil resulted from Baal's blessing and was the expression of his being. The priests and prophets of Baal took an important part in public life. The Baals of the Phoenician coastal towns were particularly revered. The Baal-Zebub of Ekron was consulted by the seriously injured King Ahaz of Judah, and the prophet Elijah reproaches Ahaz only for his disloy-alty to Yahweh; i.e., Elijah acknowledges the divinity of the foreign Baal (II Kings 1:1-3).

The fertility of Baal is symbolized by the construction of Ashera-poles, by holy trees (II Chron. 3:15-17).

The "hosts of heaven" who mediated between gods and men populated the world of the Bible. They are the offspring of Assyrian-Babylonian cultural influences (Gen. 6:4). They appear in the stories of Abraham (Gen. 18:12), and also in Jacob's dream (Gen. 28:12). Angels as divine messengers are described throughout the Bible. They are often called "the face of Yahweh" or "the name of Yahweh." These were either distinguished from Yahweh or identical with him. Another expression is "the spirit of Yahweh." The cherubim and seraphim are executives of the Holy One, and display totemistic features in their bird and serpent figures.

The sanctuaries also had in their service holy persons of a lower order, consecrated to the Deity. Children could be consecrated to God by their parents, and be later redeemed (Lev. 27); Samuel was such a child (I Sam. 1). Among these consecrated were also women (Exod. 38:8; I Sam. 2:22).

A group, working in the Temple, were the sacred prostitutes of both sexes. They paid their earnings or part of them into the temple treasury. The men were called "dogs." The women exercised their holy-evil vocation on the streets, as Tamar did (Gen. 38) or lived in the Temple precinct (Deut. 23:18). Sacred prostitution transmitted, through its heterosexual or homosexual relation, divine-magic power to the clients.

Besides Baal one of the highest Gods of the land was Moloch (Molek, Malik). The demands of Moloch, referred to in the Bible as "abominations," differ in no way from those of Yahweh, to whom every first-born must be sacrificed. The "going through the fire" was perhaps a mild form of sacrifice by fire, a form of sacred union and reconciliation with God (Lev. 18:21). King Ahaz of Judah made his son pass through fire (II Kings 16:3).

Sons were sacrificed to the god of the land and at the laying of a foundation of a house or of a city (I Kings 16:34).

The magic effect of human sacrifice is evidenced in the story of King Mesha of Moab who as a last hope in a desperate situation sacrificed his first-born son. The king thereby forced the besieging Israelites to withdraw (II Kings 3:27).

Goddesses are also mentioned. A passage in Jeremiah (44:17-19), however, shows that their worship was deeply ingrained and widespread. The text proves that at certain times, in extreme distress, the Great Goddess took first place in the divine hierarchy. The people sought Her help when they were far away from their native land as the native Baal's power did not reach beyond their country's boundaries.

There was some kind of ancestor or hero worship. The spirits of the dead could be recalled in their physical shape; thus on Saul's insistence, Samuel's spirit was summoned by the witch of Endor (I Sam. 28).

The story of the daughter of Jephtah of Gilead is an example of the worship of a local Goddess (Judg. 11).

There were minor deities, idols, who were kept in the house, carried on journeys, and consulted on everyday matters. Rachel steals her father's *teraph* and hides it in her luggage (Gen. 31:34). David possessed an idol, called a *teraph* or an ephod, which was used at one time to mislead his persecutors (I Sam. 13:13), and at another time as a God to be consulted (I Sam. 23:9).

Ritual and Priesthood

In Canaan the tribes came into close relation with the surrounding beauty and variety of nature. They attempted to free themselves from the tyranny of the demon Yahweh. Nevertheless there were circles which tried to preserve in some form the Yahweh worship, the desert ideal as a religious belief and as a social structure. It is assumed therefore that they aimed at the same unity as has already been described in the desert period. This was the kinship of the Rechabites. In the ninth century Jonadab, son of Rechab, preached a way of life which might be considered as a continuation of the Yahweh worship (Jer. 35:5-10). He supported the national and religious movement which exterminated the royal house of Omri in Israel (II Kings 10:15). One must point out that this rebellion was only against the Baals, the other idols being still worshiped officially.

The same unifying tendency created a uniform ritual of the Yahweh religion in one place, the Temple in Jerusalem. Although Leviticus, the only extant Semitic ritual, did not receive its final form till after the Exile, it is nevertheless highly probable that the main rites were already in existence in this period. Deuteronomy is the collection of these unifying Yahweh rites, as they were carried out by the reform in 622.

The development of the ritual is closely connected with the alterations in the Yahweh figure. The demon turned into a Yahweh settled in one place, a god equipped with anthropomorphic Baal features.

The indiscriminately killing demon changed into the Holy God. But this holiness acquires its ethical significance in the late prophets and in Deuteronomy. "Holy" signifies at first simply the divine and the magic; in Leviticus it is never explained in terms of ethics. Everything that comes into relation with the Divine-Magic Power is holy. God's destructiveness is no longer limitless, it affects only those who do not respect his holiness and are therefore punished.

This Holy God made his people holy, and so the evil demon becomes a God of Blessing. His jealousy and His ruthless punishing reveal the old demon (Exod. 31:14; Deut. 4:24; Num. 18:3).

The dual meaning of blessing-disastrous is well expressed in the ritual prescribed for establishing a wife's disloyalty. "Holy water may cause her belly to swell . . . her thigh to rot" (Num. 5:12-28).

Another formulation of this dual meaning is the concept of clean-unclean. The taboo of uncleanliness applies to objects which were originally connected with the deity; it is forbidden and dangerous to touch them because of their previous relation with divine "holiness." To give an important example: the fat of the entrails and the blood of the sacrificed animals were Yahweh's favorite food, and thus strictly forbidden for human use. They were ritually unclean (Lev. 3:16-17), (Lev. 22:29-39; Exod. 29:34; Lev. 2:3).

Further attenuation of the demonic quality came about through the view that it was not exercised directly but only indirectly and led into destruction in this way.

"And the Lord hardened Pharaoh's heart" (Exod. 10:20).

Then there is the story of Saul's depression (I Sam. 16:19), and Rehaboam's obstinacy (I Kings 12:24). It is not that people are wicked or unreasonable. Yahweh changes them, thereby satisfying his own vindictiveness or jealousy. "The Lord your God proveth you, to know whether you love the Lord your God with all your heart and with all your soul" (Deut. 13:3).

The appeasement of Yahweh "before Whom no one is innocent" goes on day and night, "the fire shall ever be burning upon the altar; it shall never go out" (Lev. 6:13). Animal sacrifice and priesthood are the two institutions which are instrumental in propitiation. Yahweh's evil power is turned into blessing, he accepts the animal sacrifice instead of the first-born who represented the whole people. "It is the blood that maketh an atonement for the soul" (Lev. 17:11).

The dual meaning of clean-unclean is clearly expressed in the institution of priesthood. Originally the whole people belonged to Yahweh and each one had to pay a ransom for his life (Exod. 30:12). Accordingly the whole people were considered holy (Exod. 19:6). But the order of priests and Levites took over the role of holiness (Num. 18:1-23). The magic function of the Levites consisted in staving off the slaughter of the first-born; they took over the sins of life in general (Num. 9).

This fully developed magic arrangement for protection evolved gradually and gave rise to a well-organized ruling class of priests. Originally everyone, within the limits of the prevailing social standards, could become a priest, as, for example, Micah's son in the *teraph* story (Judg. 17:5). David's two sons acted as priests.

The bearers of the "iniquity" (Num. 18:1), the priests appeased Yahweh with offerings, and the rites reveal different stages in the development of the Yahweh imago. The demon's insatiable bloodthirst was replaced by the demand for the sacrificial animal's blood and fat, Yahweh's favorite food, which was forbidden to men. The sinner placed his hand on the animal's head, thus establishing a magic continuity through contact. The animal became the bearer of the sin. Then the sacrificed animal's flesh, which had become holy through the act of offering, was eaten by the priest who thereby shared in the holy divine power. Thus the priest represented both God and people; consumer of the sacrifice and bearer of the people's iniquity.

Psychology of the Second Stage

The two factors that determined the people's God relation in the desert period were (1) the unique father relationship, (2) the repression of the mother figure.

The people were able to free themselves from the unconscious masochistic and homosexual oedipus situation by the dynamics of blessing. Thereby castration was transformed into the opposite, i.e., into fertile masculinity of the son-people blessed by the father-God.

As is generally the case, the transition period was a continuous process, but the milieu of Canaan contributed in no small measure to the development of these events.

The Canaan deities were the representatives of a manifold and limitless fantasy activity. The originally gloomy Yahweh gradually began to change into a god who dispensed blessing. The figure of Baal fitted in well with the picture of Yahweh dispensing blessing. The Canaan Goddess, acting in concert, completed the oedipus situation. She is not the rival but the harmonious completion of the father. The Canaan God relationship was a son's fairly well-balanced relation to father and mother. The return of the repressed heterosexual drives and of the mother diverted an essential part of the libido from the father. The exclusive homosexual-masochistic bondage ended.

The newly gained, or rather regained, libido positions and object relations put the ambivalence on a broader and easier basis. With the softening of the father and the lessening of the ambivalence came the decrease of castration anxiety. The son, conquered and castrated by the father in the desert, had in the new situation fairly mastered his castration anxiety.

The "Iniquity"

The transformation of the oedipal fantasies had in its turn effected a change to the usual structure of the sense of guilt, i.e., the people-son felt guilty because of love for the mother and because though he had won manhood from the father he became his rival. The sources of the sense of guilt became broadened, but at the same time the son became better protected against them due to the support from the heterosexual drives and the possibility of relying on the mother. This situation was helped by a decrease in the pressure of the strong sadistic tendencies which had helped to build the mother components of the superego and which were in Canaan abandoned. They gave way to loving fantasies which were directed toward the mother. Thus the situation differed from that of the desert period where only the father-son relation was apparent. There the sense of guilt drew its sustenance from homosexual and sadomasochistic sources. In Canaan heterosexual jealousy fantasies were projected onto the father, and then by introjection elaborated in the superego. This way, they oppressed the people in a new form of sense of guilt.

The defense measures against this sense of guilt and against the castration anxiety proper of the new relation to God found their expression in the concept of "iniquity" around which the whole ritual of appeasement revolved.

> And the Lord said unto Aaron, thou and thy sons and thy father's house with thee shall bear the iniquity of the sanctuary: and thou and thy sons with thee shall bear the iniquity of your priesthood.—And thy brethren also of the tribe of Levi, the tribe of thy father, bring thou with thee, that they may be joined unto thee, and minister unto thee [Num. 18:1-2].
> And the Lord spake unto Aaron, thou shalt have no inheritance in their land, neither shalt thou have any part among them: I *am* they part and thine inheritance among the children of Israel [Num. 18:20].

Neither must the children of Israel henceforth come nigh the tabernacle of the congregation, lest they bear sin, and die.—But the Levites shall do the service of the tabernacle of the congregation and they shall bear thy iniquity: *it shall be* a statute forever throughout your generations, that among the children of Israel they have no inheritance [Num. 18:22-23].

This implies that

1. the sanctuary itself represents a sin;
2. to be a priest is a sin;
3. to be a Levite is a sin;
4. this sin is a privilege;
5. priests and Levites have no right of legacy.

This "iniquity" belongs to the very essence of deity; it is intrinsic to his immediate servants; it is a privilege, yet entails contractions of inherited rights.

The distinction between priests and Levites was instituted in the post-exilic period along with other social changes; psychologically they had the same function.

Let us consider the Levites first since we have the clearest evidence relating to them. They were substitutes for the first-born who belonged to Yahweh (Num. 3:12-13, and elsewhere). Originally the life of everyone belonged to Yahweh and had to be redeemed (Exod. 30:12). The demon punished every living being; later on only the male first-borns were his victims. Finally the Levites were regarded as the first-borns' symbols, and had to be redeemed in order to survive. They therefore symbolized, above all, manhood, and their existence preserved the manhood of the people. Thus to be a Levite was to bear the sin of potency.

The Levitate is the "symptom" for the new oedipal attitude. The existence of the iniquity of manhood, though branded as sin, was recognized by the institution. This recognition by Yahweh concealed within itself the acceptance of the mother. Divine consent was given to the sharing of love, and to the regaining of manhood. The Levitate symbolized the victory of the oedipal incest wish.

The punishment for the sin of the oedipal success, represented by the Levites, consists in their deprivation of legacy. They were symbolically deprived of descendants, of the essence of manhood. They could exercise their power, acquired from the father, but could not hand it on. They remained the father-God's property, eternal children. Their manhood was, indeed, recognized, but at the same time nullified.

What of the punishment of the people? The people by means of the

Levitate created a barrier between themselves and Yahweh. The Levites became intermediaries between the people and their God; they bore the dangerous resentment of their God, but kept the people separate from Him. They alone could share the magic holiness of God; the people were excluded from the union which would have given them the divine power. The religious, social, and political concomitants of such an exclusion are clear.

In psychological terms it would be true to say that the defense processes have undergone a definite division. The positive aspects of the ambivalence were expressed more in the institution of priests, the negative aspects in that of the Levitate. The priests had accordingly the advantages, and the Levites the disadvantages of this defense function.

The psychological function of the priests can be understood only after discussing the problem of the sanctuary. According to the text, the sanctuary represents a sin. Since the meaning of "iniquity" is understood, it follows that even in holy places iniquity is connected wtih fertile manhood. No wonder then that the sanctuary is defined as sinful. It is holy because it represents the father's potency, and wicked because it also symbolizes the son's oedipal desires; ultimately, however, the two are identical. What is strongly forbidden to the son is holy in the case of the father. The text which appears "meaningless" displays the son's hate. The father's manhood—forbidden to the son—is marked as sinful.

Thus the sanctuary is doubly hated and sinful: first on account of the envied father qualities, and in the second place on account of the forbidden and repressed son qualities. It is also doubly holy: first because it symbolizes the beloved and respected father qualities, and in the second place because of the son's most precious instinctual demands.

This ambivalence which is inherent in the sanctuary is also an intrinsic quality of priesthood. The priests symbolize the rebellious son as well as the oppressing father. As an institution they represented a defense measure against the pressure of sense of guilt. Through their existence and activities the people are deprived of their victory; the priests interfere with the magic contact between Yahweh and people. It is the priests who enjoy the advantages of the son's victory, they are invested with Yahweh's divine power, they represent the God-father. Thus the crime the people had committed, the incest, is atoned: the people have no share in the "iniquity," i.e., in the sanctuary. At the same time the very fact of this perpetual and formalized defense measure reminds the people of incestual desires. Furthermore, the priests are the representatives of the people as well; hence their share in the sanctuary perpetuates the son's denied victory and enhances their sense of guilt.

Simultaneously the priests personify all the loving aspects of the Yahweh-people relation, as they keep alive the mutual love of son and father through their role in this ever-changing double identification series. The existence of sanctuary and priesthood secure the father's care for his people and the son's devotion to Yahweh.

The Sacrifice

The ritual of sacrifice represents the same defense measure as that of the priests: to allay Yahweh's anger, to decrease the pressure of the sense of guilt. At the same time it is a continuous though displaced repetition of the incest crime.

Numerous passages in the Bible prove that human sacrifice played an essential part in the early stages of religious worship. The institution of "men devoted unto the Lord" refers with the greatest probability to this origin (Lev. 27:28). Another example is the sacrifice of the first-born. The next step in order of development is the Levitate: its members represent the first-born sons; the description of their initiation suggests that they might occasionally have been sacrificed. They were swung like sacrificial offerings (Num. 8:6-12). In the next stage of development animals are sacrificed instead of the Levites.

This line of development toward sublimation through displacement indicates at the same time a regression as well—a regression to the archaic ritual of the totem feast. In the earliest cultural stages traceable in the Bible, the gap separating man and animal does not seem to be as great as it is later on. Animals had a soul and were responsible for their actions; certain animals were credited with supernatural powers. Totem animals were holy and represented the father.

Thus the sacrificial animal represented the father on the one hand, and the son on the other hand. In the manifest meaning of the ritual they symbolize the people-son who is sacrificed to the father-God because of his sin. This sin was transferred to the animal in a magical way, through laying on of the sinner's hands. The latent meaning—the killing of Yahweh—came into force through the regressive representation of the father. The sacrifice makes the animal's flesh holy, i.e., divine. This flesh is eaten by the priests who represent the people. In this oral-magic way the priests share the divine power, and the people have once more wrested the father's power and made it their own. The God is doubly killed: first he is murdered by his son's hands, then orally consumed. This aspect of the ritual represents a solution in the form of a regression from the phallic to the oral stage.

The subsequent pressure of the sense of guilt is apparent on two levels:

(1) the people identify themselves with the sacrificial animal; (2) they are excluded from the magic consumption of the divine meal. Again, as one aspect of this defense measure, the people were robbed of the fruit of the committed sin.

The sense of guilt arising from the iniquity of the oral killing of the father gave the people-son no peace. Yahweh had to be continually appeased (Lev. 6:6; Exod. 29:38).

THE PROPHETIC MOVEMENT

Historical Survey

The development of the prophetic movement coincides chronologically with the Canaan God relationship, but in terms of ethical and psychological development it marks the third stage in this relationship.

The prophetate of the Bible developed partly under the cultural influence of the surrounding peoples with highly developed social and religious structures. It is certain that the cultures of Mesopotamia and Egypt exercised a definite though formal influence. These influences are distinguishable (1) in the verse form of the prophecies, and (2) in Moses' character.

1. In both countries it was customary to formulate the experiences of life and wisdom in rhythmical sentences. From Egypt came the vision of Neferrehu (about 2000) prophesying times of curse and blessing. The psalms and sayings of Solomon incorporated elements, in some places word for word, and in others just the sense of passages, from the hymn of Ikhnaton IV, and from the so-called wisdom of Amenemope.

2. Moses is king of the priests, sorcerer, magician, and prophet in one person. He controls the black magic of Egypt, he knows the will of god and directs fate.

These references clearly indicate that the prophetate is as old as the history of Israel. Furthermore, the text of the Bible and other sources amply prove that most primitive forms were coexisting with the climax of prophetic monotheism. Still I would like to distinguish three stages of prophetic development in the Canaan period:

1. the "nabi," who was a seer (called "roeh" in early texts; e.g., I. Sam. 9,9), and magician in the service of one of the Gods, among them also in Yahweh's service. He was the blind servant and instrument of his God; he was always seeking the limited local advantage for this God, without any ethical implication of general human value;

2. the great forerunners, who beside their magic activities display definite ethical concepts;

3. the prophets of the Scripture who develop within 200 years the highest form of ethical monotheism, though their activities are always expressed in terms of divine magic.

The Early Stages of the Prophetate in Canaan

The prophet is called *"nabi"* in the Bible. It is rooted in the verb *"hit-nabi,"* to rage, to fume, to be crazy. The word shows that ecstasy was considered the essential characteristic of a prophet.

The first extra-Biblical description of an ecstatic scene in Canaan is to be found in the Papyrus Golenitscheff where the mission of Wen-Amon from Thebes to Byblos is described (about 1100). A young man of the city-king's retinue is seized by God in the vicinity of the harbor, falls to the ground in convulsions, and screams the divine orders which lead to a courteous reception of the previously despised envoy. This scene resembles similar ones in the Books of Samuel and Kings.

Numerous passages in the Bible prove that *nabis* were considered as mad and possessed. When the prophet Elisha sends one of his pupils on a political errand to General Jehu, his officers asked the latter: "Wherefore came this mad fellow to thee?" (II Kings 9:11).

The *nabis* lived in groups or in organized communities around holy places, for instance, in Shiloh and Beth-El, or were pupils of outstanding prophets like Samuel, Elijah, and Elisha. In Jerusalem they had their particular overseer. These communities were united not only through a leader or through a god jointly worshiped, but also through family ties. The prophets reared their sons to be prophets. There were also prophetesses (II Kings 22:14) who sometimes married prophets (Isa. 8:3).

The *nabis* wore coarse, hairy cloaks; tattooing was widely practised among them (its significance has been discussed in the section on magic).

They frequently wandered about the countryside in groups, and danced and sang during their states of ecstasy, which reached their climax in the self-infliction of wounds. Here is a typical scene (Elijah challenged the Baal prophets):

> And they . . . called on the name of Baal from morning even until noon. . . . And they leaped upon the altar. . . . And they cried aloud, and cut themselves after their manner with knives and lancets, till the blood gushed out upon them [I Kings 18:26-29].

The text describes the gradually increasing ecstasy and the successive stages of this mental state.

In Saul's story, when David flees from his revenge, the contaminating quality of this ecstasy which leads to complete exhaustion is depicted real-istically:

> Then went he also to Ramah, . . . And he went thither to Naioth in Ramah: and the Spirit of God was upon him also, and he went on, and prophesied, until he came to Naioth in Ramah.—And he stripped off his clothes also, and prophesied before Samuel in like manner, and lay down naked all that day and all that night. Wherefore they say, is Saul also among the prophets [I Sam. 19:19-24].

The examples reveal the source of this "madness," a madness in which men became "prophets, diviners, dreamers, enchanters, sorcerers" (Jer. 27:9). The source was the god, as is shown in the quotations. (Further examples are in Num. 11:16-26; I Sam. 3:21; I Kings 18:46; Amos 7:1.)

It was not only Yahweh but also the Baalim who had their prophets. Despite later editing one can see that they were honored, feared, and con-sulted. The prophets of the various gods fought and tried to destroy one another. They took part in politics. Elijah once succeeded in massacring 450 Baal prophets on Mount Carmel (I Kings 18:21-40). The prophet Elisha supported General Jehu's *coup d'état;* the dynasty was wiped out, and after the murder of Queen Jezebel the prophets of the Baal of Tyre were in their turn murdered (II Kings 9-10).

Endless disputes went on among the Yahweh prophets as to who was a false and who a true prophet. The false, deceiving prophet was not actually a liar in our sense of the term. He appeared only as such because he was possessed by an evil spirit of Yahweh.

The prophets seized and possessed by the divine-magic power had taken to themselves the qualities of Yahweh, but they were only a means by which God's intentions were fulfilled. If a prophet failed to follow Yahweh's orders exactly to the letter, he paid for his disobedience with his life (I Kings 13).

The basic principle of the prophetate, the common link between the vulgar sorcerers and the great prophets of Scripture, was their oneness with Yahweh. The most striking manifestation of this union of God and man was ecstasy, from which, as has been shown, originated the word *nabi.* Ecstasy represented the double meaning of holy-evil, cursing-blessing. It offers an explanation of the respected *and* despised status of the *nabi.* The uncanny, demonic Yahweh spoke through ecstasy, uniting divine and human qualities in the *nabi.*

The Great Forerunners

Three figures stand out in the early stages: Samuel, Elijah, and Elisha. It is immaterial from a psychological point of view whether they were historical personages or figures built up by the merging of several personalities. In reviewing them individually the line of development is made more obvious.

Samuel represents the transition from Moses' priest-king figure to the esctatic magician-prophet. His birth follows the birth pattern of the "hero": a childless marriage, divine promise of a son, the mother becomes pregnant through God's intervention, the son is offered to the God-father, and finally chosen by Him to be the leader of his people. First his figure is dignified, showing the impersonal qualities of a priest-king. Suddenly, however, when the formation of a tribal kingship removes him from the leadership, the prophetic traits appear. His history personifies the political development from priest-king to profane king. Significantly, since he is a transitional figure, he is never pictured in a state of ecstasy, he "stood" among the raving *nabis* (I Sam. 19:20). Yahweh's power emanating from Samuel sends those near him into ecstasy, though he himself remains a cool and detached figure. He does not yet have to fight the gods of Canaan; thus he symbolizes the transition from the desert period of Yahweh's absolute ruling to the Canaan period with competition from the Baals.

The prophet Elijah exhibits several general mythical features (the inexhaustible cruse of oil, resuscitation from death, his journey to heaven), nevertheless he also has individual-human qualities. His figure is undoubtedly a composite one, the separate parts representing historical and cultural developments. In Elijah for the first time are recognizable the characteristics of the great prophets. Reference is made here to: (1) his emergence in full maturity; (2) the complete emotional and spiritual identification with Yahweh; (3) the demonic qualities of god are exemplified and enforced by him; (4) his defense of the humble against the mighty (I Kings 21); (5) he is a respected, but at the same time hated, feared, and despised outsider.

The demonic qualities are personified in the prophet when he carries out a mass slaughter of the Baal prophets (I Kings 18). His magic power consumes with fire those who speak insolently to him (II Kings 1:9-15). He curses the royal house (I Kings 21:21). He brings drought on the land (I Kings 17:1). His whole figure breathes a lust for revenge. Destruction and bloodshed lead him into ecstasy: after the massacre of the Baal prophets, rain, called forth by his magic, pours down; he raves frantically through the wild storm and overtakes the king's chariot. This is a picture of the demon god himself raging through the country with storm and thunderbolt (I Kings 18:45-46).

The third figure in the series of prophets of the early stage is Elijah's pupil, Elisha. His figure and activity mark a further stage of development (II Kings 2-11). He exhibits distinctive demonic features, e.g., killing and blinding; however, the evil is overwhelmed by the blessing qualities. Whereas Elijah is put into ecstasy by bloodshed, Elisha is put into it by song. Thus, the influence of the Canaanite environment comes into the foreground.

A novel and important feature in Elisha's character is his keen participation in politics. He is a cunning instigator of internal and external political revolutions. He goads and directs the greed of Syrian and Israelite generals, and influences them to murder their rulers. This is mentioned here as a precursor of the enigmatic political activity of the prophets of Scripture.

Elisha is, despite his demonic and magic features, more human than Elijah. He worries over the misery and sorrows of his fellow men, he helps them in their need. Nevertheless his Yahweh does not differ from the Baals of Canaan. He is earthbound, capricious, jealous, but is easily placated.

The Prophets of Scripture

The great *nabis* Elijah and Elisha were representatives of the ninth century. Amos, the first great prophet of Scripture, lived in the first half or at the latest in the middle of the eighth century. Elisha died during the reign of Joash while the only known scene from Amos' life occurs in the time of Jeroboam II, Joash's son and successor. The activity of the *nabis* and their ideals, although they continued right up to the debacle of the state, never developed beyond Elijah's level. By contrast, the ideas of the great prophets underwent uninterrupted development, and this is all the more astonishing since they never founded any school. Isaiah alone seems to have been surrounded by a group of young men.

The essence of the God-relation—union with Yahweh—is, however, common to both groups. Common also is the subjective feeling of this relation and the affective experience in the ecstatic states which is bound up with various hallucinations.

The new aspect of this God relation of the great prophets is that through a series of painfully acquired and unprecedented sublimations they formed an ethical monotheism out of the demonic Yahweh-Baal who existed in Elisha's vision.

Amos

He was "among the herdsmen of Tekoa" (Amos 1:1), a fact which is important from the psychological point of view. He was a man from the lowest and least cultivated social stratum, and neither Assyrian nor Egyptian cultures can be held responsible for his progressive ideas. His intellectual achievements must be considered as having originated from the spirit of the people.

His sermons were, with the exception of the last five verses, monstrous, shattering threats, Yahweh's demonic expressions. With Amos, however, Yahweh's activity attained a moral justification. With him, it was no longer a matter of the demon's capricious bloodthirst but the punishment of a just god who was hurt by the sins of man. Yahweh was hurt because men sinned against their fellow men (2:6-7; 3:10; 4:1; 5:7).

The most astonishing of the prophet's reproaches is that he attacks hypocritical ritual, he desires real conviction (5:21-25).

The demonic in the prophet rages when he portrays the expected punishment. Yahweh's destructive nature is described realistically and elaborately:

> I saw the Lord standing upon the altar: and he said, Smite the lintel of the door, that the posts may shake: and cut them in the head, all of them; and I will slay the last of them with the sword . . . [9:1].

The demands of Yahweh are expressed by the prophet with clarity:

Seek good, and not evil . . . hate the evil, and love the good [5:14-15].

His own justification for his activity was his oneness with Yahweh. His deeds and words are those of God Who has possessed him. This identification occurs in spontaneous ecstatic states in the form of visual and auditory hallucinations. Yahweh's intentions are revealed by symbolic hallucinations:[1]

> Thus he shewed me: and, behold, the Lord stood upon a wall made by a plumbline, with a plumbline in his hand.—And the Lord said unto me, Amos, what seest thou? And I said, A plumbline. Then said the Lord, behold, I will set a plumbline in the midst of my people Israel: I will not pass by them any more [7:7-8].

The essence of the Biblical God relation is formulated with clarity. Yahweh and His people belong to each other as slayer and victim. To be chosen means to be dedicated to death.

> Can two walk together, except they be agreed?—Will a lion roar in the forest, when he hath no prey? will a young lion cry out of his

[1] Symbolic hallucinations and symbolic deeds play an important role in prophetic activities. Yahweh's desire and judgment is often experienced in such forms of magic-archaic thinking, in which thoughts and emotions are represented by concrete symbols. Similar to the operation of the dream work, as discovered by Freud, "regard for representability" plays an important role in prophetic writings and actions, as many of the quotations will show. In addition, as in our dreams and in jokes, puns are widely used.

den, if he have taken nothing?—Can a bird fall in a snare upon the earth, where no gin is for him? shall one take up a snare from the earth, and have taken nothing at all? . . . The lion hath roared, who will not fear? the Lord God hath spoken, who can but prophesy? [3:1-8].

In spite of this demonic conception of a tribally confined God, Amos made the first significant step in the direction of a true ethical monotheism.

Are ye not as children of the Ethiopians unto me, O children of Israel? saith the Lord. Have not I brought up Israel out of the land of Egypt? and the Philistines from Caphtor, and the Syrians from Kir? [9:7].

All men are equal before Yahweh. To emphasize this truly novel concept, Amos mentions the two arch-foes of Israel. Thus the concept of God's Universality appears for the first time in the history of mankind.

Hosea

The prophet Hosea, a contemporary of Amos, was a person who has presented a problem to the religious-minded as well as to the scholar. The reasons become apparent upon reading his autobiography.

The word of the Lord came unto Hosea, the son of Beeri. . . . The beginning of the word of the Lord by Hosea. And the Lord said to Hosea, Go, take unto thee a wife of whoredoms and children of whoredoms; for the land hath committed whoredom, departing from the Lord.—So he went and took Gomer, the daughter of Diblaim; which conceived and bare him a son.—And the Lord said unto him, Call his name Jezreel; for yet a little while and I will avenge the blood of Jezreel upon the house of Jehu, and will cause to cease the kingdom of the house of Israel. . . . And she conceived again, and bare a daughter. And God said unto him, Call her name Lo-ruhamah [No more mercy]: for I will no more have mercy upon the house of Israel. . . . Now when she had weaned Lo-ruhamah, she conceived, and bare a son.—Then said God, Call his name Lo-ammi [Not my people]: for you are not my people, and I will not be your God [1].
Then said the Lord unto me, Go yet, love a woman, beloved of her friend, yet an adulteress, according to the love of the Lord toward the children of Israel, who look to other gods, and love flagons of wine.— So I bought her to me for fifteen pieces of silver, and for an homer of barley, and an half homer of barley.—And I said unto her, Thou shalt abide for me many days; thou shalt not play the harlot, and thou shalt not be for another man: so will I also be for thee.—For the children of Israel shall abide many days without a king . . . without

an image. . . . Afterwards shall the children of Israel return, and
seek the Lord their God . . . [3].

Modern students of the Bible agree that actual events and not allegorical
metaphors are involved. There have been endless discussions of whether one
or two wives existed, of what was the correct sequence of events, etc. From
the text attempts have been made to reconstruct the prophet's motives as
well as his emotional life.

Here two aspects are of interest: the definite identification with Yahweh,
and the sexual interpretation of the man-God relation. Hosea not merely
becomes one with Yahweh in moments of ecstasy, but his whole life becomes
divine, his activities represent and are actually divine conduct.

The symbolism of his magic-animistic thinking preserved the original
character of the experience, the affective impact is kept in its entirety; it is
no mere form of emotional expression but is life itself.

Hosea's life is the symbol of the divinely controlled universe as well as
a manifestation of the living God. Because of Yahweh's oneness with the
prophet there exists a common interlinked causality between the fate of the
prophet and Yahweh. In consequence of the magic union, the two cycles of
events involve one another as cause and effect. Yahweh caused the prophet
to love a prostitute; the magic names "No More Mercy" and "Not My
People," influence the fate of Israel. The fidelity of his unchaste wife brings
in its train the fidelity of the people to Yahweh.

In the second chapter this fusion is completed to such an extent that it is
not possible to distinguish whether the reference is made to the prophet's
family relations or to those of Yahweh and His people (2:2-13).

The other striking characteristic is the sexual conception of the relation
to Yahweh.

> And I will not have mercy upon her children; for they be children
> of whoredoms. . . . And I will visit upon her the days of Baalim,
> wherein she burned incense to them, . . . and she went after her
> lovers, and forgat me, saith the Lord [2:4-13].

Yahweh and Israel are like husband and wife, and when the people turn
from Yahweh to the Baals, this is considered as a physical-sexual infidelity.
The rivalry of the Gods of Canaan is experienced as sexual activities. In
discussing the first two religious periods we spoke of the castration complex
and its consequences. In Hosea we come upon the final denouement of these
singular dynamics. At this stage castration is accepted, and the only possible

fantasy is chosen, namely, that of the bride. The destiny of womanhood is accepted so as to appease Yahweh, the God-father, in order to escape at his hands the threatened annihilation, and to be loved by him.

The rebellious desert tribes have become a "wanton" woman and the murderous demon a jealous but ardently loving male, a fertile God-husband. Yahweh courts Israel, promising her gifts, just as a man woos a pliant woman.

> Therefore, behold, I will allure her, and bring her into the wilderness, . . . and she shall sing there, as in the days of her youth, and as in the day when she came up out of the land of Egypt.—And it shall be at that day, says the Lord, that thou shalt call me Ishi [my husband] [2:14-16].

This hymn of love emphasizes in the same chapter that the prophet's children are Yahweh's children, the children of Israel. The sublimation of sexuality into devotion unfolds itself in the course of the poem.

Hosea's history can be approached from a clinical viewpoint. The assessment of established facts on the one hand, reconstruction on the other hand can link his way of life and his intellectual activity to his childhood. In what follows an endeavor is made to show that sublimated ethical ideas have their origin in the conflicts of childhood.

Hosea has chosen for his wives a prostitute and an adulteress, a choice which he felt as a compulsion, "the word of Yahweh." Men who make similar choices suffer from a fixation in a definite phase of the oedipus conflict, in a phase which is governed by the so-called prostitution fantasy. The very mother who gives herself to the father and repulses the son is despised and at the same time desired. She would be more approachable to the son if only he possessed sufficient power and money. These fantasies may win the upper hand in the formation of the woman ideal as the object of sexual desire. The desired woman must belong to other men, but ready to sell herself. Those men who actually marry recognized prostitutes present the extreme of this type of object choice.

We assume that Hosea could not rid himself of this despised-desired type of woman ideal, and thus enjoyed and suffered all the fulfillment and disillusionment of such a situation.

Having set out to analyze certain features of his character, let us turn to his intellectual activity. It may be summarized as follows: The universal God created by Amos acquired through Hosea a greater intensification and profundity. The progress of human thought occurred in this instance not in the widening but in the deepening of the notion. Hosea created the concept of love in man-God relations: "For I desired mercy [*chesed*], and not sacrifice; and the knowledge of God more than burnt offerings" (6:6).

Love is expressed by him through the word "*chesed*." It corresponds to the Latin "*pietas*," comprising love, tenderness, kindliness, forethought, piety—thus "love" in its noblest, deepest, and most comprehensive sense. However, in one passage in Leviticus, "*chesed*" has the meaning of incest.

> And if a man shall take his sister, his father's daughter, or his mother's daughter, and see her nakedness, and she see his nakedness; it is a wicked thing [*chesed*]; and they shall be cut off in the sight of their people: he hath uncovered his sister's nakedness; he shall bear his iniquity [Lev. 20:17].

These two meanings of *chesed* furnish the proof for the assertion that a highly intellectual activity has special instinctual origins. The word "*chesed*" shows the phenomenon which begins with Hosea's unconscious incestuous fantasies of his oedipal conflict and ends with their ethical sublimation. He chose for the highest ethical love a word designating incest, because he could never rid himself of his own incestuous conflict. His unsolved mother-prostitution fantasies determined his adult sexuality, and influenced his sublimated intellectual activity. The dynamic force of the repressed conflict associated with the yet unanalyzable power of genius achieved a particular sublimation. The ungratified incestuous love for his mother has reached a sublimated gratification on the ethical level.

The *chesed* of Hosea has become one of the most important pillars of Western civilization.

Isaiah

The prophet Isaiah who prophesied in the second half of the eighth century is a picturesque personality. He took a keen interest in high politics (1-6), he was a magician of the same type as the *nabis*, and he has suffered for years from an abnormal mental state, from what may in all probability be considered as a psychotic episode of three years' duration.

> . . . spake the Lord by Isaiah, the son of Amoz, saying, Go and loose the sackcloth from off thy loins, and put off thy shoe from thy foot. And he did so, walking naked and barefoot.—And the Lord said, Like as my servant Isaiah hath walked naked and bare-foot three years for a sign and wonder upon Egypt and upon Ethiopia;— So shall the king of Assyria lead away the Egyptian prisoners, and the Ethiopian captives, young and old, naked and barefoot, even with their buttocks uncovered, to the shame of Egypt [20:2-4].

He displayed an aristocratic bearing, despised the common people, nevertheless fought against luxury and suppression of the poor. He prophe‑ sied the end of the state and at the same time he was confident of the fate of the few good people. In him were united the respect for the ritual and the strongest emphasis on quiet, sincere belief. Through him an anthropo‑ morphic conception of Yahweh accompanied by a totemistically colored hierarchy of angels was combined with a sublime presentation of the holy universality of God.

The identification, the magic union with Yahweh, occurred in his man‑ hood, in one of his ecstasies, by means of hallucinations.

> I saw also the Lord sitting upon a throne. . . . Above it stood the seraphims . . . then flew one of the seraphims unto me, having a live coal in his hand, which he had taken with the tongs from off the altar:—And he laid it upon my mouth. . . . Also I heard the voice of the Lord, saying, Whom shall I send, . . . Then said I, Here am I; send me [6:1-8].

From the moment of his call the prophet and Yahweh became one. The prophet's children have a magic-symbolic significance, Yahweh spoke and acted through them.

> Moreover the Lord said unto me, Take thee a great roll, and write in it with a man's pen concerning Maher-shalal-hash-baz [Plunder-Hurries-Robbery-Comes-Quickly].—And I took unto me faithful witnesses to record. . . . And I went unto the prophetess; and she conceived, and bare a son. Thus said the Lord to me, Call his name Maher-shalal-hash-baz.—For before the child shall have knowledge to cry, My father, and my mother the riches of Damascus and the spoil of Samaria shall be taken away before the king of Assyria [8:1-4].

In Isaiah as in Hosea the child is the vehicle not only of divine-evil but also of divine-good. His hope for a peaceful future was based on the magic effect of one of his sons, one named Shear-Jashub (Rest-Comes-Back). Its magic meaning: after Yahweh has judged and punished, only a few remain alive. This remnant then turns faithfully and happily to Yahweh and lives to see the blessed age and regenerates the nearly extinct people.

The same principle applies to his magic through words. He certainly uses the same threats as his predecessors, but words of blessing overwhelm the tones of curse. His concepts of blessing, eternal peace and divine fulfillment display a humanitarianism and pacifism of striking purity: "I will make a man more precious than fine gold; even a man than the golden wedge of Ophir" (13:12).

The "day of Yahweh" means, for Amos, Doomsday; for Hosea, reconciliation; for Isaiah, majestic bliss. With him, the concept of "holy" lost most of its evil connotation and represented, more than with any other prophet, blessing. This is expressed by the name of those children who bring along eternal peace and bliss (God-With-Us, Prince-Of-Peace). The text does not make it clear whether these are his or Yahweh's children (Prince-Of-Peace) or those of a royal princess (God-With-Us).

Isaiah's great spiritual achievement is the deepening of the concepts of God's universality and love. This love between God and man creates the atmosphere of unshakable, deep trust, which binds through feeling and not through words. Isaiah expresses this relationship with the word "belief." The above meaning of belief appears with him for the first time in history and then later became one of the basic tenets of Christianity. A few quotations may prove his influence on the thinking and religious outlook of Western civilization: "If ye will not believe, surely ye shall not be established" (7:9). "He that believeth shall not make haste" (28:16). "In quietness and in confidence shall be your strength" (30:15).

Jeremiah

Jeremiah's activity covers the forty years of his youth, maturity, and old age. It coincides with the historical period from about 622, the reforms of King Josiah, until after 586, the destruction of the Jewish state. The prophet's inner conflicts and sufferings were presented with shattering sincerity. The force of the compelling urge he felt for communicating his thoughts was equalled by the admirable power of communication he possessed.

Yahweh called him to be his prophet in 627.

> Then the word of the Lord came unto me, saying,—Before I formed thee in the belly I knew thee; and before thou camest forth out of the womb I sanctified thee, and I ordained thee a prophet unto the nations. . . . Then the Lord put forth his hand, and touched my mouth, And the Lord said unto me, Behold, I have put my words in thy mouth [1:4-9].

This call, as it usually does in the prophets (see Amos), came in the course of symbolic hallucinations (1:11-14). He obeyed the call immediately and prophesied in his native place. Some years later he became an ardent adherent of the Deuteronomic reform, and spent thirteen years in the fulfillment of this task (622-609). Then the foolhardy King Josiah refused permission to Pharaoh to pass through his land on his march against Babylon. The king was fatally wounded in the battle of Megiddo and Judah became the vassal of Egypt. Jehoiakim, the new king, withdrew the reforms and there was a return to the polytheism of Canaan (II Kings 23).

Jeremiah proclaimed Yahweh's message at the Temple gates, and threatened the people with destruction unless they returned to Yahweh. People and rival prophets clamored for his death but the elders saved him. The court might have realized the weakness of Egyptian influence in Syria. Nebuchadnezzar, the young Babylonian heir to the throne, drove Pharaoh out of Syria in 605. In his second symbolic hallucination after his initiation by Yahweh, Jeremiah recognized that "an evil out of the north" referred to Babylon. Yahweh's threat turned into reality. Thus the prophet's voice grew sharper, his retorts to authority more frenzied.

He provoked a humiliating punishment by a symbolic action. He bought a clay jar and broke it into pieces at one of the city gates. So, he said, would Yahweh break the people and they would never be whole again. This magically dangerous action, which was carried out in an emotional storm, was followed by a corresponding official reaction. He was flogged and flung into prison for twenty-four hours. After his release he uttered a curse against the priest who insulted Yahweh through this punishment of His prophet (19-20).

The prophet was not intimidated. He prophesied an ignominious end for the king. He recognized Nebuchadnezzar as Yahweh's sword which was ready to strike. Thus he advised unconditional surrender as the only means of escape (22).

It is an idle attempt to inquire to what extent this advice should be attributed to magic thinking or to sober political consideration. Was Jeremiah influenced by his hallucinations or by his logical thinking? Men of his cultural milieu experienced their life in magic-archaic thought patterns; hence any thought was conceived to be of divine-magic origin and considered to lead to magic results; and the more it was colored by the impact of emotions, the higher was judged its value in reality. The prophets considered themselves and were considered by their contemporaries as Yahweh's servants. This fact implied identity of existence and oneness in the interpretation of events. This belief of the prophets is not specific to them. The history of mankind shows that every spiritual or political "leader" considers himself the sole representative of God or Destiny.

The prophet who had been interned somewhere in the Temple precinct read the scroll with his collected prophesies to the people. Neither the king nor the nobles and scholars dared to kill him. The king ordered his arrest but the priests hid him and his pupil Baruch. The priests' double-dealing between king and Yahweh enabled Jeremiah to utter new prophesies and curses against the king (36).

Events followed in accordance with his prophesies. Johaiakim refused tribute to Nebuchadnezzar, his revolt was quashed before the arrival of the main army, and the king's trace was lost in the defeat. His son and successor, Jeconiah, was deported with his court and with many of the priests and artisans. Among those who were deported was the later prophet Ezekiel. The third son of Josiah, Mattaniah, was then made king with the vassal name of Zedekiah.

In Judah and the other minor states there was fomenting against the Babylonian yoke. Jeremiah was never tired of emphasizing that Yahweh gave the land to Nebuchadnezzar: thus to rebel against him was to revolt against Yahweh. He walked in the streets of Jerusalem with a heavy yoke on his neck, symbolizing Yahweh's Babylonian yoke. It came to a magic-symbolic battle of wits and curses with the rival prophet, Hananiah, who broke the yoke and thus dispersed the magic spell it symbolized. Jeremiah retired but later recovered his self-assurance and prophesied Hananiah's early death "because thou makest this people to trust in a lie" (27-28).

The irresolute Zedekiah sent a reassuring message to Babylon, but let himself finally be carried away by the "hot-heads," and revolted openly. The Chaldeans besieged the city; hatred grew against the relentlessly prophesying Jeremiah. The king requested him to intercede with Yahweh for him, and ordered the liberation of the wrongfully detained Jewish slaves. This step seemed to have influenced Yahweh, the Chaldeans discontinued the siege. The king and his nobles tore off their masks, and revoked the liberation of the wretched slaves who were dragged back to slavery. The infuriated prophet raged in frenzy against them, and wanted to leave the city. He was arrested as a deserter, flogged, and thrown into prison (37).

His imprisonment was apparently not very strict. The hate was outbalanced by the fear he inspired. The undecided king secretly sent for Jeremiah and asked to be told his future. He received the same terrible answer as before: "Thou shalt be delivered into the hand of the king of Babylon" (37:17). And then came Jeremiah's bitter question, which proved that he thought himself Yahweh's embodiment with no personal existence or will: "What have I offended against thee, or against thy servants, or against this people, that ye have put me in prison" (37:18). He did not consider himself responsible for his prophesies, they were Yahweh's words.

The situation in the besieged city became desperate and the nobility asked for Jeremiah's head, since he did not cease to utter his threats. The king handed him over to the aristocrats who did not dare to kill him directly but lowered him into a cistern that served as a sewer. The desperate king saved him and asked for consolation, but Yahweh's iron decision came un-altered from the prophet (38).

> [Then] the city was broken up . . . the king of Judah . . . and all the men of war . . . fled, . . . but the Chaldeans' army pursued after them . . . and they had taken him, they brought him up to Nebuchadnezzar, King of Babylon, . . . [who] gave judgement upon him.—The King of Babylon slew the sons of Zedekiah . . . before his eyes. . . . Moreover he put out Zedekiah's eyes, and bound him with chains, to carry him to Babylon [39].

Jeremiah witnessed the tragic fate he had prophesied so many times. He stayed on in the country with the governor, Gedaliah. After the latter was murdered, the refugees took Jeremiah with them to Egypt as a pledge of Yahweh's goodwill. There he played the same tragic role of hopeless warn-ing. Here, in Egypt, the trace of him disappeared forever (39-43).

The ambivalence of good and evil, of the will to destroy and the wish to bless, reached such heights in Jeremiah, that the end of the hero, physically and mentally, was inevitable. He preached nothing that differed from the prophecies of his predecessors: disloyalty to Yahweh is punished with de-struction. But there is an important difference. The demonic quality in Amos Hosea, and Isaiah constantly threatened their people with Yahweh's wrath and revenge because of Israel's "unfaithfulness." They considered As-syria as Yahweh's punishment, but did not urge submission to her. Jeremiah demanded that his people humbly accept subjugation, he maintained that the foe was Yahweh's ally. He urged treason and desertion, he propagated self-destruction. Thus one important aspect of Jeremiah brutally and openly represented residues of the old desert-demon, whose one and only aim was destruction. Jeremiah's demonic nature was the more conspicuous for Isreal since his threats coincided with the imminent destruction of the people in reality.

This demonic quality of Jeremiah's personality tormented him more than the hatred of his fellow men. He revolted against the God he created in himself, a God Who brought him hatred, humiliation, and persecution.

> O Lord thou hast deceived me, and I was deceived: thou art stronger than I, and hast prevailed: I am in derision daily, everyone mocketh me.— . . . Cursed be the day wherein I was born. . . . Cursed be the man who brought tidings to my father, saying, A man child is born unto thee. . . . —Because he slew me not from the womb;

or that my mother might have been my grave, and her womb to be always great with me . . . [20:7-17].

He could not establish a complete identification with Yahweh. Doubt, revolt, and hunger for the love of his fellow men gnawed at his soul. The result (or rather the cause) of his inability to achieve a complete identification with Yahweh was that he stood also in the relation of son to the demon-God-father, i.e., he was in the same relation in which Israel stood to Yahweh. This was indeed a relation of weighty psychological implications. The Yahweh-demon demanded castration, and only after the people had suffered castration did he turn into a loving Baal. The same fate struck the prophet, he was humiliated and Yahweh demanded castration from him: "Thou shalt not take thee a wife, neither shalt thou have sons or daughters in this place" (16:2).

This was a demand without parallel in the Bible. The Bible in general and all the other prophets regarded sexuality as wholesome and considered it as a matter of course. Yahweh also forbade him sympathy toward his fellow men—a terrible demand: "For thus saith the Lord, Enter not into the house of mourning, neither go to lament nor bemoan them: for I have taken away my peace from this people, saith the Lord, even loving kindness and mercies" (16:5).

This conception of a cruelly jealous, unsatiable Yahweh was the basis on which by means of sublimations and reaction formations Jeremiah built his relation to God and achieved his spiritual progress.

A relationship which claimed such sacrifices, a God who accepted no rival of any sort, could be borne by Jeremiah only by means of his complete intimacy, a maximum of deepest mutuality and the warm closeness of fellowship. His aggressive drives against Yahweh were repressed and the libidinous elements assumed prominence. Jeremiah's fervor made his God relation a private and a secret one. Only Yahweh and the individual could be aware of this relation. This was a secret alliance displaying definite masochistic features: "But thou, O Lord, knowest me: thou hast seen me, and tried my heart towards thee: pull them out like sheep for the slaughter, and prepare them for the day of slaughter" (12:3).

This God relation, which was based on the innermost feelings, bore the imprint of the most personal responsibility: "In those days they shall say no more, The fathers have eaten a sour grape, and the children's teeth are set on edge.—But everyone shall die for his own iniquity: every man that eateth the sour grape, his teeth shall be set on edge" (31:29-30).

This personal responsibility implied with Jeremiah the absolute rejection of ritual: "Thus saith the Lord of hosts, the God of Israel; Put your burnt offerings unto your sacrifices, and eat flesh.—For I spake not unto your fathers, nor commanded them in the day that I brought them out of the land of Egypt, concerning burnt offerings or sacrifices: But this thing commanded I them, saying, Obey my voice . . . and walk ye in all the ways that I have commanded you, that it may be well to you" (7:22-23).

The only way to Yahweh lay in sincere devotion. Jeremiah attained for himself, for his people, and for humanity, the God Who Loves (14:17; etc.).

Ezekiel

Ezekiel was a priest, one of the prisoners who were deported to Babylon with King Jeconiah in 597. In the fifth year of their deportation, apparently in the open air, his first hallucination came to him, that of his "call." Yahweh appeared before him with a half-human, half-animal retinue. The word of Yahweh was taken physically through his mouth:

> And when I looked, behold, a hand was sent unto me; and, lo, a roll of a book was therein;—And he spread it before me; and it was written within and without: and there was written therein lamentations, and mourning, and woe.—Moreover he said unto me, Son of man, eat that thou findest; eat this roll, and go speak unto the house of Israel.—So I opened my mouth, and he caused me to eat that roll. —And he said unto me, Son of man, cause thy belly to eat, and fill thy bowels with this roll that I give thee. Then did I eat it; and it was in my mouth as honey for sweetness [2:9-10; 3:1-3].

The ecstasy of the "call" was followed by seven days of negativism. The prophet sat in silence among other people. This state of stupor was resolved through further hallucinations; under their influence a catatonic phase ensued which lasted a year. It consisted of autistic regression which was time and again interrupted with phases of manic excitement. During these periods Ezekiel carried out symbolic acts, besieged Jerusalem, stormed the city with word and eye, both actions having had magic effects. When he was hungry, Yahweh's voice ordered him to cook his meal on dried human excrement. He worked magic through his hair and beard. All his actions represented and caused the downfall of Jerusalem and the dispersal of Israel (3-7).

He interpreted his catatonia as Yahweh's punishment for Israel's sins. He felt himself chained, lay rigid and speechless, turned alternately to right and left.

He lived and prophesied during this psychotic episode in public. The nobles came to his house, sat attentively and horror-stricken around him, watched his rigor, and listened to his raving prophecies. His psychosis tormented and blessed the prophet in front of his people.

This severe catatonic period is resolved in a new series of exciting hallucinations and magic actions that mostly symbolized the destruction of Israel (8-12).

Four years later, in 588, there came a new psychotic episode which coincided with his wife's death, and was very probably precipitated by it. This lasted three years and was marked by negativistic phenomena.

> Also the word of the Lord came unto me saying,—Son of man, behold, I take away from thee the desire of thine eyes with a stroke: yet neither shalt thou mourn nor weep, neither shall thy tears run down.— . . . So I spake unto the people in the morning: and at evening my wife died; and I did in the morning as I was commanded [24:16-18].

This psychotic episode which coincided with his wife's death resolved itself three years later under the traumatic effect of the same symbolic value, the fall of Jerusalem.

> And it came to pass . . . that one that had escaped out of Jerusalem came unto me, saying, The city is smitten.—Now the hand of the Lord was upon me in the evening, afore he that was escaped came; and had opened my mouth, until he came to me in the morning; and my mouth was opened, and I was no more dumb [33:21-22].

Ezekiel spent out of some eleven years roughly four years in a state which nowadays would certainly entail confinement in a mental hospital. His thinking not only displays the magic-archaic thought symbolism of his culture, but also clearly presents the thought disorder of a schizophrenic. Complete openness of the ego boundaries, grave disturbances of the body image, and permanent hallucinations mark his regression. His oneness with Yahweh develops along the dynamics of oral devouring. Also clinging trends (Hermann, 1936) are discernible in his magic with hair and beard.[2]

The precipitating effect of his wife's death and the clearing-up of the acute symptoms after the loss of the symbolic mother, Jerusalem, point to the loss of the mother representatives as pathogenic factor in his psychosis. It

---

[2] I. Hermann, the Hungarian analyst, maintains that clinging is one among the infantile partial drives, its erotogeneous zone being the hand. Its most conspicuous phylogenetic prototype is the newborn ape who clings in the first months of his life to the mother's hairy body. According to Hermann, this infantile drive and its derivatives are important carriers of early and mature object relationships. Picking the skin, nail, and hair are autoerotic activities of this partial drive to cling.

should be also mentioned that his first recorded episode occurred during his stay in Babylonian exile after the enforced loss of his homeland and his beloved Jerusalem.

While Hosea's case history allows the assumption of a particular oedipal phase as a pathogenic factor, in Ezekiel's case the reconstruction of his development has no special material to rely upon. The above-mentioned reference to the archaic object loss, the loss of the mother, offers only a general known pathogenic factor in schizophrenias.

An individual feature of Ezekiel's prophetic activities was that he was preoccupied with the ritual (40-48). Some authorities even regarded him as one of the editors of Deuteronomy. This is in sharp contrast with the other great prophets who all spurned the ritual. It is a fair assumption that he followed here a path of defense which is well known and often found in schizophrenics. The obsessional superstructure in such cases is in the service of warding off the psychotic dynamics. Apart from their defensive purposes obsessional dynamics may well conceal intellectual and emotional defects that result from the progress and scars of a psychotic process. Preoccupation with ritual may have served similar defensive functions in Ezekiel's case.

Ezekiel's ethical views and his concept of God do not differ from those of the other prophets.

Deutero-Isaiah

This is the name given to the great poet and thinker whose work is collected in Chapters 41-55 of Isaiah. The years 550-538 are put as his probable period of activity, but scholars are far from unanimous.

In his work a new note is sounded: the demonic has disappeared, Yahweh's attributes are love and grace, his justice is mild and forgiving. Ecstasy had completely disappeared from the sphere of prophetic activities and the communication of Yahweh's desires was most probably achieved no longer by preaching but only by writing.

A significant change is marked by the description of Yahweh's representative, the leader of the people: "He shall not cry, nor lift up, nor cause his voice to be heard in the street.—A bruised reed shall he not break, and the smoking flax shall he not quench: he shall bring forth judgement unto truth" (42:2-3).

This is a figure who differs fundamentally from that of his predecessors, though some slight resemblances with Isaiah and Ezekiel might be discerned. The grace, which had already been propagated by Jeremiah and Ezekiel, becomes with Deutero-Isaiah the focal point of his relation to God (41:14; 43:25; 48:11).

Grace is the basis of a new form of "being chosen." Prophet and Israel who are identical in the text become Yahweh's mundane agents to spread the light of Yahweh throughout the world and down through the ages. The prophet enters no longer into identification with Yahweh but into a secret father-son relationship, a form that has already appeared in Jeremiah (1:5). This new psychic constellation conditions the new type of identification with Israel (49:1-6). The universality of Yahweh—the great spiritual achievement of Amos—is here restricted. Yahweh is not obviously and immediately the God of mankind but only indirectly through the medium of His own people. Deutero-Isaiah represents the point at which—after all his predecessors' bitter struggles—a decisive regressive turn is taken.

From the basic sharing of all people in the universality of God there is a regressive turn to a concept where the "chosen" people becomes the primary carrier of the God concept. This then is conveyed by the chosen people to all other nations. Thus there is a return, though a sublimated one, to the tribal God, who is originally one with his own people only.

This regressive change is reinforced by the reappearance of the sado-masochistic demon component with prevailing masochistic features of the son. It creates the figure of the self-sacrificing mediator. "I gave my back to the smiters, and my cheeks to them that plucked off the hair; I hid not my face from shame and spitting" (Deut.-Isa. 50:6). This sufferer takes up the position between God and mankind. He must take the whole brunt of divine wrath, but also becomes the sole, immediate recipient of God's love. While the previous prophets visualized the people-God relationship as that of the bride's to the bridegroom, Deutero-Isaiah's mediator disrupted this relationship, since he took a position between people and God. It is obvious that one important function of this disruption was to allay the anxiety and guilt, which arose from the ambivalence we discussed in the previous chapters. But this lessening of anxiety went hand in hand with weakening of the feeling of individual responsibility, as it was attained by the sublimations of Deutero-Isaiah's predecessors.

Masochism and lessening of self-responsibility are heightened by the picturesque portrayal of this "servant" who takes on himself the sins and sufferings of mankind (52-53).

Israel had once again endured and overcome castration. Out of the wife-Israel of the great prophets has arisen the son-Israel, the man. But a price had to be paid for this, the masochistic component came into its own, though displaced unto the "servant": "But he was wounded for our transgressions, he was bruised for our iniquities: the chastisement of our peace was upon him; and with his stripes we are healed" (53:5).

The Yahweh of the great prophets was no longer a castrator either from hate—as the demon—or from love—as the lover Baal. With Deutero-Isaiah, Yahweh permitted his son to be just a son and loved him as his son. This love was dearly bought. The son becomes a "sufferer," and with this concept a new trend of development comes into force—new for ethical monotheism, but not new for mankind whose various religions display the same solution of the oedipus conflict.

The Psychology of the Prophets

The psychological investigation of a cultural achievement must consider the cultural environment as a decisive factor for "secondary elaboration," i.e., for the selection and formulation of contemporary sublimation. It means that every civilization and every epoch of it has its own spiritual problems that represent the contemporary attempt to solve basic human emotional conflicts.

The prophets lived in a magic-animistic culture. The projection of emotions and thoughts created a world that was fundamentally different from that of so-called Western civilization. Inner psychic events and external happenings were connected by emotional experience and thinking processes. A whole culture lived—as so many other cultures have done—with its ego boundaries "open." Subject and objects were not clearly separated, microcosm and macrocosm were fused. God's existence was not only known but also felt. His living and operation was conceived as a real sensorily experienced fact.

The affects had free access to the activity of the higher thought processes. Mental activity aimed not at purifying ideas of their affective origin or coloring, but on the contrary, the value of thoughts was determined by their affective admixture. The stronger this was the greater the thinker's and his audience's moral conviction. Decisions were carried out not under the pressure of our "logic" but under that of "magical logic," i.e., under affective impact. Isaiah's self-esteem and reputation were not in the least disturbed by the fact that many of his political prophecies did not come true. The impetus of his affect storm was equivalent with reality.

Through this merging of ego and outer world—like in the case, among others, of Hosea—man lost his independence but at the same time, as a representative of divine power, he won the power of directing destiny. Prophetic identification was an example of this process and its consequences.

The prophets were considered by their contemporaries as being mad, whether they were dervishlike *nabis* or major prophets (II Kings 9:11; Jer. 29:26). The prophets themselves never protested against this opinion. They were indeed "possessed" by Yahweh and in this state they "raged" (*"hitnabi"*). Jeremiah describes realistically his inner experience: "his word was in mine heart as a burning fire shut up in my bones" (20:9). What was considered and treated as madness would today be described as a confusional state of the mind. What we today term psychic abnormality was in those times regarded as the manifestation of divine power. This fact explains the respected-despised status of these men. The double meaning of the word *"sacer"* illuminates this point.

The cultural environment in which the prophets lived had its own particular manifest form of neurosis and psychosis. The prophets properly "chose" this culture's particular type of illness. The mental disorder of this culture in its most favored form, though other types existed, was characterized by the syndrome of (a) ecstasy, (b) hallucination, and (c) symbolism. The above-discussed openness of the ego boundaries in this magic-animistic culture explains the choice of this syndrome.

(a) Ecstasy was the essence of the prophetate, the mark of the "Man of God," of the man who was seized by Yahweh. The discharge of affect was brought about either spontaneously or artificially (II Kings 3:15). Whether these attacks were hysterical or psychotic with different prophets and at different times cannot be answered in every case.

(b) These ecstasies were accompanied by hallucinations and delusions. The case histories proved that some of the prophets were undoubtedly psychotics (Isaiah, Ezekiel). Others, like Hosea and Jeremiah, cannot be diagnosed as psychotic, since we lack the proof of definite psychotic signs. Their hallucinations and their thinking may have been solely determined by the above-mentioned cultural factor of a magic society, and, in addition, by a neurotic disorder. Its main recorded symptom was extreme acute or chronic emotional tension, which conspicuously distinguished them from their contemporaries. In such cases a magic culture readily offers its main forms of highly charged emotional expression to neurotic symptom formations, which we also often observe in patients. The transference neurosis often induces ephemeral hallucinations and delusions which come and go within a single analytical session at times of extreme emotional stress during therapy.[3]

[3] Experiments carried out by Schilder (1918) proved that hallucinations may appear in normal or neurotic individuals under the impact of emotional upheavals. He invited normal subjects to imagine things highly tinged with affect. Schilder did not particularly emphasize the fact, but he wished to stimulate thoughts that provoked castration anxiety. His male subjects had to imagine to possess female breasts or the lack of an arm. Thereupon there emerged intensive bodily sensations in the affected parts of the body.

(c) The third factor in this syndrome was symbolism which played a more important part in this culture, particularly in the prophetic activity, than it does in Western cultures. Symbolism was a sign of the prophets' magic thinking; through their symbolism their emotions and thoughts were brought into causal relation with external events. They practiced magic by means of their symbolism. When Jeremiah broke the jar, this action symbolized and was considered to bring about the downfall of Israel. Thus the despair of the people and their thirst for revenge become intelligible.

Another example: Jeremiah conjured up catastrophe by carrying a yoke on his shoulders; thereby he set into motion a train of events destined to end in the subjugation of Israel. The prophet Hananiah opposed him and broke the heavy yoke in an emotional storm. Jeremiah retreated downcast and vanquished. Hananiah proved by breaking the yoke that he had more divine power than his opponent. His countermagic turned the scales, and the jubilant people felt liberated from the magic curse of Jeremiah.[4]

In the affect storms of the prophets the primary processes won the upper hand over the secondary processes. Thus abstract ideas of high ethical value were expressed in affect-charged symbol language of ecstatic hallucinations. Our culture has officially discarded this language under the influence of scientific developments in the course of the last 300 years. For a magic culture this language was the only effective and acceptable one.

Concerning the psychic conflicts that caused the "prophetic syndrome" we must be content with surmises and restrict ourselves to inferences that arise from general psychoanalytic experience. Uncontrolled aggression was common to all. Had their aggressive fantasies been fulfilled, the whole people would have been destroyed. This aggression was so powerful that in spite of far-reaching ethical sublimation, it appeared clearly in its brutality. Prophetic aggression and their ecstasies were closely linked up. Their aggression was directed not only against their environment but against themselves as well. It is common analytic clinical experience that men who create a strict ethic, in the first place create it as the final complex elaboration of strong aggressive drives. The ensuing superego gives opportunity to the gratification of sadistic as well as masochistic tendencies.

Amos seems to have been normal. Isaiah's "going naked" for three years suggests a psychotic episode. Hosea's sex life proves that he could never develop beyond a certain stage of his oedipal conflict. His fixation manifested

---

[4] The well-known self-observations of Silberer (1911) led to the discovery that when predisposing conditions of open ego boundaries exist, then abstract ideas may appear in the ego as "autosymbolic hallucinations." The Silberer phenomenon points to the close relationship between projection, hallucination, open ego boundaries, and animistic thinking.

itself in his neurotic choice of a partner. Jeremiah denied himself sexual life. There cannot be any doubt about Ezekiel's schizophrenia.

Narcissism played a prominent part with the prophets. This is evident from the life and writings of these men who were raised above their fellow men by their identification with Yahweh and at the same time were isolated from the people through the very same identification. Their honored-despised status resulted from their narcissistic isolation which gave rise to their own as well as to their environment's ambivalent attitude. Their secondary narcissism attracted and repelled their contemporaries. It served as protection against their inner conflicts and was useful as a way of instinctual gratification of sexual but mainly of aggressive trends.

In the formation of their secondary narcissism two main factors must be considered: (a) the already discussed strength of their instinctual drives with the subsequent conflicts and character formations, and (b) their creative genius.

The great prophets' inborn creative sublimating talent within the sphere of ethics discriminated these men from the other raving *nabis* of their culture. The latter were *only* neurotic or psychotic and lacked the intellectual capacity of these few geniuses—a capacity which for the time being is not further analyzable.

The attempted clinical analysis of these cases proved that the prophets' ethical sublimation was from their individual point of view far from satisfactory; their illness overwhelmed them in several sectors of their lives. They were incapacitated in the emotional and social sphere either for their whole life or for long periods.

Psychology of the Third Stage

The development of ethical monotheism appears to have been connected with just a few personalities, isolated from the community, whose ideas were strongly resisted. Their ideas spread slowly in the postexilic period when external circumstances favored this God relationship. Though there was a spiritual gap between the prophets and the people during their lifetime and even later, they must be regarded as true representatives of collective thoughts, otherwise their ideas would never have become the heritage of their people. The prophets' isolation at the beginning, the extremely slow but final acceptance of their thoughts symbolizes the people's hard and unsuccessful struggle to resolve their oedipal conflict in the usual way. This battle was fought out between the people and the prophets, the former fighting to retain the Canaan God relation, the latter to regain the "desert ideal," i.e., the

God relation of the desert which under the prophets underwent an ethical reshaping.

The prophets' particular ethical demands are the outcome of the individual characteristic qualities of each of them, but the common and central point of their demands is the return to the nomadic ideal. The form of life, the social and religious structure of the desert period is the desired one, and is conceived as the only possible one for Israel. The God relation of the desert period brought prosperity, harmony, and divine grace, while the Canaan God relation meant disloyalty and "adultery," the sin that will be punished by their political downfall.

The analysis of the first and second stages revealed the unconscious meaning of these prophetic assertions. If the prophets demand the return to the desert, they are demanding nothing less than the re-establishment of a unique oedipal situation, the sources of which were specific traumata, and in particular one based on sadomasochistic father and mother fantasies. The re-establishment of the former relation to God would involve the renewal of the old ambivalence, which had already reached its climax. The son is conquered and castrated and is compensated by the blessing of being chosen. The prophets fully confirm this concept in always speaking of Israel as "wife" (particularly Ezekiel). The masochistic bondage is clearly expressed by Amos, among others, when he speaks of the relation of beast of prey and victim.

The sin of the second period is clearly visible analytically. In Canaan the people have won back their manliness in their success against the father and in the regaining of the mother. "Iniquity" proved to be the incest complex. The character of the sense of guilt changed and assumed usual features and elaborations.

The new mental trend, manifested by the great prophets, was prompted by the sense of guilt. This anxiety, originating in the oedipus situation of the Canaan period, received its rationalization from the external political situation. The prophets interpreted the looming menace of Assyria and later that of Babylon as the punishment for the people's changed attitude. Assyria and Babylon represented Yahweh's revenge, symbolized the pressure of the superego. In this way an external political event became intelligible from the magic viewpoint. Assyria and Babylon, therefore, were the late external traumata that brought a new series of psychic conflicts.

The overwhelming power of Assyria and Babylon and the terror they exerted evoked, as the Bible testifies, feelings of impotence in Israel. The psychological result must have been the disbelief in their own manliness, the manliness which had been achieved in Canaan. The power, won back from the father, was refused them. They lost confidence in their own ability.

Up to this point the whole situation and the prophets' slogan of "back to the past" have their parallels in many other historical times. Usually an old constellation cannot be reinstated, or, if it can, then, at the most, the reinstatement is short-lived and superficial. The case of Israel, however, is quite different. Israel actually did return to the oedipus constellation of the desert period, though with a sublimation corresponding to the progress made. Still the psychological basis remained unaltered.

The might of Assyria-Babylon represented the outer world onto which the inner processes could be projected. Assyria destroyed the minor states as the demon in the desert destroyed men. So in Assyrian might was repeated the desert trauma caused by the unsuccessful revolts. The people were as helpless against this great power as they were in the revolts of the desert against the Demon God Yahweh. When the prophets demanded submission, they desired the repetition of the old fixated situation.

The victory of the son in Canaan did not correspond to the line of development foreshadowed in the desert. The superego, Yahweh, nurtured by the sadomasochistic fantasies, demanded its old rights. The fixation on the failure of the desert revolts could not be overcome.

These psychic circumstances explain the conduct of the prophets, exhorting their own people to accept their subjugation voluntarily. The son renounced his victory and resumed the position of the ever-conquered child bound *only* to the father by hate-love, seeking to overcome his castration anxiety through the defense of being "chosen." Israel became, as the prophets show at every stage, the castrated son, the wife.

The renunciation of manhood was not possible without violent reactive feelings of revenge and hate. These feelings were projected upon the God figure, and, after introjection which followed in the process of the building up of the newly formed superego, the sense of guilt increased. Both these stages are observable in the prophets. The projection stage is visible in the mercilessly destructive severity of Yahweh, and the introjection stage in the ever-growing feeling of responsibility of the prophets, culminating in Ezekiel. Hand in hand with this went the demand that the entire people should accept Yahweh's wrath, i.e., the yoke of Assyria-Babylon. This incredible demand of the prophets indicates the extent of the projected aggression toward Yahweh, and also the following introjection which strengthened the cruel pressure of the superego.

The dynamics of these conflicts, the struggle between the oedipus situation in the desert and that in Canaan are represented by the hard contest carried on between Israel and the prophets. In the "prophetic" oedipus situation, the libido—after the repeated repression of the mother—could only cathect the father. Thus with growing love for the father, the father's love for his son—as a consequence of projection—was also intensified. In this way the mobilization of the heterosexual libido in Canaan has finally strengthened the father cathexis.

There arose a fresh ambivalence which in its nature was similar to that of the desert. The castration anxiety had to be alleviated, the father-God had to be conquered, but his love had to be preserved. Two conflicts awaited solution: (1) to avoid the father's aggression, (2) at the same time to assuage the sense of guilt arising from the son's wish to leave the tender loving father. The conflict was the more involved as defenses against the son's hate *and* against his love for the father had to be mobilized within the frame of the God relation.

The main defense measure was a complex chain of sublimations on the ethical level. Two trends are discernible in these sublimatory processes: (1) denials which achieve a loosening of a close people-God relationship and reduce the libidinal ties as well as the immediate experience of aggression; and (2) the countertrends which create an extreme emotional and intellectual intimacy, causing a high degree oneness between people and God.

The prophetic ethical development showed the prevailing of denial at its beginning. Nonpresence of Yahweh was dominant. That corresponded to the cruelty of the Yahweh imago. Only later when a certain distance had somewhat lessened the anxiety, appeared the sublimation of approach and alliance.

Yahweh's Universality

The first phase of denial is represented by Amos, who portrays Yahweh's destructive, demonic quality. He compresses into a few sentences the essential of "being chosen" of the oedipus conflict, of the libidinous sadomasochistic son-father relation: "You only have I known of all the families of the earth: therefore I will punish you for all your iniquities" (Amos 3:2). There follows the salvation from this desperate situation by the defense measure of ethical sublimation: Yahweh's universality (Amos 9:7).

Flight results in the concept of the universality of god. Sublimation by means of universality sought to cope with castration anxiety in three ways: (1) by diminishing the opportunity for divine aggression, (2) by renunciation of the excessive love tie, and (3) by decreasing the sense of guilt.

1. As a result of Yahweh's universality the father's cruelty, which has been related so far only to the chosen son, spread to other people also, and thereby lost a great deal of its destructive force. When a father is cruel, an only child suffers more than when the father's aggression is distributed over

several children. Collective defense and revolt are more likely to be successful than individual attempts. Israel's greatest enemies, the Philistines and Syrians, are equally the cherished sons of Yahweh; thus "new booty" is offered to "the beast of prey" (Yahweh) (Amos 3:4). Israel's greatest enemies are recognized as brethren and so become allies in the struggle against the father. The oedipal hate of every nation was directed against Yahweh.

2. Universality considerably relaxed the love tie to Yahweh. This intimate and unique relation was now available to others. Jealousy, so often stressed by Yahweh, had to be eliminated from this relation. If Yahweh had other children, his fatherly love would not be absolute and undivided. Subsequently the divine-fatherly love was no longer accepted as a matter of course but was dependent on conditions which arose in consequence of the sublimation. The affable relation between Yahweh and Israel was thus lost. God needed no more the love of his son, having other objects available for his love.

These considerations show that owing to universality the ambivalent homosexual sadomasochistic God relation decreased in intensity. Yahweh's love grew more indifferent but also less dangerous. The relaxation in the God relation lessened the fear of castration, still demanded by Yahweh.

The very same trends, however, had their countertrends that pressed for the strengthening of the love tie. The sublimation process of universality rendered God greater, nobler. Yahweh became God-father of the whole world, the tribal father changed into a world ruler. His son's love for him, and his love for his son grew in significance and value. Yahweh had all people for His children, thus the "chosen" child's significance and power increased. He gained distinction from His exalted love.

Though the people were raised through this sublimation, at the same time they humbled themselves by accepting the position of being one of many. This forced them into a continuous effort of winning Yahweh's love which depended henceforward on definite criteria. In this way the masochistic sublimated component came into force.

3. The feeling that they were one among many, that they had brothers, quieted their conscience. As other people had the same relations to Yahweh, their oedipal sins were the same. On the other hand the renunciation of the old exclusive love link between father and son affected also the ambivalence in these lines. The attempt of withdrawal—as expressed and achieved in universality—stimulated self-reproaches, since it implied the abandonment of the old object relation. A further increase in the pressure of the sense of guilt was reached through the following psychic fact: Israel became a member of a group of children and so He took upon Himself the sins of others.

But this side of the sublimation—the feeling of enhanced responsibility—developed only later.

Yahweh's Love

The pendulum of the sublimatory defense measures swung first toward denial. This achievement was represented by the concept of Yahweh's universality as it was expressed by Amos.

The next phase of this development brought to the fore the countertrend of intimacy. The sublimation of this clinging tendency to God produced the sublimated, prophetic love, which is demanded by Yahweh from his people and by the people from Yahweh.

The first representative of this trend is the prophet Hosea. He represents the affirmation of love in the most elevated and warmest approach to God.

The homosexual instinctual background manifested itself in its final setting. This drive and its vicissitudes are represented by Hosea. The castration became irrevocable and Israel turned into Yahweh's wife (2:18-25).

We attempted to show that this love as propagated by Hosea in the form of *chesed* had the unconscious meaning of incest. With the concept *chesed,* Hosea described the castrated son's love to his father with the complete exclusion of the mother. It represented, in our analysis, the negative, incomplete oedipus conflict. The word "love" is used by the prophets with two connotations, viz. the father's love for his son, and the lover's love for his bride. Thus Israel, the first-born, became Israel, the bride who was wooed by Yahweh, the father-bridegroom.

Tenderness, devotion, piety as expressed by *chesed* went further in the unconscious feminization of Israel. Yahweh's wooing displayed the expectation of womanhood on the part of Israel with all of its female attributes as described in detail in the prophetic writings. The final developmental stage of the notion *pietas* became one of the main pillars of prophetic doctrine and consequently of Western religious thinking. In *chesed,* in prophetic love, the submissive love to Yahweh reached its climax; the deepening and broadening of this concept led to the heights of ethical monotheism.

Israel was no longer the subjugated son in the desert but—after having accepted castration—the loving bride. It was through *chesed* that the trauma of the desert revolts and that of Assyria-Babylon could be handled. The involved dynamics represent a striking example of the return of the repressed. The repressed mother returned after manifold vicissitudes. Its qualities and cathexes were represented by the tender loving son-people who became Yahweh's bride.

This acceptance of the bride role indicated the penetration of the repressed mother qualities into the oedipus situation. Through the defenses of projection-introjection not only the people but also Yahweh had changed his features under the influence of "prophetic love." The gentler the bride the more refined were Yahweh's qualities whose softening had in turn affected the features of the son. A definite femininity entered into the Yahweh figure, marking the return of the repressed mother. The wooing Yahweh of the prophets and the subtly refined God figure in Deutero-Isaiah's writings represent the above dynamics.

This positive, approaching, clinging trend of the sublimatory process found in Hosea's contemporary, Isaiah, a broader and deeper interpreter than his predecessors. The two basic achievements of Isaiah's sublimation were: (1) belief i.e., a quiet firm feeling which dismissed the formal approach; (2) love for one's fellow men. The ethical sublimation of the father-son relation mitigated the castration anxiety in these lines and this new oedipal situation brought along a new adjustment in all object relations.

1. Out of the sadomasochistic bondage of the desert grew a deep confidence in the father who no longer castrated, who forgave, and who yearned for the son's attachment to him (Isa. 5). The libidinous ties which united father and son became deeply intimate. Quiet belief and confidence are by no means demonstrative. They are noticeable only by the other partner. The God figure grew in strength not by way of aggression but by love and belief.

2. The reduction of castration anxiety brought about a further ethical demand, namely, love for one's fellow men (Isa. 13:12). The refined feelings of the father-son relation were expected in every object relation. In this way the love of God was sublimated and extended into love of man. It did not stop here but was widened to love for animals, nature, and ended at the concept of eternal peace (Isa. 2:4). This last stage is not unique in the history of mankind; it is found in the form of prophecies in other ancient oriental religions.

The tender, refined ethical love that unites Yahweh and his people, God and the individual with intimate ties of belief and confidence prevails with Jeremiah more than with Isaiah (Jer. 14:17).

Jeremiah completed the trustful unification of God and man. Yahweh had become so tender, loving and harmless, that the individual could turn in solitude and silence to him in his private troubles. No barriers were needed between Yahweh and his son; fear has apparently been driven from the world. Man was directly bound to his God-father, nothing must be kept secret from this father any more (Jer. 12:3). The road to God is marked by unconditional frankness (Jer. 29:13).

With this achievement the cup became too full; neither the people nor the individual could bear such a degree of proximity, however ethically sublimated. This excessive emotional surrender aroused new anxiety. Yahweh won much more power by this love than the demon of the desert possessed. The people again became powerless against him. The notes of this highly sublimated love echoed the threats of the demon: "Circumcise yourselves to the Lord, and take away the foreskins of your heart" (Jer. 4:4).

Yahweh's Absolute Justice

The countertrends of approach—as described above—and of flight are symbolized in Jeremiah's thoughts and emotions. Though the whole conflict is carried out on an ethical level, the original instinctual trends are still preserved in his curses, reproaches and quandaries in his struggle for and against Yahweh. The resulting sublimation once again aimed at flight, i.e., removal and avoidance of Yahweh. The results of this sublimatory process were: (a) Yahweh's absolute righteousness; and (b) his imperceptibility; he could not be perceived by the senses, he could not be represented by any symbolic image.

The absolute righteousness of a father like Yahweh, who demands such an unselfish, "self-circumcising" love, must necessarily be considered by the people-child as disappointing. Only loving care and exceptional position can compensate for such a father's numerous commands and demands.

How difficult it was to accept Yahweh's absolute justice is proved by the fact that it is ambiguously expressed in the older (Exod. 34) as well as in the later (Exod. 20) edition of the Decalogue, though both received their final form in postprophetic times ("I am a jealous God visiting the iniquity of the fathers upon the children . . ." Jeremiah's formulation is clear and simple: ". . . every one shall die for his own iniquity . . .") (Jer. 31:30).

The ethical sublimation of absolute justice warded off the anxiety that had been aroused by the close emotional tie of "love." In place of the warm atmosphere of *chesed* came the ice-cold severity of justice. This defense measure led further than that of universality. A father who must be shared with others remains, despite this fact, a father; but a father who is absolutely just, inspired not by love but by righteousness, is no longer a father but a judge without any leniency. Here again we may observe the return of the repressed. The old desert-demon returned in the image of the ethically absolutely just Yahweh. They are both absolutely void of love, consideration, and pity. Yahweh who exercises justice indiscriminately does not differ—in terms of the unconscious—from the demon who kills indiscriminately. The demon strove to kill everyone; merely being alive was equivalent with being in mortal danger. The God who is absolutely just threatens everyone in the same degree, since no one can be without sin. The "iniquity" of the oedipus sin is common to all. Absolute justice as a defense measure in the service of withdrawal contains in itself the punishment for its operation. The further the people moved away from Yahweh, and the less love was there in their relation to God, the more dangerous God became to his "unfaithful" son. Yahweh was tied to his son exclusively by aggression in the form of absolute justice.

The pressure of the superego was increased through a further development in which the ruthless superego acquired greater significance. In Ezekiel's concept of personal responsibility men were absolutely at Yahweh's mercy. They were handed over to him more than they had been to the demon. The demon demanded life, while Yahweh who was absolutely just made his son responsible even for the life and deeds of others (Ezek. 33:8).

Yahweh's Imperceptibility

Parallel with the function of absolute justice operated another process of ethical sublimation which was in the service of denial. The development of absolute justice can be traced from Amos to its climax in the ethical teaching of the last great prophets. A similar process can be observed in the concept of the God's image. The concept of representability passed through a process that ended in absolute unrepresentability and imperceptibility. This sublimation was in the service of denial. It protects against Yahweh and—at the same time—preserves Yahweh from his son's aggression. It leads on this level of the ambivalence, by way of total sensory denial, to a considerable decrease of castration anxiety and of sense of guilt.

As Yahweh became inconceivable and unapproachable through the sense organs, he could not be represented physically. Thus the emotional conflicts that referred to him could be considered as nonexistent, could be denied. "Out of sight, out of mind."

The Bedouin tribes of Syria created simple representations of deities in the shape of uncarved blocks of stone. Hosea still accepted the existence of idols in Israel (Hos. 3:4). Isaiah thundered only against the gold and silver images. In Jeremiah, however, 100 years later, figurative representation was no longer mentioned. For Jeremiah, this problem no longer existed.

The concept of imperceptibility aided the denial and therewith the decrease of anxiety due to proximity through love. Nevertheless it implied simultaneously the countereffect, i.e., the increase of anxiety. It paved the way for the omnipresence of the deity. As Yahweh was neither in any definite place nor was he representable in any perceptible form, the people lost all control over him, because he was everywhere (Jer. 23:23). He could be omnipresent without being noticed. The people could never be sure, never be protected against him (Jer. 11:20; 16:17).

This defense measure made Yahweh uncontrollable. The demon of the desert returned from repression and was more dangerous than ever before.

BIBLIOGRAPHY

Allwohn, A. (1926), *Die Ehe des Propheten Hosea in psychoanalytischer Beleuchtung*. Giessen: Töpelmann (In Referat).

Arlow, J. A. (1951), The Consecration of the Prophet. *Psychoanal. Quart., 20*: 375-397.

Baeck, L. et al. (1927), *Entwicklungsstufen der jüdischen Religion*. Giessen: Töpelmann.

Beer, G. (1927), *Welches war die älteste Religion Israels?* Giessen: Töpelmann.

Benedict, R. (1934), *Patterns of Culture*. Boston: Houghton Mifflin.

Bidney, D. (1953), *Theoretical Anthropology*. New York: Columbia University Press.

Bonkamp, B. (1939), *Die Bibel im Lichte der Keilschriftforschung*. Recklinghausen: Viranus.

Breasted, J. H. (1936), *Geschichte Ägyptens*. Zürich: Grosse illustrierte Phaidon Ausgabe.

Caiger, S. L. (1936), *Bible and Spade*. London: Oxford University Press.

Cambridge Ancient History (1923). Cambridge: University Press.

Church, B. (1953), *The Private Lives of the Prophets and the Times in Which They Lived*. New York: Rinehart.

Cook, S. A. (1903), *The Laws of Moses and the Codex of Hammurabi*. London: Black.

—— (1930), *The Religion of Ancient Palestine in the Light of Archeology*. London: British Academy.

Fisch, S. (1950), *Ezekiel*. London, Bournemouth: Soncino Press.

Free, J. P. (1950), *Archeology and Biblehistory*. Wheatin, Ill.: Van Kempen Press.

Freud, S. (1939), *Moses and Monotheism*. London: Hogarth Press, 1951.

Gressmann, H. et al. (1911-1914), *Die Schriften des Alten Testamentes in Auswahl, neu übersetzt und für die Gegenwart erklärt*. Göttingen: Vandenhoek & Ruprecht.

Gunkel, H. (1930), *Zum religionsgeschichtlichen Verständnis des Neuen Testamentes*. Göttingen: Vandenhoek & Ruprecht.

Hermann, I. (1936), Sich-Anklammern, Auf-Suche-Gehen. *Int. Z. Psychoanal., 22*:349-370.

Hirsch, W. (1910), *Religion und Zivilisation vom Standpunkt des Psychiaters*. München: Bonsels.

Hölscher, G. (1914), *Die Propheten*. Leipzig: J. C. Hinrichs.

Jeremias, A. (1929), *Handbuch der altorientalischen Geisteskultur*. 2. Auflage. Berlin-Leipzig: Gruyter.

—— (1930), *Das Alte Testament im Lichte des alten Orients*. 4. Aufl. Leipzig: J. C. Hinrichs.

Junker, H. (1927), *Prophet und Seher in Israel*. Trier: Paulinus.

Kellermann, B. (1917), *Der ethische Monotheismus der Propheten in seiner sociologischen Würdigung*. Berlin: Schwetschke.

Kittel, R. (1910), *Die alttestamentarische Wissenschaft in ihren wichtigsten Ergebnissen*. 5. Aufl. Leipzig: Quelle & Meyer.

Lange-Eichbaum, W. (1928), *Genie-Irrsinn und Ruhm*. München: E. Reinhardt.

Lods, A. (1930), *Israel*. Paris: La renaissance du livre.

—— (1935), *Les prophètes d'Israel*. Paris: La renaissance du livre.

Meyer, E. (1896), *Die Entstehung des Judentums*. Halle: Niemeyer.

—— (1906), *Die Israeliten und ihre Nachbarstämme*. Halle: Niemeyer.

—— (1924), *Ursprung und Anfänge des Christentums*. Vols. 1-3. Stuttgart-Berlin: J. G. Cotta.

Oesterley, W. O. E. (1927), *The Wisdom of Egypt and the Old Testament*. London: Society for the Promotion of Christian Knowledge.

Otto, R. (1932), *Das Heilige*. München: C. H. Beck.

Pedersen, J. (1926), *Israel, Its Life and Culture*, Vols. 1-2. London-Kopenhagen: H. Milford-P. Branner.

Reik, T. (1919), *Ritual*. New York: International Universities Press, 1958.

—— (1923), *Der eigene und der fremde Gott*. Wien: Internationaler Psychoanalytischer Verlag.

Schilder, P. (1918), *Wahn und Erkenntnis*. Berlin: Springer.

Schneider, H. (1910), *Kultur und Denken der Babylonier und Juden*. Leipzig: J. C. Hinrichs.

Silberer, H. (1911), Symbolik des Erwachens und Schwellensymbolik überhaupt. *Jahrb. Psychoanal.*, 3:621-660.

Smith, S. (1928), *Early History of Assyria to 1000 B. C.* London: Chatto & Windus.

Smith, W. Robertson (1889), *The Religion of the Semites*. London: Stanley A. Cook.

Spinner, S. (1933), *Herkunft, Entstehung und Umwelt des hebräischen Volkes im Lichte der alten Urkunden, Neuausgrabungen, etc.* Wien: Vernay.

Storch, A. (1932), *Das archaisch primitive Erleben und Denken der Schizophrenen*. Berlin: Springer.

Wallis, L. (1913), *Sociological Study of the Bible*. Chicago: Chicago University Press.

Weigall, A. (1923), *Echnaton*. Basel: Schwabe.

Woolley, L. (1929), *Ur of the Chaldees*. London: Allen & Unwin.

—— (1936), *Abraham*. London: Faber & Faber.

INDEX